D1559605

THE ECONOMICS OF COMPUTERS

The Economics of Computers

WILLIAM F. SHARPE

COLUMBIA UNIVERSITY PRESS

NEW YORK AND LONDON   1969

William F. Sharpe, a RAND Corporation Consultant,
is Professor of Economics in the University of California
at Irvine, California.

56,091

PREFACE

It is not a simple matter to describe this book. Briefly, it attempts to provide and apply a set of concepts from economic theory that may prove valuable to those who are now or may become decision-makers in the selection, financing, and/or use of computers. Only theory relevant for such decision-makers is presented here. This means that the effects of computers on the economy as a whole lie outside the scope of this book, as do a number of related issues. We deal, thus, with microeconomic, not macroeconomic, theory: our focus is on the small (industry, firm, computer) and not the large (gross national product, consumer price index, unemployment).

The book is intended to appeal to three groups of readers. First, and of the most immediate importance, are those who now manage or set policy for computer installations. The second group consists of students in programs leading to degrees in computer science (or information science); such programs are becoming widespread and seem destined to remain permanent fixtures on most university campuses. Finally, the book is aimed at economists interested in the computer industry; only a minimal knowledge of computers per se is assumed here, and most of the material of interest to an economist requires no such knowledge.

Although the book has been neither designed nor tested as a textbook, it should prove useful for a one- or two-semester course for computer scientists. As the profession matures, I hope that a course dealing with economic matters would be considered an essential part of the computer science curriculum. Perhaps this book will play a part in gaining acceptance for this view.

The book is written for a reasonably sophisticated audience. The reader is assumed to be familiar with mathematics through introductory calculus. More important, however, is the requirement that the reader be sympathetic to the use of relatively simple but rigorous models for analyzing economic problems confronting computer users and producers. No prior knowledge of economic theory is assumed; such knowledge is an output, not an input.

The book is divided into two major sections. Part I is organized around techniques; Part II, around applications. The dichotomy is not complete, however. The techniques in Part I are presented with illustrative examples concerning computers, and some new theoretical concepts are introduced in Part II. The division is primarily one of convenience: applications are included in Part I whenever they can serve to illustrate a particular theoretical construct, and theoretical techniques are used in Part II as appropriate for the applications discussed.

This is not a book about economic theory or even one about microeconomic theory. The reader interested in a broad background in the subject is advised to read instead, or in addition, one of the many general textbooks on the subject (e.g., Alchian and Allen's excellent *University Economics**). The theory included here is limited to that portion which, in my opinion, is of prime importance to the computer scientist. No apology is intended for this statement—some economic theory is better than none, and this book is meant to provide a means whereby a particular group of people can efficiently obtain a core of such theory selected with their needs and interests in mind.

Empirical results have been included, wherever possible, to illustrate the theory and to provide numerical estimates for key relationships. To some extent it has been necessary to rely on the work of others, since time and resources did not allow extensive independent empirical research to be conducted specifically for this book. This means that there is a less than perfect correlation between the importance accorded various subjects and the empirical research performed to date and described here. It also means that some important subjects must be treated briefly since little empirical material is available. Hopefully the recognition of such imbalances will lead to further research aimed at their correction.

The book is long. The reader with broad experience in the computer industry may prefer to skip Chapters 6, 7, the first part of 8, and 12. The professional economist interested primarily in applications of economic theory to the computer industry should omit Chapters 1–6. The pragmatic reader interested primarily in obtaining a general familiarity with the industry may wish to skip Chapters 1–5, 8, and 11.

---

* Armen A. Alchian and William R. Allen, *University Economics,* Second edition, 1967, Wadsworth Publishing Co., Belmont, California.

The Appendix is included for those with little or no exposure to the technique of regression analysis. A minimal understanding is required to benefit fully from some of the discussion in Chapters 9 and 10.

Most books reflect the background, the interests, and, we hope, the comparative advantage of the author. This one is no exception. I have included material that seems to me both relevant and interesting. I make no claim to have exhausted the subject of computer economics or even to have remained within its bounds. I do hope that I have provided material that will prove useful to those for whom the book is intended.

William F. Sharpe

May, 1969
Irvine, California

ACKNOWLEDGMENTS

This study was undertaken by the RAND Corporation as a part of its research program for the United States Air Force. The book was written over a period of three and a half years. During that time I received help, advice, data, criticism, and support from a great many people. Those to whom I am especially indebted are listed here.

Betty Armstrong, Jean Anderson, Lani Levine, Sally Robison, and Sharon Stanger provided secretarial help on schedule and with good cheer.

Nancy Jacob did much of the empirical work described in Part II. She also listened patiently to some of my ideas and helped sort out the ones worth pursuing.

Mrs. Lynn De Shong prepared all the illustrations with accuracy and dispatch.

I was fortunate to be able to persuade a number of graduate students at the University of Washington to do research on subjects relevant for this book. Some of this work was done in connection with seminars that I gave in 1965, 1966, and 1967. Some was performed for research papers submitted to fulfill the requirements for the Master of Business Administration degree. I have used much of this work, with suitable references, in the chapters that follow.

Particular thanks are due the following, who helped me form my own ideas and also provided important results: Susan Allerdice, Paul Giese, Larry Granston, Bob Johnson, Terry Lee, Gordon Parkhill, Jim Patrick, Bob Robinson, Stein Skattum, and Steve Takaki.

The RAND Corporation staff has provided both moral and practical support. I owe particular thanks to John Hogan and Terry Halverson.

Empirical information about the computer industry cannot be efficiently collected without the cooperation of the members of this industry, which I have been fortunate to have. Representatives of all the major manufacturers have been helpful. Special thanks are due Bob Knight, Bill Lull, and Ron Muecke of IBM's Seattle office.

My greatest debt is owed to Paul Armer of Stanford University, formerly associate head of the RAND Computer Sciences Department, who first suggested that I write this book. Through three years of missed (self-imposed) deadlines, he has remained firm in his conviction that the author knows best. Most hold this view of their own work; Paul Armer is one of the few people who apply it to the work of others. I cannot adequately express my gratitude for his support. He urged me to continue the project and encouraged the RAND Corporation to make it possible for me to do so. I have tried to produce a book worthy of his support.

The Center for Research in Management Science of the University of California, Berkeley, provided support during the summer of 1966 for some of the preliminary work on the cost and effectiveness of memory devices. I am particularly grateful for the assistance provided by Emmanuel Sharon during that period; his ideas furnished much of the direction for my subsequent work.

A number of my colleagues have expressed interest in this book, and many have contributed to it, either directly or indirectly (perhaps unknowingly). C. B. McGuire and Ralph Miller of the University of California, Berkeley; Kenneth Knight of the University of Texas; Edward Fiegenbaum of Stanford University; Fred Tonge and Julian Feldman of the University of California, Irvine; Martin Solomon of the University of Kentucky; Seymour Smidt of Cornell University; J. Fred Weston of The University of California, Los Angeles; Bob Blechen of California Oceanography, Inc.; Jim Tupac of Planning Research Corporation; and Bob Patrick, a RAND consultant, have been particularly helpful. My greatest debt in this respect is to Ken Knight.

What merits the book may have are due in large part to the careful and detailed reviews of an earlier version provided by John McCall of the University of California, Irvine, and Norman Nielsen of Stanford University. Needless to say, the usual limitations on liability for error apply.

W. F. S.

CONTENTS

PART I: Theory

CHAPTER **1** **MICROECONOMIC THEORY**

AN INTRODUCTION

A. MICROECONOMICS

Anyone who feels that he can precisely define the boundaries of his profession either possesses a skill of little importance or is incredibly naive. Hence we will not attempt to define rigorously the scope of economics. Dictionary definitions typically state that economics is the social science dealing with the production, distribution, and transportation of goods and services. Many feel that its domain should be limited to activities in which money plays a role. But economists often concern themselves with social and business systems in which monetary transactions are of little importance. A better definition might thus include activities in which money *could* play a role.

Whatever economics may be, it is typically divided into two parts. *Macroeconomics* deals with the large questions. What determines the gross national product, the percentage of unemployment, the overall price level? *Microeconomics* deals with the small. What determines the price of a particular computer, the rental terms offered by IBM, the optimal usage of a computer in a particular firm? As these examples suggest, the techniques of microeconomics are the more valuable for computer scientists acting in their professional capacities. As an enlightened citizen, the computer scientist may well be concerned with the broad aggregate measures of a society's welfare and the influence of major policy decisions on them. But we will not attempt to provide here the requisite education for the latter role. Our concern is primarily with microeconomic theory.

One of the goals of this chapter is to provide the reader with a feeling for the approach an economist takes to problems. To accomplish this, a number of important subjects will be treated, often in a rather cursory manner. In subsequent chapters we will build our models more carefully, deal with complications and special cases at greater length, discuss more fully the manner in which the models can be put to practical use, and, wherever possible, provide relevant empirical data.

At this point it is more important to prepare the reader emotionally for the rest of the book.

B. POSITIVE VERSUS NORMATIVE THEORY

One may differentiate positive theory from normative. *Positive* theory attempts to predict. What types of rental terms *will* a computer manufacturer enjoying a monopoly position offer? What type of costing system *will* a firm adopt for internal computer use, and how *will* people react to it? *Normative* theory provides guides for decisions. What types of rental terms *should* such a manufacturer offer? What type of costing system *should* a firm adopt, and how *should* people react to it? Normative theory must of course be supplemented by value judgments (e.g., *if* the manufacturer *wants* to maximize profits, *then* he should . . .). Positive theory, in principle, is free of value judgments: it deals with what will happen, not what should happen given some set of values as to the relative desirabilities of various outcomes.

As a social science, economics deals more with positive theory. But economists attempting to construct models of the economy early found it useful to utilize submodels of firms that made decisions as if they sought to maximize profit, produce a given output at minimum cost, etc. Such models can clearly be adapted for normative applications with similar goals. When cast in the latter role, the models are often given a new name — for example, managerial economics, business economics, or even systems analysis.

The dichotomy between positive and normative theory is based more on the use to which the theory is put than on the theory itself. For example, we will examine in some detail the optimal types of behavior for a computer manufacturer attempting to maximize profit. To the extent that computer manufacturers do attempt to maximize profit and are successful at it, such behavior may be observed; we thus have a good positive theory. To the extent that manufacturers want to maximize profit but do so only rarely, the theory is less useful in a positive role. But obviously it can be utilized to help the manufacturer attain his goal and is thus a good normative theory.

In this book we will consider a number of situations, each involving an objective, certain decision variables, and a set of constraints (technical relationships, those imposed by market conditions, those imposed by competition, etc.). The optimal behavior in each case will be derived by manipulating the resultant model. In some instances we will propose the model as more valuable in a positive role; the appropriate test of its value in such a role is the extent to which observed behavior is consistent with the implications of the model. In other cases we will propose a model as more valuable in a normative role. Here the appropriate test of its value is consistency between the assumptions of the model (particularly those concerning objectives) and those relevant to the decision-maker for whom it is proposed. From time to time we will even confront one type of model with another. For example, we will ask, What policy *should* a user adopt with regard to rental versus purchase of a machine if the manufacturer *does* indeed arrange his terms so as to maximize his profit?

In general our concern will be with the user; to the extent that normative models are developed they will be directed primarily to his problems. Models dealing with manufacturers are intended to be used more often in a positive context, to shed light on the situations faced by the typical user so that his decision rules may be formulated in a sensible manner. However, as this section has indicated, the dichotomy between positive and normative models is never complete; the distinction is at best a matter of degree.

C. COST/EFFECTIVENESS

In the last few years economics has been employed increasingly as one of the decision-making techniques utilized within the federal government. The names assigned to the products of government economists are varied, but one in particular has been the focus of much controversy: cost/effectiveness. Like most key ideas, this one is almost trivially simple and thus should produce little controversy once understood.

Figure 1–1 illustrates the general procedure. Assume that many different techniques are available to perform computation for some organization (é.g., an aerospace firm or a university). Each technique has some cost and provides computation with some amount of "effectiveness" (somehow measured). In Fig. 1–1 each point represents one of the alternative techniques. Obviously:

    (1) among techniques with equal cost, the one with the greatest effectiveness is best; and

    (2) among techniques with equal effectiveness, the one with the least cost is best.

These criteria define a set of *dominant* techniques, illustrated by the circled points in Fig. 1–1. No rational decision-maker would consider any of the other techniques. We say that the circled points represent *efficient* techniques; the others are dominated by them and are *inefficient*.

If there are many efficient techniques, they may be represented by a continuous curve as illustrated in Fig. 1–1. Cost/effectiveness analysis is designed to locate this curve (i.e., efficient techniques). Obviously all the power of cost analysis, statistics, operations research, engineering, and many other fields, as well as (perhaps most important) knowledge of the process being studied, must be brought to bear if this exercise is to be performed correctly. Equally obviously the difficult part

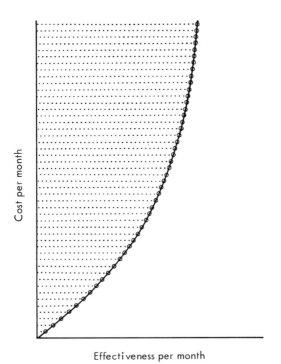

Effectiveness per month

FIGURE 1–1. Cost/effectiveness combinations.

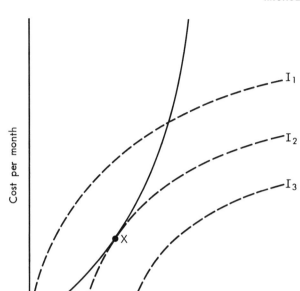

FIGURE 1-2. Cost/effectiveness combinations and preferences.

is the enumeration of all the interesting techniques and the estimation of their cost and effectiveness; the rest of the exercise (up to but not including the final decision) is completely straightforward.

Given a set of efficient techniques, which should the ultimate decision-maker select? Clearly he should not choose (or be advised to choose) the cheapest—this technique usually involves doing nothing, with both cost and effectiveness equal to zero. Equally clearly only the ultimate decision-maker or someone who knows his preferences can make the final choice. If the decision-maker himself is to choose, the cost/effectiveness curve (or points) can be presented to him and his decision made directly. If someone else is to choose, the relevant preferences must be captured in advance.

Figure 1-2 shows one possible mapping of preferences. Equally desirable combinations of cost and effectiveness are connected: thus combinations lying along curve I_1 are equally desirable, those lying along I_2 are equally desirable and also preferable to those along I_1, etc. If sufficiently many of these *indifference* curves are obtained from a decision-maker in advance, the optimal cost/effectiveness combination can be determined without further consultation (in Fig. 1–2 this combination is shown by point X). In practice this is rarely done; it is more convenient to ask a decision-maker to simply choose among the efficient techniques rather than to make choices among many hypothetical techniques so that his entire range of preferences can be identified in advance. But constructs such as those shown in Fig. 1–2 are often useful for depicting the factors at work when choices ultimately are made, and we will employ them in the chapters that follow.

Note that the final selection from among alternative techniques may be the most difficult part of the entire decision process. Usually the decision-maker has been delegated the task by a group that will ultimately bear the consequences of his decision. Moreover, the preferences of the members of the group are hardly likely to be identical, and the weights to be given to the preferences of various individuals are rarely obvious. Thus the Secretary of the Air Force may have to attempt to choose the best technique for the nation as a whole, or the president of a firm may have to attempt to choose the best technique for the firm's stockholders as a body. Just as reasonable men may disagree about the cost and effectiveness of various techniques, so too they may disagree about the relative values of alternative combinations in the eyes of the group for whom the decision is being made. All will agree to avoid vertical portions of the cost/effectiveness curve (i.e., portions in which additional cost gives no additional effectiveness). But the manager of a computer center may well believe that the stockholders' interests are best served by moving very close to such a vertical portion (which may occur at a high level of cost), whereas the firm's president may feel that the optimal expenditure on computer facilities is considerably smaller.

To summarize, we can say that cost/effectiveness as a method for decision-making is clearly above criticism (i.e., it is sufficiently trivial to be obviously correct); in practice, however, there is ample room for disagreement, criticism, and assertions that the method implemented incorrectly is worse than no method at all.

D. REQUIREMENTS

Cost/effectiveness analysis is very much at variance with another approach to decision-making that can best be termed the "requirements" approach. The latter recommends that the decision-maker (1) determine his requirements and then (2) find the cheapest way to satisfy them. Such a procedure, if followed literally, can lead to optimal decisions only by chance. Indeed the concept of a requirement or need is completely foreign to an economist. Firms "need" the biggest and best computer available. Researchers "require" an almost unlimited amount of computer time with the very highest priority. Central processors "need" a large number of peripheral devices to ensure that they will be used to capacity. In short, needs are either unlimited or so large that they can hardly ever be met in practice.

The harsh reality that must be faced by all decision-makers is simply that desirable consequences are usually accompanied by undesirable consequences. One user's need for computer time is satisfied by reducing the time allotted to another. The purchase of a bigger and better computer is accomplished by reducing expenditures on other items. Greater effectiveness is accompanied by greater cost (at least if only efficient techniques are considered). In a narrow sense the sacrifice involved in obtaining increased effectiveness is the dollar outlay required. In a broader sense it is the loss of other desirable uses for which the resources in question could have been employed.

The dangers associated with the requirements approach are illustrated in Fig. 1–3. Assume that a decision-maker somehow determines that he requires the level of effectiveness OR, and that this determination is made in complete ignorance of the relative costs of various levels of effectiveness. The second step of the procedure will ensure that he adopts an efficient technique, but will it be the best of all possibilities? Probably not. For example, if the true cost/effectiveness relation is that shown by curve CE_1, the optimal level of effectiveness may be greater, since increases in effectiveness are accompanied by small increases in cost. On the other hand, if the true relation is that shown by curve CE_2, the optimal level may be smaller, since major reductions in cost can be obtained by reducing the required effectiveness slightly. Clearly the appropriate level of effectiveness will depend on the alternatives available (consider, for example, curves such as CE_3 and CE_4).

This is not to say that the requirements approach should be dismissed out of hand. Information is seldom a free good; the cost of finding the relationship between cost and effectiveness will typically depend on the precision with which the relationship is determined. Thus it may prove worthwhile to:

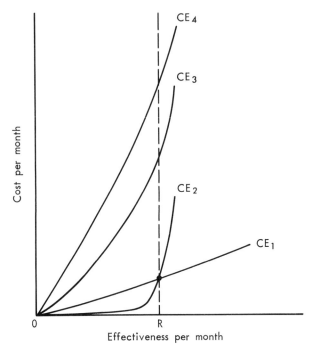

FIGURE 1–3. Cost/effectiveness versus the requirements approach.

(1) obtain rough estimates of the relationship between cost and effectiveness (assuming efficient techniques are utilized);
(2) estimate the range within which the optimal combination will lie;
(3) obtain improved estimates of the relationship within the range selected in step 2; and
(4) then, if the results of step 3 are sufficiently precise, formulate a required level of effectiveness and determine the least-cost method of obtaining it. If the results are not sufficiently precise, return to step 2.

Needless to say, the number of iterations, the extent to which results are refined (in steps 1 and 3), and the size of the range selected in step 2 should depend on the cost of obtaining better information relative to the cost of making a nonoptimal decision. In practice the decision-maker may possess sufficient knowledge to avoid repeated iterations; indeed he may even be justified in stating requirements without explicitly engaging in the earlier steps of the procedure. Thus the experienced computer manager who knows (if only intuitively) what equipment can be obtained at various costs and how it can best be utilized may well be acting rationally when he proposes a set of specifications and accepts the lowest bid consistent with his requirements. As always, it is not the form but the substance of the approach that matters.

E. MAXIMIZING NET VALUE

Often it is possible to simplify the cost/effectiveness approach by estimating the values of various levels of effectiveness. We can define *gross value* as the maximum amount (in dollars) that the decision-maker is willing to pay to obtain any given level of effectiveness. Presumably higher levels of effectiveness will have greater gross values. Figure 1–4 illustrates one possible relationship between gross value

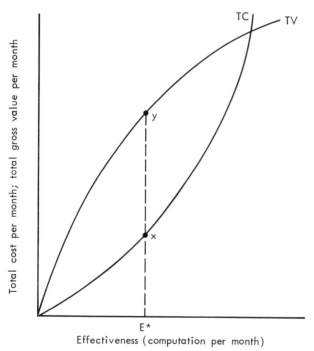

FIGURE 1–4. Maximizing net value.

and effectiveness (here assumed to be some measure of computation per month). Since both gross value and cost are expressed in the same dollar metric, it is possible to compare various levels of effectiveness directly. The goal is to select a level of effectiveness that maximizes *net value,* defined as gross value minus cost. In Fig. 1–4 the optimal level is clearly E^*, giving the cost shown by distance E^*x, the gross value shown by distance E^*y, and the (maximal) net value shown by distance xy.

Although the net value approach is useful in a wide variety of contexts, it is particularly relevant for a firm selling a product or a service and attempting to maximize its profits. The decision variable is usually output or volume of sales (the term *effectiveness* may not be the most appropriate in this situation). The gross value of any given level of output is simply the revenue it provides, and net value equals gross revenue minus cost, a measure according with the usual (accounting) definition of profit. Thus Fig. 1–4 might stand very well as a model of a profit-maximizing service bureau selling computation capability to outside customers.

We have chosen to present the case of the profit-maximizing firm selling in the open market as a rather special example of a more general approach. Historically, models were developed for this case with little or no regard for alternative situations. Indeed, models of profit-maximizing firms form a major part of the classical economist's overall model of a free-enterprise economy.

Many have raised objections that real firms do not accept such a simple one-dimensional goal, and thus that models of profit-maximizing firms are of little use in a positive (or, for that matter, normative) context. In reply the proponents of such models present three arguments. First, these models yield predictions that appear to be more consistent with observed behavior than do any other models of comparable generality and parsimony. In fact, many competitive models are not even operational: they are consistent with any type of behavior and thus predict nothing. Second, under the forces of market competition the maximum profit obtainable may be no profit at all; a firm that does not maximize its profit may thus sustain a loss — maximizing profit may be equivalent to avoiding loss. Finally, a Darwinian process may be at work. Firms that inadvertently adopt policies consistent with profit maximization will prosper, expand, and be emulated by others.

Those that do not will falter, contract, and not be emulated. Thus observed behavior may tend to follow that predicted by a model based on the assumption that firms consciously and efficiently set out to maximize profits.

Other arguments can be made against the profit-maximizing assumption. Many of them rest on a misunderstanding of the assumption itself. Suffice it to say here that by "profit-maximizing" we do not mean short-sighted, get-as-much-as-possible-now-with-no-regard-for-later-consequences policies. What we do mean will be developed in later chapters.

F. MARGINALISM

If a frequency count of words used by economists were made, *marginal* would certainly appear very near the top of the list. Laymen are advised, for example, to "set marginal revenue to marginal cost," "equalize marginal productivity per dollar," and "set marginal profit to zero." In casual conversation (and beginning textbooks), the marginal concept is defined in terms of increments. For example, assume a relationship between total cost and some level of output (q):

$$TC = f(q)$$

For a given level of output, what is marginal cost? The informal description implies that it is the change in total cost brought about by a one-unit change in output:

$$MC \equiv \frac{\Delta TC}{\Delta q}$$

where $\Delta q = +1$ or -1. But of course the change in total cost may be different when Δq is $+1$ from when it is -1. The more satisfying definition, and the one we adopt, uses the derivative

$$MC \equiv \frac{dTC}{dq}$$

In general:

$$\text{Marginal} \langle \text{something} \rangle \equiv \frac{d(\text{total} \langle \text{something} \rangle)}{d \langle \text{some decision variable} \rangle}$$

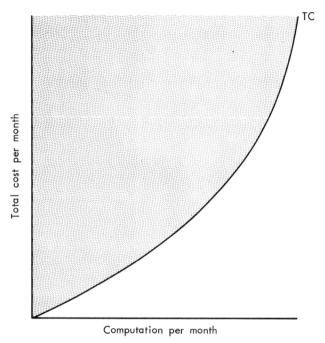

Computation per month

FIGURE 1-5. Total cost versus computation.

Figures 1–5 through 1–7 illustrate a typical (and important) application of marginalism. We assume that a number of techniques are available for producing computation; each is represented by a point in Fig. 1–5 with the efficient techniques shown by a smooth and continuous curve (TC). We assume also that there are a number of ways in which various amounts of computation can be employed; each is represented by a point in Fig. 1–6. Only the points lying on the upper-left border of the region are efficient; and they are also represented by a smooth and continuous curve (TV).

Efficiency dictates that any given amount of computation be obtained at the (least) total cost shown by curve TC and utilized in the manner that will give the (greatest) total value shown by curve TV. Only one decision remains: what is the optimal quantity of output (computation)? We wish to maximize net value ($TV - TC$). Obviously net value is related to output as shown in bottom part of Fig. 1–7. Equally obviously, it reaches its maximum value at q^*. In general, a necessary condition for a maximum is that the curve be flat. In this case

$$\frac{dNV}{dq} = 0$$

Here the condition is also sufficient. Thus we could recommend the following decision rules:

1. If marginal net value is positive, expand output.
2. If marginal net value is negative, contract output.
3. If marginal net value is zero, output is optimal.

These rules may be reformulated. The change in net value brought about by a small change in output equals the change in total value less the change in total cost:

$$dNV = dTV - dTC$$

Thus:

$$\frac{dNV}{dq} = \frac{dTV}{dq} - \frac{dTC}{dq}$$

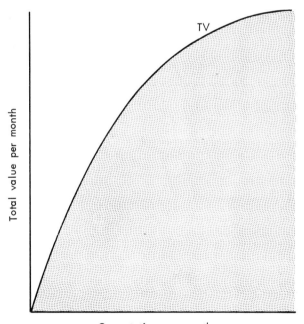

FIGURE 1-6. Total value versus computation.

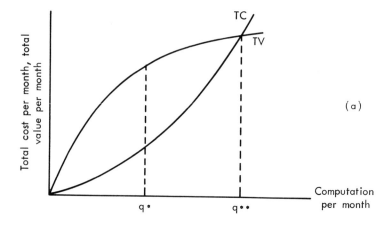

(a)

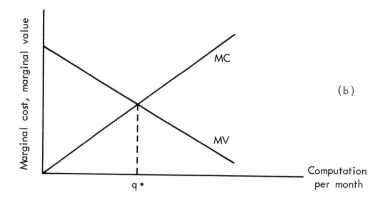

(b)

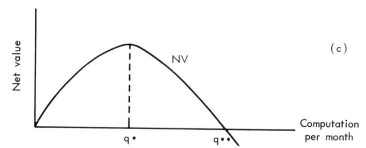

(c)

FIGURE 1-7. Maximizing net value.

The necessary condition for maximizing net value is that marginal net value be zero:

$$\frac{dNV}{dq} = \frac{dTV}{dq} - \frac{dTC}{dq} = 0$$

Rearranging, we have the following equivalent condition:

$$\frac{dTV}{dq} = \frac{dTC}{dq}$$

that is,

Marginal value = marginal cost

The marginal value and marginal cost curves derived from Fig. 1–7a are plotted in Fig. 1–7b. In this case the following decision rules are obviously appropriate:

1. If marginal value exceeds marginal cost, expand output.
2. If marginal value is less than marginal cost, contract output.
3. If marginal value equals marginal cost, output is optimal.

A number of objections can be made about the economist's use of marginalism. For example, it is argued that total cost and total revenue curves need not be smooth and continuous with first derivatives defined at all points; the curves may have kinks, steps, or even discontinuities. Moreover, even if the curves are well behaved, the condition specified (marginal net value $= 0$, or, equivalently, marginal cost $=$ marginal value) may not be sufficient to determine the optimal level of output.

We consider the latter type of objection first. In theory the maximal net value may not lie at a local optimum at all (i.e., net value may increase continually as output either increases or decreases); and the optimal level of output is infinite. However, this could hardly be the case in any real economic situation. Thus the maximal net value can be assumed to lie at some local optimum; the condition specified will find that optimum if the total cost and total value curves are well behaved. Of course it is only a necessary condition and will be satisfied by local minima and inflection points as well as local maxima. Thus additional tests must be invoked when more than one output level satisfies the condition (i.e., when the marginal value curve crosses the marginal cost curve more than once). Moreover, in such situations the decision rules given above may prove untrustworthy (i.e., it may be desirable to expand output in some cases even though marginal cost exceeds marginal value). But these complications can be accommodated easily within the general framework; the necessary modifications are described in Chapter 2.

The decision rules may also prove inadequate if the optimal policy is not to produce at all. Thus an additional test must be invoked to determine whether or not the maximal net value is negative; if it is, obviously the optimal output is zero.

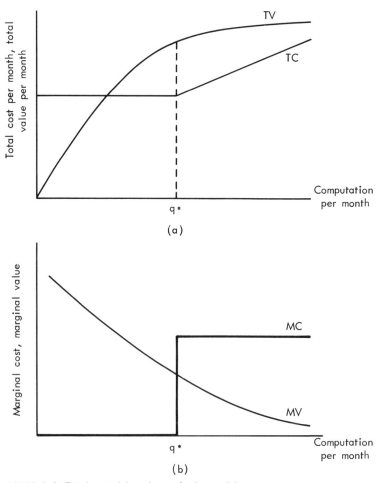

FIGURE 1-8. Total cost (a) and marginal cost (b) curves.

The argument that marginal values may not even exist at some levels of output is somewhat more difficult to overcome. However, a slight modification of the definition of a marginal value helps considerably, making the decision rule much more robust than might be expected.

Consider the situation illustrated by the total cost curve of Fig. 1–8a (Chapter 3 shows that users renting equipment during the period 1955–1965 faced such a situation). If computation per month is below q^*, marginal cost is well defined; it is zero, as shown in Fig. 1–8b. For computation in excess of q^*, marginal cost is also defined; it is positive and constant, as shown in Fig. 1–8b. But at q^* the derivative (dTC/dq) is not defined, since the curve has a "kink" at that point. We get around such problems by a very obvious procedure: if the total curve has a kink, the marginal curve is constructed by simply connecting the segments on either side of the quantity at which the kink occurs in the total curve. Thus the total cost curve in Fig. 1–8a gives rise to the marginal cost curve in Fig. 1–8b. Moreover, the decision rules lead to the optimal output (q^*). We will not attempt to prove this here or to examine the conditions under which such a procedure will allow the marginalist approach to be used in practice. It suffices to say that many real-world complications can be accommodated successfully within the framework of marginal analysis.

G. MATHEMATICAL PROGRAMMING [1]

A mathematical programming problem has the following characteristics:

1. One or more *decision variables:* $X_1, X_2, \ldots, X_n$.
2. An *objective* to be either maximized or minimized, the level of which is a function of the values of the decision variables:

$$Z = f(X_1, X_2, \ldots, X_n)$$

[1] The reader who is not mathematically inclined may wish to skip this section, although he is encouraged to give it at least a cursory reading. Other readers are encouraged to investigate the three previous RAND books dealing with the subject:

Robert Dorfman, Paul A. Samuelson, and Robert M. Solow, *Linear Programming and Economic Analysis,* McGraw-Hill, New York, 1958.

David Gale, *The Theory of Linear Economic Models,* McGraw-Hill, New York, 1960.

George B. Dantzig, *Linear Programming and Extensions,* Princeton University Press, Princeton, N.J., 1963.

3. One or more *constraints* that must be observed, at least one of which is expressed as a weak inequality: [2]

$$g_1(X_1, X_2, \ldots, X_n) \begin{Bmatrix} \geq \\ = \\ \leq \end{Bmatrix} b_1$$

$$g_2(X_1, X_2, \ldots, X_n) \begin{Bmatrix} \geq \\ = \\ \leq \end{Bmatrix} b_2$$

$$\vdots$$

$$g_m(X_1, X_2, \ldots, X_n) \begin{Bmatrix} \geq \\ = \\ \leq \end{Bmatrix} b_m$$

Often a set of constraints restricting the decision variables to nonnegative values is assumed to be implicit in the problem statement, but this is not an essential characteristic.

Problems of this type can be subclassified into various groups. A *linear programming* problem is one in which all the functions (i.e., all constraints plus the objective function) are linear. A *nonlinear programming* problem contains at least one nonlinear constraint and/or a nonlinear objective function. Additional constraints may also be placed on such a problem. An *integer* problem is one in which some or all of the decision variables are restricted to integer values instead of being allowed to take on any values consistent with the set of constraints; thus we speak of an integer linear programming problem, as opposed to a (standard) linear programming problem.

Formally, many economic problems have these characteristics or can be put into this form without making unreasonable assumptions or modifications. However, if the solution can be predicted to some extent, it may be possible to determine in advance which of the constraints will in fact be binding (i.e., hold as equalities) and which will not (i.e., hold as strict inequalities). The former constraints can then be stated as equalities, and the latter disregarded completely. Thus transformed, the problem can in many cases be solved by the methods of the classical calculus (using Lagrange multipliers as needed). Such a transformation was utilized for solving the problem described in Section F; in fact this type of approach underlies most of the tradi-

[2] That is, one that can be satisfied by equality.

tional marginal analysis. To illustrate the use of mathematical programming and to contrast its approach with that of marginalism we will
briefly reconsider the problem represented in Figs. 1–5 through 1–7.

Let X_i represent a technique for producing computation; if used
fully ($X_i = 1$), the technique will produce q_i units of computation per
month and cost C_i dollars. Assume that there are n such techniques.
Obviously each point in Fig. 1–5 gives the coordinates (q_i, C_i) of one
such technique.

Now let Y_j represent some method for allocating computation; if
used fully ($Y_j = 1$), Q_j units of computation will be allocated, giving a
total value of V_j. Assume that there are m such methods of allocation.
Obviously each point in Fig. 1–6 gives the coordinates (Q_j, V_j) of one
such method.

The original formulation required the adoption of just one technique
and one method of allocation; these constraints may be stated as follows:

(1–1)
$$\sum_{i=1}^{n} X_i = 1$$
(1–1)

(1–2) $\quad 0 \leq X_i \leq 1 \quad$ for each i from 1 to n (1–1a)

(1–3) $\quad$ Each X_i integer (1–1b)

(2–1)
$$\sum_{j=1}^{m} Y_j = 1$$
(1–2)

(2–2) $\quad 0 \leq Y_j \leq 1 \quad$ for each j from 1 to m (1–2a)

(2–3) $\quad$ Each Y_j integer (1–2b)

The amount of computation produced (Q_p) will be

(3–1)
$$\sum_{i=1}^{n} X_i q_i = Q_p$$
(1–3)

The amount utilized (Q_u) will be

(4–1)
$$\sum_{j=1}^{m} Y_j Q_j = Q_u$$
(1–4)

Obviously the amount utilized cannot exceed the amount produced:

(5–1)
$$Q_u \leq Q_p$$
(1–5)

Subject to these constraints, we wish to maximize net value:

(6-1) $$\text{Maximize: } Z = \sum_{j=1}^{m} Y_j Q_j - \sum_{i=1}^{n} X_i q_i$$ (1-6)

This formulation casts the decision as an integer linear programming problem. We will defer the discussion of such problems until Chapter 2. Here we consider the problem without constraints 1-1b and 1-2b; in this form it is a standard linear programming problem. In essence we have allowed partial adoption of any production technique (i.e., $0 \leq X_i \leq 1$) and/or any allocation scheme (i.e., $0 \leq Y_j \leq 1$).

Figure 1-9 shows the q_i, C_i values for three techniques. If $X_1 = 1$, we have point q_1, C_1. If $X_2 = 1$, we have point q_2, C_2. But if some intermediate combination is desired, a mixture of the two techniques can be utilized; for example, if $X_1 = 0.5$ and $X_2 = 0.5$, we have point q', C'. A mixture of such a combination and technique 3 will, in turn, provide a combination along the line connecting points q', C' and q_3, C_3. Obviously, by taking an appropriate mixture of techniques, any point in

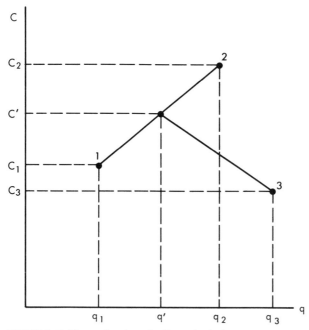

FIGURE 1-9. The q, C values for three techniques.

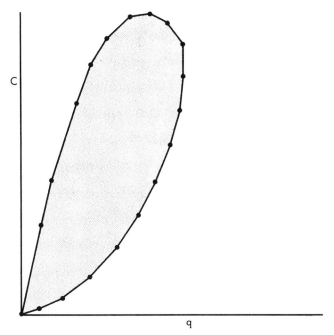

FIGURE 1-10. Feasible q, C values.

the region shown in Fig. 1–10 can be obtained without violating constraints 1–1 and 1–2.[3] The region is simply the convex hull of the original points — that is, the smallest convex region[4] containing all the points. Of course only points lying on the lower border of the region need be considered as candidates for the solution, since cost is an undesirable element in the objective function. Using our previous definitions, points on the boundary are efficient, and the boundary itself is the total cost curve. Note that it will be composed of linear segments and that the segments increase in slope as greater quantities are reached.

A similar argument can be made with regard to alternative methods for allocating computation. The region of possible combinations will

[3] Not all possible techniques have been included in the figure. One can always spend inordinate amounts to produce a given output. With all possible techniques included, the region would extend upward virtually without limit.
[4] For purposes of this discussion, a region can be said to be convex if a line-segment connecting any two points in it lies wholly within the region.

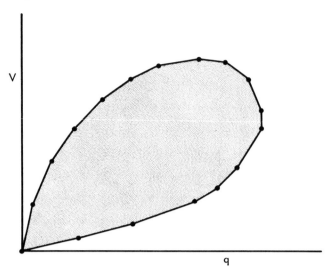

FIGURE 1–11. Feasible q, V values.

be convex, as shown in Fig. 1–11,[5] but only the upper border need be considered. Points on this border are efficient, and the border itself constitutes the total value curve. It too is composed of linear segments, but the segments decrease in slope as greater quantities are reached.

The situation is summarized in Figs. 1–12a and b. Since the extent to which each technique may be utilized is assumed to be variable, it will always prove desirable to produce just the amount utilized (i.e., $Q_p = Q_u$); thus the problem can be reduced to one in a single decision variable, $q(= Q_p = Q_u)$. Figure 1–12a shows the total cost and the total value as functions of Q, while Fig. 1–12b gives the derived marginal cost and marginal value curves. The optimal quantity (q^*) is shown in both figures.

Several comments are in order here. As this example illustrates, the classical economics method obtains the optimal solution in three separate stages. First, alternative production techniques are investigated, inefficient ones rejected, and the efficient techniques used to

---

[5] Not all possible allocation methods have been included in the figure. One can always throw away a portion of the quantity available or devote it to worthless uses. With all possible methods of allocation included, the region would extend down to the horizontal axis and rightward virtually without limit.

form a total cost curve. Next, alternative methods of utilizing output are investigated, inefficient ones rejected, and the efficient methods used to form a total value curve. Finally, the two sets of efficient processes are examined concurrently and the overall optimum is determined. The mathematical programming method, by contrast, combines the operations: all the many production techniques and allocation

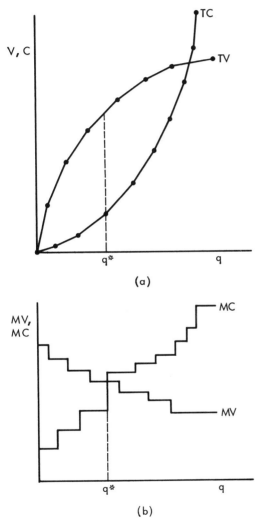

(a)

(b)

FIGURE 1-12. Total cost and total value (a); marginal cost and marginal value (b).

methods are enumerated and included as decision variables, and then the problem is solved directly.

A second comment concerns the shape of the curves obtained. Note that the linear programming formulation implies directly that the slope of the total cost curve will increase [6] with the rate of output and that the slope of the total value curve will decrease.[7] Putting it somewhat differently, we can say that both marginal curves will be monotonic: marginal cost will never decrease with increases in the rate of output, and marginal value will never increase. We will argue these characteristics independently on economic grounds in subsequent chapters, but this brief example provides an alternative way to make the point.

Finally, note that the greater the number of allocation methods and production techniques, the smoother will be the total value, total cost, marginal value, and marginal cost curves. Thus curves such as those shown in Fig. 1–7 may be regarded as limiting cases for curves similar to those of Fig. 1–12. One may take the position that the real world provides a virtual continuum of alternatives and that the linear programming approach represents an approximation to the true situation (as reflected in the smooth curves of classical economics). Alternatively, one may feel that opportunities do in fact come in discrete units and that it is the classical economist who is approximating reality. Whatever the correct position, we will utilize both approaches in this book, usually letting expository convenience govern the emphasis accorded each one. Throughout, however, we will attempt to emphasize the similarities of the two techniques rather than the differences between them.

H. PRICE AS A RATIONING DEVICE

One of the first sentences in most economics textbooks describes the task of allocating *scarce* resources among *competing* uses. As we have argued, rarely will there be sufficient computer time, remote consoles, disk space, etc., to meet everyone's "needs." Whatever amount of some desirable resource may exist at any point of time, some method must be adopted to *ration* it.

Many schemes can be utilized to accomplish this purpose. The de-

---

[6] More precisely: will not decrease.   [7] More precisely: will not increase.

cision-maker may simply allocate the supply to people he considers worthy of it. Thus a computer center manager may grant priority to scientific users, relegating data-processing applications to periods in which no scientific computation needs to be performed. Debugging runs may be given priority over production runs. Universities may establish schemes under which faculty members take precedence over graduate students but the latter have priority over undergraduates. Short runs may be given priority over long ones.

All these schemes have one common attribute: they are generally inflexible. Once the rules have been established, jobs are rigidly classified. No provision is made for the unusual case in which some job in a lower classification is more important than one in a higher classification. Thus the *typical* short job may be more important than the *typical* long job (at least relative to the computer time required), but exceptions will occur and some procedure should be available to handle them.

To solve such problems, one needs a reasonably reliable method to evaluate the intensity of a person's desire to obtain an item. Typically this is accomplished by requiring the user to engage in some unpleasant activity. Thus remote consoles may be allocated simply by adopting a first-come, first-served philosophy. A person whose desire to use a console is sufficiently strong will endure long periods of waiting in line to get one. The console is thus allocated on the basis of patience and endurance. Hopefully, such a scheme will result in its use by those with the most important problems (although it is entirely possible that the console may simply go to those whose time is the least valuable).

In a broad sense the term *price* can be used to represent all the disagreeable things that one must do to obtain an item. Thus we might include, for example, waiting, political capital expended, enemies made, and effort devoted to currying favor with the personnel running the computer center. Certainly we would include any required payments of money. Given a price, people will be willing to pay for some specific amount of an item. And the higher the price, the smaller is the amount. Thus there exists some price that will ration the existing supply completely, without any additional restrictions.

We will generally use the term *price* in its narrower sense to refer to *transfers* of money or resources from the user to the supplier of an item. Conceptually the entire rationing function can be accomplished by setting such a price at an appropriate level. A scheme of this type has significant advantages. Like some of the other methods, it forces a person to engage in a disagreeable activity (paying) if he wants to use the item. But this activity is agreeable for the supplier, since the control of some amount of resources is simply being transferred from one party to another; on net, no unproductive activity is required. This contrasts sharply with the first-come, first-served method of allocation. The user finds waiting disagreeable, but his "payment" of time rarely improves the well-being of the item's supplier; on net, the society (or firm) loses the value of the user's wasted time. Monetary transactions (or intrafirm transfers of budgeted funds) thus provide major advantages over other rationing schemes: resources are transferred from the user to the supplier, not expended or consumed.

We will focus on the use of prices throughout this book. To avoid confusion it is important to think of price first in its role as a device to ration an existing supply. Obviously the relationship between the price of an item and the cost of altering its supply will prove important in determining whether the supply will expand, contract, or remain constant over time. But even if supply were totally unaffected by it, price could fill an important role.

We will be particularly interested in *equilibrium prices*. A *short-run* equilibrium price is simply the price that will serve to adequately ration an existing supply of an item. A *long-run* equilibrium price performs the short-run function and has the further characteristic that no one has an incentive to add to or subtract from the total supply as time passes. In normative contexts we will propose methods for finding such equilibrium prices. In positive contexts we will show that market forces will often lead to the establishment of these prices.

Prices are important in microeconomic theory. In fact, the subject is often called price theory.

A. INTRODUCTION

In Chapter 1 we suggested that a decision-maker might attempt to measure the maximum gross value associated with alternative levels of effectiveness and then choose the level that gives the maximum net value. This chapter is concerned with methods for assigning such values and with some important implications of the overall procedure. The reactions of a decision-maker to various situations concerning the cost and availability of the good or service are of particular interest; several cases—those forming the core of the theory of demand—are dealt with here.

Consider a firm attempting to decide whether or not to utilize computers for its data processing. Assume that the possible applications are well understood and stable from month to month. Moreover, assume that there is sufficient flexibility in scheduling the applications for jobs to be spread out evenly through the month with no undesirable consequences. Restating these assumptions, we can say that any hour per month of computation can be viewed as equivalent to any other and service can be measured simply in total hours per month. Admittedly this is not a very realistic case. We will deal with more complex situations later. But a simple cardinal measure of service (or output or utilization, etc.) makes sense only if the items in question are truly homogeneous; by assumption, this is such a case.

We assume that computation service will be measured in terms of the number of hours required to provide the service with a particular computer (X). If only one computer is to be considered, this causes no complications. If another (Y) is to be considered, there may or may not be complications. If the ratio of the time required to perform a job on machine Y to that required to perform it on machine X is the same for all jobs, an hour on machine Y can obviously be expressed simply as an equivalent amount of time on machine X. But if the relative effectiveness of the two machines varies from job to job, no simple equivalence can be established. To retain the homogeneity of our measure of service we thus assume that the capability of each machine being considered can be expressed in terms of equivalent hours of time on the base computer (X).

Finally, note that we have assumed nothing about the manner in which service will be provided. Time may be obtained from a service bureau, one or more machines may be leased, one or more machines may be purchased, or any combination of such alternatives may be chosen. At this point only the value associated with various levels of service is of interest. We will bring cost and availability into the analysis later.

B. VALUE AND ALTERNATIVE COST

Let there be N jobs that might be performed on a computer. Each job can be characterized by the required computer time (assuming efficient programming) and the value associated with running it. We represent the time required (per month) to run the ith job by T_i, and the value (per month) associated with running it by V_i.

The time required to run a job will obviously depend on the details of the job (how much output is to be printed, how much precision is to be retained during calculations, etc.) and the manner in which it is programmed. Moreover the time required may not be easily predicted in advance and may even depend on the jobs with which the job in question is run (e.g., in a multiprogrammed machine). We abstract from these problems at this point, assuming that each job can be precisely defined and its time estimated exactly in terms of the hours required per month if the base computer is utilized. Furthermore, we assume that times are additive: the total time required to run any set of jobs is simply the sum of their individual time requirements.

How might the value associated with running a job be assessed? The simple answer is that V_i is the most that the decision-maker is willing to pay each month to have the job run on a computer. A more complete answer goes farther. What would be done if the job were not run? Perhaps the operation might be dropped entirely. This could be the case for some management reports. Alternatively, the job might be performed, but in some other way. We can formalize this as follows. Let

V_i^* be the value of performing job i (somehow) and C_i the lowest alternative cost; then

$$V_i = \min (V_i^*, C_i)$$

V_i^* is the most that the decision-maker is willing to pay to have the job performed at all. This value will not be infinite. Even a task essential for the firm's existence, such as preparing the payroll, is not worth an infinite amount of money — at some point it becomes cheaper to go out of business. Needless to say it may be extremely difficult to measure the value of a job. In practice it usually suffices to determine whether this value is more or less than some relevant cost. However, for purposes of understanding the overall process it is preferable to assume that the decision-maker actually estimates the value explicitly. The similarity of the two approaches will become clear later in this chapter. Practical aspects of the process are taken up in subsequent chapters.

Typically there are many ways to perform any given job; the use of a computer is just one of them. Of course the manner in which the job is performed should depend on the method utilized (e.g., clerks should rarely simulate a computer, simply following the same program). Each possible method presumes that the resources in question are employed efficiently, and major practical problems are associated with estimating the costs of alternative methods. But conceptually at least, one can enumerate the alternatives and estimate the cost of each one. The cheapest is the best, and its cost is used for C_i. The method associated with this cost could represent the use of some computer other than those being considered. For the present, however, we assume that all eligible computers are contained in our measure of computation through the expedient of equivalent capabilities; thus C_i is associated with the cheapest method using some means other than a computer. Although this figure may be very large, it will rarely be infinite, since many very complicated operations can be performed without a computer.

The value associated with running job i on a computer (V_i) depends on the next best alternative. If $V_i^* > C_i$, the best alternative is to perform the job by the cheapest available method. Thus, if computation is not used, C_i will be spent. Using the computer gives a (gross) saving equal to C_i; thus $V_i = C_i$. On the other hand, if $V_i^* < C_i$, it is not worth the cost to perform the job by any other method; if the computer is not used, the job will not be done. The value of running the job on the computer is clearly the value associated with having it done at all: $V_i = V_i^*$. Finally, of course, if $V_i^* = C_i$, then $V_i = V_i^* = C_i$.

To summarize, the value of running job i is the lesser of V_i^* and C_i. We assume for now that the value of each of the N jobs can be determined with precision. Moreover, we assume that they are independent in the following sense: the *value* of running job j is not affected by any decisions made concerning job i (e.g., whether it is run, or how much must be paid to run it).

C. ALLOCATING TIME

There are N jobs, each of which requires a given amount of time and has a given value. For convenience we define the value per unit of service (i.e., the value per hour) as the ratio of these two characteristics:

$$v_i \equiv \frac{V_i}{T_i}$$

Now assume that the firm has somehow obtained T hours of computation per month; neither more nor less will be available, and cost is thus determined and invariant. The only decision to be made concerns the appropriate utilization of the available time.

Let t_i be the amount of computer time allocated to job i each month. Since both total time and cost are fixed, the problem is to select values for the t_i's that maximize the value of jobs run. In linear programming terms,

$$\text{Maximize:} \quad \sum_{i=1}^{N} t_i v_i \tag{2-1}$$

Subject to

$$\sum_{i=1}^{N} t_i \leq T \tag{2-2}$$

and subject to

$$0 \leq t_i \leq T_i \quad \text{for each } i \tag{2-3}$$

Note that this statement of the problem does not require that each job be run completely if it is run at all (i.e., $t_i = 0$ or T_i). We allow a job to be allocated only a portion of its required time per month; moreover, in such a case a proportionate amount of value is attributed to it ($v_i t_i$). Fortunately the solution of the problem will treat at most one job (and often none) in this way. Furthermore, it may even be meaningful to operate in this manner. An allocation of 6 hours per month to a job requiring 18 hours to complete is consistent with running the job completely every third month. In any event, for now we allow this sort of allocation.

The problem stated in expressions 2-1, 2-2, and 2-3 could, of course, be solved with any general-purpose linear programming code. However, it is trivially simple and can be solved almost by inspection. There is but one scarce resource—computer time (T). It is to be allocated among competing jobs so as to maximize value. Any allocation scheme subdivides the jobs into two subsets: those that get computer time (i.e., are run) and those that do not (i.e., are not run). Let R be the set of jobs that are run (not necessarily completely) and NR the set of jobs that are not run. The following condition is necessary for an efficient allocation of time:

(a) $\qquad\qquad v_i \geqq v_j \quad$ for each i in R and each j in NR

This states that the value per hour of any job that is run must exceed (or, as a special case, equal) that of any job that is not run. Imagine an allocation in which this does not hold; obviously the time should be reallocated, with some time taken away from job i and given to job j, since this will increase total value; thus the original allocation could not have been efficient.

Figure 2-1 shows the problem in a convenient graph. Each job is represented by a block, with the height indicating the value of the job per hour (v_i) and the width indicating the time required for its completion (T_i). The blocks are arranged in order of decreasing height (v_i); for convenience the jobs have been numbered in the same order.

Note that the arrangement of blocks in Fig. 2-1 ensures compliance with the requirement for efficient allocation. Given scarce computer time, we take first the best job (i.e., the one with greatest v_i). Only when there is more than enough time to complete this job do we consider the next best. Jobs are simply taken in order of decreasing value

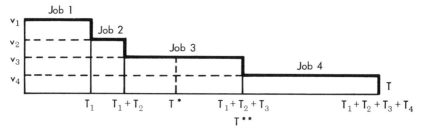

FIGURE 2-1. Marginal value as a function of available time.

per hour until the available time is used up. This obvious rule for efficient allocation implies that diagrams such as those in Fig. 2–1 can be used directly to show how available time should be allocated.

Assume that T^{**} hours per month are available. Which jobs should be run? Obviously jobs 1, 2, and 3. Moreover, each can be run completely $(t_i = T_i)$. The total value obtained from the available time will be maximal and equal to the values of jobs 1–3 $(V_1 + V_2 + V_3 = v_1 t_1 + v_2 t_2 + v_3 t_3)$. Graphically the total value is shown by the sum of the areas of the blocks to the left of T^{**} — since for each job the height of its block represents its value per hour and the width represents hours, the area must represent its value $(v_i t_i)$.

Now assume that T^* hours per month are available. Jobs 1 and 2 should be run to completion with the remainder of the available time allocated to job 3. Total value will again be maximal and equal to the areas of the blocks to the left of the available time. This follows from the assumption that jobs can be given partial allocations of time.

Figure 2–2 shows total value as a function of available time. As usual, the curve is constructed on the assumption that time is utilized efficiently (i.e., value is maximal for any given time). But Fig. 2–1 was constructed to show how to allocate time efficiently. Obviously the *height* of the total value curve for any given value of T in Fig. 2–2 is simply the *area* of the blocks lying to the left of T in Fig. 2–1.

We define the upper right-hand border of the blocks in Fig. 2–1 as the *marginal value curve* (*MV*). The reason is simple. Consider time T^*. If the available time were altered slightly (either up or down), efficiency would dictate that only the time allocated to job 3 be changed. The height of the *MV* curve at T^* is, of course, the value per hour of job 3. For small changes in the neighborhood of T^* this is precisely the change in total value per unit change in available time:

that is, the marginal value. In linear programming terms, the marginal value is a *shadow price,* the one associated with constraint 2–2 (a shadow price shows the change in the optimal level of the objective per unit change in the constant of a constraint, assuming that the rest of the problem is unchanged).

Strictly speaking, the marginal value is not uniquely defined when the curve is vertical, since the change in total value per unit change in time will depend on whether the latter is increased or decreased. However, we follow our previous convention, utilizing vertical segments for connections and defining the resultant curve as the marginal value curve.

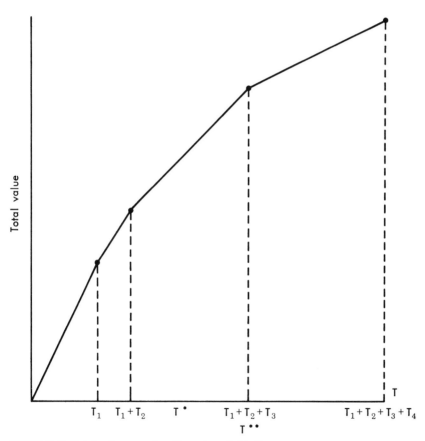

FIGURE 2–2. Total value as a function of available time.

Figure 2–1 was constructed on the basis of the obvious rule for efficiency — first things first. Clearly this implies that the marginal value curve must be downward-sloping (more properly, it must not be upward-sloping). Alternatively we may say that the total value curve must decrease in slope (more properly, it must not increase) as time available increases. This is consistent with the conclusion reached in Chapter 1.

D. ALL-OR-NONE RESTRICTIONS

As long as the partial completion of jobs is allowed, the total value curve will be similar to that shown in Fig. 2–2: continuous and kinked. Note, however, that it will be flat (marginal value $= 0$) only when the available time is so great that all valuable jobs can be run with time to spare.

Consider a situation in which each job must be run to completion each month or not run at all. This takes us out of the domain of standard linear programming problems. The problem can, however, be stated as an integer linear programming problem. A set of new decision variables, $X_1, X_2, \ldots, X_N$ is added, along with the following set of constraints:

$$X_i = \frac{t_i}{T_i} \quad \text{for each } i \text{ from 1 to } N \tag{2–4}$$

Now, if all decision variables are restricted to integer values, the solution to the problem will give the desired result. Constraints 2–3 require that $0 \leq t_i \leq T_i$ for each i; thus X_i must lie between 0 and 1 (by constraint 2–4). But X_i is allowed to take on only integer values; thus it can only be 0 or 1. This effectively restricts t_i to be either 0 or T_i: each job must be given all the time required to complete it or none at all.

Computer codes are available for solving integer linear programming problems, but their performance is often unpredictable. One desirable possibility is that the solution to the basic problem (i.e., without the integer restriction) will turn out to involve only integer values. If so, the total value obtained from the computer time in question will not be affected by the all-or-none requirement. If not, the value will be decreased, since a situation can never be improved by adding further

restrictions. The total value curve consistent with all-or-none requirements must thus lie below and/or coincide with the total value curve derived in the manner shown in Section C.

One solution to the all-or-none problem is simply to utilize the
standard procedure, throwing away any time that would otherwise be
utilized to partially complete a job. The result would be a step-function
total value curve, coinciding with the unrestricted curve at the corners.
However, this is not necessarily the best procedure. In fact there may
be situations in which the best allocation violates our "obvious" rule
for efficiency: it may pay to run some jobs having a smaller value per
hour than that of one or more jobs that are not run.

Figure 2–3 illustrates the point. There are four jobs:

Job (i)	V_i	T_i	v_i
1	24	3	8
2	12	2	6
3	24	6	4
4	14	7	2

The marginal value curve is that shown in Fig. 2–1. The corresponding
total value curve was shown in Fig. 2–2 and is repeated in Fig. 2–3
as the upper solid curve; it shows the total value that can be obtained
in the absence of all-or-none restrictions. Only some of the points on
this curve will meet the all-or-none requirement; there will be at least
N: T_1, $T_1 + T_2$, etc. (i.e., the circled points in Fig. 2–3).

If the all-or-none requirement is met by simply utilizing the standard
allocation technique and throwing away time that would otherwise be
used to partially complete a job, the total value curve is that shown by
the lower (step-function) solid curve in Fig. 2–3. Obviously the efficient total value curve consistent with all-or-none restrictions is
bounded by this curve and the unrestricted total value curve. But it
may be necessary to enumerate all 2^N combinations [1] of jobs to find its
precise location. Each point in Fig. 2–3 represents one of the possible
combinations in this simple case. The dashed step function is the

---

[1] Assume that an N-bit binary number is used to represent a combination of jobs: a 1 in
position i indicates that job i is in the combination; a 0, that it is not. Obviously there are
2^N combinations. Note that we have been examining only N of them: those represented
by binary numbers with a string of K ones followed by a string of $N - K$ zeros (where
$0 \leq K \leq N$).

desired total value curve. It includes allocation schemes that do not meet requirement (a). For example, point *y* shows that a total value of 48 can be obtained if 9 hours per month are available. This is accomplished if (and only if) the time is used to run jobs 1 and 3; jobs with values of \$8 and \$4 per hour will be run, whereas jobs with values of \$6 and \$2 per hour will not. One cannot characterize such an allocation in terms of any simple subdivision based on value per hour (e.g., all jobs with v_i greater than or equal to some amount are run, but the others are not).

This discussion should serve to indicate that all-or-none restrictions,

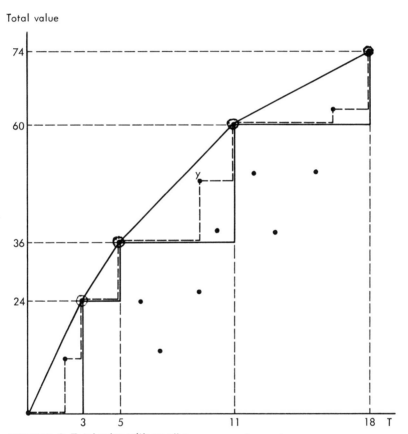

Total value

FIGURE 2-3. Total value with an all-or-none requirement.

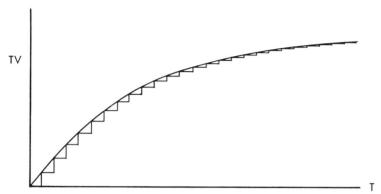

FIGURE 2–4. All-or-none constraints with many jobs.

if strictly adhered to, can cause substantial problems in optimally allocating time. The magnitude of the problem increases, of course, with the number of jobs. But so does the utility of bothering about it at all. Figure 2–4 illustrates this. If there are many jobs, the two curves that bound the actual total value curve are very close together, and either could serve as a good approximation to it. We utilize the upper curve in such cases. The reason is illustrated by the curves in Figs. 2–5a through 2–5d. In each case the marginal value is defined over the entire range of time except at points T_1^*, T_2^*, T_3^*, and T_4^*. But in the case of Fig. 2–5a we can connect the marginal value segments and obtain a curve (Fig. 2–5c) with the desirable property indicated earlier: the area under the curve up to any value of T will equal the maximal total value for that time. No construction in the world can give a sensible marginal value curve with this property for a total value curve with vertical segments, such as that shown in Fig. 2–5b (as Fig. 2–5d illustrates).

In some cases we will have to acknowledge the existence of all-or-none constraints and deal (reluctantly) with total curves containing vertical segments. Whenever possible, however, we avoid such complications, using instead total curves that are kinky but never vertical. Such curves may or may not represent reality. However, even in cases in which all-or-none restrictions really are relevant, such curves may still be perfectly adequate approximations of reality.

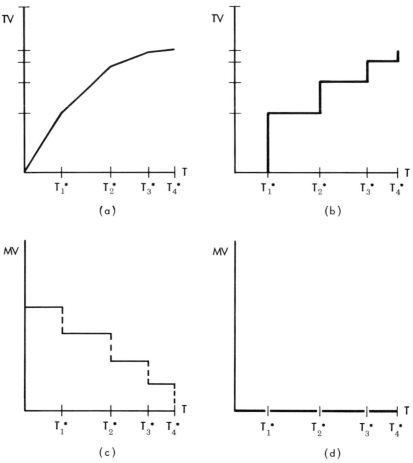

FIGURE 2-5. Total and marginal value curves.

E. SMOOTHING THE MARGINAL VALUE CURVE

As shown in Section D, if many jobs are available we may reasonably approximate the total value curve with a continuous but kinky curve, the derivative of which (marginal value) plots as a step function. But why stop there? Why not go all the way, making the total value curve smooth, thereby obtaining a correspondingly smooth marginal value curve? In fact this is precisely what economists do whenever possible. Such a transformation greatly facilitates exposition and avoids the problems of derivatives that are, strictly speaking, undefined.

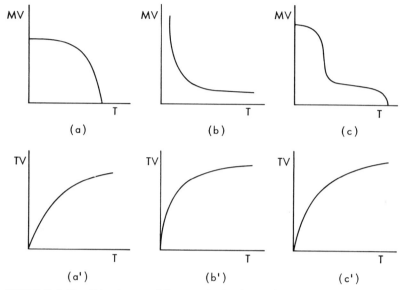

FIGURE 2-6. Possible shapes of the marginal value and total value curves.

As mentioned in Section C, the rule for efficient allocation of time guarantees that the marginal value curve will be downward-sloping (at least it will never be upward-sloping). But the rule implies nothing more. For example, any of the shapes shown in Figs. 2–6a, b, and c is perfectly plausible.[2] As a corollary, the slope of the total value curve must decrease with increases in T (at least it must not increase). But any of the shapes shown in Figs. 2–6a′, b′, and c′ is perfectly plausible. Finally, the marginal value curve is the derivative of the total value curve, while the latter is the integral of the marginal value curve.

F. THE DEMAND CURVE

Imagine a situation in which a firm can obtain any desired number of hours of computer time each month at a specified price per hour (P). Total cost is thus PT. The objective is to maximize net value (total

---

[2] Some feel that certain shapes are more plausible for certain applications than are others. For example, Donald V. Etz has asserted that Fig. 2–6c represents best the marginal value of information to be processed on a computer. However, he provides no empirical evidence, and this is primarily an empirical issue. See letters to the Editor, *Datamation*, October, 1965.

value less total cost). As shown in Chapter 1, the appropriate time per month can be determined simply enough in this case: select the value of T for which marginal value equals marginal cost. Since price is a constant, marginal cost is equal to price.

Figures 2–7a and a' show the solution using a kinky total value curve and the corresponding step-function marginal value curve. Figures 2–7b and b' show a comparable situation with smooth curves. In each case T^* is the optimum amount of time per month, TC is the total cost of that time $(= PT^*)$, TV is its total value when utilized efficiently, and NV is the difference or net value.

The simple rule for optimal utilization and for selecting the appropriate amount of time to be purchased is best illustrated in Fig. 2–7a'. If the value per hour (v_i) of a job is greater than or equal to the

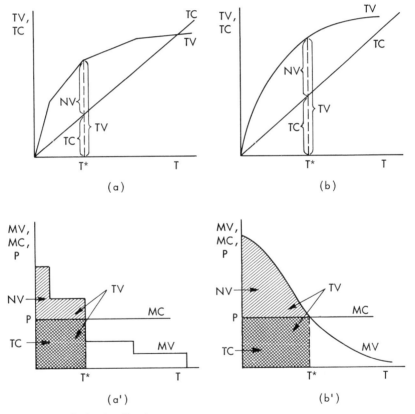

FIGURE 2–7. Optimal utilization.

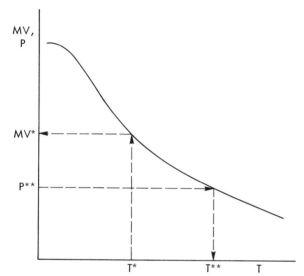

FIGURE 2-8. The marginal value curve as a demand curve.

given price per hour, the job should be run; otherwise it should not. As long as the firm follows this rule, the marginal value curve can be used to predict its response to any given price. Given a fixed price per hour of computer time, how much will the firm buy? Such a relationship forms part of a demand function:

$$q_d = f(P, \ldots)$$

where q_d is the quantity demanded, P is the price, and the dots represent other relevant factors.

Figure 2-8 illustrates the dual role of the marginal value curve. It can be used to find the marginal value of any given amount of time (e.g., T^*) and also to find the time that will be demanded (purchased) at any given price (e.g., T^{**} at price P^{**}). We thus may refer to it as either a marginal value curve or as a demand curve, depending on the manner in which it is being used; but it is the same curve, regardless of the name assigned.

G. THE LAW OF DEMAND

We have established that the marginal value curve is downward-sloping. Therefore the demand curve is too. This is one of the most important relationships in microeconomic theory. Its importance is indicated by the dignified title assigned to it: *the law of demand.* The law states simply that the lower the price the greater is the quantity demanded (purchased), and the higher the price the smaller the quantity demanded (purchased), all other things being equal. In other words,

$$\frac{\partial q_d}{\partial P} < 0 \quad \text{for all } P$$

Needless to say, this law holds strictly only in the case of a smooth demand curve (e.g., Fig. 2–7b'). Step functions (e.g., Fig. 2–7a') accord with the law only in a gross sense, since quantity demanded will not change as price changes along a vertical segment (and the curve is not downward-sloping along horizontal segments). But significant changes in price will elicit changes in quantity demanded, and the changes will be of the type predicted. A more general statement of the law accommodates all cases: demand curves are never upward-sloping.

Economists argue that the law of demand holds for virtually all goods and services. The assertion is based on overwhelming empirical evidence, although the argument we have given for a firm's demand for computer time can be generalized to buttress the case.[3] A simpler argument merely points to an absurd implication of denying that the law holds at all. Assume that the quantity demanded would never decrease as the price of some item is increased. What would be the most profitable price for the item? Clearly infinity. We observe no goods priced in this manner.

H. SHORTAGES AND SURPLUSES

We return to the case of a firm attempting to allocate a fixed amount of computer time among competing users. For convenience we assume

[3] However, the argument depends on the assumption that the value of each application (job in our example) is unaffected by its cost or that of any other application (job). Recall that the value depends, among other things, on the most that the decision-maker is willing to pay. It has been asserted that in Ireland in the nineteenth century a rise in the price of potatoes led to an increase in the quantity demanded. Because of the higher price of potatoes, the peasants could purchase less meat; this in turn increased the value they assigned to potatoes, leading them to buy more, even at the higher price. In the jargon of the economist, the "income effect" of the price increase more than offset the "substitution effect." Needless to say, this was an extreme case, one hardly likely to prove relevant for the problems facing the computer scientist.

that each user can estimate the value associated with running each of his jobs, and that the value as estimated by the user is consistent with that based on the overall objectives of the firm. Finally, we assume that, if a user is "charged" for computer time, he acts as if the charge were a true cost, running only jobs with values greater than the "price" he is charged for computer time. These are heroic assumptions, rarely met in practice. We consider them at length in Chapter 11, but at this point we blithely assume that they all hold.

Figure 2–9 represents such a situation. If users are not charged for computer time, they will collectively demand (need, require) OT_0 hours per month—many more than are available (OT^*). There will be a "shortage" of computer time (equal to T^*T_0). However, the quantity demanded (used) can be decreased by instituting a charge; the higher the price per hour, the fewer the jobs submitted. Imagine that the computer center, in a fit of zeal, sets a price per hour of OP_2. Now only OT_2 hours are demanded and there is a "surplus" of computer time (equal to T_2T^*). The appropriate price is obviously OP^*—the one that elicits the number of jobs that just use up the available computer time. As we have shown before, the time will be utilized in the most efficient

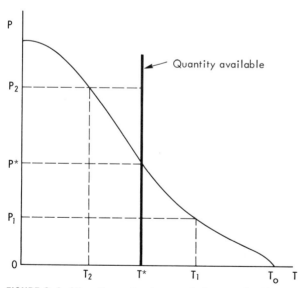

FIGURE 2–9. Allocating a fixed amount of computer time.

manner possible: total value will be maximized (and equal to the area under the demand curve to the left of T^*).

This example illustrates the economist's meanings for the terms *shortage* and *surplus:*

Shortage: the price is too low.

Surplus: the price is too high.

A common complaint made by some firms is the following: "There is a critical shortage of good programmers." What does this mean? Perhaps that the firm would like to get more programmers than it now has. But at what salary? Taking the broad view, there is a "shortage" of everything good: there is just not enough to go around if everyone is to get the quantity he would like to have (at zero price). The limited supply is typically rationed on the basis of price. Does the firm want more programmers? All that it has to do is to raise the salary offered. Hence the only sensible interpretation of its complaint is this: "We would like to hire more programmers than we can get at our current salaries, but either (1) we don't want them badly enough to raise our salaries significantly or (2) we are precluded from raising them by some institutional or legal constraint." The first situation is not a shortage in any economic sense. The second is, but the problem is more evident if stated directly: "We are not allowed to raise the salaries of programmers as much as we desire." This type of situation often prevails in governmental organizations, since civil service systems frequently fail to deal adequately with job classifications subject to major and sudden increases in average industry-wide salary. Union regulations often have a similar effect. These problems are real and significant, but the issue is only confused by using the term *shortage.*

I. EQUILIBRIUM PRICE

The price that equates quantity demanded with that available is often called an *equilibrium price,* since under certain conditions free-market forces will operate to return price to such a level if it temporarily diverges. A good example is provided by the market for used computers.

Assume that there is a given stock (N_s) of computers of a particular type. For concreteness assume further that this type of computer is no longer being produced, all computers are owned by users, and brokers actively promote sales between users. Needless to say, every seller tries to get the highest possible price and every buyer the lowest possible price.

Let there be N potential users of such computers; in theory each can estimate the value of owning a machine of this type, giving rise to values $V_1, V_2, \ldots, V_N$.[4] Assume that the brokers send out newsletters requesting calls from prospective buyers and sellers of such computers. Present owners will sell if and only if they receive more than the equipment is worth to them (V_i); nonowners will buy if and only if they have to pay less than it is worth to them (V_i).

Equilibrium is defined as a situation that will be maintained once it is attained. The equilibrium situation for the case described is reached when the N_s computers are owned by the users for whom such machines are most valuable (i.e., those with the N_s greatest values of V_i). If this were not the case, at least one nonowner would be willing to pay more than the minimum required to get at least one owner to sell his machine. If a broker *or* buyer *or* seller is clever, the parties will come together and conclude their business.

Once equilibrium is attained, brokers find themselves unable to promote any transactions. The lowest price acceptable to any owner exceeds the highest price any prospective buyer is willing to pay. Brokers sometimes reveal such figures: the former is called the "ask" price, the latter the "bid."[5] There is thus in a sense a range of equilibrium prices. But the greater the number of prospective users, the smaller will be this range. As a special case we may speak about "the" equilibrium price when the demand curve is assumed to be smooth. The two situations are illustrated in Figs. 2–10a and b.

The key point illustrated in these figures is that the results are precisely those obtained earlier, even though no central agent purposefully manipulates price, allocates equipment, etc. This is an illustration of the somewhat overadvertised "invisible hand"[6] at work: individuals motivated by self-interest and operating in a free market may often

---

[4] Some users might find it worthwhile to own more than one machine if the price were sufficiently low. Such alternatives can be treated as additional "users." Value, as used here, has the meaning given earlier: it is the smaller of (1) the value of the applications and (2) the cost of doing them in some other way.

[5] One or both may include allowances for the broker's commission.

[6] The term was introduced by Adam Smith in *The Wealth of Nations* in 1776.

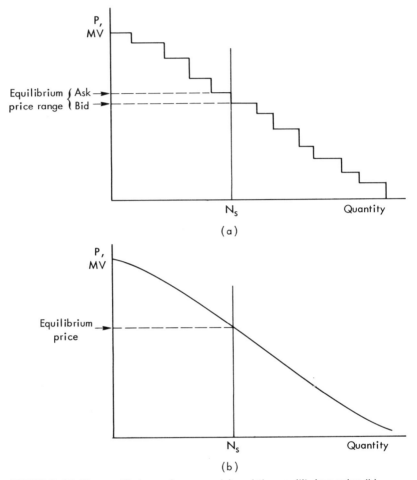

FIGURE 2-10. The equilibrium price range (a) and the equilibrium price (b).

(unwittingly) obtain the same results that a clever central authority would choose to impose on them. This example illustrates another oft-quoted principle: in a free market, prices are set by the forces of demand and supply.

Fortunately for computer brokers, conditions change rather frequently. Yesterday's equilibrium is today's disequilibrium. Suppose that a current owner decides to go out of business; the value of a computer to him may be supposed to become zero. The situation is illustrated in Figs. 2-11a, b, and c. The user in question is the one

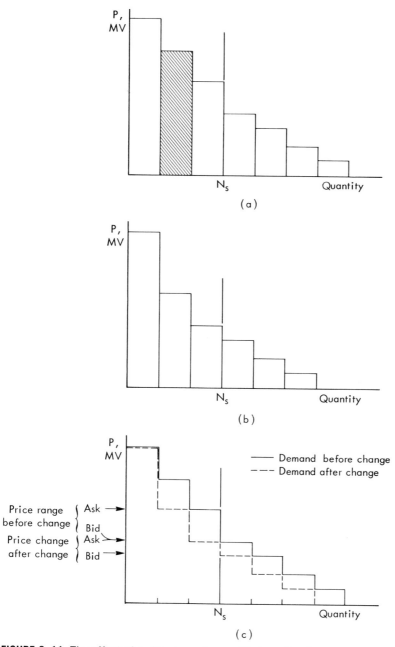

FIGURE 2-11. The effect of a change on the equilibrium situation.

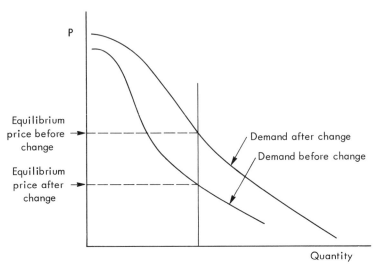

FIGURE 2-12. Equilibrium price before and after a shift in demand.

represented by the shaded block in Fig. 2–11a. When he leaves the scene, the blocks to the right move over, as shown in Fig. 2–11b. As expected, he will sell his machine to the highest bidder. The new equilibrium situation is shown in Fig. 2–11c: the new range of prices is lower than before (in this case the new ask price is the old bid price, since only one computer changed hands).

Figure 2–12 illustrates a comparable situation with continuous curves. When the demand curve shifts left, we say demand has decreased; in such cases equilibrium price also decreases. When the demand curve shifts right, we say demand has increased; in such cases equilibrium price also increases. The relevant shifts, of course, are those in the neighborhood of the current price.

J. CHARACTERISTICS OF DEMAND CURVES

Let us modify the case of Section I; we now assume that the computer is in production and that any number can be purchased at a given price (P^*). In equilibrium every user for whom the computer is worth at least P^* will have ordered one. The number of computers installed or on order will thus be Q^*, as shown in Fig. 2–13.

It is unlikely that every user will attempt to determine the precise value of such a computer in his installation. Instead he may try only to determine whether it is "worth the cost," i.e., whether $V_i \geq P^*$. Similarly, it is unlikely that every nonuser will attempt to determine the precise value of such a computer in his installation; he too may try only to determine whether it is worth more or less than P^*.

Assume now that the manufacturer of the computer unexpectedly cuts the price to P^{**}. Some of those who decided against ordering a machine at the higher price will undoubtedly find it worthwhile to order one now (i.e., all those for whom $P^* > V_i > P^{**}$), but it may take some time for these persons to identify themselves as falling in this category. Before, there was no reason to spend the time and money required to determine anything more about value than whether it was more or less than P^*. Now it is desirable to know whether it is more or less than P^{**}. But the evaluation will take time (most likely, the closer V_i to P^{**}, the longer will be the time required). Thus the initial response to the price cut will typically fall short of the eventual response, since only those who are virtually certain that the computer is worthwhile at the new price will act immediately. The total quantity installed or on order at the end of a month will increase, say to Q_m. It may take a year, however, for the full response to be felt; the quantity installed or on order at the end of a year may thus be considerably larger, say Q_y.

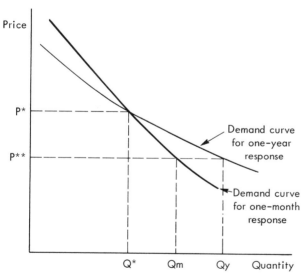

FIGURE 2-13. Long-run and short-run demand curves.

Obviously one can draw a great many demand curves; the two shown in Fig. 2–13 provide just a sample. The relevant curve depends on the initial position and the time lapse before the response is to be observed. The important point is that adjustment takes time. If price falls, quantity demanded will increase; the longer the time allowed, the greater will be the increase. If price rises, quantity demanded will decrease; the longer the time allowed, the greater will be the decrease.

Another characteristic of demand curves concerns the effect of alternatives. Roughly speaking, the better the substitutes for the item in question, the lower will be the demand curve. Remember that the curve is derived from estimates of the value of the item in various uses. But the values are, in turn, affected by the costs of alternatives.

This is illustrated in Fig. 2–14. The upper (dashed) curve represents the demand of a firm for computer time (this is similar to the example used at the beginning of the chapter). The other curves illustrate two possibilities for the firm's demand for computer time from a nearby service bureau. In each case the firm is assumed to be able to rent time from another, somewhat more distant service bureau at a price of P' per hour. If the latter were a perfect substitute for the nearer bureau, the relevant demand curve would be perfectly flat at price P' over a considerable range, as shown by the lower dashed curve. But use of

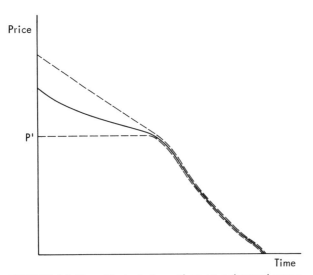

FIGURE 2–14. The effect of alternatives on a demand curve.

the more distant service bureau will typically result in transportation or communications costs. For some jobs these will be of little importance; the firm will use the nearer service bureau for such jobs only if it charges no more than P' per hour. For other jobs, however, the difficulties associated with using the distant service bureau will be significant, and the nearer bureau will be chosen even if its price is somewhat greater than P'. Thus the demand curve is likely to have some slope, as shown by the solid curve in Fig. 2–14. In any event, the demand curve faced by the nearer service bureau is obviously affected by the presence of the other (competitive) bureau. Competition is thus manifested in the demand curve facing the seller.

K. OPTIMAL COMPUTER UTILIZATION

Demand (marginal value) curves can be usefully applied to the problem of determining optimal computer utilization. Some simple cases are considered here to illustrate the method; a more complete discussion is provided in Chapter 11.

One case has already been discussed: that faced by a firm purchasing computer time from a service bureau at a fixed price per hour. Diagrams based on a smooth demand curve are shown in Figs. 2–15a and b. The optimal utilization is that at which marginal value (demand) equals marginal cost (which equals price in this case), as shown in Fig. 2–15a. Alternatively, it is the utilization for which the total value curve is parallel to the total cost curve (TC_1), as shown in Fig. 2–15b.

Now assume that, in addition to the hourly charge (P^*), the service bureau requires a fixed fee each month. What will be the optimal utilization? The answer is that it will be either unchanged or zero. This is best seen in Fig. 2–15b. The fixed fee per month merely shifts the total cost curve upward by a constant amount, for example, to TC_2 or TC_3. Either the optimal utilization is the same as before (e.g., if TC_2 is the new curve), or it is zero (e.g., if TC_3 is the new curve).

An alternative way of viewing this relationship uses Fig. 2–15a. The imposition of the fee does not affect the *marginal* cost of computer time. If any time is used, the fee must be paid. Given the decision to use computer time, it is desirable to maximize total value less total *variable* cost, where the latter refers to all costs that vary with utilization once the fixed fee has been paid. Figure 2–15a can be used directly

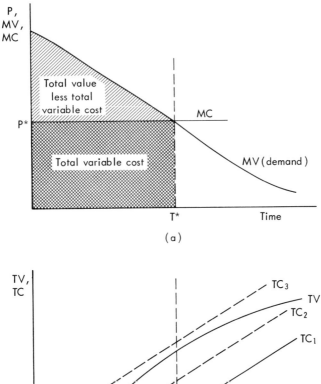

FIGURE 2–15. The determination of optimal computer utilization.

to find the optimal utilization viewed in this manner, regardless of the fee charged. But the net value (the upper shaded area) is now total value less total variable cost. The true net value equals this amount less the fixed fee. If the fee exceeds the upper shaded area in Fig.

2–15a, no time should be utilized; if it does not, T^* hours should be used.

The practical implication of this case is quite important. When all-or-none decisions are required (e.g., whether or not to pay a fixed fee, whether or not to buy a computer, whether or not to add a second-shift operator), it is often useful to analyze the problem by asking the following questions in order:

1. If the step is taken, what is the optimal way of utilizing the added capability?
2. Is the value that will be obtained if the step is taken and the added capability used optimally sufficiently larger than the variable costs to justify the expense of taking the step at all?

A useful construct formalizes the results of this decision process for the case of a user faced with a fixed fee plus a constant hourly charge. Let F be the maximum fee that the user is willing to pay if the hourly charge is P. A typical relationship between P and F is shown by the curve in Fig. 2–16c; it is derived from the demand curve shown in Figs. 2–16a and b. At a price per hour of P' the user will purchase no computer time and F will be zero. If time is free ($P = 0$), the user will pay any fee up to F', the area under his demand (marginal value) curve. At prices P_1 and P_2 he will pay fees up to F_1 and F_2, respectively. Since demand curves are downward-sloping, the P-F curve must be both downward-sloping and convex to the origin. The reason for this latter characteristic is seen in Figs. 2–16a and b. A drop in price per hour of ΔP increases F by an amount shown by the shaded area ΔF_1 in Fig. 2–16a when $P = P_1$ and by an amount shown by the shaded area ΔF_2 in Fig. 2–16b when $P = P_2$. Clearly ΔF_2 must be larger than ΔF_1; thus the curve in Fig. 2–16c must be convex to the origin.

Diagrams of the type shown in Fig. 2–16c are particularly interesting from the seller's viewpoint. If the service bureau wishes to retain this user as a customer, it must choose a P, F combination represented by some point in the shaded area under his P-F curve. This relationship will prove valuable in later discussions of pricing policies for not only service bureaus but other sellers as well.

The final case is both more complex and more realistic. The seller requires a fixed fee (F) each month if any time is to be utilized. This fee entitles the buyer to some number of hours per month at no additional charge; the number is called the basic monthly utilization (B).

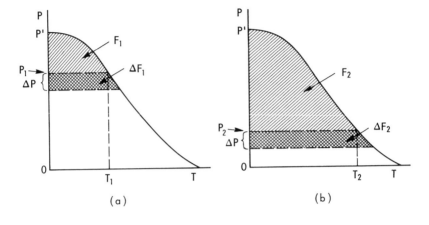

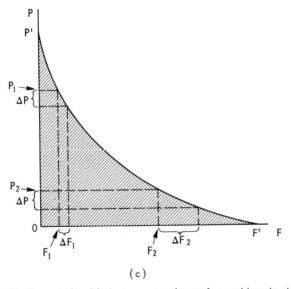

FIGURE 2–16. The relationship between maximum fee and hourly charge.

Additional hours may be obtained, but at some constant cost per hour (P).[7] The buyer is assumed to use an internal charge of C^* per hour to regulate the utilization of computer time. As before, we heroically

---

[7] This is equivalent to a scheme in which the seller charges a constant price per unit (P) but requires a minimum utilization for billing purposes. The (implicit) fee is simply $F = BP$.

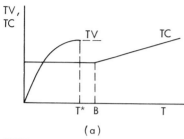
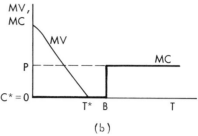

(a)
(b)

FIGURE 2–17. Hypothetical relationship between cost and value: optimal internal charge equals zero.

assume that only jobs with a value per hour in excess of C^* will be submitted.

The costs faced by the firm are shown by the total and marginal cost curves in Figs. 2–17, 2–18, and 2–19. Three possibilities regarding the relationship between total cost and total value are illustrated.[8] In the case shown in Fig. 2–17 the basic monthly utilization is sufficiently large to run all jobs worth anything at all. The optimal utilization (T^*) is thus less than B, and all valuable jobs should be run. The internal charge (C^*) should be zero.

The case shown in Fig. 2–18 is one in which the optimal utilization per month is exactly equal to the basic monthly utilization. The internal charge must be set so as to ration this time; it will lie somewhere between zero and P.

[8] Only cases in which total value exceeds total cost over some range have been included. In all other situations the optimal policy would be to abandon the computer entirely.

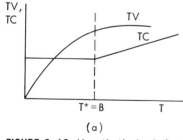
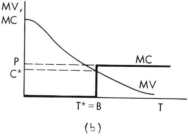

(a)
(b)

FIGURE 2–18. Hypothetical relationship between cost and value: optimal internal charge lies between zero and P.

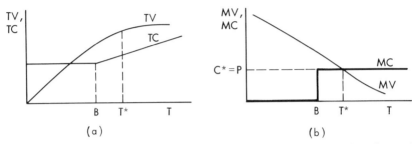

FIGURE 2–19. Hypothetical relationship between cost and value: optimal internal charge equals P.

Finally there is the type of situation shown in Fig. 2–19. Here the optimal utilization exceeds B; all jobs with values per hour exceeding or equaling P should be run. The correct internal charge thus is equal to P.

In a formal sense it can be said that in each case the appropriate internal charge equals marginal cost. One often sees prescriptions to engage in "marginal cost pricing." But such a recommendation is of limited value in cases of this sort; marginal cost varies with utilization, and at B it is not even uniquely defined. The correct view is that proposed earlier: the price should be set to ration the (optimal) supply.

Conditions	C > P	●									
	C = P		●	●	●						
	O < C < P					●	●	●			
	C = O								●	●	●
	T > B	●				●			●		
	T = B			●			●			●	
	T < B				●			●			●
Action	Lower C	●			●			●			
	Raise C					●			●		
	Do not change C		●	●			●			●	●

FIGURE 2–20. Decision table for setting an internal charge. *Definitions:* C = Internal charge per hour of computer time; P = Cost per hour of computer time in excess of basic monthly utilization; B = Basic monthly utilization: hours per month available with no surcharge; T = Total time required to run all jobs submitted at charge C.

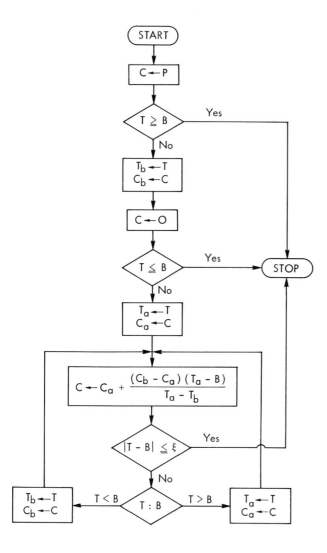

FIGURE 2-21. An iterative process for setting an internal charge. *Note: T_b and C_b* refer to the most recent observation of the demand curve giving a value of T below B; T_a and C_a refer to the most recent observation giving a value of T above B. The iterative procedure recomputes the charge by assuming the demand curve is linear through these points and finding the charge at which such a curve would give $T = B$. The process terminates when T is within some prespecified tolerance (ξ) of B.

Note that there need be no particular relationship between the "receipts" obtained from charges and the desirability of utilizing the computer at all in these cases. All three diagrams represent situations in which total value exceeds total cost at some levels of utilization (and, a fortiori, at the optimal level). But charges may or may not cover total costs. In the case shown in Fig. 2-17 the charge required to induce optimal utilization is zero, and total "receipts" will clearly not cover costs. Later we will explore this apparent paradox more extensively; at this point we simply remark that an excess of receipts from internal charges over costs may be a sufficient but not necessary condition for a valuable activity.

The analysis based on Figs. 2-17, 2-18, and 2-19 assumes that some central agent knows the values of all the firm's possible jobs. If this were the case, there would be no need to utilize a system of internal charges to select appropriate jobs: the agent would know which ones to run. A more likely situation occurs when the central agent (e.g., the manager of the firm's computer center) knows only the costs of computation to the firm, that is, the total and marginal cost curves. He must then experiment with internal charges until an optimal utilization is found.

Figure 2-20 provides a decision table that shows the direction in which the charge should be altered under various conditions. Figure 2-21 suggests one possible iterative process for coming close to the actual optimum by changing the charge periodically (e.g., every month) until an approximate solution is obtained. As usual we must remark that formidable practical problems are associated with implementing such a process; problems of this type are considered in Chapter 11.

This particular three-parameter (F, B, P) pricing policy has been discussed at considerable length here because its use has been so widespread. Service bureaus offering time-shared service often follow such a policy, and similar schemes were commonly used by manufacturers for contracts involving the rental of computer equipment before 1965. To understand why sellers often select policies of this type we must temporarily adopt their point of view; this is the task of the next chapter.

A. REVENUE VERSUS VALUE

We have argued that many decisions can usefully be cast as problems in which the objective is to maximize net value, the difference between total value and total cost. For such analyses to be meaningful, of course, both total value and total cost must be measured in a manner relevant for the decision-maker in question. The total value must be the total value *to him,* as must total cost. However, in some cases total value (or cost) may be the value (cost) to someone else as well. For example, in Chapter 2 we dealt with cases in which a firm's computer center "sold" computation service to users within the firm. The decision-maker was the manager of the computer center, and total value from his viewpoint was assumed to be the value to the firm of the jobs run. But since the value to each user was similarly defined, the value to the buyer was also relevant for the seller. Thus we could discuss "total value" without specifying whether it applied to the buyer or the seller.

In most cases there is no neat identity of the goals of the seller with those of the buyer. The seller may wish to maximize the value received by the buyer for a particular service, and in this regard their goals are similar. But the seller may also want to obtain as much of that value as possible from the buyer in fees; in this regard their interests diverge sharply.

This chapter deals with cases in which the seller is concerned primarily with the money paid by the buyer, and only indirectly with the value of the benefits the buyer obtains. To simplify the analysis we assume that only the revenue received is relevant and use the term *total revenue* to indicate the total value to the seller. This makes it possible to let the term *total value* represent total value to the buyer(s). Note that, given this definition of total value, the marginal value curve can still stand as a demand curve.

The objective of the seller must now be stated as follows: maximize total revenue minus total cost; or, defining the difference as profit, maximize total profit. The marginal conditions are straightforward. Marginal revenue is defined as the derivative of total revenue with respect to the decision variable in question. To maximize profit, we find the value of the decision variable for which marginal revenue equals marginal cost. Needless to say, the earlier discussion concerning kinks, discontinuities, steps, etc., and their effects on marginal conditions applies here as well.

B. PERFECT PRICE DISCRIMINATION

Assume that a software firm has completed a particularly elegant general-purpose program (e.g., a linear programming code). The development cost has been incurred, and the marginal cost of providing extra copies is insignificant; thus total cost is essentially unaffected by the number of copies, as shown in Fig. 3–1. Although there may be many potential users of the program, its value will vary considerably among them. The situation can thus be represented with the familiar total and marginal value curves, as shown in Figs. 3–1 and 3–2 (for convenience we use smooth curves).

How should the software firm price the program? Obviously the firm cannot sell it to any given customer for more than it is worth to him; the maximum price that can be charged is thus the value of the

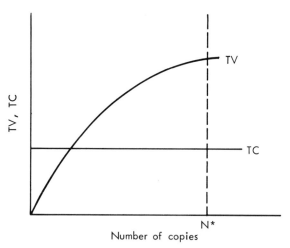

FIGURE 3-1. Total cost and total value versus number of copies of a program.

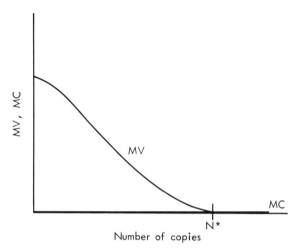

FIGURE 3-2. Marginal cost and marginal value versus number of copies of a program.

program to him. If the software firm can accurately estimate this value, and if resale of the program can be prohibited, then each buyer can be charged a price just slightly below the value he attributes to the program.

Economists use the term *discriminatory pricing* to refer to policies of this sort, in which the prices charged different users differ in a manner unrelated to the seller's costs. No connotation of necessarily antisocial behavior should be assumed at this point; the term simply indicates that the seller discriminates among buyers on the basis of the value they receive from the item. Price discrimination is *perfect* if each buyer pays an amount only slightly below the value of the product for the use in question.

If the seller is particularly successful at price discrimination, the amount sold may approach that obtained under circumstances in which the seller acts in a more benevolent capacity. Perfect discrimination allows him to capture virtually all the value of the item to the buyer. Thus total revenue will equal total value. The seller is keenly interested in the value of his product to the user since he plans to capture almost all of it. In this case, perfect discrimination will lead the software firm to sell N^* copies of the program; it will be used in every installation in which it is worth anything at all, clearly a sensible situation from the standpoint of society as a whole since the marginal cost of an additional copy is zero. In general discriminatory pricing is efficient, since it allows the seller to base his decisions on the value of his product. Note, however, that all the fruits of this efficiency accrue to the seller.

If information were perfect and free, and if contracts could be enforced at no cost, extensive price discrimination would be used for most goods and services since such a policy provides the greatest possible revenue from any given quantity sold. Of course information is neither perfect nor free, and it may be very expensive (perhaps even illegal) to enforce contracts to prohibit resale. Thus no firm finds it profitable (or even possible) to engage in perfectly discriminatory pricing. But in many situations it proves both possible and profitable to discriminate to some extent. We will consider some important cases later. First, however, the full range of possibilities must be defined. Perfect discrimination lies at one end of the spectrum; a single-price policy lies at the other.

C. A SINGLE-PRICE POLICY

Consider a company manufacturing a small computer so inexpensive that the administrative cost associated with renting it is very large relative to the value of the equipment. Under these conditions the additional revenue obtained through discriminatory pricing is likely to be less than the cost of enforcing the policy. If the equipment is to be offered to different users at different prices, they must be prohibited from trading with one another. If a computer were worth, say, $20,000 to user A and only $10,000 to user B, the manufacturer might attempt to make corresponding offers. But there would be a substantial incentive for B to purchase a machine for $10,000 and sell it (or time on it) to A for some amount between $10,000 and $20,000. By renting equipment the manufacturer could prevent resale and thus enforce a policy of discriminatory pricing. When equipment is sold outright, however, it is much more difficult to make such a policy effective. In this case we assume that the manufacturer has decided to adopt the simplest of all possible policies: a single price will be set, with any buyer allowed to purchase one or more computers at that price.

This is, of course, precisely the type of situation in which the marginal value curve can be interpreted as a demand curve. Thus in Fig. 3–4

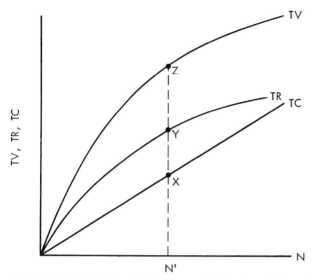

FIGURE 3-3. Total value, total revenue, total cost and the maximum-profit quantity.

the marginal value (demand) curve shows that N' computers will be purchased if the (single) price is P', having a total value equal to the entire shaded area under the demand curve up to N' (shown also as distance $N'Z$ in Fig. 3-3). Total revenue, however, will be less. Total revenue is price times quantity; it will equal the cross-hatched area of rectangle $OP'AN'$ (Fig. 3-4), the sides of which measure price (OP') and quantity (ON'). In Fig. 3-3 the total revenue associated with quantity N' is shown by the distance $N'Y$. The full relationship between total revenue and quantity sold is indicated by curve TR in Fig. 3-3.

The optimal behavior for the firm is shown in Figs. 3-3 and 3-4: N' computers should be sold at a price of P' each. This can be seen in Fig. 3-3; profit (the distance between the total revenue and total cost curves) is maximized at N'—the amount is shown by distance XY. In Fig. 3-4, the optimal output is found by invoking the marginal conditions; marginal revenue equals marginal cost at output N'. The price to be charged is, of course, the greatest that can be obtained for the quantity, as shown by the demand curve; for N' the appropriate price is P'.

Figure 3-4 shows marginal revenue everywhere below the demand

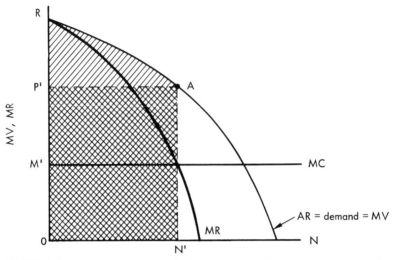

FIGURE 3-4. Marginal value, marginal revenue, marginal cost and the maximum-profit quantity.

curve. This is not accidental. The demand curve indicates the maximum price that can be charged for any given quantity if the entire amount is to be sold:

$$P_d = f(Q)$$

The maximum total revenue that can be obtained from any given quantity is thus

$$TR = Q \cdot P_d$$

and marginal revenue is

$$MR \equiv \frac{dTR}{dQ} = P_d + \frac{dP_d}{dQ} \cdot Q$$

The derivative dP_d/dQ (the slope of the demand curve at Q) is generally negative; this *is* the law of demand. Thus marginal revenue must be less than price for any given quantity. Moreover, the steeper the demand curve, the greater will be the disparity between price and marginal revenue. Figures 3–5a through 3–5d illustrate this relationship, including the special case in which the demand curve is virtually horizontal and marginal revenue equals price. Note that it is entirely possible for the marginal revenue curve to be upward-sloping, but it may not rise above the demand curve.

This relationship may be made even more obvious by assigning yet another name to the demand (marginal value) curve. *Average* revenue is defined as total revenue divided by quantity, but it clearly must equal price per unit if a single-price policy is used:

$$AR \equiv \frac{TR}{Q} = \frac{P \cdot Q}{Q} = P$$

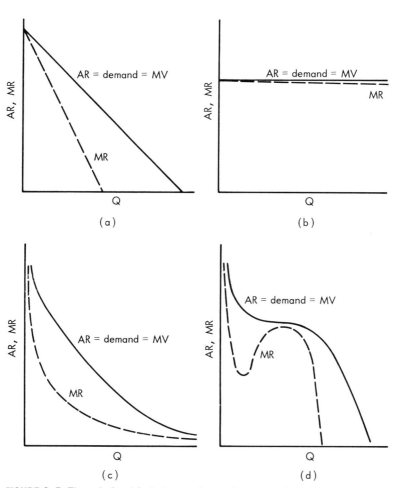

FIGURE 3–5. The relationship between demand and marginal revenue.

The demand curve can thus be considered an average revenue curve in this case. To make an average value decrease, one must add a marginal value below the current average (the analogy with grades is obvious). And the greater the desired decrease in the average, the lower must be the marginal value relative to the current average.

This is an important case, and a number of its characteristics warrant discussion. First note that the price of the computer is determined by the number available (N'). Had the manufacturer set a price above P' it would have been unable to sell the entire output; eventually a reduction would have been required to bring price down to P'. On the other hand, had the firm set a price below P' the entire stock would have been sold, and very rapidly. If the buyers had not been those for whom the computer was most valuable, some reselling would have taken place, but sooner or later the computers would be owned by those with the N' most valuable applications, and the bid and ask prices would converge to P'. The computer manufacturer, by setting a price below equilibrium, only provides a windfall to those fortunate enough to obtain the underpriced equipment, at the cost of a reduction in his own profit.

A second point concerns the relationship between value and price. The market equilibrium price for N' computers is P'. Any customer who chooses to purchase a computer accords it a value at least as great as P'. But in the absence of discriminatory pricing most buyers can be expected to receive a bargain—the value of the computer will exceed its price, perhaps by a large amount. This is easily shown if the marginal value curve is drawn as a series of blocks, as in Fig. 3–6. The shaded area in each block represents the difference between the value of the computer to the customer and its price (P'). Only the marginal buyer finds the machine just worth P'. In a market in which products can be freely traded, price will equal the marginal value for the existing supply; if N units are available, the price will be the value of the item in the Nth most valuable use.

We have repeatedly argued that price is determined by the available supply and not by cost. However, the available supply is typically affected by someone's estimate of the relationship between price and cost. In this case supply will be set so that marginal revenue equals marginal cost. But the manufacturer will consciously avoid producing enough computers to bring price down to marginal cost. This may seem

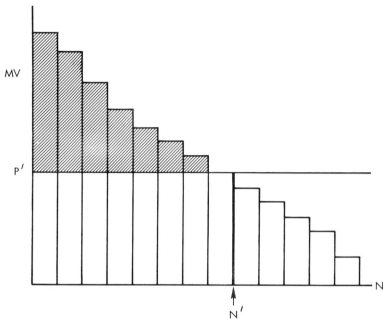

FIGURE 3-6. The relationship between value and price.

perverse. At an output of N' the marginal value of an additional computer is P', but the marginal cost is only M' (Fig. 3–4). Why not plan to produce $N' + 1$ computers? Because this amount cannot be sold at a price of P', and the total revenue obtainable from an output of $N' + 1$ computers does not exceed that obtainable from N' by an amount large enough to cover the additional cost.

Profit-maximizing firms will find it desirable to produce a quantity for which marginal cost equals marginal revenue. This implies that the marginal cost of production will be less than the price of the item. But how much less? The answer depends on the slope of the demand curve: the flatter the curve, the less is the disparity between price and marginal cost, as illustrated in Figs. 3–7a through 3–7c. In Chapter 2 we suggested that typically the greater the competition facing the seller, the flatter will be the demand curve for his product. The implication is obvious: the greater the competition, the smaller is the difference between price and marginal cost.

Note that disparity between price and marginal cost need not imply

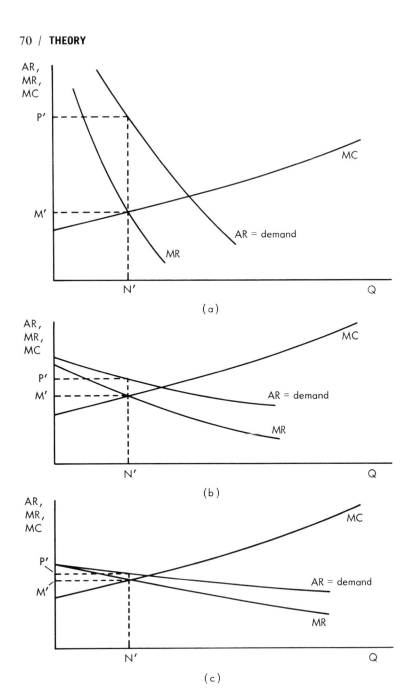

FIGURE 3-7. The disparity between price and marginal cost.

that the manufacturer is making an exorbitant profit. In the case illustrated in Figs. 3-8a and b the seller makes no profit at all, even though
price differs considerably from marginal cost. In fact it may be impossible for the seller to avoid loss with a single-price policy. In the situation shown in Fig. 3-8c some price discrimination is required to cover
costs. In the situation shown in Fig. 3-8d perfect price discrimination
is essential for this purpose. These cases illustrate the reason for not
labeling price discrimination as clearly antisocial. Figure 3-8c may
represent rather well the relationship between cost and value that held
for certain large scientific computers produced between 1955 and 1965.
Had the manufacturers not been able to engage in some type of price
discrimination,[1] such computers might not have been developed at all.
Price discrimination increases the seller's profit, but it may raise it
only from a negative amount (i.e., a loss) to zero.

D. A TWO-PRICE POLICY

We have covered the two extreme cases. The total value curve provides an upper bound — it indicates the maximum revenue that can be
obtained for each possible quantity (with perfectly discriminatory
pricing). The total revenue curve associated with a single-price policy
provides a lower bound. Between these two curves lie points that can
be obtained with an almost unlimited variety of pricing policies. Here
we consider a policy in which buyers can be divided into two groups
with resale between the members of different groups either prohibited
or so costly that it is not worthwhile.

Assume that a manufacturer is selling (or renting) large scientific
computers to two types of buyers. The first type is best represented by
a large aerospace firm, for which the computer may be considered very
important. The second is best represented by a university, for which
the computer is desirable but perhaps less important. Educational institutions are, of course, readily identified and categorized. Moreover, it
is relatively simple to prohibit such an institution from selling equipment or time to an industrial user at bargain rates. The manufacturer
simply specifies in the sale or rental contract that "noneducational"

---

[1] Many forms were used; some of the more important are described in the remaining sections of this chapter.

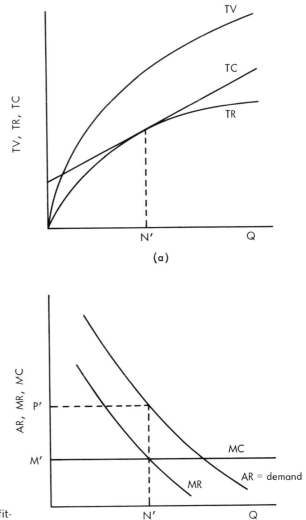

FIGURE 3–8. The profitability of a single-price policy.

(a)

(b)

use requires additional payment to the manufacturer. Since educational institutions are typically nonprofit organizations, there is little temptation to cheat by not reporting such outside use. Thus all the conditions for a viable policy of price discrimination are present.

The situation is shown in Figs. 3–9a and b. The demand curve for

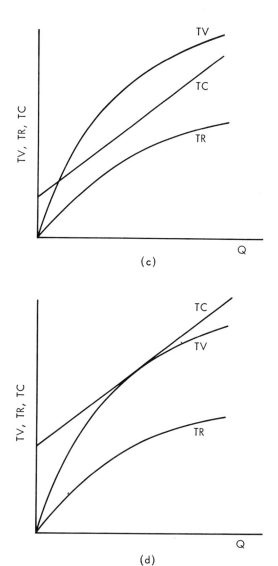

(c)

(d)

educational use is assumed to be flatter than that for industrial use: thus the marginal revenue is closer to average revenue in Fig. 3–9a than in Fig. 3–9b.

The manufacturer must decide (1) how many computers to sell (Q_T), (2) how many to sell to educational institutions (Q_e), (3) how many to

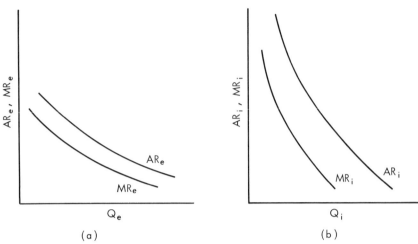

FIGURE 3-9. Demand conditions for two users.

sell to industrial users (Q_i), and (4) what prices to charge (P_e and P_i). Of course these decisions are interrelated.

What are the characteristics of the optimal solution? First, the marginal revenues in the two markets must be the same. Assume that some total quantity has been allocated so that $MR_e > MR_i$; obviously total revenue can be increased by reallocating the existing supply, increasing Q_e and decreasing Q_i. Conversely, if $MR_e < MR_i$ it will pay to sell more computers to industrial users and fewer to educational institutions, since increased industrial sales will add more to total revenue than the required decrease in educational sales will subtract. Thus the rule for the optimal allocation of any given total quantity is as follows:

Select Q_e and Q_i so that

$$(1) \ MR_e = MR_i$$

and

$$(2) \ Q_e + Q_i = Q_T$$

This rule can be used to construct a curve relating quantity and marginal revenue. In Fig. 3-10a the two diagrams of Fig. 3-9 are drawn back to back. Consider a situation in which $MR_e = MR_i = M^*$. This will be the case only if $Q_e = Q_e^*$ and $Q_i = Q_i^*$. The total quantity required is the sum $Q_T^* = Q_e^* + Q_i^*$. Thus the quantity Q_T^*, when properly allocated between educational and industrial users, will give marginal revenue equal to M^*, as plotted in Fig. 3–10b. If the desired marginal revenue is M^{**}, the appropriate quantity is Q_T^{**}, also shown in Figs. 3–10a and b. Repeating this procedure leads to the construction of curve MR_T, relating marginal revenue to total quantity under the assumptions of optimal allocation between the two markets. The best total quantity is obviously that for which marginal revenue equals

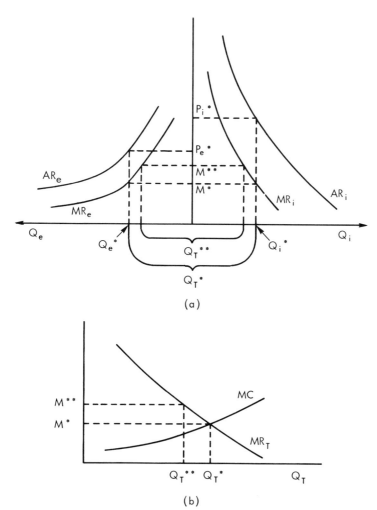

(a)

(b)

FIGURE 3–10. Maximizing profit with a two-price policy.

marginal cost; in Fig. 3–10b it is $Q_T{}^*$. The appropriate allocation is shown in Fig. 3–10a ($Q_e{}^*$ to educational institutions and $Q_i{}^*$ to industrial users), as are the prices ($P_e{}^*$ and $P_i{}^*$).

Optimal allocation requires that marginal revenues in the two markets be equal (and equal to marginal cost). But it does not require that prices be equal. Quite the contrary, the price charged in the market characterized by the steeper demand curve should be greater than that charged in the other market. The desirability of a price increase depends on the size of the resulting decrease in quantity demanded. The smaller this decrease, the more desirable will be the price increase. Thus the steeper the demand curve, the greater is the optimal price.

This example is intended primarily to illustrate a particular form of price discrimination. However, computer manufacturers do offer educational "discounts," and they do impose restrictions on the sale of equipment and time to outside users at low rates. Obviously, such behavior may be perfectly consistent with profit maximization.

E. ELASTICITY OF DEMAND

Thus far we have used the slope of the demand curve to represent the responsiveness of quantity demanded to changes in price. In practice it is often desirable to use a different measure, the price elasticity (or simply elasticity) of demand. This can be defined as the ratio of (1) the percentage change in quantity demanded brought about by a change in price to (2) the percentage change in price. Alternatively,

$$E_d \equiv \frac{dQ/Q}{dP/P}$$

One advantage of this measure is its lack of dependence on the units in which price and quantity are measured: it is a pure number. Moreover, actual demand curves often exhibit relatively constant elasticities over substantial ranges (and hence varying slopes).

Assume that a seller has obtained several price-quantity combinations from market surveys, test marketing in various areas, and other sources, and wishes to estimate the demand curve for his product. Typically regression analysis is used to find the best-fitting equation of a particular form. One possible form is simply linear (i.e., has a constant slope):

$$Q = a + bP$$

But there is no reason to assume a priori that this is the best form. A particularly interesting alternative plots as a linear equation on log-log graph paper.

$$\ln Q = a + b(\ln P)$$

The coefficients a and b can be found simply by using $(\ln Q)$ and $(\ln P)$ as the observations and applying standard techniques of linear regression.[2] The corresponding equation using Q and P can then be reconstructed:

$$e^{\ln Q} = e^{a + b(\ln P)}$$

or

$$Q = a'P^b$$

where $a' = e^a$. If this type of equation fits the data reasonably well, one can meaningfully discuss *the* elasticity of demand (b), since it is constant over the relevant range of prices and quantities. Figures 3–11a and b illustrate this relationship for three sample curves. Note that in general, however, elasticity (like slope) may vary from point to point along the demand curve.

Elasticities are often categorized as follows:

$E_d = 0$ to -1:   demand is inelastic;
$E_d = -1$:   demand is unitary elastic; and
$E_d = -1$ to $-\infty$: demand is elastic.

It is a simple matter to show that no producer will find it profitable to operate in a region in which demand is inelastic. Recall the formula for marginal revenue:

$$MR = P + \frac{dP}{dQ} \cdot Q$$

Rearranging, we obtain

$$MR = \left(1 + \frac{dP}{dQ} \cdot \frac{Q}{P}\right) P$$

$$= \left(1 + \frac{1}{E_d}\right) P$$

Now, if demand is inelastic, $0 > E_d > -1$, and marginal revenue will be negative. But marginal cost can never be negative; thus the optimal

[2] Such techniques are described in the appendix.

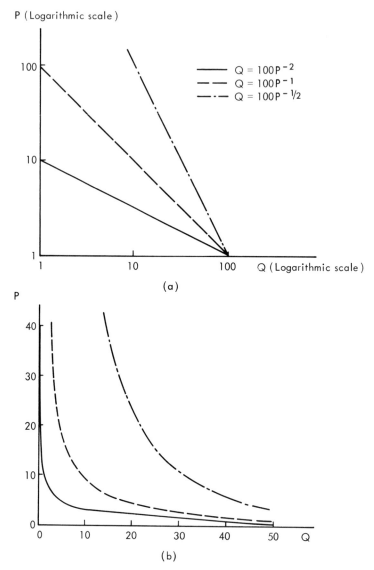

P (Logarithmic scale)

$Q = 100P^{-2}$
$Q = 100P^{-1}$
$Q = 100P^{-1/2}$

Q (Logarithmic scale)

(a)

(b)

FIGURE 3-11. Constant-elasticity demand curves.

output can never occur at a point at which the demand for the seller's product is inelastic. We note in passing that this formulation indicates clearly that the more elastic the demand curve, the closer will marginal revenue (and hence marginal cost) be to selling price.

There are other measures of elasticity. For example, the total number of computers sold might be related to the average price per computer and the level of the national income (Y) as follows:

$$\ln Q = a + b(\ln P) + c(\ln Y)$$

Equivalently,

$$Q = a'P^bY^c$$

where $a' = e^a$. As before, b is the price elasticity of demand. The coefficient c measures the income elasticity, the ratio of (1) the percentage change in quantity demanded caused by a change in income to (2) the percentage change in income. In empirical work demand functions of this type are used extensively.

F. QUANTITY DISCOUNTS

Price discrimination can lead to increased profit for a seller but only if it is possible to differentiate among buyers (at least roughly) on the basis of the value they attribute to the product. In practice it is often impossible to identify a priori those buyers willing to pay high prices. In such cases an alternative approach may prove fruitful. The seller offers the same *terms* to all buyers, but the terms are arranged so that buyers pay *amounts* that vary in a manner related less to the seller's costs than to the value received by the individual buyer.

An obvious example of this policy is the quantity discount. Consider a manufacturer of small process-control computers. Depending on the price, any given buyer may want one or more of the computers. The total demand (marginal value) curve for the product will thus reflect the addition of both new users and new uses as price is lowered. Figure 3–12a shows an overall marginal value curve (step function) that includes three possible uses for computers in a particular firm (indicated by the shaded blocks). Each buyer has a rudimentary demand curve of his own; for the firm in question it is that shown in Fig. 3–12b. The seller can increase his profit by treating each customer as a separate market. For example, this particular firm could be offered one computer at a price of P_1 and a second at a price of P_2; since the value of a third would be less than marginal cost, purchase of additional computers should be discouraged (e.g., by setting their price equal to marginal cost).

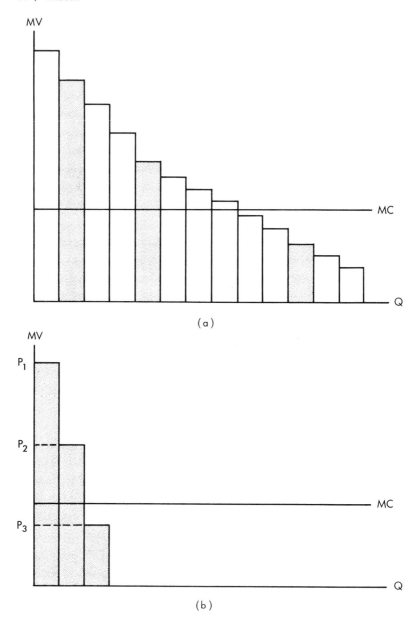

FIGURE 3–12. Total demand (a) and one firm's demand (b) for small computers.

Needless to say, if the seller knew the values of various applications in each customer's firm, he would offer a special set of terms to each potential buyer. In fact he must operate under conditions of considerable uncertainty. In many cases he will try to find a single pattern of prices that provides some of the advantages of discrimination and then offer this pattern to all buyers. Since demand curves are downward-sloping, the pattern will involve lower prices for additional units — in other words, quantity discounts. The lowest price offered should not, of course, be below marginal cost.

It is important to note that the type of pricing policy discussed here is characterized by a decreasing marginal cost *to the user* as quantity is increased. This need not reflect a comparable decrease in the seller's marginal cost. Indeed, even if the seller's marginal cost increases with output, such a pricing policy may prove profitable.

Quantity discounts are often attributed to the reduced cost per unit of administrative tasks, transportation, and maintenance. However, many actual cases exhibit characteristics inconsistent with any explanation other than that attributable to the advantages of price discrimination. Quantity discounts are used by computer manufacturers and service bureaus, among others.

In this case, as in others, discriminatory pricing need not imply high profits. Without quantity discounts a manufacturer may not find it worthwhile to develop a computer, or a service bureau to provide service.

G. RENTAL CHARGES

Even more complicated types of price discrimination can be adopted when a computer is rented. The value of the computer can be assumed to be related to its use, and the rental fee varied accordingly. The number of possible arrangements is almost infinite, and it is very difficult to predict which one will prove best in any given case. However, it is instructive to consider some policies that have actually been used in computer rental contracts. We focus here on situations in which the same terms are offered to all buyers. Such policies are particularly important in practice because they appear to be acceptable to those charged with enforcing antitrust laws. Manufacturers concerned with potential legal action under such legislation thus have good reasons to favor this type of price discrimination.

Consider a manufacturer renting a number of computers of a particular model to various users. Assume that the computer is sufficiently valuable to warrant rather extensive record-keeping and administrative costs (since the potential gain from discriminatory pricing is substantial). Rental is paid monthly. Although not essential to the argument, we assume that the costs of the manufacturer are virtually unaffected by the utilization of any given machine. Thus the marginal cost of an hour is zero up to some practical limit per month (H_L), as shown in Figs. 3–13a and b.

Consider a user with the applications represented by curve MV_1 in Fig. 3–13a; the total monthly value of a computer if used optimally is shown by the shaded area. This value will be obtained only if the marginal cost to the buyer equals that to the seller (i.e., zero up to H_L hours). For the user represented in Fig. 3–13b the maximum total monthly value (shown by the shaded area) will be obtained as long as the marginal cost to him does not exceed C_b.

We wish to consider three types of policies that a manufacturer might adopt for such users. The first involves a price for each hour the computer is used plus a basic monthly fee; the second exempts some number of hours per month from the hourly charge; the third adds an upper limit to the total monthly cost. These will be termed two-part, three-part, and four-part policies. Chapter 2 discussed the optimal behavior for a user faced with such pricing policies. We now consider the optimal behavior for a seller attempting to maximize profit by using policies of this type.

Consider first situations in which the manufacturer makes a two-part offer to his customers: a basic monthly fee (F) plus a surcharge for every hour utilized (P). We assume that the same terms are offered to all buyers. Needless to say, outright sale is not possible under such a scheme; only if the manufacturer retains ownership of the computer, can he extract additional fees for its utilization. It has been alleged that IBM's pre-1956 policy of only renting its equipment and requiring the use of its own punched cards at purportedly inflated prices was an effective two-part policy.[3]

---

[3] Armen A. Alchian and William R. Allen, *University Economics*, Second Edition, Wadsworth Publishing Company, Belmont, Calif., 1967, pp. 331–332.

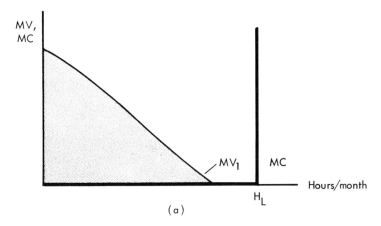

(a)

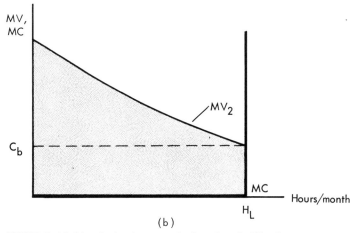

(b)

FIGURE 3-13. Marginal value, marginal cost and utilization.

Figure 3-14 illustrates a situation involving three hypothetical customers. The three feasible regions divide the figure into six subregions (U through Z). Any combination of terms lying within a given region results in the same set of customers accepting the offer and thus the same number of computers being installed. To find the overall optimum set of terms the manufacturer must determine the optimum set within each of these subregions; the overall optimum is then simply the best of those found in the initial stage.

We shall not describe in detail the method for finding the optimum

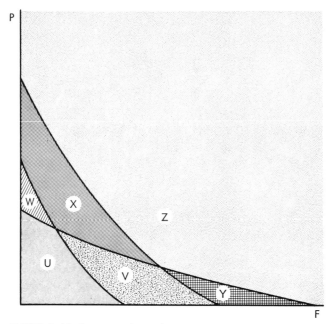

FIGURE 3-14. Customers' reactions to fee-price combinations.

set of terms within a subregion. However, it is not too complex. The cost of the computer can be disregarded since within the subregion the number of installations is constant. Moreover, the solution must lie on the right-hand boundary of the region. This follows from the facts that (1) for any given P the payments for hours utilized are determined and (2) total revenue is the sum of these payments plus N times F, where N is the number of customers for the region. Obviously, for any given P, total revenue is maximized by selecting the maximum value of F within the region. Since cost is not altered as long as the terms remain within the selected region, only points along the right-hand boundary are efficient.

Unfortunately the analysis cannot be generalized simply. The overall optimum may lie within the quadrant, but it may also lie along the horizontal axis (i.e., involve only a one-part pricing policy). In the general case one would expect that the optimum terms would involve the use of an hourly surcharge, but the conditions required for this result are not easily specified.

The following example will illustrate that the optimum policy can involve a true two-part pricing approach. Figures 3-15a and b show the marginal value curves for two customers. We are interested in finding the two-part pricing policy that will maximize total revenue subject to the constraint that both customers accept the offered terms. One possible two-part policy is shown in Fig. 3–15a. The cost per hour is P', leading to hourly charges from customer 1 equal to the area of rectangle C and to charges from customer 2 equal to the area of rectangles C plus D. In order to keep both customers, the basic monthly fee must be less than or equal to the area of triangle B. Total receipts for the best two-part policy based on P' will thus be

$$R_a = 2B + C + (C + D) = 2B + 2C + D$$

Figure 3–15b shows a three-part pricing policy in which the same hourly charge (P') is levied, but only on hours in excess of H_1^*, the maximum use for customer 1. In this case a basic fee equal to the sum of areas B, C, and E can be levied. No hourly charges will be collected from customer 1, but the amount shown by area A will be received from customer 2. Total receipts for this policy will be

$$R_b = 2(B + C + E) + A = 2B + 2C + 2E + A$$

Note, however, that area D is equal to the sum of areas E, F, and A. And if the MV curve for customer 1 is linear (as we assume here), areas E and F must be equal. Thus $2E + A = D$ and the revenues under the two policies must be precisely equal.

The identity of the revenues under the two pricing policies implies that the optimum two-part policy can be found by investigating the conditions for the optimum corresponding three-part policy. This is a particularly simple matter since under such a policy only the hourly charges received from customer 2 will be affected by changes in P. The solution is obvious if customer 2's MV curve is also linear: the optimum price is the one which leads customer 2 to a monthly utilization of H_2', midway between his maximum use (H_2^*) and that of customer 1 (H_1^*). This will certainly be a positive value, and thus the optimum two-part pricing policy must also include a positive level of P (the same one).[4]

---

[4] Of course, it is possible that the overall optimum might involve terms under which only customer 2 accepts the offer. If so, the appropriate policy would degenerate into a one-part offer equal to the total area under customer 2's MV curve. The argument given here needs some extension to cover fully some additional possibilities. Prices above P_1 need not be considered, since they would lead customer 1 to refuse the offer. Also, prices higher than the level of customer 2's MV curve at H_1^* hours can be shown to lead to smaller total revenue than prices below that level.

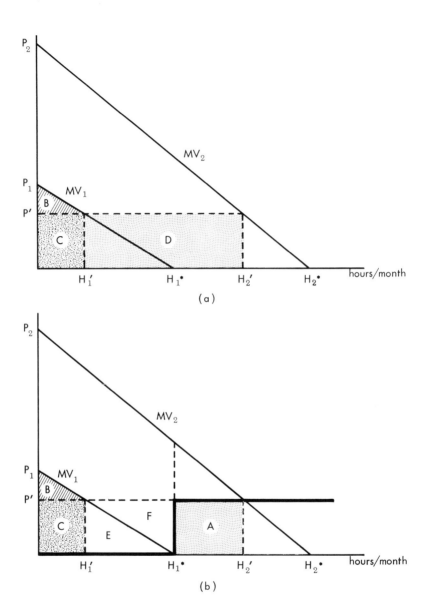

FIGURE 3-15. An optimum two-part (a) and the corresponding three-part (b) pricing policy.

This example certainly does not prove that a manufacturer contemplating a two-part policy will always find it advantageous to charge the user for monthly utilization. However, it does provide presumptive evidence. Note that the policy will cause inefficiency. All customers that install computers will use them inefficiently, since a possible application with a positive marginal value will not be run if its value per hour is less than the hourly surcharge imposed by the manufacturer. The customer will not obtain the total value possible from the computer (nor, for that matter, will the manufacturer). All parties could improve their positions if separate negotiations were held with each user to move toward a more discriminatory pricing policy. This is but another example of the efficiency of discriminatory pricing.

We now consider pricing schemes in which the manufacturer explicitly sets three separate terms: a basic monthly fee (F), an hourly surcharge (P), and an amount of time exempt from the surcharge (X). The standard rental contracts used from 1955 to 1965 conformed to this pattern. Needless to say, two-part pricing schemes can be considered special cases $(X = 0)$, as can one-part pricing policies $(X = 0$ and $P = 0)$.

We have shown that, for the case illustrated in Figs. 3–15a and b, identical revenues could be obtained under either the optimum two-part policy or a corresponding three-part policy based on the same value of P. Thus a true three-part policy can yield at least as much revenue as the optimum two-part policy. We now show that for the example a better three-part policy exists.

Figure 3–16 shows P', the optimum value of P for the two-part pricing policy. As shown earlier, total revenue will equal that obtained with a three-part policy in which the maximum use of customer 1 is exempt $(X = H_1{}^*)$. Total revenue for such a policy is the sum

$$R_{H_1}{}^* = 2(D + C) + A = 2D + 2C + A$$

Now consider the effect of a small reduction in the exemption, to H''. The basic fee must be reduced to retain customer 1; it will equal area D. But the extra-use charges from customer 2 now equal the sum of areas A, B, and C. Total revenue is therefore

$$R_{H''} = 2D + A + B + C = 2D + (B + C) + A$$

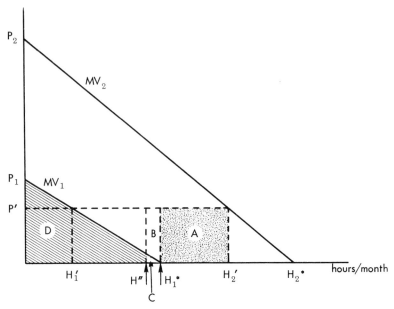

FIGURE 3-16. Improving a three-part pricing policy.

Note that, for the small change in the exemption, $B > C$. Therefore the revenue for H'' must exceed that for H_1^*. The optimum solution is clearly to set the exemption midway between customer 1's maximum-use level (H_1^*) and the level he would select at P' (H_1').[5] Interestingly enough, this policy involves inefficient use of both computers. Customer 2 pays an extra-use charge and thus does not run some jobs with positive marginal values per hour. Customer 1 does not pay any extra-use charges, choosing instead to stop at the level of the exemption. However, some of the jobs that he does not run have positive marginal values. Thus the situation is inefficient, and all parties could gain by renegotiation to a more discriminatory scheme. Note, however, that the manufacturer's profit is greater than it would be if he used a two-part policy. Presumably this applies in more realistic situations as well.

For either two-part or three-part pricing schemes to be effective the manufacturer must not allow resale of his equipment from low-utilization customers to high-utilization ones.[6] For that reason only rental is

[5] Since only at that point will the area above his MV curve up to P' equal that below the MV curve for a small change in X. In terms of the example, for small changes above or below such a level, the area of trapezoid B will equal that of trapezoid C.

[6] Restrictions on the sale of computer time may also be required.

appropriate. But antitrust policy requires that manufacturers offer equipment for sale. Under these conditions what policy should the manufacturer adopt if he wishes to maximize profits?

One alternative would involve compliance with the requirement in a manner meeting the letter but not the spirit of the law: setting the price at a sufficiently high level to be clearly undesirable for any customer. However, such a policy would not be the most desirable from the standpoint of the manufacturer even if it could be implemented. A preferable strategy would utilize the purchase price as a fourth component, augmenting the type of three-part rental offer described previously.

Figure 3–17 illustrates such a four-part policy. For users with monthly utilization below the exempt amount X, the machine is available for the basic monthly rental of F. Customers who choose to rent must, however, pay a surcharge of P (shown by the slope of the portion of the curve to the right of X) for each hour in excess of X. A user determined to rent would incur total costs shown by the curve that is horizontal up to X hours and then rises at a rate of P per hour for all

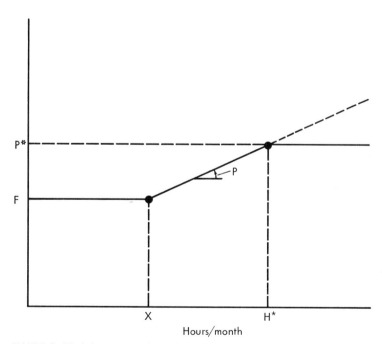

FIGURE 3–17. A four-part pricing policy.

hours over X. However, an alternative is available; he may purchase the computer for a cost equivalent to some basic monthly charge P^*. The manner in which such an equivalent charge might be found is discussed in Chapter 4. At this point we merely assume that it can be determined. Thus the possibility of purchase, with the accompanying zero marginal cost of all hours used, may dominate the rental offer over some range of utilization. In the case illustrated in Fig. 3–17 the minimum cost for each possible level of utilization is shown by the solid curve. For utilization below H^* hours per month the optimum policy involves rental; for utilization above this level it involves purchase.

The question we now seek to answer concerns the manner in which the manufacturer should set the values of the four parameters if he wishes to maximize profit. No attempt will be made to derive a general solution; instead we will simply present an argument for the thesis that profit-maximizing behavior involves setting a price such that purchase will in fact be preferable for certain classes of users.

Recall that throughout the previous discussion we have shown that pricing policies involving hourly surcharges are inefficient since the users are induced to stop short of realizing the total values of their available jobs. Moreover, we have shown that both the manufacturer and the user could benefit by renegotiating to terms involving no marginal cost to the user. However, such benefit will accrue to the manufacturer only if the renegotiated policy does not apply to all users.

Consider a situation in which the manufacturer has implemented a three-part rental policy; assume that all his customers have selected monthly utilization rates less than or equal to H^* (in Fig. 3–17). If the alternative of purchase at a cost equivalent to P^* is now announced, the manufacturer cannot possibly be any worse off, since he receives no more than P^* from any of his rental customers at present. Nor can any of his customers be worse off, since the previous rental terms are still available to them. But some customers will certainly be better off. In particular consider the user shown in Fig. 3–18, who had chosen to utilize his equipment H^* hours per month under the rental policy. Since that policy involved a surcharge of P per hour, some portion of his valuable jobs was not being run. By replacing the rented machine with a purchased machine, he maintains his monthly costs unchanged (at P^*) but he now faces a zero marginal cost. This makes it worthwhile

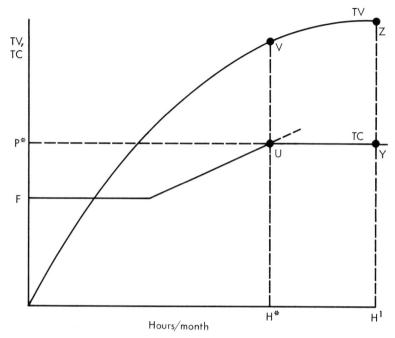

FIGURE 3-18. A four-part pricing policy providing benefits for a user.

to run all valuable jobs (unless doing so would exceed capacity), thus increasing the total value of the machine to him. In Fig. 3–18, the new net value is shown by distance YZ; it is considerably greater than the old value, represented by distance UV. The change will thus benefit the user, although not the manufacturer.

There are, however, other changes that will benefit both parties. Consider the user shown in Fig. 3–19, who had elected a monthly utilization of H'' ($<H^*$) hours under the rental contract terms, paying a total monthly rental of R. Faced with an offer involving a zero marginal cost for hourly usage, he might well increase the number of jobs run and thus the total value of the computer in his installation. In the case shown, purchase will prove advantageous, giving the user a net value of YZ, greater than that associated with rental (UV). The change will also benefit the manufacturer, since he receives an amount equivalent to P^* instead of the smaller quantity R. Clearly the manufacturer's best interests dictate a policy in which purchase is preferable for some

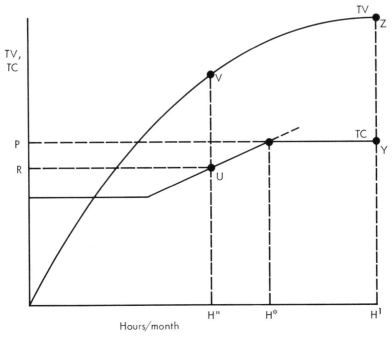

FIGURE 3-19. A four-part pricing policy providing benefits for the manufacturer and a user.

users—those planning high utilization. And since other users will be offered preferable terms only if they choose to rent the equipment, there is no danger that resale operations will destroy the scheme.

We have discussed but a few of the many alternative policies that might be utilized to obtain increased revenue from any given stock of computers. They are important because they correspond closely to actual practice during the first decade in which computers were widely sold commercially.

H. THE VIABILITY OF DISCRIMINATORY PRICING

Discriminatory pricing depends on information and enforcement for success, and both cost money. Thus the smaller the potential gains from discrimination, the less is the likelihood that it will prove profitable. The potential gains depend, in large part, on the elasticity of the demand for the seller's product. The closer the substitutes and the greater the competition, the less is the potential gain from discriminatory pricing. In a highly competitive industry, prices will approximate marginal cost, and discrimination on the basis of value will disappear. Indeed the disappearance of certain discriminatory pricing schemes can be taken as strong evidence of increasing competition; in some cases it may even be the only obvious evidence.

In the domain of highly standardized, homogeneous products sold by many competitive sellers one may assume that goods are sold for a single price and that the price virtually equals marginal cost. In the computer industry such an assumption is hazardous at best. Instead the seller may be expected to experiment with all sorts of pricing schemes in the hope that he will be able to increase his profit. Since information is imperfect, some of the schemes may actually reduce profit. Also, some manufacturers may adopt policies that seem at first clearly inefficient. However, as this chapter has illustrated, such policies may be perfectly consistent with profit-maximizing behavior under a set of reasonable assumptions about market demand. Manufacturers are often accused of behavior inconsistent with profit maximization, but in some cases the analyst may be more naive than the manufacturer.

CHAPTER **4   TIME AND RISK**

□   □□

□

□

□

A. PRESENT VALUE

Assume that a firm has decided it must use a particular computer for a 24-month period until next-generation equipment can be delivered. The only decision concerns financing: should the computer be rented or purchased? Rental (including maintenance) costs $10,000 per month. The purchase price of the machine is $450,000, the monthly cost of a maintenance contract is $1200, and the computer's estimated market value 24 months hence is $270,000. A simple analysis might suggest that it would be cheaper to purchase than to rent:

Rental:
  $10,000 per month for 24 months   = $240,000
Purchase:
  Purchase cost   = $450,000
  Maintenance ($1200 per month for 24
    months)   =   28,800
  Less sales value   =   270,000
        Net cost   = $208,800

Unfortunately the conclusion may be incorrect. The error lies in the addition of dissimilar amounts. A dollar spent 24 months from now is not the same as a dollar spent now. Adding together expenditures occurring at different points of time is as unreasonable as adding together punched cards and reels of paper tape on the grounds that both are input-output media.

In virtually all times and places, goods and services in the present have been considered preferable to equivalent amounts in the future. Two factors account for this: time preference and risk aversion. People prefer something now to the same thing later, since the number of alternative uses to which it can be put is thus enlarged. Moreover, the present good is certain, as is the existence of its owner, whereas the future good usually rests on promises, the fulfillment of which is less than certain; also, the needs of the recipient in the future are uncertain, as is his presence to enjoy the good.

Returning to our example, assume for now that the firm is absolutely certain that the figures given above are correct. Thus no element of risk enters the problem; we need only account for differences in timing.

The concept of present value is the key to understanding problems of this sort. The sum of X dollars received in the future is less valuable than X dollars received now. Some larger amount, however, will be considered equally valuable. Let Y_N represent such an amount received N periods in the future. Obviously,

$$Y_N > X$$

In well-developed capitalist economies there are markets for trading present dollars for future dollars and vice versa. As in other markets, the terms of trade will adjust until quantity demanded equals quantity supplied. The underlying determinants of demand and supply and hence of the market terms of trade concern people's preferences for present goods over future goods. As collective preferences change, the terms of trade will change. But at any given point of time there will be a reasonably standard set of terms for trading present dollars for future dollars ("lending") and vice versa ("borrowing").

Assume, for example, that \$1.00 today can be traded for \$1.22 available 40 months from today. A succinct description of the terms would be as follows:

$$Y_{40} = 1.22X$$

or

$$\frac{Y_{40}}{X} = 1.22$$

However, an alternative description is far more common. If X dollars were placed in an account returning $r\%$ interest per month compounded monthly, the value at the end of N periods would be

$$Y_N = \left(1 + \frac{r}{100}\right)^N X$$

There is, of course, some value of r for which $[1 + (r/100)]^{40} = 1.22$;

it is, in fact, slightly less than one-half of 1% per month. Thus we may describe the terms of trade as follows:

$$r_{40} = \frac{1}{2}\%$$

If the terms are applicable to trades involving virtually certain payment in the future, we designate this the *pure* rate of interest, since it reflects only preference for present over future goods and services, and not the preference for certainty over uncertainty.

At any point of time there will be a set of terms on which present money can be traded for virtually certain money 40 months hence, a set of terms on which present money can be traded for money 20 months hence, etc. There will thus be a large set of pure interest rates: $r_1, r_2, \ldots$, the values depending on people's relative preferences for goods and services at various times. No theoretical basis can be given for making the assumption that all these rates will be equal. At some times short-term interest rates have exceeded long-term rates, although the converse is more typical. However, there is no particular reason to assume that short-term rates will be either higher or lower than long-term rates. For this reason, and in order to simplify the analysis, it is usually assumed that all rates are equal. We thus omit the subscript and refer simply to *the* pure rate of interest. In the United States it has varied between 2% and 8% per annum (i.e., between approximately $\frac{1}{6}$ of 1% and $\frac{2}{3}$ of 1% per month) since 1929.

Now assume that Y_N dollars must be spent N months from now and that the pure rate of interest is $r\%$ per month. The *present value* (X) of the expenditure is defined as a present amount of equal value:

$$Y_N = \left(1 + \frac{r}{100}\right)^N X$$

or

$$X = \left\{\frac{1}{[1 + (r/100)]^N}\right\} Y_N$$

The term in the braces is called the *discount factor;* it will always be less than 1 (as long as r and N are positive). Multiplying the actual amount (Y_N) by this factor to compute present value is termed *discounting.*

An economic interpretation of the present value in this case is straightforward. Instead of spending Y_N dollars N months in the future, X dollars can be spent now. The X dollars would be placed in a bank paying the market rate of interest ($r\%$ per month). At the end of N months the account would have grown (because of interest compounded monthly) to Y_N; the total amount could then be withdrawn and the required payment made.

The overwhelming advantage of the concept of present value is that it gives an analyst the ability to express diverse items (cash flows occurring at different points of time) in terms of a common denominator. This is simply an extension of the use of a money measure of value. We cannot add reels of paper tape and punched cards, but equivalent amounts of money can be determined through market trading ratios (prices) and added to compute total value (or total cost). Although seldom stated, here too the common denominator is money *today* – in other words, present value.

We are now in a position to deal with the problem posed earlier. Assume that the current market pure rate of interest is $5/12$ of 1% per month (approximately 5% per annum). The policies of renting versus purchasing can be compared by computing the sum of the present values of the required cash flows. We represent outflows (costs) by negative values, and inflows (receipts) by positive values:

Rental:

Month (N)	Cash Flow	Present Value of $1	Present Value of Cash Flow
1	−10,000	0.995851	−9,958.51
2	−10,000	0.991718	−9,917.18
⋮	⋮	⋮	⋮
24	−10,000	0.905025	−9,050.25
Total present value			= −227,938.98

Purchase:

Month (N)	Cash Flow	Present Value of $1	Present Value of Cash Flow
0	−450,000	1.000000	−450,000.00
1	− 1,200	0.995851	− 1,195.02
2	− 1,200	0.991718	− 1,190.06
⋮	⋮	⋮	⋮
24	$\begin{cases} - 1,200 \\ +270,000 \end{cases}$	0.905025	$\begin{cases} - 1,086.03 \\ +244,356.75 \end{cases}$
Total present value			= −232,995.93

Purchase no longer appears to be the cheaper policy. When the timing of the cash flows is taken into account, rental is shown to be preferable.

The effect of discounting is shown in Fig. 4–1. The bars represent the actual cost each month for the rental policy ($10,000). The undiscounted sum of the actual payments—$240,000—is the total area under the curve showing the time pattern of payments (it can also be considered the present value of the payments when $r = 0$). The height of the shaded portion of each bar represents the present value of the corresponding actual payment, based on an interest rate of ⁵⁄₁₂ of 1% per month. The total present value is thus represented by the shaded area.

Discounting clearly alters the relative importance of payments occurring at different points of time. Earlier payments are made relatively more important than later ones; the greater the interest rate, the more pronounced the effect becomes. At an interest rate of zero, timing is irrelevant. At an extremely high interest rate, only initial

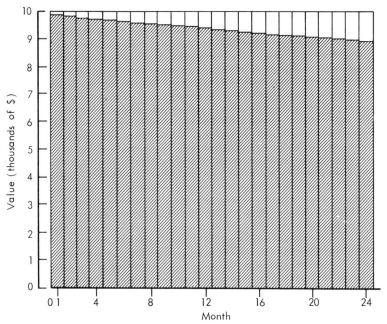

FIGURE 4–1. The effect of discounting on value.

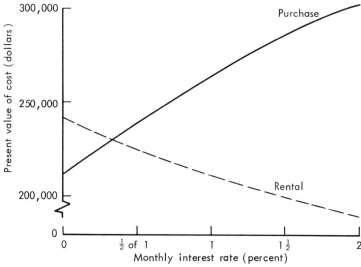

FIGURE 4-2. Present value versus the rate of interest for two policies.

payments matter much. Of course, the larger the applicable interest rate, the smaller is the present value of any future payment.

Figure 4-2 illustrates the effect of the rate of interest on the present values of the two policies. The present value of the stream of rental payments decreases when larger interest rates are used, approaching zero as an asymptote. However, the present value of the cost of purchase increases as r is raised. Recall that the major cash flows for the purchase policy were the initial cost ($450,000) and the final receipt ($270,000). The former is unaffected by discounting. The final receipt, however, is definitely affected. The higher the interest rate, the less important is the relatively distant receipt and the more costly (in present value terms) the purchase of the machine. For this reason the present value of cost approaches $450,000 as an asymptote.

We have approached the problem posed by comparing the present values of the costs of the two policies, basing the present values on the relevant rate of interest. However, Fig. 4-2 suggests an alternative approach. One might ask, At what rate of interest are the two policies equally costly (in terms of present value)? In this case the rate is about ⅓ of 1% per month. Since the relevant rate of interest is assumed to be greater than this, rental is thus preferable. Note, however, that the rate of interest at which the policies are equally costly may not, by itself, provide sufficient information on which to base a decision. More information of the type shown in Fig. 4–2 may be needed. Note also that the rate in question is the root of a Nth-degree polynomial;[1] thus it may not be unique (i.e., the curves may cross more than once) and it will typically be difficult to calculate. In many cases it is no more difficult to compute the data required for a reasonably complete diagram showing present value versus rate of interest than it is to calculate the rate(s) of interest at which two policies are equivalent. As a general rule policies should be evaluated on the basis of present values computed at some relevant rate of interest. If supplementary information is desired (e.g., for a sensitivity analysis to estimate the consequences of errors in measurement), diagrams of the type shown in Fig. 4–2 may prove useful.

B. TIME PREFERENCE

It is important to recognize that the relevance of present value is based entirely on the availability of a market in which patterns of cash flows over time can be converted into other patterns. For a given interest rate, a virtually infinite number of patterns of cash flows (receipts and/or expenditures) can be found that have the same present value. If it is really possible to borrow or lend money at the specified interest rate, any one of the patterns may be converted into any of the others. The one chosen will depend on the preferences of the person in question. But whatever his preferences, the more attractive the present value of the original pattern, the more desirable is the eventual pattern obtained.

Figure 4–3 illustrates the principle for a simple case. Two alternative investment policies are available. Investment A gives $150 now and $42 a year hence; investment B gives $100 now and $105 a year hence. The market rate of interest is 5% per annum. The parallel

---

[1] Letting X_i be the cash flow in period i from one alternative and Y_i the cash flow from the other, a positive value of r must be found that satisfies

$$X_0 + \frac{X_1}{[1 + (r/100)]} + \frac{X_2}{[1 + (r/100)]^2} + \cdots + \frac{X_N}{[1 + (r/100)]^N}$$

$$= Y_0 + \frac{Y_1}{[1 + (r/100)]} + \frac{Y_2}{[1 + (r/100)]^2} + \cdots + \frac{Y_N}{[1 + (r/100)]^N}$$

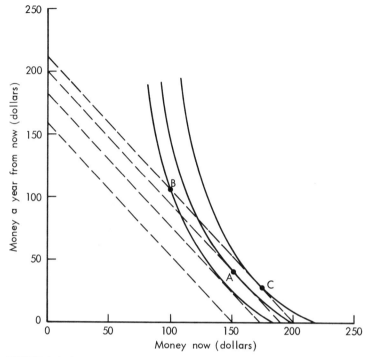

FIGURE 4-3. Choosing the pattern with the higher present value.

lines show combinations of equal present value. The equation of such an *isovalue* line is

$$\frac{y}{1.05} + x = k$$

where k is the present value represented by the line (it is, of course, equal to the x intercept).

The indifference curves in Fig. 4-3 are assumed to represent the preferences of the decision-maker. Combinations lying along any given curve are equally desirable; those above and/or to the right are preferable.

At an interest rate of 5%, the present value of investment B exceeds that of A ($200 as opposed to $190); B should thus be chosen. This appears to conflict with the preferences of the decision-maker. In the absence of a market he would prefer investment A, since it gives preferred cash flows (its point lies on a higher indifference curve). But the ability to trade with the market enlarges the set of available opportunities. Investment A's cash flows can be traded for any combination on the isovalue line through point A. Investment B's flows can be traded for any combination on the isovalue line through point B. Clearly the line through point B dominates that through point A. No matter what the decision-maker's preferences, investment B is the better choice. In the case shown the pattern of receipts finally obtained is given by point C—$180 now and $21 next year. The details are:

Now:

Received from investment B:	$100
Borrowed at 5%:	80
	$180

One year hence:

Received from investment B:	$105
Less payment on loan ($80 × 1.05)	−84
	$ 21

C. PRESENT-VALUE FORMULAS

The present value of any pattern of cash flows can, of course, be computed directly from the basic formula. Let X_i represent the cash flow in period i, and r the relevant interest rate, expressed as a ratio rather than as a percentage (e.g., as 0.05 instead of 5%). Then the present value of all the flows that occur during N periods will be

$$PV = \sum_{i=0}^{N} \frac{X_i}{(1 + r)^i} \qquad (4\text{-}1)$$

Fortunately, in many cases the pattern of cash flows is relatively simple, allowing special formulas to be used.

Consider a stream of flows of equal amounts beginning in period 1 and extending through period N:

$$X_1 = X_2 = \cdots = X_N$$

Letting X represent the cash flow each period, the total present value will be

$$PV_{X,r,N} = \frac{X}{(1 + r)} + \frac{X}{(1 + r)^2} + \cdots + \frac{X}{(1 + r)^N}$$

Note that the terms can be considered successive terms in a geometric progression:

$$\text{First term } (A) = \frac{X}{1 + r}$$

$$\text{Common ratio } (R) = \frac{1}{1 + r}$$

The sum of the first N terms of a geometric progression is

$$S_N = A \left(\frac{R^N - 1}{R - 1} \right)$$

Substituting and simplifying, we obtain

$$PV_{X,r,N} = X \left\{ \frac{1 - [1/(1 + r)^N]}{r} \right\} \tag{4-2}$$

The term in the braces is the formula for the present value of an annuity of \$1 per period received for N periods, given an interest rate of r per period. Tables giving values for wide ranges of r and N are available.

An interesting corollary concerns the value of a perpetual annuity. Obviously,

$$PV_{X,r,\infty} = \underset{N \to \infty}{\text{limit}} \, (S_N)$$

But

$$\underset{N \to \infty}{\text{limit}} \, (S_N) = \frac{A}{1 - R} \quad \text{if } R^2 < 1$$

The required condition is met for any positive interest rate since $R = 1/(1 + r)$. Substituting and simplifying gives

$$PV_{X,r,\infty} = \frac{X}{r} \tag{4-3}$$

In other words, the present value of an annuity of \$1 approaches $1/r$ as the length of time over which it is to be received is increased.

Consider next a stream of payments in which the cash flow grows by a constant proportion (g) each period:

$$X_1 = (1 + g)X$$

$$X_2 = (1 + g)^2 X$$

$$\vdots \qquad \vdots$$

$$X_N = (1 + g)^N X$$

The total present value of the payments received over N periods will be

$$PV = \left(\frac{1+g}{1+r}\right) X + \left(\frac{1+g}{1+r}\right)^2 X + \cdots + \left(\frac{1+g}{1+r}\right)^N X$$

This can also be considered the sum of the first N terms of a geometric progression. Its limit as N approaches infinity is defined if the growth rate is less than the applicable rate of interest:

$$[g < r] \leftrightarrow \left[R = \frac{1+g}{1+r} < 1\right]$$

The present value of such a stream of payments extending over a long time period will thus approach

$$PV = \frac{X_1}{r - g} \qquad (4\text{-}4)$$

When $g = 0$, equation 4–4 reduces to equation 4–3.

Consider next a series of payments increasing by an equal absolute amount each period and extending over an infinite number of periods:

$$X_1 = A$$
$$X_2 = A + B$$
$$X_3 = A + 2B$$
$$\vdots \qquad \vdots$$

This can be considered a perpetual annuity of A dollars per period beginning in period 1, plus a perpetual annuity of B dollars per period beginning in period 2, plus another perpetual annuity of B dollars per period beginning in period 3, etc. The value in period i of a perpetual annuity of B dollars per period beginning in period i is

$$V_i = \frac{B}{r}$$

The present value of such an annuity will equal its value in period i times the present value of a dollar in period i:

$$PV = \left[\frac{1}{(1+r)^i}\right] V_i = \frac{B}{(1+r)^i r}$$

Thus the present value of the stream of payments is

$$PV = \frac{A}{r} + \frac{B}{(1+r)r} + \frac{B}{(1+r)^2 r} + \cdots$$

$$= \frac{A}{r} + \frac{B}{r}\left[\frac{1}{(1+r)} + \frac{1}{(1+r)^2} + \cdots\right]$$

The sum indicated in the brackets is simply the present value of a perpetual annuity of \$1 (=1/r). Hence the present value of the original stream of payments is

$$PV = \frac{A}{r} + \frac{B}{r^2} \qquad (4\text{-}5)$$

In practice, cash flows appear at discrete points of time, and interest is calculated and compounded periodically. However, calculations are often simplified by assuming that interest is calculated and compounded continuously. At an annual rate of interest r, compounded annually, a dollar will have grown after N years to

$$V = (1+r)^N$$

Now, if the interest is compounded n times each year and the interest rate adjusted accordingly, we have

$$V = \left(1 + \frac{r}{n}\right)^{nN}$$

$$= \left[\left(1 + \frac{r}{n}\right)^n\right]^N$$

What is the effect on this value as n becomes very large? It can be shown [2] that

$$\lim_{n \to \infty} \left(1 + \frac{r}{n}\right)^n = e^r$$

[2] The proof requires only that we show

$$\lim_{n \to \infty} \left(1 + \frac{r}{n}\right)^{n/r} = e$$

Letting $Z = n/r$, this is equivalent to proving that

$$\lim_{Z \to \infty} \left(1 + \frac{1}{Z}\right)^Z = e$$

But this is a definition of e. Q.E.D.

Thus the amount after N periods, at an interest rate of r per period, compounded continuously, will be

$$V = e^{rN} \qquad\qquad (4\text{-}6)$$

As a corollary, the present value of a dollar received N periods hence will be

$$PV = \frac{1}{e^{rN}} = e^{-rN} \qquad\qquad (4\text{-}7)$$

Needless to say, the assumption of continuous compounding overstates the growth of funds at compound interest and thus understates the present value of future cash flows. However the approximation may prove satisfactory in some cases. For example, let $r = 0.12$ and $N = 1$.

Interest Compounded	n	Amount after 1 Year
Annually	1	1.1200
Semiannually	2	1.1236
Quarterly	4	1.1255
Monthly	12	1.1268
Weekly	48	1.1273
Continuously	∞	1.1275

One can, of course, derive additional present-value formulas. Only a few of the more useful ones have been presented here.

D. THE RATE OF RETURN

We have shown the appropriate method for evaluating competing alternative flows of cash over time: calculate the present value of each, using an appropriate rate of interest. Our example involved a choice between two expenditure patterns, but the method can be used for a wide variety of problems. Perhaps the most common application involves acceptance or rejection of an investment. Here the two mutually exclusive alternatives are (1) to undertake the investment or (2) to not undertake it. The former will involve both negative and positive cash flows; its net present value may thus be either positive or negative. Alternative 2 involves no cash flows at all; its present value is zero. In accordance with the rules stated earlier, the better alternative is the one with the higher present value. Restating the rule for this case, we can say that an investment should be undertaken if and only if its cash flows have a positive net present value when discounted at the appropriate rate of interest.

Consider the following simple example. A service bureau is considering renting a computer for 24 months at $10,000 per month. The first 11 months will be required to test software for the particular application to be offered by the firm. During each of the remaining 13 months the service is expected to yield $20,000 in revenue. Ignoring other items of cost and revenue, the investment involves the following flows:

Month	Flow(s)	Net Flow
1	−10,000	−10,000
⋮	⋮	⋮
11	−10,000	−10,000
12	$\begin{Bmatrix} -10,000 \\ +20,000 \end{Bmatrix}$	+10,000
⋮	⋮	⋮
24	$\begin{Bmatrix} -10,000 \\ +20,000 \end{Bmatrix}$	+10,000

If the appropriate rate of interest is $5/12$ of 1% per month, the investment should be undertaken, since the present value of the stream of flows is positive:

(1) Present value of an annuity of $1 for 11 months at $5/12$ of 1%   = $10.7299

(2) Present value of $10,000 per month from month 1 through month 11 [(1) times $10,000]   = $107,299

(3) Present value of an annuity of $1 for 13 months at $5/12$ of 1%   = $12.6286

(4) Present value of an annuity of $10,000 for 13 months [(3) times $10,000]   = $126,286

(5) Present value of $1 received in 11 months at $5/12$ of 1%   = $0.9553

(6) Present value of $10,000 per month from month 12 through month 24 [(4) times (5)]   = $120,641

(7) Present value of investment [(6) − (2)]   = +$13,342

The present value will, of course, depend on the appropriate rate of interest. Figure 4–4 shows the relationship for the example. The present values of the alternatives are equal (i.e., the present value of the stream is zero) if the interest rate is approximately $1\frac{1}{3}\%$ per month. This is called the investment's *rate of return*.

Although the rate of return is an extremely useful measure for some purposes, it is quite inappropriate for others. It is inappropriate when choosing among mutually exclusive investments: although several may have rates of return exceeding the relevant rate of interest, the one giving the greatest present value may not be the one with the greatest rate of return. It is also inappropriate when it is not unique: an investment's cash flows may have a zero net present value at two or more rates of interest.

The rate of return can prove useful, however, when it is possible to undertake an investment without affecting the firm's ability to undertake other investments, and when the curve relating the present value of its cash flows to the rate of interest is monotonic downward. The latter condition is met if the investment involves a series of net out-

Present value of investment

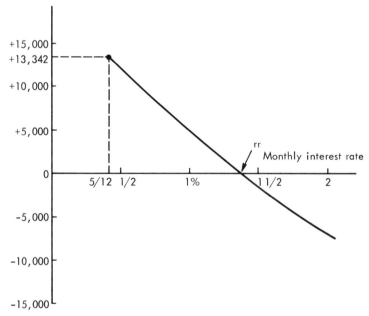

FIGURE 4–4. The relationship between present value and the rate of interest.

flows followed by net inflows. Letting F_i be the net flow in period i, we have

$$\begin{bmatrix} F_i < 0 & \text{for } i = 1 \text{ to } i^* \\ F_i > 0 & \text{for } i = i^* + 1 \text{ to } N \end{bmatrix} \rightarrow [PV(F) \text{ is inversely related to } r]$$

Fortunately this condition holds for many investments. In such cases we have

$$[rr > i] \leftrightarrow [PV > 0] \leftrightarrow [\text{Invest}]$$

$$[rr \leqq i] \leftrightarrow [PV \leqq 0] \leftrightarrow [\text{Don't invest}]$$

where rr = the rate of return on the investment, i = the relevant rate of interest, and PV = the present value, using the relevant rate of interest (i). Expressed more succinctly, the decision rule becomes: Invest if and only if the rate of return on the investment exceeds the relevant rate of interest.

The concept of an investment's rate of return provides a useful and familiar rule for decision-making. The user must, of course, recognize its limitations, applying it only to situations in which these limitations are unimportant. Fortunately such cases appear to be in the majority.

E. SUBJECTIVE PROBABILITIES

Thus far we have focused on the element of time, assuming that future events could be predicted with certainty. Of course this is rarely the case. We must now account for the element of risk.

Assume that a programming staff has been assigned a particularly complicated problem. If the project leader were asked whether the program would be completed within 12 months, he might respond, "Almost certainly" or "Probably" or "Perhaps" or "Not likely" or something equally unquantifiable. However, it may be possible to obtain a much more precise idea of his beliefs. Ask him to consider a bet, with given odds, that the program will be completed within the specified period. He must indicate how he would bet (we assume that his bet would not affect the outcome). His choice of sides will, of course, depend on the odds. For example, if the odds were even − 1 to 1 − he might bet on completion, as shown in Fig. 4–5. But if the odds were 4 to 1, he might bet against completion. There will be some set of odds that he considers "fair"; that is, he will not care which side he bets

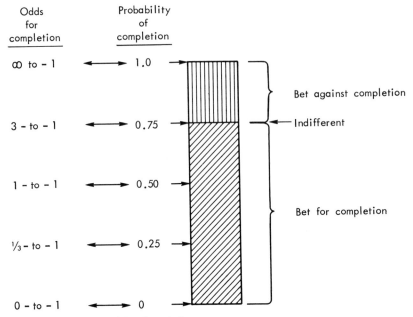

FIGURE 4-5. Odds and betting choices.

on (or whether he bets at all). We define his subjective probability estimate in terms of this set of odds:

$$P = \frac{\text{odds}}{\text{odds} + 1}$$

In Fig. 4–5 the "fair" odds [3] are 3 to 1; the person's subjective probability estimate for completion in 12 months is thus $3/(3 + 1) = 0.75$.

It is important to note that a person's subjective probability estimate may be based on vague feelings, limited knowledge, or, at the other extreme, extensive analyses of past data. My subjective probability that a coin will come up heads is in a sense quite objective. My subjective probability that a computer will malfunction at a particular time may not be very objective at all. But from the standpoint of decision-making the difference is unimportant: the probability is rele-

---

[3] There may be a range of odds over which the individual will refuse to bet. If the range is small, it may be reasonable to use its midpoint as a subjective probability estimate and proceed in the manner described in the text. If the range is large, some other procedure may be required.

vant, not the basis on which it is determined. Having argued the point, we now drop the adjective "subjective," referring in the subsequent discussion simply to probabilities.

The discussion can easily be extended to include probability distributions. Assume that the project leader is asked to consider a set of bets based on completion within 1 month, another set based on completion within 2 months, etc. Let P_i be the probability of completion within i months, obtained in the manner described previously. Given a sufficient number of choices of hypothetical bets, we can derive the project leader's *cumulative probability distribution,* relating P_i to i. An example is shown in Fig. 4–6a. Needless to say, P_i cannot decrease as i increases.

For some purposes a cumulative probability distribution best presents feelings about the likelihood of various outcomes. But for other purposes a different presentation proves useful. Figure 4–6a indicates that $P_{12} = 0.75$, while $P_{11} = 0.60$. This implies that the probability of completion *during* month 12, represented as p_{12}, is 0.15. Figure 4–6b shows the relationship between p_i and i. It is simply a probability distribution. Note that the cumulative distribution can be considered the integral of (area under) the (plain) probability distribution.[4]

Figures such as 4–6a and b provide explicit statements of a person's beliefs about alternative future events. However, it is seldom convenient to deal with such detailed assessments. Summary measures are used to characterize an entire probability distribution. The two most important indicate its location (*central tendency*) and the extent to which it is dispersed (*spread*).

Measures of central tendency include the arithmetic mean, the median, and the mode. The *mode* is the most likely outcome (in Fig. 4–6b it is month 12). The *median* has the characteristic that an outcome below it as likely as one above it — in other words, $P_i = 0.50$. The median can best be seen in Fig. 4–6a; it is not unique — any number between 10 and 11 can be used. The *arithmetic mean* is simply the weighted average of the possible outcomes, using the probabilities of the outcomes as weights. For the example it is 9.65.

---

[4] That is, $P_{i*} = \int_{i=0}^{i*} p_i \, di$. In more formal terminology, Fig. 4–6a can be said to illustrate a cumulative distribution function, and Fig. 4–6b a probability distribution function.

Probability of completion
within i months (P_i)

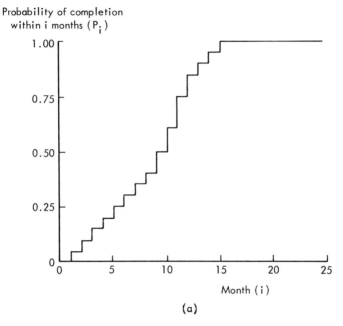

(a)

Probability of completion
during month i (p_i)

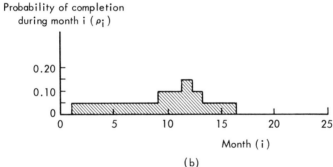

(b)

FIGURE 4–6. Cumulative probability distribution (a) and the associated probability distribution (b).

Although the three measures of central tendency differ in the example shown here, they may coincide. In particular, if the probability distribution is symmetric and unimodal (i.e., has a unique mode), the three measures will be identical. Whatever the distribution, we will adopt the arithmetic mean as the preferred measure of central tendency, since it is always uniquely defined and has desirable properties.

We use terms such as *expected value* and *expected outcome* to refer to the mean. Formally

$$E \equiv \sum_{i=1}^{N} p_i X_i$$

where $X_1, \ldots, X_N$ are alternative outcomes, and $p_i =$ the probability of outcome $i (\Sigma p_i = 1)$.

Several measures of spread are also available. We will use the *standard deviation* since it also has desirable properties and is consistent with the choice of the arithmetic mean as a measure of central tendency.[5] The standard deviation (S) is the square root of the variance (V); the variance is the average squared deviation from the mean (expected value), using the probabilities as weights:

$$S = \sqrt{V}$$

$$V = \sum_{i=1}^{N} p_i(X_i - E)^2$$

For the example the variance is approximately 15.5, and the standard deviation approximately 3.95.

If the shape of a probability distribution is known, its expected value and standard deviation may suffice to indicate precisely the probability that the actual outcome will fall within any specified range. For example, this will be the case if the probability distribution is normal, that is, follows the familiar bell-shaped curve. However, even if nothing is known about the shape of the distribution, some limits may be given, as shown here: [6]

Range of Outcomes		Probability That the Actual Outcome Will Fall within the Range	
From	To	If Distribution Is Normal	Whatever the Shape
$E - S$	$E + S$	0.6826	≥ 0
$E - 2S$	$E + 2S$	0.9546	≥ 0.7500
$E - 3S$	$E + 3S$	0.9974	≥ 0.8889

[5] The standard deviation measured from the arithmetic mean is less than that measured from any other value.
[6] The figures in the right-hand column are based on Chebyshev's inequality, which states that the probability that a value lies outside the range $E \pm NS$ does not exceed $1/N^2$ for $N \geq 1$.

The discussion that follows does not depend on any particular assumption about the shapes of probability distributions. It does assume that the expected value and standard deviation adequately characterize a probability distribution for purposes of decision-making. The role of expected value will depend on the case in question. For example, the lower the expected value of a project's completion date the more desirable is the project; the higher the expected value of future receipts from an investment, the more desirable is the investment. However, the role of risk is generally the same—the greater the standard deviation (risk), the less desirable is the activity. All other things being equal, people typically prefer certainty ($S = 0$) to risk ($S > 0$): they exhibit risk aversion. In other words, they demand (and receive) compensation to bear risk. Risky ventures will be undertaken only if they carry promises of greater rewards (more desirable expected values) than less risky ventures. In addition to the pure interest rate (the "price of time"), there is a price of risk.

F. CERTAINTY EQUIVALENTS

Consider the general problem of evaluating an investment: the cash flow in each period of time is uncertain—instead of a single estimate there is a probability distribution. In terms of the previous discussion, we have:

E_i = the expected value of the cash flow in period i, and

R_i = the risk associated with the cash flow in period i (measured by the standard deviation of the distribution).

How can the set of probability distributions (or E, R values) be summarized in a single measure of merit (present value)? An obvious possibility is to estimate a certainty-equivalent cash flow for each period. Let F_i^* be a cash flow in period i such that the decision-maker is indifferent between (1) receiving F_i^* with certainty in period i and (2) the prospects he actually faces in period i (i.e., the probability distribution characterized by E_i and R_i). For a given set of certainty-equivalent flows $F_1^*, \ldots, F_N^*$, the present value of the investment can presumably be found by discounting with the pure rate of interest.

A certainty equivalent can be estimated directly, without actually formulating a probability distribution: the decision-maker simply uses a "pessimistic" estimate in his calculations; in practice this is a very common method for accounting for risk. Alternatively, the certainty equivalent may be based on an "unbiased" estimate (E_i) and a separate measure of risk (R_i). Although the exact relationship will depend on the preferences of the decision-maker, it will have this form:

$$F_i^* = f(E_i, R_i)$$

$$\frac{\partial F_i^*}{\partial E_i} > 0; \quad \frac{\partial F_i^*}{\partial R_i} < 0$$

The idea of a certainty-equivalent cash flow is appealing; however, it provides relatively little information about the true prospects of an investment. Assume, for example, that the actual outcome from an investment in year i is related to the outcome in year $i - 1$: if the cash flow is larger than expected in one year, it will also be larger in other years; if it is smaller than expected in one year, it will also be smaller in other years. Such an investment is clearly more risky than it would be if the outcomes in various years were unrelated. The certainty-equivalent approach makes it difficult to take such differences into account. For this reason (and others) it provides an imperfect method for measuring value.

G. DISCOUNTING FOR RISK

As suggested in Section F, one approach to investment evaluation involves the choice of pessimistic forecasts discounted at the pure interest rate. An alternative approach uses unbiased (expected) values, accounting for risk by discounting with an appropriate rate of interest. More specifically,

$$PV = \sum_{i=1}^{N} \left[\frac{F_i}{(1 + r)^i} \right]$$

where $r = r_p + r_r$,
    F_i = the *expected* cash flow in period i,
    r_p = the pure interest rate, and
    r_r = an appropriate discount for the risk associated with the investment.

No precise rule is provided for the choice of the discount rate. Since the overall risk of the investment is to be considered, the relationships among cash flows as well as their individual risks can be taken into account. Certain general relationships can be given. Let R_i represent the risk associated with the cash flow in period i. Then:

$$[r_r = 0] \leftrightarrow [R_i = 0 \quad \text{for all } i]$$

$$\frac{\partial r_r}{\partial R_i} > 0 \quad \text{for each } i$$

and r_r will be greater, the greater is the (positive) correlation among cash flows.

An alternative statement of the procedure holds that the rate of discount used (r) should equal the expected rate of return on investments of equivalent risk. Although this captures the essence of the problem, the statement begs the question instead of answering it. The key questions remain: (1) what is the relevant measure of risk, and (2) what is the relationship between an investment's risk and its expected rate of return?

H. RELATIONSHIPS AMONG INVESTMENTS

We have suggested some of the problems associated with investment evaluation but cannot yet provide final solutions. Instead we introduce a further complication: any given investment will typically account for only a portion of the total wealth of an individual; thus the risk associated with a proposed investment must be evaluated in the light of the owner's other sources of wealth.

In order to focus on the problem of the relationships among investments we assume that each investment can be described in terms of a probability distribution of rate of return. An obvious case involves two-period investments (buy now, sell later), although more general cases can be accommodated. In any event, the probability distribution for investment i can be characterized by its mean or expected rate of return (E_i) and its standard deviation of rate of return (S_i).

The relationship between any two investments can be described by a correlation coefficient (ρ). Two special cases are of interest. If $p_{ij} = +1$, investments i and j are perfectly correlated; the actual return from one will be related to the actual return from the other by a precise linear equation:

$$A_i^R = a + bA_j^R \quad (b > 0)$$

On the other hand, if $\rho_{ij} = 0$, investments i and j are uncorrelated. A prediction of the actual return on one will not aid the decision-maker in predicting the actual return on the other.[7] Most cases lie between these extremes. In unusual situations there may be negative correlations: the outcome from one investment is actually inversely related to the outcome from the other. Thus correlation coefficients can, in theory, range from +1 to −1.

Assume that two investments are available, with the expected rates of return and standard deviations of rate of return shown in Fig. 4–7. Now, if both investments are undertaken, the owner will be in a new position, characterized by some overall expected rate of return (E^*) and some overall standard deviation of rate of return (S^*). The new combination depends on (1) the correlation between the two investments and (2) the proportion of total funds invested in each. For example, if $\rho_{ij} = +1$, the overall combination (E^*, S^*) will lie along the straight line connecting points (E_i, S_i) and (E_j, S_j); if $\rho_{ij} = 0$, it will lie along the curve indicated in Fig. 4–7. In general, the larger (algebraically) the correlation coefficient, the closer will be the relevant curve to the straight line connecting the two points (as shown in Fig. 4–7). Whatever the curve, the greater the proportion of funds allocated to investment j, the closer point (E^*, S^*) will be to point (E_j, S_j).

Now assume that investment j represents a firm's overall prospects, given its present commitments, and that i represents a new investment under consideration. Will the new investment prove desirable? The answer may depend on the extent to which its prospects are related to those of the firm's other commitments. If the new investment is closely related to the others (i.e., $\rho_{ij} \approx 1$), it may prove undesirable. But if it is unrelated (i.e., $\rho_{ij} \approx 0$), it may prove very desirable. In short, not only the expected return and standard deviation of return are relevant; the investment's relationship to other commitments is

---

[7] This is not precisely true unless qualified by adding "assuming that a linear relationship between the two rates of return is to be used for the prediction." In general, let the best linear estimate of the relationship be

$$A_i^R = a + bA_j^R$$

Assume that the probability distribution assigned to a has a zero standard deviation. If $b > 0$, $\rho_{ij} = +1$. If $b < 0$, $\rho_{ij} = -1$. But if the distribution assigned to a has a positive standard deviation, then, if $b > 0$, $0 < \rho_{ij} < +1$; if $b < 0$, $0 < \rho_{ij} < -1$; and if $b = 0$, $\rho_{ij} = 0$.

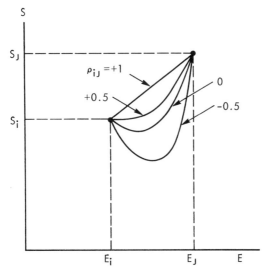

FIGURE 4-7. Combinations of E and S attainable by undertaking two investments.

also important. In fact, the latter may be a more crucial component of risk than the standard deviation.

The relevance of this relationship depends upon the viewpoint of the decision-maker. The manager of a small project will be interested primarily in the total risk (measured by the standard deviation) of anything he undertakes, since it will represent virtually the whole activity of his project. Rightly or wrongly, he expects to be judged on the actual outcome of the project. Although it may prove desirable from the standpoint of the firm to have him undertake a high-return, high-risk project, he may be most reluctant to do so, preferring instead a low-return, low-risk project that will minimize the probability of a disastrous (to him) outcome.

From the standpoint of the manager of a firm, the correlation of a proposed investment's outcome with the other commitments of the company becomes an important component of risk. He may thus seem less conservative than his subordinates, since he will expect disappointing outcomes on some projects to be offset by better-than-expected outcomes on others. However, the manager may still seem more conservative than his stockholders, for they are primarily interested in the extent to which an investment is correlated with all

investments taken as a whole. For them, the extent to which an investment's outcome is affected by (moves with) the overall business cycle
is the most relevant measure of risk. If the firm's manager is solely
concerned with the interests of the owners, and if the owners' wealth
is spread over diverse commitments, the "responsiveness" of the

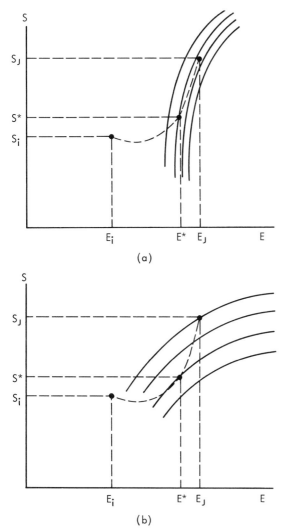

(a)

(b)

FIGURE 4–8. Indifference curves showing attitudes towards risk and expected return.

rate of return on an investment to changes in the overall level of the economy should be the major item considered when evaluating risk. Needless to say, these conditions may rarely be met.

A final complication concerns the decision-maker's attitude regarding overall risk. Presumably this can be represented by a family of indifference curves, with each curve indicating combinations of E and S among which he is indifferent. Figure 4–8a shows a family of such curves. They are upward-sloping, indicating that the investor is risk averse—to remain indifferent as risk is increased he must receive a greater expected return. Combinations on curves lying to the right are preferred, since they provide a higher expected return for a given risk. The curvature suggests that the additional expected return required to compensate for additional risk increases as the total risk rises.

Figure 4–8b shows a set of indifference curves for a different decision-maker. In a rough sense, he is more risk averse, requiring greater increases in expected return to compensate for added risk.

Now assume that the firm's present position is indicated by point (E_j, S_j) and that a new investment having prospects represented by point (E_i, S_i) is proposed. If the investment is undertaken, the firm's overall prospects will be those shown by point (E^*, S^*), reflecting the proposed investment's correlation with the firm's present commitments and its importance as a determinant of the company's value.

Should the new investment be undertaken? No, given the values of the individual pictured in Fig. 4–8a. Yes, from the point of view of the more risk-averse individual shown in Fig. 4–8b. Thus the decision-maker's attitude toward risk may also play a role in the final decision.

I. CAPITAL VALUE

We have discussed at length the problem of investment evaluation. Underlying the discussion was the assumption that the present cost (or price) of the asset(s) was given. We now wish to alter the approach to determine the highest price that the individual is willing to pay for the asset(s). This is, by definition, his estimate of its (their) *capital value*.

Consider an investment to be evaluated without concern for other holdings. Let F_0 be the cash outflow representing the cost of acquiring the assets required for the investment. Then, given F_0, we have

$$PV = \sum_{i=0}^{N} \frac{F_i}{(1 + r)^i} = F_0 + \sum_{i=1}^{N} \frac{F_i}{(1 + r)^i}$$

where r = the appropriate discount rate for investments of equal risk. The investment should be undertaken as long as its present value is nonnegative:

$$PV = F_0 + \sum_{i=1}^{N} \frac{F_i}{(1 + r)^i} \geqq 0$$

Obviously the highest price (negative F_0) that should be paid for the asset is the present value of all other flows:

$$V_0 = \sum_{i=1}^{N} \frac{F_i}{(1 + r)^i}$$

Consider next an investment being evaluated in the context of other sources of wealth. It will have an expected rate of return, standard deviation of rate of return, and correlation with other sources of wealth. But these are to some extent dependent upon its initial cost. In particular, the lower the cost, the greater is the expected rate of return.[8] At some sufficiently low price, the asset(s) will typically become attractive enough to purchase. By definition, this is the capital value in the environment being considered.

In general, an individual's estimate of the capital value of an asset or group of assets will depend on the following:

1. His expectations (best single estimates) concerning future prospects.
2. His assessment of the risk associated with the asset (i.e., the extent to which actual outcomes may diverge from those predicted).
3. The context within which the asset is evaluated—that is, other sources of wealth and the extent to which the proposed investment's prospects are affected by the factors that influence these other sources.

---

[8] The standard deviation of rate of return may or may not be affected by current price, depending on the relationship between the individual's estimate of the future and the current price. The correlation coefficient will probably not be affected by current price.

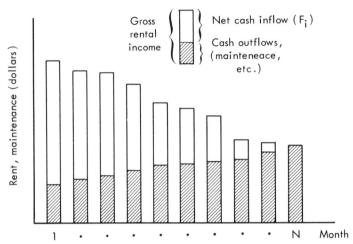

FIGURE 4-9. Anticipated cash inflows and outflows for a rented computer.

4. The attitude toward risk of the decision maker or the individuals for whom he acts.

A clear example of the importance of capital value is provided by the relationship between a computer's projected rental income and the price at which the manufacturer will sell it outright rather than retain ownership and rent it. Figure 4-9 shows the streams of gross inflows (rental income), gross outflows (maintenance, modifications, etc.), and net inflows (gross inflows less gross outflows) anticipated if the computer is retained and rented. The estimated rental payments decline over time, reflecting an assumption that innovations will lead to new computers with improved price-performance ratios, requiring this computer to be offered at a lower rental rate to remain competitive. Gross outflows are expected to increase over time, primarily because of heavier maintenance requirements. Of course the inflow and outflow streams can be varied as a matter of policy. For example, the manufacturer may keep the computer competitive by constant improvements. If so, the rental income may not decline over time,[9] but costs will increase substantially. Figure 4-9 should be interpreted as showing the most desirable set of inflow and outflow streams of all those possible. Given these streams, after some point the net inflows

---

[9] Rental charges have, in fact, tended to remain constant over time; additional explanations and a detailed examination of the issue can be found in Chapter 8.

become negative: the cost of maintaining the computer's effectiveness will exceed its value to users. At this point (month N in Fig. 4–9), the value of the computer will become zero. This is, by definition, the end of its *economic life*.

What is the computer's capital value at the present time? Formally it will equal the present value of the stream of net inflows, discounted at the appropriate interest rate. Probably the manufacturer will be willing to sell the equipment at a price equal to his estimate of its capital value. Under such conditions what attitude should the user take toward rental versus purchase? The answer depends on whether or not his assessment of the computer's capital value exceeds that of the manufacturer (reflected in the purchase price). The user's attitude toward risk may differ from that of the manufacturer, as may his assessment of this risk and the context within which it is evaluated. The problems associated with the issue of rent versus purchase are clearly complex. For this reason we defer further discussion; the subject is covered in Chapter 8.

Figure 4–9 can be used to illustrate another important relationship. At time zero (the present), the estimated capital value of the computer will be

$$V_0 = \sum_{i=1}^{N} \frac{F_i}{(1 + r)^i}$$

After one period has elapsed, assuming that no change is made in the estimates of the remaining cash flows or the degree of risk, the value will be

$$V_1 = \sum_{i=2}^{N} \frac{F_i}{(1 + r)^{i-1}}$$

Thus the present value is

$$V_0 = \frac{F_1}{1 + r} + \frac{V_1}{1 + r}$$

In other words, the present value of an asset may be estimated either directly, by discounting the entire stream of the cash flows during its economic life, or, indirectly, by considering only its cash flow in the next period and its estimated value at the end of the period. In fact, any cutoff point can be used, with the asset's residual value at this point

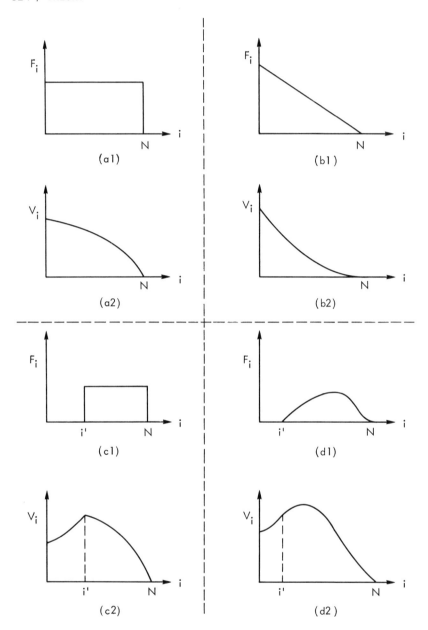

FIGURE 4–10. Relationships between predicted cash inflows and predicted capital value.

considered a final cash inflow. If the residual value is assumed to represent the capital value (at that time) of all remaining flows, the estimated present capital value will be the same, regardless of the choice of horizon. The methods are thus logically equivalent.

J. DEPRECIATION AND OBSOLESCENCE

Given a set of estimates of cash flows $(F_1, \ldots, F_N)$ of the type described in Section I, one can estimate the capital value of an asset at any given time. In general,

$$V_{i^*} = \sum_{i=i^*+1}^{N} \left[\frac{F_i}{(1 + r)^{i-i^*}} \right]$$

Figures 4–10a(1) and a(2) illustrate the relationships between predicted net inflows [4–10a(1)] and predicted capital value [4–10a(2)] for one simple pattern of flows. The value declines over time because fewer inflows remain as time goes on. However, there is a counteracting factor: although fewer inflows remain, they are closer at hand. In the case shown in Figs. 4–10a(1) and a(2), the latter factor is not as strong as the former. This is also the case for the pattern illustrated in Fig. 4–10b(1); the net effect is to cause the capital value to decrease over time, as shown in Fig. 4–10b(2).

Figures 4–10c(1) and c(2) illustrate a case in which capital value does rise over time (through month i'). The reason is obvious: until month i', each month brings the expected inflows closer without reducing the set of those that remain. This explains why common stocks not currently paying dividends (but expected to do so in the future) often increase in market value over time.

Figures 4–10d(1) and d(2) provide another example of the relationship between cash flows and predicted capital value.

Anticipated declines in capital value [e.g., those shown in Fig. 4–10a(2)] are termed *depreciation*. Anticipated increases in capital value [e.g., those shown through month i' in Fig. 4–10c(2)] are termed *appreciation*. But the actual capital value may not equal that originally anticipated. At any given time there will be a predicted set of cash flows and a corresponding set of predicted capital values. For example, the solid curve in Fig. 4–11 shows V_i^0, the predicted capital value for month i based on flows $F_{i+1}, \ldots, F_N$ estimated in period 0. When month i actually arrives, there will be a new set of predictions con-

Capital value

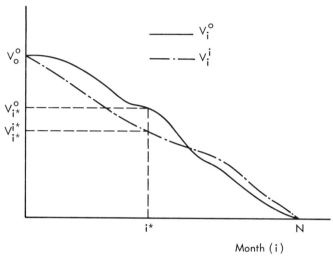

FIGURE 4-11. Predicted and actual capital values.

cerning flows $F_{i+1}, \ldots, F_N$. The capital value based on these flows (V_i^i) will be the actual capital value at the time. Thus the pattern of actual capital values may depart considerably from that predicted (e.g., it may follow the dotted curve instead of the solid curve in Fig. 4–11).

If the actual value falls below the predicted value, we term the difference *obsolescence*. Thus in month i^* we have depreciation of $(V_0^0 - V_{i*}^0)$ and obsolescence of $(V_{i*}^0 - V_{i*}^{i*})$. There is no comparable term in common use for the difference between actual value and predicted value when the former exceeds the latter, although such cases will be as likely as those involving obsolescence if predicted values are truly unbiased estimates.

K. DEPRECIATION FORMULAS

In view of the complexity of the problem of predicting capital values over time, it is not surprising that, in practice, simplified models are adopted. Three are of particular importance, since they are used regularly by accountants and are accepted by the U.S. government for purposes of corporate income tax calculations. All three methods assume that the initial value of an asset equals its cost and base the depreciation calculations on an estimated "useful" life (N).

The *straight-line* method assumes a constant absolute decrease in value, with value reaching zero in N periods:

$$V_i = V_{i-1} - \frac{V_0}{N}$$

The *double-declining-balance* method assumes a constant percentage decline in value:

$$V_i = V_{i-1} - \left(\frac{2}{N}\right) V_{i-1}$$

The *sum-of-the-years'-digits* method [10] is more complicated:

$$V_i = V_{i-1} - \left[\frac{N+1-i}{(N^2+N)/2}\right] V_0$$

The first and third method give a value of zero in period N; the double-declining-balance method yields a small positive value in period N. If desired, the formulas may be modified so that value will reach a specified salvage value in a given year.

Tax regulations suggest an economic life of 10 years for computers. However, corporations are allowed to use other estimates if a reasonable precedent can be cited; 5 years is quite common. Figure 4–12a shows the estimated value of a computer costing $100,000 as a function of age for each of the three depreciation methods, based on an assumed life of 5 years. Figure 4–12b shows estimated values based on an assumed life of 10 years.

As the figures illustrate, both the double-declining-balance method and the sum-of-the-years'-digits method provide greater depreciation in the earlier years and less in the later years than the straight-line method. For this reason they are termed *accelerated* depreciation methods. Since the amount by which an asset is estimated to have depreciated during a year is considered an expense, taxable income is reduced by an equivalent amount. Thus, although total depreciation will be virtually the same regardless of the method chosen, accelerated methods imply lower incomes (and hence taxes) in the early years and higher incomes (and hence taxes) in the later years. For this reason

---

[10] The name refers to an alternative method for calculating the denominator in the depreciation formula:

$$\frac{N^2+N}{2} = 1 + 2 + 3 + \cdots + N$$

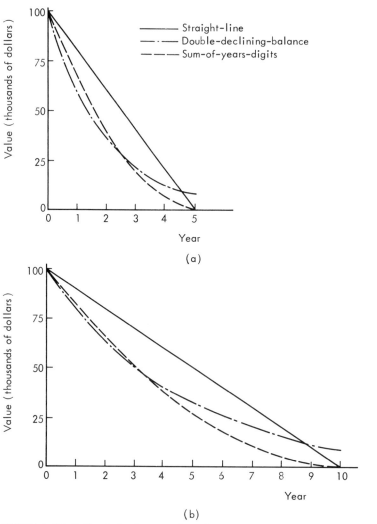

FIGURE 4-12. Estimated value as a function of age for each of three depreciation methods, based on an assumed life of (a) 5 and (b) 10 years.

accelerated methods (and the shortest allowable economic life) are almost always used for tax purposes, since the present value of a tax payment is less, the farther in the future it is made.[11] However, finan-

[11] This is but one case in which cash flows for tax payments must be included in the analysis. In practice such considerations may be overriding. No change is required in the procedures described in this chapter; the problems arise primarily in understanding the full implications of all the applicable tax regulations.

cial reports furnished to stockholders may (and often do) use different procedures. The first three columns of Table 4–1 indicate those used in 1966 by the eight major computer manufacturers for estimating the depreciation of owned computers.

It is important to note that only by chance will capital values estimated in accordance with simple depreciation formulas provide correct estimates of the total value of a firm. Financial services report a figure described as book value per share of common stock (shown in column 4 of Table 4–1). This is obtained by summing the values of the assets of the firm (calculated with standard depreciation formulas in the case of fixed assets), subtracting total liabilities (debts), and then dividing the remainder by the number of shares of stock outstanding. In theory this should provide a reasonably accurate estimate of the value of a share of ownership of the firm. In fact, the owners rarely believe that it does. The final column in Table 4–1 shows the market price per share for each of the eight manufacturers on the last market trading day in 1966. Stockholders evidently attached considerably greater values to these firms than did their accountants.

Why do standard depreciation techniques fail to provide reasonable estimates of the value of a firm? In a real sense a firm is a unique capital asset. It is a composite of physical facilities and equipment, technical

TABLE 4-1. Depreciation Data, 1966 *

Company	Depreciation Method †	Estimated Life (years) †	Book Value per Share ‡	Market Price per Share §
Burroughs	Straight-line	4–5	$26.44	$ 87.75
CDC	Straight-line	?	7.44	32.38
GE	Accelerated	10ⁱⁱ	23.72	88.50
Honeywell	Straight-line	8	22.19	66.38
IBM	Sum-of-the-years'-digits	3–17	60.88	371.50
NCR	Sum-of-the-years'-digits	4–6	33.09	67.50
RCA	Accelerated	3–10	11.26	42.75
Sperry Rand	Accelerated	2–16	13.16	29.75

* Sources: *Moody's Industrial Manual,* June, 1967; Investment Services Listing, October–November–December, 1966.

† Depreciation methods and estimated lives are those used for financial reports. Methods and lives used for tax purposes may differ. Data refer to computer equipment on lease.

‡ Net tangible asset value per share as of Dec. 31, 1966, or the company's regular reporting date in 1966.

§ As of Dec. 30, 1966.

ⁱⁱ Company states that it follows the Internal Revenue Service guidelines.

skills, good will, innovations, debts, and general know-how. The composite is capable of producing a great many alternative streams of cash flows of varying risk over time. The value of the firm is the capital value of the best stream from the set of possible streams. There is no reason to believe that this overall value is related in a simple way to *any* values assigned to its individual components. Imagine a completely new firm. Traditional accounting techniques would assign values to the assets equal to their costs. The book value of the firm would thus equal the total cost of its assets. But the whole should be greater than the sum of its parts; otherwise why begin the firm at all?

The value of a firm must, in the final analysis, be based on people's estimates of its (uncertain) future prospects. Opinions will differ on this score. However, one set of opinions, backed by financial commitments, can be observed. Undoubtedly the best available estimate of the value of the ownership of a firm can be obtained by simply multiplying the market price of a share of the firm's common stock by the number of shares outstanding.

If the accountants' estimates of book value have relatively little economic meaning, what about their estimates of income, earnings, and profit? Without entering into the details, we merely assert that these are also subject to serious problems. A useful alternative procedure builds on the market measure of value.

Let the value of the ownership of a firm in period i be V_i and the value in period $i + 1$ be V_{i+1}. Assume that at the end of period i the firm provides its owners with an amount D_i in cash. Then the actual wealth of the owners at the beginning of period $i + 1$ is

$$W_{i+1}^a = V_{i+1} + D_i$$

Let r_i^e be the rate of return expected by the owners at the beginning of period i; we assume that r_i^e is equal to the expected rate of return on investments of equal risk. The wealth expected at the beginning of period $i + 1$ is

$$W_{i+1}^e = (1 + r_i^e)V_i$$

If the actual wealth exceeds the expected wealth, the difference is *profit*. If the actual wealth is less than expected, the difference is a *loss*. The expected increase in wealth $(r_i^e V_i)$ is *income*.

L. THE COST OF CAPITAL

It is often asserted that large computer manufacturers enjoy an unfair competitive advantage because of their low "cost of capital"; for example, it is said that IBM can afford to retain ownership of the computers it produces, renting them to users, whereas smaller manufacturers must attempt to sell their products outright. Although there may be an important element of truth in this assertion, it is concealed, rather than revealed, by the oversimplified concept of the cost of capital.

Firms can obtain capital from a wide variety of sources subject to a wide variety of conditions. To simplify, we aggregate all sources into two major classes: creditors and owners. Creditors are promised specific payments and given prior claims on the firm's earnings and/or assets. Owners are residual claimants — they get whatever is left after the creditors have been paid. Debt instruments (bonds, notes, etc.) are evidence of the claims of creditors, and common stock certificates represent ownership claims.[12]

A firm may obtain capital from creditors or owners or both. When the firm is first established, a financing mix is chosen. And by default, at least, the choice concerning capital is made continuously during the life of the firm.[13] Earnings may be paid to stockholders or retained for reinvestment. Additional funds may or may not be borrowed. Capital thus comes from all sources and is used for all the firm's undertakings. The idea that the nominal interest cost of debt can be considered representative of a firm's cost of capital is clearly in error. Although the actual cash for a new project may come from a new bank loan, it would be foolish to link the two events together by asserting that the rate of interest required by the bank is the cost of capital for the new

---

[12] There are, of course, many mixed types (debt convertible into stock, preferred stock, etc.). However, the key concepts can best be illustrated by considering only the two pure types of capital.

[13] Certain sources of capital, such as bonds and new stock issues, require rather large fixed costs (underwriting, advertising, registration, etc.). The firm may thus wait until its capital structure diverges considerably from the optimal mix before resorting to these sources, and may anticipate future needs when the sources are used. The divergence allowed before such sources are utilized may be larger, the smaller is the total value of the firm. The problem is similar to that of selecting an economic order quantity for inventory items and can be analyzed with models similar to those developed for inventory problems.

project. This might be the case if all funds for payment of the principal and interest were required to come from the proceeds of the project. But this is rarely so. Typically, creditors are given a prior claim on all the earnings and/or assets of the firm; and the smaller the extent to which the firm is financed by debt, the less risky is the creditors' position. Whatever the relevant cost of capital may be, it is typically higher than the nominal interest rate required by creditors.

Consider the situation faced by a group of entrepreneurs planning to start a new firm. For convenience we assume that the only available alternative would involve a present outlay of $100 and that total proceeds would be realized a year hence. The entrepreneurs' probability distribution is shown in Fig. 4–13a; the expected value of the dollar payoff is $110, giving an overall expected rate of return of 10%. If the firm were financed entirely by its owners, Fig. 4–13a would, of course, show the probability distribution of rate of return on equity as well as the firm's overall rate of return.

Assume that the entrepreneurs choose instead to finance the firm partly with debt. In particular assume that $70 is obtained from creditors and only $30 from owners. Let the nominal rate of interest on the debt be 5%. This means that the firm promises to pay *no more than* 5% over and above the initial amount borrowed: creditors will receive $73.50 (1.05 times $70) or the total amount that the firm obtains, whichever is smaller.

Figure 4–13b shows the probability distribution of the amount paid to creditors and the implied rate of return. The expected rate of return is approximately 2.6%, considerably less than the nominal rate of 5%. Moreover, there is considerable risk. The actual prospects faced by creditors are clearly less desirable than the nominal rate of interest suggests. If the creditors require an expected rate of return of 5%, the nominal rate must be set at approximately 7.8%. Even if this were done, there would be substantial risk. If the current pure rate of interest is 5%, an even greater nominal rate might be required (e.g., 10%) to bring the expected rate of return far enough above 5% to compensate for the risk involved.

This is, admittedly, an extreme case. Consider the situation if only $30 had been raised by debt financing at a nominal rate of 5%. There is no chance that the firm cannot repay both capital and interest; thus the nominal rate equals the expected rate and there is no risk. But note that this is so only because the debt provides a relatively small amount

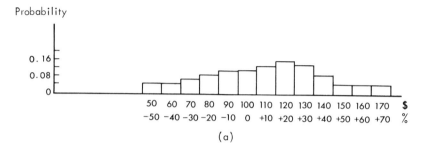

(a)

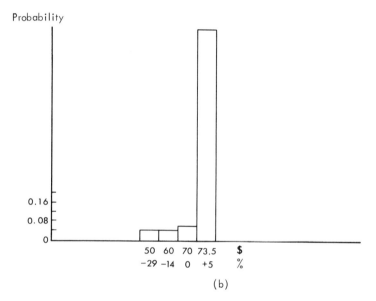

(b)

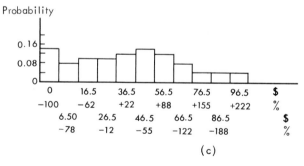

(c)

FIGURE 4-13. Probability distributions for earnings (a) payments to creditors (b) and payments to owners (c).

of the total capital. The cost of debt is low only because it is accompanied by equity financing.

The example could be extended, but the point should be clear enough: neither the nominal rate of interest nor the expected rate of return on debt can be considered the relevant cost of capital for a firm. By and large, the cost depends on the prospects and risk of the proposed uses to which the capital is put, not the source(s) from which it is obtained. If IBM enjoys a low cost of capital, this is so because investors feel that its activities involve relatively small risks. If small manufacturers must pay more for capital, the reason is that investors consider their activities more risky. Needless to say, the investors may be wrong, overrating IBM's prospects and underestimating those of small manufacturers. However, errors of this sort may be corrected over time as additional evidence is obtained.

M. LEVERAGE AND RISK

The overall risk associated with a firm's future prospects depends on the activities of the firm. But the risk borne by the firm's owners depends on both the overall risk and the extent to which the firm is financed by debt. The point can be illustrated with the example of Section L. Consider the case in which 70% of the initial capital was provided by creditors at a nominal rate of 5%. Figure 4–13c shows the probability distribution of returns to the owners. The expected amount is $38.19, giving an expected rate of return of 27.3%. But note the large element of risk. A small variation in the overall rate of return will cause a large variation in the rate of return on equity. The firm is said to be highly *levered*, since it has such high fixed charges for servicing and repaying debt.

The risk borne by owners can be shown to be related to both the percentage of the firm that is financed by owners and to its overall risk. Let r_0 be the overall rate of return on total assets (T); and let F be the total fixed charges for debt. Then the owners' actual rate of return on equity (E) will be

$$r_e = \frac{r_0 T - F}{E}$$

$$= \frac{r_0}{E/T} - \frac{F}{E}$$

It follows that [14]

$$S(r_e) = \frac{1}{E/T} S(r_0) \tag{4-8}$$

where $S(r_e)$ = the standard deviation of the rate of return on equity (i.e., its risk),

$S(r_0)$ = the standard deviation of the firm's overall rate of return on assets (i.e., its risk), and

E/T = the proportion of the firm's total value represented by equity (ownership claims).

In the example, $E/T = {}^{30}/_{100}$. Thus the stockholders' risk is 3.33 times as great as the firm's overall risk.

There is nothing inherently bad about a company heavily financed by debt. Although ownership claims will be risky, they will generally provide a high expected return (otherwise no one would hold them). To be sure, when expectations of the firm's overall prospects are revised downward, the effect on the value of the ownership claims may be extreme. For example, during June, 1965, the market price of Control Data Corporation's common stock fell over 30% (from $56.75 on June 1 to $38.63 on July 1), in response to news of unexpected difficulties encountered in the production and sale of some of the firm's large computers. At the time Control Data had large amounts of debt outstanding.

In theory the risk provided by a firm to its owners may not be particularly important as long as high risk is accompanied by high expected returns. In practice, however, a firm may attempt to maintain roughly the same overall position in terms of stockholders' risk over time.[15] This need not imply that the firm invests only in projects of roughly equal risk. A particularly risky venture can be undertaken along with an unusually safe one. Moreover, the firm's financing can be adjusted to compensate for its activities. An increase in the firm's overall risk can be accompanied by a decrease in the importance of

[14] The derivation of equation 4–8 shown here is based on a continuing situation—F represents only the annual charges for servicing the firm's debt. However, the relationship holds even in the extreme case in which the firm is liquidated at the end of one period.

[15] Otherwise the present owners would either have to (1) sell their stock every time the firm's risk position diverged to any major extent from their preferred position, incurring transactions costs, or (2) retain the stock, even though it had become more or less risky than they considered optimal.

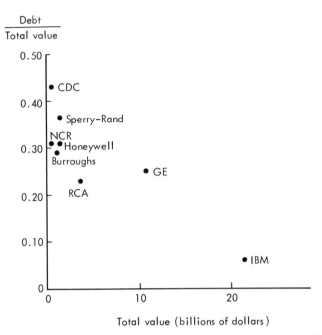

FIGURE 4-14. Total values and ratios of debt to total value for eight manufacturers, 1966.

debt financing; for example, new projects can be financed entirely through retained earnings or even a new issue of stock.

There is no reason to suppose a priori that all firms in a given industry will attempt to provide roughly equal degrees of risk to their stockholders. In fact the evidence suggests quite the contrary for the computer industry. Figure 4-14 shows the ratios of debt to total value and the total values [16] of the eight major manufacturers in 1966. In general, the larger the firm, the less it relied on debt financing. Large firms may be less risky than small, other things being equal: the sheer number of IBM's customers and products reduces the impact of a disappointing reaction by an individual customer and/or an unprofitable product. Thus, in a rough sense, Fig. 4-14 suggests that the more risky firms chose to add even more risk to be borne by their stockholders, through reliance on relatively heavy debt financing.

[16] Total values are based on the market value of common stock as of Dec. 30, 1966, and the book value of all other components of capital as of Dec. 30, 1966, except that (1) the balance sheet for Control Data Corporation was dated June 30, 1966, and (2) the balance sheet for Sperry Rand was dated Mar. 31, 1966. All capital items other than common stock were classified as debt and evaluated at book value.

CHAPTER **5** **COSTS, INPUTS, AND OUTPUTS**

A. INTRODUCTION

Thus far we have dealt with value, revenue, methods for comparing streams of cash flows, and optimal behavior under various assumptions concerning costs and market situations. This chapter builds on the earlier discussion. We consider how inputs should be combined to efficiently produce outputs, suggest typical relationships between costs and outputs, and extend the previous discussion to include cases of joint products and pricing under conditions of uncertainty.

B. OUTPUT PATTERNS

Assume that a firm is planning to produce a particular computer. Let period zero be the present. The manager of the firm wishes to select the best possible output pattern $o_1, o_2, \ldots, o_n$, where o_i represents the number of units available for sale in period i. How should he proceed?

In the most general possible terms, the answer is as follows. Consider a particular output pattern; it can undoubtedly be produced in many ways, each involving a certain pattern of input requirements and hence cash outflows (and possibly some inflows) over time. Each of the possible methods for producing the given output pattern has an associated total cost, measured in present value (using the techniques described in Chapter 4). The best method for producing the specified output pattern is the cheapest, that is, the one with the lowest total present value of cost. And its cost is the total cost of the pattern. Repeating the procedure for different output patterns provides for each an associated minimum present-value total cost.

Consider now the revenue situation. There will typically be many ways of marketing any given pattern of output. Each will give rise to a pattern of cash inflows (and possibly some outflows). The optimal marketing method is the one giving the greatest total revenue measured in present value. By repeating the procedure, an associated maximum present-value total revenue can be obtained for each output pattern. The optimal pattern is simply the one for which the difference between total revenue and total cost is the greatest.

Needless to say, it may be extremely difficult to consider the full range of alternatives open to a firm, be it a producer of computers, computer time, or computer programs; add the possibility of multiple outputs (e.g., some firms produce all three of these) and the problem becomes almost totally intractable at a formal level. For purposes of exposition we thus consider only a few possible forms of output patterns. We have already treated some simple cases. We now consider both these and a few others in detail.

All patterns discussed here can be characterized by a *starting point* (S), a constant *rate* of output per period (R), a total *volume* (V), and a *time* or length of production (T). More precisely,

$$o_i = 0 \quad \text{for } 0 \leqq i < S$$
$$= R \quad \text{for } S \leqq i \leqq S + T$$
$$= 0 \quad \text{for } S + T < i$$

Note that an output pattern is completely described by three parameters (S and two of the others) since

$$V = RT$$

Patterns involving a constant rate of output are not often encountered in practice. Output usually builds up to some peak rate and eventually tapers off toward the end of the production period. However, we wish to concentrate on the key relationships between cost, rate, and volume; thus it is useful to deal with somewhat artificial patterns of output.

C. COST AND OUTPUT

Consider a pattern of output $\phi = o_1, o_2, \ldots, o_n$. Let $F^\phi = f_0, f_1, \ldots, f_n$ be a set of cash flows that will purchase resources capable of producing ϕ. Let $PV(F^\phi)$ be the present value of F^ϕ. Then the total cost of output pattern ϕ is simply

$$TC(\phi) = \min PV(F^\phi)$$

Note that the *total* cost of the output is stated in terms of present value.

The actual pattern of cash flows that will produce a pattern of output at minimum cost may be quite different from the pattern of the output itself. However, it is possible to construct an equivalent set of flows that will be similar to the pattern of output. Simply select a constant (A) that satisfies the following relationship:

$$\sum_{i=0}^{n} \frac{Ao_i}{(1 + r)^i} = TC(\phi)$$

The value A is defined as the *average cost* (cost per unit) for the output pattern. The actual set of cash flows is equivalent to (has the same present value as) a pattern involving an outlay of A dollars every time a unit of output becomes available for sale.

It is a simple matter to compute the average cost. Rewriting the formula above, we obtain

$$A = \frac{TC(\phi)}{\sum_{i=0}^{n} \frac{o_i}{(1 + r)^i}}$$

Thus the average cost per unit of output can be obtained by "discounting" the output pattern and then dividing the result into the present-value total cost.

How is average cost related to the characteristics of the output pattern? Consider first the effect of variations in the starting date. Among alternative patterns of output, each involving the same rate, volume, and length of production, average cost is typically smaller the later the point at which production is to begin, approaching some lower bound as an asymptote, as illustrated in Fig. 5–1.[1] The reason is simply that the longer the time available for preparation, the more efficient production can be. The firm can "shop around" for lower prices for its inputs, study alternative technologies in detail, etc. The relationship is stated rather well in the proverb "Haste makes waste."

Consider next the effect of varying volume, holding constant the rate of output and the starting date. Among alternative patterns, each starting at the same point of time and involving the same rate of output

---

[1] *Total* (discounted) cost will, of course, continue to decrease as S increases, approaching zero as an asymptote.

but differing in length of production and hence volume, average cost is typically smaller the greater the volume (and production time), approaching some lower bound as an asymptote, as illustrated in Fig. 5–2. Two factors account for the relationship: the learning effect and economies of scale.

For a given technique of production, learning occurs over time; fewer man-hours will be required per unit of output during the second year of production than during the first. The average cost per unit will thus be smaller if production continues for two years (at a given rate of output) than if it stops after one year. The learning effect may also reduce the material required per unit and perhaps effect other economies. But there is a limit to the extent to which learning can lower costs; for a sufficiently large volume (long period of production), average costs will be affected little by further increases in volume.

The learning effect is extremely difficult to isolate. For example, learning may be at least partially transferable: production of additional units of computer model A may lower the costs of producing model B. The importance of the volume of a particular model produced in lowering average cost as a result of learning is typically greater, the smaller is the similarity among models and the less automated the production technique utilized.

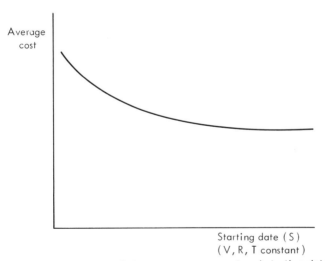

FIGURE 5–1. Relationship between average cost and starting date.

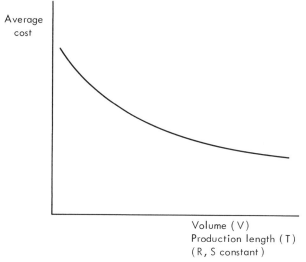

Average
cost

Volume (V)
Production length (T)
(R, S constant)

FIGURE 5–2. Relationship between average cost and volume, given rate.

The second factor accounting for decreasing average cost as volume and production length increase is summed up in the term *the economies of large-scale production.* Figure 5–3 illustrates the general principle.[2] Three techniques of production are available. Each involves some learning; thus total cost rises less than proportionately with volume. However, the techniques differ with respect to initial outlay and variable costs. Technique A requires no initial outlay, has rather high variable costs, and exhibits a rather large learning effect; it is represented by curve OA'. Technique B requires an initial outlay (OB), has lower variable costs, and benefits less from learning, as shown by curve BB'. Technique C is the most suitable for large-volume production; its total cost is shown by curve CC'.

If the firm knows with certainty the desired volume of output, the cheapest technique should be utilized (A if $0 < V \leqq V_1$, B if $V_1 < V \leqq$

---

[2] The total cost in Fig. 5–3 is measured in present value. The volume indicated should thus be the discounted value of actual outputs

$$\sum_{i=0}^{n} \frac{o_i}{(1 + r)^i}$$

rather than the total (undiscounted) volume. With this interpretation, average cost is simply the total cost (y axis) divided by the volume (X axis).

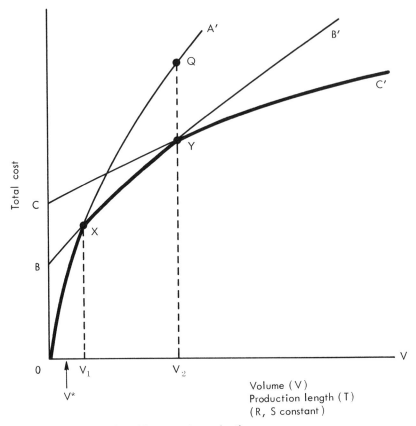

FIGURE 5-3. Economies of large-scale production.

V_2, and C if $V_2 < V$). The total cost is thus represented by the lower envelope $OXYC'$. As volume increases, total cost increases less than proportionately because of both the learning effect and the economies of large-scale production (i.e., the ability to obtain a lower average cost by using a technique involving large fixed but low variable costs). Average cost thus decreases with volume, approaching some lower bound (as shown previously in Fig. 5–2).

It is important to interpret Fig. 5–3 correctly. The envelope $OXYC'$ shows total cost as a function of the volume of production under the assumption that planned and actual volumes are equal. If this is not the case, total cost will be greater. For example, assume that planned volume was V^*, involving a rate of R^* for T^* periods ($V^* = R^*T^*$). Obviously technique A was optimal and would have been selected. Now assume that after production began a decision was made to produce for a longer time (T_2), giving a total volume of V_2 ($= R^*T_2$). At the time the new decision was made it might not have been profitable to switch to technique B, since its lower variable costs would apply only to the remaining volume. The lowest total cost possible at the time of the decision to extend production might thus have been as high as V_2Q; in any event it undoubtedly exceeded V_2Y. Whenever possible, it pays to plan ahead.

In practical situations it is difficult to predict the optimal production pattern. Thus it may be profitable to invest little, choosing a technique involving rather high variable but low initial costs. After the fact, the choice may prove to have been suboptimal (e.g., if technique A was selected and actual production exceeds V_1), but this in no way implies that the decision was incorrect given the situation at the time it was made.

The relationship between total cost and volume of production applies in a wide variety of situations. Consider the problem of writing programs. The larger the number of programs to be written, the more reasonable it becomes to prepare efficient compilers, train programmers in more complex languages, etc.; the higher initial costs are more than compensated for by the corresponding reductions in variable cost per program. Note also that economies of scale can arise in marketing, maintenance, software support, and other areas as well as in the actual production of hardware. In fact, these other areas may provide greater economies of scale than hardware production for manufacturers of full lines of general-purpose computers.

Average cost is often related to volume (given a rate of production) in a manner approximated well by a log-linear function: [3]

$$\ln A = a - b \ln V$$

or

$$A = aV^{-b}$$

[3] This form does not explicitly allow fixed costs. It thus may only approximate the true relationship over a limited range of values.

The coefficient b is easily interpreted; for example, if $b = 0.15$, a 100% increase in volume will reduce average cost by 15%.[4]

Consider now the relationship between average cost and rate of production, holding constant the volume of production and the starting date. Among output patterns having the same starting date and total volume of production but differing in rate of output and production period, average cost typically is higher the greater the rate of output (and the shorter the period of production). This follows from the existence of variations in efficiency among resources and the obvious decision rule that the most efficient resources should be used for any given rate of production. For example, assume that several programmers are available for employment by a software firm. Programmer i is capable of producing L_i lines of code per year and requires a salary (cost) of C_i dollars per year. His cost per line of code is thus C_i/L_i. For a given rate of output, programmers should be hired in order of efficiency, that is, in order of increasing values of C_i/L_i. Assume that the programmers have been numbered accordingly, so that $C_1/L_1 < C_2/L_2 \cdots < C_n/L_n$. Assume further that it is possible to hire any programmer for a fractional part of a year. Then efficient (least cost) production implies the costs illustrated in Fig. 5–4. Marginal cost rises with rate of output as less and less efficient resources must be utilized, and of course average cost rises as well.

The argument given for the relationship shown in Fig. 5–4 is analogous to that presented earlier to justify the law of demand. If several alternatives are available, the rational decision-maker will take the best one first. The best uses are the most valuable: thus the marginal value (demand) curve falls with increases in quantity. The best resources are the cheapest per unit of output: thus marginal cost rises with increases in the rate of output if volume is held constant. Again the familiar proverb may be invoked: "Haste makes waste" (but it may be profitable).

No particular form is typical for the curve relating average cost to rate of output (for a given volume); a priori, one can argue only that it is upward-sloping. However, the curve may be presumed to become quite steep as rate of output becomes very large. There will be some

[4] This figure has been used for planning purposes by at least one manufacturer of magnetic core memories.

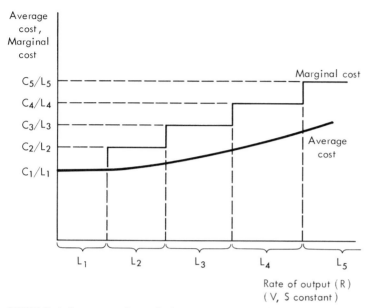

FIGURE 5-4. Average and marginal cost versus rate of output, given volume.

practical upper limit to the possible rate of production for any given product, with the average cost curve becoming vertical at this rate of output.

We turn finally to the most important case from a practical standpoint. Consider output patterns involving identical starting dates and production periods, but differing in both rate and volume. Two counteracting forces apply here. Greater volumes imply lower average costs, *ceteris paribus*. But greater rates of output imply higher average costs, *ceteris paribus*. The net effect of varying rate and volume concurrently can be deduced from the shape of the curve relating average cost to volume when rate of output is held constant (Fig. 5-2). When volume is small, increases in volume lead to substantial absolute declines in average cost. Thus the volume effect can be expected to dominate the rate effect, leading to a net decrease in average cost. But when volume is large, economies of scale and learning account for relatively small decreases in average cost; the rate effect can be expected to dominate, leading to a net increase in average cost. Thus average cost will be related to the rate and volume of output in the manner shown in Fig. 5-5: the curve will be U-shaped.

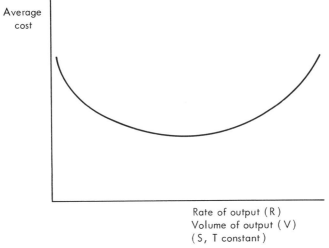

FIGURE 5-5. Average cost versus rate and volume, given the production period.

The greater part of the discussion thus far, and most of that which follows, should be interpreted in the manner suggested by Fig. 5-5. We refer simply to "output" or "quantity" without specifying precisely whether rate or volume or both are assumed to vary. The answer is both: implicitly, a specified length of production is assumed. Strictly speaking, demand curves must be interpreted in a similar manner for complete consistency. Moreover, total cost and total revenue must be redefined slightly. However, these subtleties are of secondary importance; the interested reader is referred to the footnote.[5]

Although average cost will, in theory, fall and then rise with increases in output (rate *and* volume), it is an empirical question whether the range of interest in any particular case is that in which cost per unit is falling, constant, or increasing. Moreover, it is perfectly possible

---

[5] Average cost is determined by dividing the present value of total cost by the discounted sum of outputs. Average revenue is calculated in a similar manner: the optimal marketing scheme for each pattern of output is found, and the resulting present value of total revenue divided by the discounted sum of outputs. To obtain total cost and total revenue curves consistent with the average revenue curves, simply multiply average cost (revenue) by total volume. The resultant figures can be regarded as the present value of total cost (revenue) calculated as of some time K during the production period. If production begins in period $S + 1$ and extends through period $S + T$, given an interest rate r,

$$K = S + T - \left\{ \frac{\ln[(1 + r)^T - 1] - \ln T - \ln r}{\ln(1 + r)} \right\}$$

that the minimum average cost can be obtained with a wide range of outputs. Whether or not this is the case, there is no reason, a priori, for a firm to produce at a level giving the lowest cost per unit. Figures 5–6a through 5–6c illustrate three possible situations. In each case a

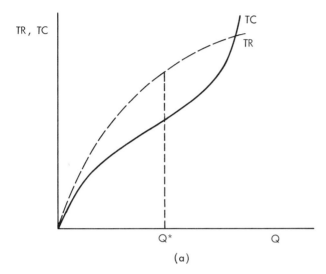

(a)

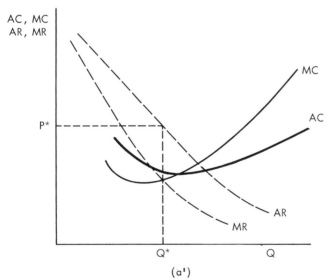

(a')

FIGURE 5–6. Three possible relationships between optimal output and average cost: a, a'; b, b'; c, c'.

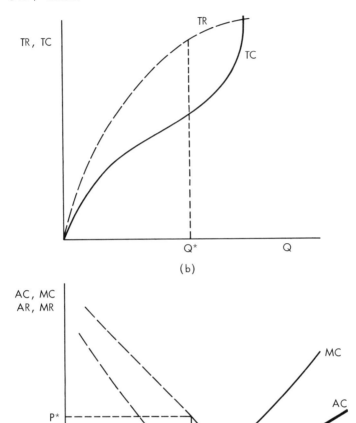

(b)

(b')

FIGURE 5-6 (continued)

total cost curve has been derived from the average cost curve (total cost = average cost times output) and a marginal cost curve derived from the total cost curve. In the situation shown in Figs. 5–6a and a′, the maximum profit output occurs in the range of decreasing average

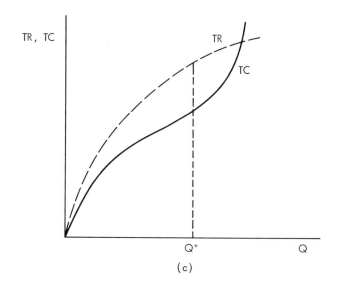

(c)

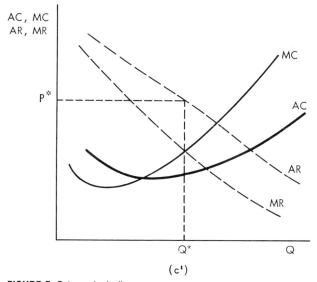

(c')

FIGURE 5–6 (concluded)

costs. Figures 5–6b and b′ show a situation in which the optimal output occurs in the range of minimum average cost. Figures 5–6c and c′ illustrate a case in which the optimal output is in the range of increasing average costs.

Relationships such as those shown in Figs. 5–6a through 5–6c can be used to illustrate the so-called *natural monopoly* situation. Assume that several firms can make a particular type of computer and that their costs will be roughly the same. Figure 5–7 shows the relationship between average cost and output for any firm choosing to manufacture the computer. The demand (average revenue) curve represents the entire demand for such computers. Obviously one firm can manufacture the machine profitably. Any output between X_1 and X_2 will give a cost per unit below the price for which the total output can be sold. But note that two or more firms cannot manufacture the computer without at least one of them sustaining a loss. For example, if each of two firms produces X_1 units, total output will equal $X_2(=2X_1)$, requiring sale at a price of OP. But average cost will be OC_1, leading to a loss for both firms. In such a situation the first firm entering production enjoys a major advantage over competitors. By virtue of its large output, it can undercut the competitors' prices and still cover its average costs. Demand is sufficiently small relative to the minimum average cost output to provide a monopoly position for the first firm in the market. Since no artificial (legal) barriers account for the firm's ability to preclude new entrants, we say that such a firm has a natural monopoly.

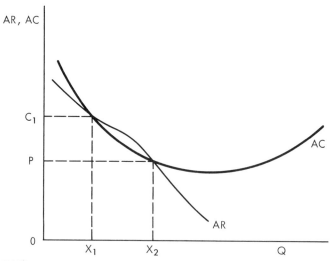

FIGURE 5–7. Natural monopoly.

In the computer industry, the factors leading to economies of scale often apply over large ranges of alternative outputs. Basic software can be used on many models of computers. Sales and maintenance staffs can be responsible for a wide range of equipment. Production lines can be adapted to produce different models without the expenditure of too much time or effort for the changeover. Also, learning is at least partially transferable from model to model. For all these reasons, economies of scale may dominate the difficulties caused by increased rates of output over a rather large range of outputs. This may or may not lead to a condition of natural monopoly, depending on the position of the demand curve relative to that of the average cost curve of a single firm. The question is, of course, an empirical one. We return to it in later chapters.

D. COST AND INPUTS

Assume that a software firm has contracted to produce a large compiler within a one-year period. The major inputs are programmers and computer time. Each must be purchased: programmers cost P_p dollars per hour; computer time costs P_c dollars per hour. The production of the specified compiler within one year can be considered one of many possible levels of output (Q_o^*). The firm's problem is to produce Q_o^* at the lowest possible cost. Let Q_p be the number of programmer-hours utilized during the year and Q_c the number of computer-hours. Then the firm must

$$\text{Minimize:} \quad P_p Q_p + P_c Q_c$$

Subject to

$$Q_o \geqq Q_o^*$$

Figure 5–8 shows some of the alternatives available. Each point represents a combination of inputs (Q_p, Q_c) that will provide the specified output (Q_o^*); such points indicate *technologically feasible* production methods. The firm can, of course, use any linear combination of such methods; thus any point within the shaded area is technologically feasible (i.e., capable of producing Q_o^* units of output). Although only a few basic technologies have been enumerated, all feasible alter-

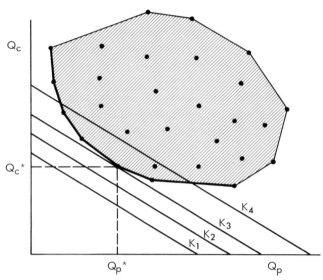

FIGURE 5-8. Producing a given output for the least possible cost.

natives may readily be obtained by assuming combinations of technologies.

Within the set of technologically feasible combinations of inputs there is a *technologically efficient* subset: in Fig. 5-8 such combinations lie on the left-hand border of the shaded area. A combination of inputs is technologically *in*efficient if another combination exists that (1) can produce as much output, (2) uses less of at least one input, and (3) uses no more of any other input(s). A combination is technologically efficient if it is not technologically inefficient.

The locus of technologically efficient combinations giving a specified level of output is called an *isoquant* (equal quantity of output) curve. As illustrated in Fig. 5-8, such a curve is typically downward-sloping and convex to the origin. Both characteristics concern the substitutability of inputs. With few exceptions, inputs can be substituted for one another (to a greater or lesser extent). At universities, where computer time is often free to the user and turnaround time small, programmers rely heavily on diagnostic messages and high-level languages, substituting computer time for their own. But companies purchasing computer time from outside sources encourage their programmers to desk-check extensively and to use relatively low-level languages, hoping thus to substitute relatively cheap programmer time for relatively expensive computer time.

Although substitution among inputs is usually possible, the extent to which one input can be used in place of another depends typically on the initial proportions utilized. In general, the more an input is utilized, the less its ability to substitute for others. This is reflected in the convexity of the isoquant in Fig. 5–8. Points near the top of the curve represent combinations using relatively little programmer time and relatively large amounts of computer time. For such a position, an increase in programmer time allows a substantial reduction in computer time: the curve is quite steep. On the other hand, if the initial position is relatively labor-intensive (i.e., the point lies toward the bottom of the curve), additional increases in programmer time allow only small reductions in computer time: the curve is relatively flat.

It is a simple matter to show the solution to the software firm's problem graphically. In order to meet the requirement $Q_o \geqq Q_o{}^*$, a combination of inputs lying on the $Q_o{}^*$ isoquant must be selected. But which one? Obviously the cheapest. In fact, we define a combination of inputs as *economically efficient* if it is the cheapest (has the least cost) among the technologically efficient combinations. To find such a combination we construct a series of isocost lines. Each has the form

$$P_p Q_p + P_c Q_c = K$$

where K is a parameter representing total cost. The optimum combination obviously lies at the point at which an isocost line is tangent to the $Q_o{}^*$ isoquant.[6] In Fig. 5–8, the appropriate input quantities are $Q_p{}^*$ and $Q_c{}^*$, and the total cost is $K_3 (= P_p Q_p{}^* + P_c Q_c{}^*)$.

Note the division of decision-making labor implicit in this view. The person or persons familiar with the firm's technology can be expected to isolate a relatively few interesting (technologically efficient) production processes. But only a decision-maker who knows the costs (prices) of various inputs can make the final choice among these possibilities. As long as inputs are substitutable, and as long as they are scarce (i.e., command a price), it will be impossible to choose the "best" programming language, the "most efficient" compiler, or the

[6] In the sense that the isocost line touches but does not intersect the isoquant. If the latter is smooth at the point of tangency, the two curves will have equal slopes; but if tangency occurs at a kink, the isoquant's slope is not even defined.

"optimal" computer configuration without explicitly considering the relative costs of various inputs. This may seem obvious, but the principle is often overlooked in practice.

Figures 5–9a and b show the relationship between inputs and outputs in the more general case in which output can be varied. For each possible output there is a set of technologically efficient input combinations. In Fig. 5–9a each such set is represented by an isoquant (drawn as a smooth curve to show a situation in which there are a great many technological possibilities). Given the current prices of the inputs, there will be an economically efficient combination for each output (e.g., the points shown in Fig. 5–9a). The minimum cost for each output is that associated with the economically efficient combination of inputs for the output, as shown in Fig. 5–9b.

The relationship between output and inputs, assuming that only technologically efficient combinations are employed, is called the firm's *production function*. The isoquants in Fig. 5–9a show it graphically. For a firm producing one type of output with N types of inputs we have

$$Q_o = f(Q_I^1, Q_I^2, \ldots, Q_I^N)$$

For a firm producing several types of outputs the function can be given implicitly:

$$f(Q_o^1, Q_o^2, \ldots, Q_o^M; Q_I^1, Q_I^2, \ldots, Q_I^N) = 0$$

Stated in the most general form, the firm's problem is to maximize profit – the difference between revenue (related to outputs) and cost (related to inputs) – given its production function:

$$\text{Maximize:} \quad \text{Profit} = R - C$$

subject to

$$R = r(Q_o^1, Q_o^2, \ldots, Q_o^M) \tag{5-1}$$

$$C = c(Q_I^1, Q_I^2, \ldots, Q_I^N) \tag{5-2}$$

$$f(Q_o^1, Q_o^2, \ldots, Q_o^M; Q_I^1, Q_I^2, \ldots, Q_I^N) = 0 \tag{5-3}$$

Restriction 5–1 reflects the conditions (demand, competition) in the markets for the firm's outputs; restriction 5–2 reflects the conditions (supply, competition) in the markets for the firm's inputs; and restriction 5–3 represents the technology available to the firm.

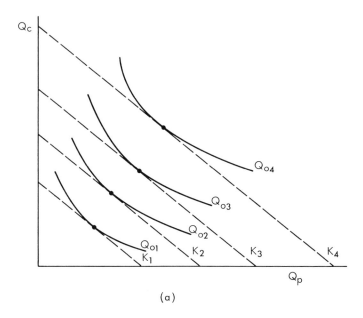

(a)

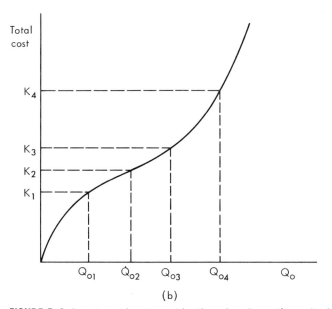

(b)

FIGURE 5-9. Least-cost input combinations for alternative outputs.

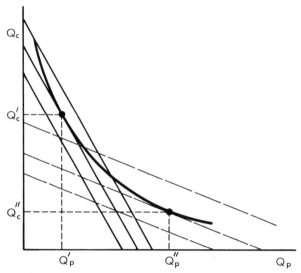

FIGURE 5-10. The effect of a change in relative input prices holding output constant.

We have shown how a firm should choose inputs for a given set of prices; it is a relatively simple matter now to trace the effect of a change in the price of one input. Recall the situation of the software firm committed to produce a specified output. The original prices for its two inputs are reflected in the family of solid isocost lines in Fig. 5-10. Given these prices, the firm would have planned to use input combination (Q_p', Q_c'). Now assume that either (1) the price of computer time has risen or (2) the price of programmers has fallen. The cost of programmer time *relative* to that of computer time is now less, and the firm should substitute more of the now cheaper programmers for the now more expensive computer time. Figure 5-10 shows that this will indeed be the case. The new family of isocost lines will be flatter, since the slope of such lines depends solely on the relative input prices; [7] and

[7] The equation of an isocost line is

$$P_c Q_c + P_p Q_p = K$$

Thus

$$Q_c = \frac{K}{P_c} - \left(\frac{P_p}{P_c}\right) Q_p$$

The slope equals $-P_p/P_c$.

the optimum combination will therefore include more programmer time and less computer time, because isoquants are assumed to be convex to the origin.

The conclusion to be drawn from this example is clear. If output is held constant, a change in input prices will cause firms to substitute the inputs whose relative prices have declined for those whose relative prices have increased. Thus, for the case in question, an increase in programmers' wages will cause a decrease in the use of programmers and an increase in computer time. A decrease in the cost of computer time will elicit the same response. The extent of this *substitution effect* depends, of course, on the substitutability of the inputs. Figure 5–11a illustrates a situation in which the inputs are very good substitutes: a change in relative prices leads to a major revision of inputs used. Figure 5–11b shows a situation involving less substitution, and Fig. 5–11c represents the extreme case in which no substitution is possible — input proportions are fixed and hence are unaffected by changes in relative prices.

Typically a change in the price of one or more of a firm's inputs will lead to other changes. In particular, the firm's optimal output will change, giving rise to a *scale effect*. Consider the more general case for a software firm. Assume that the firm has selected the optimal (maximum profit) levels for output and inputs. Now the cost of computer time falls. The firm's total cost curve will certainly fall; in all likelihood so will its marginal cost curve.[8] The optimal output will increase, for example, from Q_{o1} to Q_{o2} in Fig. 5–12b. The initial situation is shown by point 1 in Fig. 5–12a: Q_{p1} units of programmer time are used, along with Q_{c1} units of computer time. If the firm had continued to produce Q_{o1} units of output, computer time would have been substituted for programmer time, giving combination $(Q_p{}^*, Q_c{}^*)$. But the firm chose instead to increase output, using more of both inputs (relative to $Q_c{}^*$ and $Q_p{}^*$). We thus have

$P_c\downarrow$:

substitution effect:	$Q_c\uparrow$	$Q_p\downarrow$
scale effect:	$Q_c\uparrow$	$Q_p\uparrow$
net effect:	$Q_c\uparrow$	$Q_p\downarrow$

[8] Although this need not necessarily be the case.

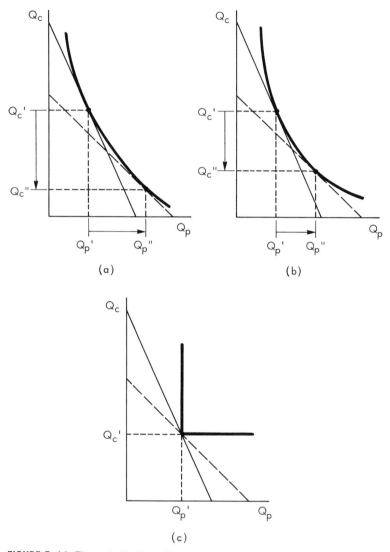

FIGURE 5–11. The substitution effect: (a) major, (b) moderate, (c) nonexistent.

In general a fall in the price of an input will lead a firm to buy more of the input, because of both substitution and scale effects. The effect on the demand for other inputs depends on the relative strengths of the two counteracting effects. The greater the extent to which two inputs are substitutes, the more likely it is that the price of one will be directly

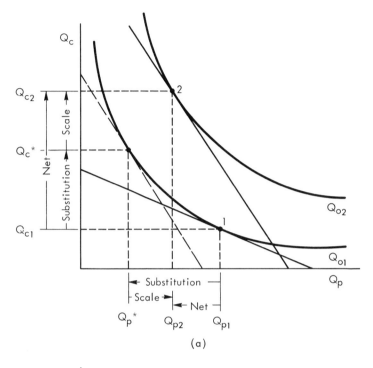

(a)

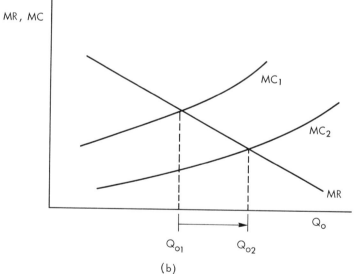

(b)

FIGURE 5–12. Substitution and scale effects.

related to the demand for the other (i.e., the substitution effect will be greater than the scale effect).

The key result of this analysis is the conclusion that the demand curve for any input is downward-sloping; we have thus provided a more elegant argument for the basic assertion of the law of demand. Two related points bear restatement. First, the demand curve can also be interpreted as a marginal value curve. Second, the longer the period available for adjustment to a new input price, the greater is the adjustment (i.e., the flatter the demand curve for the input).

Substitution may take time; hence it may be difficult to assess its importance empirically. An increase in the rates charged by a service bureau may not affect sales for months. Moreover, the demand for the firm's services may have increased in the interim, so that the quantity demanded at the new price actually exceeds that at the former price. It is even possible that the price increase may have been anticipated long before it took place: the adjustments may thus have occurred before the price change. For all these reasons it may appear that inputs are not substitutable and that the quantity of an input demanded is not affected by its price. But evidence offered to support such an assertion is not likely to stand up under careful analysis.

The discussion thus far has assumed that inputs are purchased in competitive markets; the firm is assumed to be able to buy as many units of each input as desired at a given price per unit. Of course this may not be the case; instead the firm may have to pay higher prices to attract larger quantities (i.e., the supply curve for the input will be upward-sloping).

Assume that several programmers are available to a firm, but that they differ in cost per unit of output. If possible, the firm will pay each programmer just the amount required to keep him. For simplicity, we consider a case in which programmers are equally productive but require different minimum salaries. Thus in Fig. 5–13, programmer 1 must be paid C_1 or more; programmer 2, C_2 or more; etc. Under these circumstances, the firm will hire four programmers (Q_p*). The step function represents the *marginal* cost of programmers; the firm selects a quantity for which marginal cost equals marginal value. Of course *average* cost will be less; in Fig. 5–13 it is $A*$.

An equally important case arises when all units of an input must be paid an equal amount. Assume that the programmers form a union and

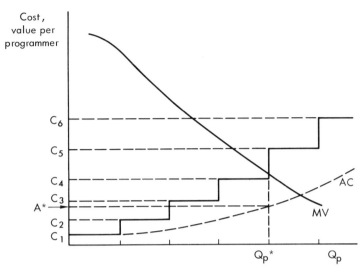

FIGURE 5-13. Marginal value, marginal cost and average cost for inputs.

require the firm to adopt an equal-pay policy. Now the step function in Fig. 5–13 shows the *average* cost of programmers. The marginal cost is higher. For example, to hire a fourth programmer adds $C_4 + 3(C_4 - C_3)$ to total costs, since all programmers must be paid C_4 if the new man is to be attracted to the firm. Total employment will thus be less than Q_p*.

These brief examples only hint at the complications inherent in understanding the behavior of collective bargaining groups (unions). With rare exceptions, such groups can raise wages only at the expense of decreases in employment (because of the law of demand). However, the decrease may fall only partly (or not at all) on union members. If the wage increase comes during a period of enlarging demand, total employment may actually rise; if not, employees lost through normal attrition may simply not be replaced. Moreover, if a union represents the employees of many firms, total wages paid may increase even though union members become unemployed. In this case the members who are still employed can support those who become unemployed, through union dues or special assessments. Alternatively, the union can require that employment be spread among all members (e.g., so-called railroad "featherbedding" rules and dockworkers' hiring halls). Of course a union with substantial monopoly power can be expected to engage in activities similar to those discussed in earlier chapters: it may offer all-or-none arrangements (e.g., guaranteed annual wages), "quantity discounts," etc. The major problem facing the officers of such a union concerns the division of the gains — some method must be found that will keep the union intact.

The extent to which a union can exploit its monopoly power depends, at base, on the extent of its monopoly and the slope of the demand curve for its members' services; and the latter depends greatly, of course, on the substitutability of other inputs for those services.

Unionization does not appear to be a particularly important phenomenon in the computer industry. The reasons may rest as much on sociological as on economic grounds. In any event, we will merely note here in passing that, in the future, attempts may be made to unionize computer programmers (among others) and that it is difficult to predict the outcome of such efforts.

E. MULTIPRODUCT FIRMS

The following artificial problem is typical of a class found in introductory explanations of linear programming. A firm produces two types of computers: A and B. Three hundred man-hours of labor will be required to produce one model A machine; 600 man-hours, to produce one model B. Twenty hours on the automated assembly line will be required for each model A; 80 hours for each model B. During the next year 30,000 man-hours and 3200 hours on the automated assembly line will be available for production. Model B computers can be sold for $3000 each; model A machines for only $1000. Since costs are given, the firm wishes to maximize revenue.

A graphical solution to the problem is shown in Fig. 5–14. The feasible combinations of the two outputs lie within or on the borders of the shaded area. The efficient combinations of outputs lie on the right-hand border of the region. The optimal combination lies at the point at which an isorevenue line is tangent to the border of the feasible region ($Q_A = 40$; $Q_B = 30$).

The example is contrived, but it illustrates a general relationship that holds for all multiproduct firms. In very short-run situations, such as this, all inputs may be fixed; in more realistic cases some or all are variable; in any event, given a specified total cost, the firm can

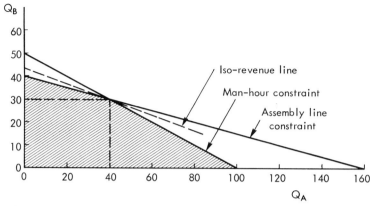

FIGURE 5-14. The optimal combination of two outputs.

produce any one of a number of efficient combinations of outputs. As might be expected, a combination is *in*efficient if another exists that (1) costs no more, (2) provides more of at least one output, and (3) provides no less of any other output(s). A combination is efficient if it is not inefficient.

For expository purposes we consider only cases in which the firm can produce two types of output. For a given total cost, there will be a set of efficient combinations, for example, those shown by curve C_1 in Fig. 5-15 (drawn as a smooth curve to represent a situation in which there are many inputs, several of them capable of being used to produce either output). Without laboring the point, we merely assert that such curves are typically downward-sloping and concave to the origin; each is called a *production possibility* curve. The second curve in Fig. 5-15 shows efficient combinations available for $C_2(= C_1 + 1)$ dollars.

Now assume that the firm is producing Q_A' and Q_B' and spending C_1 dollars. What is the marginal cost of A? Approximately $1/\Delta Q_A$ (where $\Delta Q_A = Q_A'' - Q_A'$), as shown in Fig. 5-15. Similarly, the marginal cost of B is approximately $1/\Delta Q_B$, where $\Delta Q_B = Q_B'' - Q_B'$. This follows from the fact that the curves are downward-sloping: given some quantity of output A, additional units of output B can be obtained only by either (1) adding to total cost or (2) giving up some units of output A. If the production possibility curve is smooth, marginal cost is well defined and measurable. Multiple products need not lead to major modi-

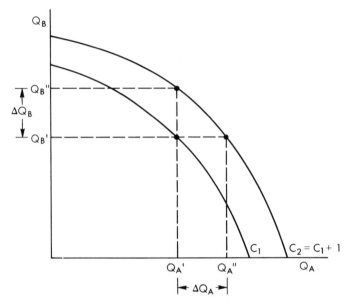

FIGURE 5-15. Production possibility curves.

fications in the analysis presented earlier: the *marginal* cost of each output is relevant when questions concerning price, level of output, etc., must be answered; given optimal policy (i.e., answers to all such questions), the firm must obtain enough revenue to cover its total costs—otherwise it should not be in business.

However, this rule may not apply if the production possibility curve has significant "kinks"; an extreme case arises when the output of one product must always be proportionate to the output of another. Cases involving such *joint products* require a different approach.

The situation is illustrated in Fig. 5-16. At a cost of C_1, Q_A' units of A and Q_B' units of B can be produced. The only other available combinations are obtained by simply throwing away some of Q_A' or some of Q_B'. Similarly, at a cost of C_2, $Q_A''(= kQ_A')$ and $Q_B'(= kQ_B')$ can be produced, with some of either one thrown away if desired. Obviously it is senseless in this situation to speak of the marginal cost of either product separately. All that can reasonably be said is that, by spending one dollar more, the firm can obtain $\Delta Q_A(= Q_A'' - Q_A')$ *and* ΔQ_B $(= Q_B'' - Q_B')$. Any attempt to "allocate" such a joint cost to specific products is likely to be either useless or perverse. This does not imply that rational decision-making is impossible under such circumstances. To show that rational decisions can be made, we consider an important example.

Assume that a corporation is considering the establishment of a service bureau. Since plans call for a rather large-scale operation, it is reasonable to measure computing power installed as if it were a continuous variable. The analysis is complicated, however, by the fact that computation during normal working hours is considered more valuable by customers than computation at night. Installation of X units of computing power thus yields a joint product: X units of daytime computing power and X units of nighttime computing power. To keep the problem simple we assume that total cost is unaffected by the use made of installed capability and that the demand for nighttime computation is independent of that for daytime computation (and vice versa). We also assume that the firm must set a single daytime price and a single (but possibly different) nighttime price.

The solution to the problem is indicated in Figs. 5–17a, b, and c. Figure 5–17a shows the demand for daytime computing power and the associated marginal revenue curve. The latter differs slightly from that previously defined: at $Q_d{}^*$, total revenue is maximal; marginal

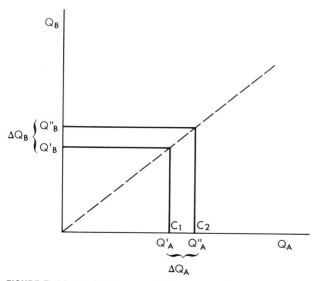

FIGURE 5–16. Production possibility curves: joint products.

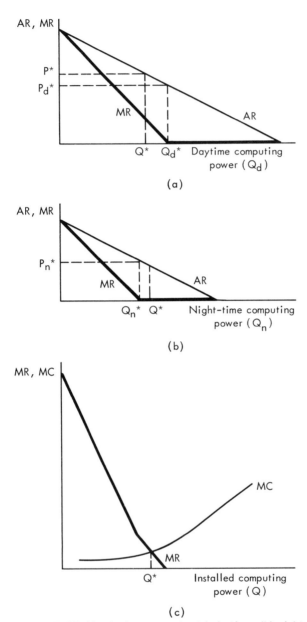

FIGURE 5–17. Marginal revenue for (a) daytime, (b) night-time, and (c) installed computing power.

revenue for larger quantities would thus be negative if such quantities had to be sold (and the price reduced accordingly). But a clever manager, given any quantity in excess of $Q_d{}^*$, would simply set the price at $P_d{}^*$, thereby maximizing total revenue; the excess $(Q - Q_d{}^*)$ would go unused. Assuming such rational behavior, we indicate that marginal revenue is zero for quantities exceeding the maximal revenue quantity. This procedure is also employed to obtain the marginal revenue curve in Fig. 5–17b for nighttime computing power; it becomes horizontal at $Q_n{}^*$.

The problem is easily solved. A unit of installed computing power yields one unit of daytime and one unit of nighttime computing power. Thus the marginal revenue associated with installed computing power (Fig. 5–17c) is the sum of the marginal revenues associated with the two joint products (Figs. 5–17a and b). The optimal amount of installed computing power is, of course, that for which marginal revenue equals marginal cost (Q^* in Fig. 5–17c). The appropriate use of this capability is indicated in Figs. 5–17a and b. During the day the equipment should be used to capacity ($Q_d = Q^*$; $P_d = P^*$). At night it should not ($Q_n = Q_n{}^* < Q^*$; $P_n = P_n{}^*$).

Figures 5–17a through 5–17c indicate the optimal policy for the corporation if it does set up a service bureau. The final stage in the analysis involves the go/no-go decision. If total revenue ($P_d{}^*Q_d{}^* + P_n{}^*Q_n{}^*$) exceeds total cost for Q^* units of computing power, the venture is desirable. Otherwise it is not.

A word of caution is in order concerning this example. There is no reason, a priori, to assume that optimal policy will lead to excess capacity in some periods. It is entirely possible that it will pay the firm to lower price enough during less attractive periods to make *every* period a "peak-load" period.

The key point illustrated here is simply that, in cases involving joint products, it is neither necessary nor possible to base decisions on the "cost" of the separate products.[9] Cost is associated with the joint products and is best treated as such.

---

[9] Except in special cases: such a procedure may prove sensible if demands are not certain but the shape of the distribution is known. Under these conditions, and given a number of other limiting assumptions, meaningful marginal (expected) costs can be attributed to the individual products.

In general, demands for joint products are interrelated. For example, computing power demanded during the day might depend on both the rate charged during the day and the rate charged at night. So might the amount demanded at night. Moreover, costs may be associated with the use of capacity, as well as with its creation. A more general formulation of this problem would be as follows:

$$\text{Maximize:} \quad P_d Q_d + P_n Q_n - C$$

where
$$\left.\begin{array}{l} Q_d = f_d(P_d, P_n) \\ Q_n = f_n(P_d, P_n) \end{array}\right\} \quad \text{demand conditions,}$$

$$C = c(Q, Q_d, Q_n) \text{ cost conditions,}$$

$$\left.\begin{array}{l} Q_d \leqq Q \\ Q_n \leqq Q \end{array}\right\} \quad \text{capacity conditions.}$$

Other problems arise. Should the output be considered two, three, or even more (joint) products; for example, should computation be performed in the evening for a different rate than that required for work done at night? The answer depends on the relative magnitudes of (1) the cost of administering a detailed and complicated pricing scheme, and (2) the advantages it might offer. Trial and error will usually be required to find the best policy.

Perhaps the most difficult problem of all is that of properly classifying costs. Many apparently joint costs disappear on closer examination, proving to be related to the outputs of specific products after all.

F. OVERHEAD COSTS

We have repeatedly argued the importance of marginal costs for making decisions concerning output, prices, etc. For most products marginal cost is simply the derivative of total cost with respect to the quantity produced. For joint products the relevant output is a "package" of the jointly produced products, and the marginal cost is defined as the derivative of the total cost with respect to the quantity of such packages produced. In either event, given smooth and continuous functions, a necessary condition for optimal policy is the equality of marginal revenue and *marginal* cost.[10]

[10] Except that if the decision-maker wishes to maximize net *value* (total value less total cost), the condition is that marginal value equals marginal cost.

This approach in no way implies that total costs must not be covered by total revenue. After determining optimal policy (outputs, prices) based primarily on marginal considerations, the firm must determine whether this policy is better or worse than stopping production of some or all of its products. Decisions of this sort must be made by enumerating the alternative combinations of products, finding the optimal policy for each combination, and comparing the results case by case.[11]

These remarks serve as a preface to the assertion that little can be gained (and much may be lost) from attempts to allocate so-called *overhead costs* to specific products.

Assume that a firm produces N products. Let Q_i be the quantity of the ith product and MC_i its marginal cost (i.e., dTC/dQ_i, given $Q_1, \ldots, Q_N$). Let $TC(Q_1, \ldots, Q_N)$ represent the total cost associated with a set of outputs; we define overhead cost as follows:[12]

$$OC(Q_1, \ldots, Q_N) = TC(Q_1, \ldots, Q_N) -$$

$$[MC_1Q_1 + MC_2Q_2 + \cdots + MC_NQ_N]$$

Roughly speaking, overhead cost is the difference between total cost and the costs "attributable" to the individual products. The process of "allocating" overhead cost is simply a method for finding some set of "full costs"$-F_1, \ldots, F_N-$that will account for the total cost:

$$F_1Q_1 + F_2Q_2 + \cdots + F_NQ_N = TC(Q_1, \ldots, Q_N)$$

Often the full cost for each product is calculated by adding a proportionate "burden" to each "direct" (marginal) cost:

[11] That is, if there are N possible products, consider each of the 2^N possible combinations; for each combination determine the optimal set of outputs and find the associated difference between total revenue and total cost. The best combination is the one for which the difference is the greatest.

[12] Overhead cost as defined here may be positive, zero, or negative. For a one-product firm these possibilities have simple and obvious interpretations. If overhead cost is positive, marginal cost is less than average cost; the firm is operating in the range of decreasing (average) costs. If overhead cost is zero, the firm is operating in the range of constant average cost; since average cost curves are typically U-shaped, this implies that a least-cost output is being produced. Finally, if overhead cost is negative, the firm is producing in the range of increasing average cost. This definition of overhead cost is by no means universally accepted. Often "direct cost" is used instead of marginal cost, in order to attribute fixed costs associated with a particular product to that product. Such procedures are, at best, vaguely understood. The definition given here comes reasonably close to the popular notion behind the term without unduly sacrificing precision.

$$F_i = (1 + \alpha)MC_i$$

What value can be attached to such calculations? In theory, none. If the full-cost figures are to be utilized for decision-making, they will generally lead to erroneous conclusions: the marginal cost of product i is MC_i, not F_i. If the figures are not to be used for decision-making, why compute them at all?

As always, it is important to make the distinction between form and substance. Crude, short-sighted analysis may lead to serious underestimates of marginal costs. The correct figures may thus be closer to the calculated full costs (F_i) than to the erroneously estimated marginal costs. So-called fixed costs are often fixed only in the very short run. As a practical matter, the addition of an overhead burden to those variable costs that are easily identified may provide fairly reasonable estimates of true long-run marginal costs. But this sort of approach is clearly second-best; it is obviously preferable to attempt to identify actual marginal costs explicitly and to make decisions accordingly.

G. BREAKEVEN ANALYSIS

By and large, the price-output models presented in the earlier chapters ignored the possibility that demand or cost conditions might be uncertain. The firm was assumed to know the demand curve for its product(s) and the costs of various levels of output(s). With this information, the optimal price-quantity combination could be readily determined. Under conditions of certainty this is equivalent to either (1) selecting a quantity and then selling it at the maximum obtainable price, or (2) selecting a price and then selling the quantity demanded at that price.

Once uncertainty is introduced into the analysis, the equivalence of these approaches disappears. The firm may select a quantity and then sell it at the maximum price obtainable, but the exact level of this price cannot be predicted exactly. Or the firm may set a price and then sell whatever quantity may be demanded at that price; in this case the quantity is uncertain. Finally, the firm can select both a price and a quantity; if the quantity demanded exceeds that produced, only the latter is actually sold; otherwise the quantity demanded is sold and the excess held as inventory or disposed of. All three of these possibilities are of interest; however, we concentrate on the second, since it forms the basis for the widely used "breakeven analysis."

Assume that a firm is considering the introduction of a new computer model. If the computer is introduced, the firm will take any and all orders placed at the announced price (although delivery dates may differ). For simplicity we assume that, within the relevant range, total cost is linearly related to quantity sold: [13]

$$TC = a + bQ$$

Total revenue will, of course, be proportional to quantity sold, depending solely on the price (P):

$$TR = PQ$$

The relationships are indicated on the breakeven chart in Fig. 5–18a. If quantity demanded equals Q^*, revenue will just cover costs, and the firm will "break even"; quantities larger than Q^* will give profits, and smaller quantities will lead to losses.

It is important to recognize that the quantity on the horizontal axis in Fig. 5–18a is *not* a decision variable; it is a random variable subject to some probability distribution such as that shown in Fig. 5–18b. Since both total revenue and total cost are linear functions of quantity, so is total profit. Thus the axis of Fig. 5–18b can be rescaled to represent profit, as shown.

The firm's decision problem is now clear. First, it must select a price. This will determine the slope of the total revenue curve in Fig. 5–18a as well as the location (and perhaps the shape) of the probability distribution in Fig. 5–18b. The higher the price, the steeper is the total revenue curve but the farther to the left the probability distribution (because of the law of demand). Second, the firm must select a production policy—in other words, a total cost curve. Each possible set of decisions will give a corresponding probability distribution of profits. The managers or owners must choose among them on the basis of their

---

[13] The exact relationship between total cost and quantity will depend, of course, on the manner in which orders are accepted and filled. The firm may hold the rate of output constant, filling new orders by lengthening the production period. If so, some learning effects may be obtained with larger quantities (but economies of scale may not appear since increased volume may not have been anticipated). On the other hand, the firm may meet orders by increasing the rate of output as well as (or instead of) the production period, giving rise to counteracting increases in cost. Needless to say, the method chosen will affect the orders received—more may be obtained if early delivery is available than if delivery is far in the future. Although these aspects are of crucial importance to the computer manufacturer, we abstract from them here.

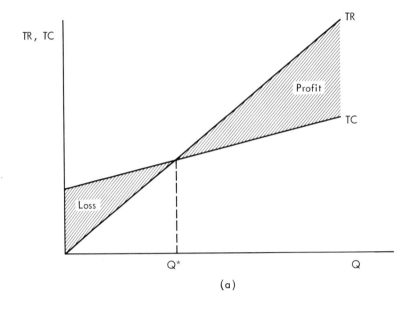

(a)

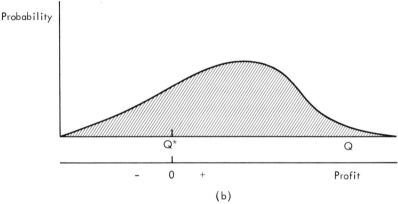

(b)

FIGURE 5-18. Breakeven chart (a) and associated probability distribution (b).

attitudes toward risk, the relationship between this decision and others, and other relevant factors.

In practice probability distributions are rarely stated explicitly. Breakeven charts are drawn, and the desirability of the decision is evaluated subjectively. Our characterization should thus be regarded as a formal description of the process.

Before leaving this example, it is instructive to consider a special case in which uncertainty, though present, may be ignored. Assume that the *expected* quantity demanded (Q_e) is inversely related to price, as represented by the "usual" demand curve. *Actual* quantity demanded (Q_a) is related to the expected quantity as follows:

$$Q_a = kQ_e$$

where

the expected value of $k = 1$, and
the standard deviation of $k = S_k > 0$.

Cost is assumed to be a linear function of the quantity actually demanded (and subject to no additional uncertainty):

$$TC = a + bQ_a$$

The only decision to be made concerns the price (P). The measures of interest are assumed to be the expected profit (E_π) and the standard deviation of profit (S_π).

It is a simple matter to show that

$$E_\pi = (P - b)Q_e - a$$
$$S_\pi = (P - b)Q_e S_k$$

where $Q_e = f(P)$.

Substituting, we obtain

$$S_\pi = S_k a + S_k E_\pi$$

This relationship is illustrated graphically in Fig. 5–19. The axes show expected profit (E_π) and standard deviation of profit (S_π), both measured in dollars. However, if the cost of the firm is given, the equivalent expected rates of return (E_r) and standard deviation of rates of return (S_r) can be determined and the axes relabeled as shown in Fig. 5–19.[14]

Each point along the line *VW* can be obtained by an appropriate selection of price. It might appear that the optimal point (and hence

---

[14] Let C be the cost of the firm. Then

$$E_r = \frac{E_\pi}{C}, \quad \text{and} \quad S_r = \frac{S_\pi}{C}$$

As shown in the text, the optimal policy for the firm is to select the price that maximizes E_π, giving the combination represented by point W in Fig. 5–19. The firm can thus be viewed as an asset providing a distribution of dollar values with this expected value and standard deviation. The value of such an asset depends on the factors described in Chapter 4; given an efficient market, the cost of the firm (C) will equal this value.

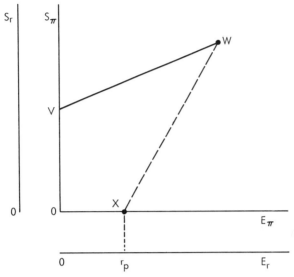

FIGURE 5-19. Relationship between expected profit (or rate of return) and standard deviation of profit (or rate of return).

price) depends on the decision-maker's attitude toward risk. But this is not the case. The firm and/or its owners can invest in risk-free assets (e.g., buy bonds at the "pure" interest rate). Point $X(E_r = r_p$, the pure rate) represents such an alternative. By investing in this firm and in a risk-free asset, an investor can obtain any (E_r, S_r) combination along the line XW if (and only if) the firm operates so as to maximize its expected profit (i.e., at point W). This policy is clearly dominant—for any level of risk (S_r), line XW provides a greater expected return (E_r) than line VW. The firm should thus maximize expected profit; in other words, ignore the risk entirely.

Needless to say, this is a very special case; in general, uncertainty, when present, must be dealt with explicitly. On the other hand, there are situations in which uncertainty may be safely ignored or handled by very simple methods. One cannot argue a priori that the analysis of classical economics is inapplicable whenever there is uncertainty.

H. COMPETITORS' REACTIONS

Thus far we have said relatively little about the competitive conditions facing a seller, simply assuming that they have been incorporated in the demand curve. In two extreme cases this assumption is obviously reasonable. If there are many independent competitive firms in an industry, the actions of one may be expected to induce no reactions from the others; the policies of the firm's competitors may be assumed to be unaffected by any of the firm's decisions. At the other extreme, if the firm enjoys a virtually complete monopoly over a product, there are (by definition) no competitors; here too, the firm need not concern itself with reactions to its decisions.

As usual, most cases lie between the extremes. The typical firm must at least consider the possibility that its actions may evoke reactions from competitors. Under certain circumstances it may prove reasonable to act as if competitors' reactions can be predicted with certainty. We will briefly discuss a simple model incorporating such an assumption and then comment on approaches to the problem that deal explicitly with uncertainty about reactions.

Assume that a firm is producing a computer, selling Q^* units per year at a price of P^*, as shown in Fig. 5–20a. Only single-price policies are to be considered (i.e., customers will be allowed to buy one or more units at a stated price). The firm believes that, if it raises its price, competitors will not react; the demand curve is thus relatively flat for prices above P^*, since many customers will switch to the products of competitors if the firm raises its price. On the other hand, the firm believes that, if it lowers price, competitors will react, at least to some extent, perhaps by lowering their prices, increasing service, providing better software, or offering more attractive financing. Thus the demand curve is relatively steep for prices below P^*.

The asymmetry in the firm's assumptions concerning competitive reactions introduces a kink in both the demand (average revenue) and total revenue curves at Q^*. And because of the kink in the total revenue curve (shown in Fig. 5–20b), the marginal revenue curve exhibits a step at Q^*, as shown in Fig. 5–20a. At the optimal output, marginal revenue equals marginal cost, as usual; in Fig. 5–20a the optimal output is Q^*, given the marginal cost curve MC.

Now consider the effect of a change in the firm's marginal cost curve from MC to either MC' or MC''. The optimal price and output are unchanged. This implication is often asserted to be consistent with observed behavior in many industries characterized by few sellers (so-called *oligopolies*). Casual empiricism would suggest that it applies rather well to the computer industry: list prices set by manu-

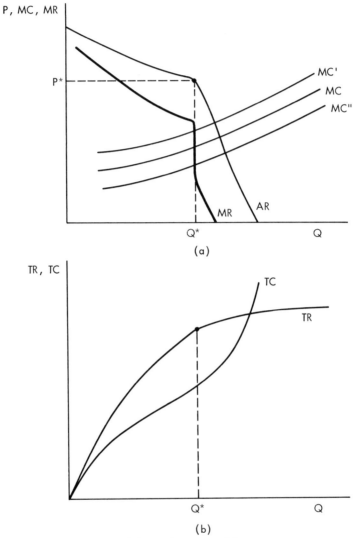

FIGURE 5–20. The kinked demand curve model.

facturers change seldom if at all. But the relevant measure is not the list price but the cost (relative to effectiveness) of the item actually received. A decrease in cycle time, with no change in price, is equivalent to a price cut. Indeed a change in any of the many dimensions of the relationship between user and manufacturer can be regarded as equivalent to a change in price. Viewed more broadly then, computer prices do change, and rather often.

A key deficiency of the kinked-demand-curve model concerns the initial price-quantity combination (P^*, Q^*): the model does not specify the manner in which it is established. Interestingly enough, at least one view of IBM's pricing policy appears to be consistent with the model and also suggests a manner in which the initial position might be reached.[15]

The argument is as follows. IBM is said to attempt to offer equipment similar to any sold by its competitors, at prices equivalent to those set by the other firms. Sales and marketing efforts are directed toward selling as many units as possible at these prices. Cost is virtually ignored. Because of its reputation and efficient service organization, IBM expects to receive the bulk of the orders placed, given equal prices. On the assumption that, within the range of interest, the volume effect will dominate any rate effect, IBM's unit costs will clearly be the lowest in the industry; if another firm thinks that it can make a profit at the given price, then surely IBM will too. On the other hand, there is no point in charging a different price: a higher price would cause an undesirable loss of orders, and a lower price would elicit retaliatory actions by competitors and lead to only a small increase in the total quantity demanded (and hence sold by IBM).

Is this model consistent with observed behavior? Not entirely; but it may contain some elements of the true situation.

The kinked-demand-curve model discussed here is but one of many that can be constructed under the assumption that competitors' reactions can be predicted with certainty; each reaction model gives rise to a corresponding model for optimal behavior. In practice, however, reactions that cannot be ignored are likely to prove very difficult to predict. In such situations the decision-maker may well abandon formal models; the positive economist, attempting to predict industry behavior, may or may not find it useful to do so. An alternative approach involves an attempt to incorporate uncertainty, complicated reaction patterns, and a host of other features in a large but nonetheless completely specified model. Analytic models of the type presented

---

[15] This view may or may not represent informed opinion; it is attributed to a knowledgeable person with no training in economics.

thus far are not well suited for such an approach; computer programs and Monte Carlo methods are better for this purpose.

At a level of great generality, a model of the computer industry might have the following form. Assume that time is divided into discrete periods. Let there be I types of computers, J manufacturers, and K potential and actual customers. Then let:

P_{ij}^t = the price charged for a computer of type i by manufacturer j at time t: a value of infinity indicates that the manufacturer does not produce this type of computer at this time,

P^t = the set of P_{ij}^t values for time t,

Q_{ijk}^t = the number of computers of type i ordered from manufacturer j by customer k at time t, and

Q^t = the set of Q_{ijk}^t values for time t.

Consider a customer k. Given this customer's applications, financial situation, prejudices, experience, location, etc., his behavior can be represented by some sort of submodel (program) relating his orders to existing prices and historical information, as shown in Fig. 5–21a. The submodel need not be deterministic. Actions may be predicted probabilistically, with the action taken made to depend on the value of a random number. For example, the submodel might specify that for a particular set of prices P^{*t} there is a probability of 0.3 that the customer will order a computer of type 5 and that, if he does order a computer, it is as likely that he will choose manufacturer 1 as manufacturer 2. Let R represent a random number drawn from a uniform distribution ranging between 0 and 1. Then this part of the submodel could be implemented as shown in Fig. 5–21b.

More complicated relationships can also be modeled. Samples may be drawn from prespecified probability distributions, and the distribution utilized can be made to depend on other results, actions taken, etc. The possibilities are almost limitless. Use of probabilistic relationships and random numbers identifies a model as a member of the class of Monte Carlo models (for obvious reasons).

The general model of the industry is completed by a set of manufacturer submodels. Given a firm's cost situation, production techniques, goals, guesses about competitors' strategies, concern about possible antitrust actions, and general policy, one can specify the relationship

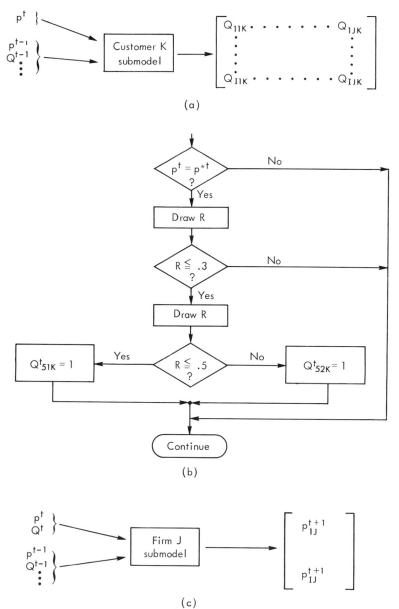

(a)

(b)

(c)

FIGURE 5-21. Submodels (a) representing a customer's behavior, (b) predicting a customer's actions, and (c) representing a firm's behavior.

between the firm's offerings in the next period and current prices, orders, and historical data, as shown in Fig. 5–21c. Again the sub-model may include probabilistic relationships of varying complexity.

No really general model of this type could ever be fully implemented, but it is entertaining to speculate on the use that could be made of one if it were available. Given complete specifications and a set of initial conditions, one could predict actions over time with one run of the model. If the model includes probabilistic relationships, a second run would typically produce different results. A great many runs would produce a great many results. For the specified world view, such a set of results captures the (probabilistic) implications for future outcomes. Now assume that the model for firm i^* is changed in some way; that is, the firm's overall policy (strategy) is altered. A new set of runs will provide the (probabilistic) implications of the new policy, assuming that all other parts of the world (model) remain unchanged. In the most general sense, the problem facing firm i^* is to select the set of rules (policy, strategy) that will provide the best set of (probabilistic) outcomes, given the goals of the relevant individuals.

This brief discussion suggests the complexity of the problem faced by anyone wishing to understand, predict, profit from, or merely exist in the computer industry (or any other, for that matter). It also provides a powerful argument for abstraction. Abstraction is, after all, the key characteristic of any formal theory, including that presented in Part I (Chapters 1–5). The utility of the theory can only be gauged by confronting it with reality (and vice versa). This is the task of Part II.

PART II: Applications

A. MAJOR SECTORS

When speaking of the computer industry people sometimes mean only the relatively few firms that sell medium-to-large general-purpose computers. We use the term in a more general context, to include sellers of many types of equipment and/or services. Part II of the book will be concerned with several sectors of the industry.

1. *Computer manufacturers.* More aptly called computer assemblers, these firms offer general-purpose computers for sale to the general public. For convenience we restrict our attention to producers of digital computers.

2. *Component manufacturers.* These firms manufacture computer components (e.g., logic modules, core memories, and disk drives) for internal use and/or sale to others. The large number of such firms makes it possible for a computer "manufacturer" to manufacture very little, choosing to simply select and assemble components manufactured by others.

3. *Service bureaus.* These firms purchase or lease computer equipment and hire staffs of programmers, analysts, and operators. They offer computer services to others, providing an alternative or supplementary source of computation for users who prefer not to obtain equivalent equipment directly.

4. *Time-sharing vendors.* We differentiate firms offering time-shared services from more traditional service bureaus. In essence the difference concerns the use of remote input/output stations—time-sharing services give the illusion of concurrent use by several (sometimes many) customers, causing complex problems concerning fees, priorities, etc. Such time-shared services (often called "computer utilities") are of increasing importance, offering substantial competition to traditional service bureau operations (among others).

5. *Used-computer brokers.* There is a growing market in used computers. Some firms simply act as marriage brokers, attempting to bring

together a buyer and a seller. Others hold inventories of used equipment, bearing the associated risk.

6. *Computer-leasing companies.* Many computer users prefer to lease equipment rather than purchase it, while some manufacturers would rather sell their computers than lease them. Although the situation is much more complex than these statements suggest, they do indicate the general basis for the rapid growth of an independent computer-leasing industry. Such firms purchase equipment either from present users or directly from the manufacturer and then lease it to users. Terms vary widely, from month-to-month rentals to full-cost contracts. Needless to say, the risk borne by the leasing company varies accordingly.

7. *Software firms.* The cost of computer hardware has fallen dramatically over the last 15 years, but the decline in the cost of software production has been smaller.[1] Thus software (the production of programs, compilers, operating systems, etc.) looms ever larger as a component of total costs. Recent years have witnessed considerable growth in the number and size of independent suppliers of software. Such firms sell and lease their services and products to users as well as to computer manufacturers.

It is important that the complexity of the computer industry be understood. Many firms compete in several of the sectors described above. Burroughs, for example, sells its own line of computers as well as memory modules for use by other computer manufacturers. C-E-I-R provides both a conventional and a time-shared service bureau. Data Products manufactures disk files and, through a subsidiary, offers software and consulting services. IBM, together with its wholly owned subsidiary, The Service Bureau Corporation, covers almost the entire spectrum. IBM manufactures virtually all its components, writes much (but not all) of its own software, and leases equipment to any user who prefers not to purchase it. The Service Bureau Corporation provides computer services of a conventional variety and offers time-shared services. In practice, then, boundaries among sectors are seldom clear, and the activities of individual firms may range over several boundaries.

---

[1] Some would assert that the cost of producing software has actually increased, primarily because of the complexity of current computers and their operating systems.

B. THE COMPUTER MANUFACTURING INDUSTRY

It is traditional to trace the origins of the digital computer to the British mathematician Charles Babbage (1792–1871). Babbage completed one working calculator (the "difference engine") and began construction of another with support from the British government (about £17,000 over 19 years). Neither of these calculators was a computer in the modern sense, but the "analytical engine," conceived in 1833, was comparable to present-day devices. It was to have an internally stored program and to be capable of executing conditional transfers and modifying both data and program steps. Available technology made it impractical to construct a complete working model, however, since mechanical techniques were unreliable, slow, and expensive.

The first working computer of substantial size was the Mark I (or Automatic Sequence Controlled Calculator), developed from 1939 to 1944 by Howard Aiken at Harvard University. It was built by IBM engineers from standard business-machine parts at a cost of approximately $500,000.[2] The Mark I and an improved machine, the Selective Sequence Electronic Calculator, completed in 1947, were considered showcases for IBM engineering talent and gifts to science and engineering. Neither was offered commercially. Indeed, Thomas J. Watson Sr., the president of IBM at the time, is purported to have believed that computers had no commercial possibilities.[3]

The world's first all-electronic computer was put into operation early in 1946. Developed and built for the U.S. Army at the University of Pennsylvania, the ENIAC (Electronic Numerical Integrator and Computer) was designed to speed up the computation of firing tables. The machine was used for this purpose at the Aberdeen Proving Ground from 1947 through 1955. ENIAC lacked a stored program, not because the idea had not occurred to its designers, John W. Mauchly and J. Presper Eckert, but because available types of storage were considered too expensive. The idea of using a mercury delay line resolved this problem, however, and a number of stored-program machines were soon constructed.

Many of the key ideas for these (and later) machines were developed

---

[2] T. G. Belden and M. R. Belden, *The Lengthening Shadow, the Life of Thomas J. Watson,* Little, Brown, Boston, p. 259.
[3] George Schussel, "IBM vs. Remrand," *Datamation,* May and June, 1965.

in a course held at the University of Pennsylvania during the summer of 1946. The EDVAC (Electronic Discrete Variable Automatic Computer), designed by Eckert and Mauchly in 1945 but not completed until 1952, provided the basis for the EDSAC (Electronic Discrete Sequential Automatic Computer), completed in 1949 at the University of Cambridge in England, and the SEAC (Standards Eastern Automatic Computer), built by the National Bureau of Standards from 1948 to 1950.

Important machines were constructed at other universities during this period, often under government sponsorship. A computer completed at the Institute for Advanced Study at Princeton in 1952 followed the design specified by Von Neumann and others in a classic paper.[4] The University of Manchester (England) built the first machine using a cathode-ray tube memory. Some of the most important contributions were made by Project Whirlwind, supported jointly by the Office of Naval Research and the U.S. Air Force and conducted at the Massachusetts Institute of Technology. The Whirlwind I computer was the first (in 1952) to successfully incorporate a coincident-current magnetic core memory, replacing its original cathode-ray tube memory.

Until 1951 the computer industry was essentially noncommercial: each machine was one of a kind, and support came primarily from universities and government. In fact, it can plausibly be argued that without government (and particularly military) backing, there might be no computer industry today.

In 1946 Eckert and Mauchly, the developers of the ENIAC, left the University of Pennsylvania and set up a company to produce a new machine based on the EDVAC design. This computer, the UNIVAC I, was to be the first commercial electronic computer. However, it too received considerable governmental support. The Eckert-Mauchly Corporation began with a contract from the National Bureau of Standards, and the first UNIVAC was to be delivered to the Bureau of the Census. In 1950 the Remington Rand Corporation bought out Eckert-Mauchly, but the original group continued to operate as a separate division of the Corporation until 1955, when Sperry Instrument merged with Remington Rand. In 1952 Remington Rand purchased Engineer-

[4] A. W. Burks, H. H. Goldstine, and J. von Neumann, "Preliminary Discussions of the Logical Design of an Electronic Computing Instrument," reprinted in *Datamation,* September, 1962.

ing Research Associates, a small Minnesota firm, and with it the rights to the ERA 1101, the first computer to use a magnetic drum memory. The ERA group also operated as a separate division until 1955, when it was merged with the Eckert-Mauchly group.

Deliveries of UNIVAC I began in 1951. The first sale to a commercial customer, however, did not take place until 1954; the first six machines were all sold to government agencies (two to the Atomic Energy Commission, one each to the Bureau of the Census, the Air Force, the Army, and the Navy's Bureau of Ships).

In 1952 the CRC-102 computer was introduced by the Computer Research Corporation, a firm purchased shortly thereafter by the National Cash Register Company. In 1953 IBM offered its first machine, the IBM 701, for general sale. In late 1954 the IBM 650, a small drum-memory system, became available. The 650 was the first machine to be produced in quantity (well over a thousand were sold). By the end of 1955 computer manufacturing was a recognized commercial industry.

Figure 6–1 illustrates the changing nature of the industry during the period 1944–1962. Over these years the percentage of new models manufactured by users (i.e., one-of-a-kind machines built by universities, government agencies, laboratories, etc.) declined dramatically. During the period 1960–1962, 95% of all new models were built for commercial sales. The percentage of *machines* (as opposed to *models*) was, of course, much higher—about 99.9%.

One qualification is in order concerning these figures. The data refer only to general-purpose digital computers. The production of special-purpose and analogue computers constitutes a lucrative source of business for firms offering general-purpose machines and for other firms as well. Many of these machines, such as airborne computers and radar system computers are produced to order. However, accurate information on this segment of the industry is not available, partly because of security regulations. For this reason our attention, both here and throughout the book, is focused on general-purpose digital computers. And, as Fig. 6–1 shows, such computers are now manufactured primarily as commercial ventures.

Figure 6–2 is an attempt to illustrate the rate at which new models have been developed over time. Three series are shown. The first, covering the period from 1944 through 1962, includes all general-purpose machines. The other two series, covering the period 1960–

Percentage of new models
manufactured by users

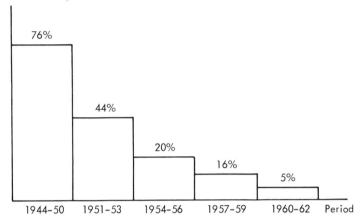

FIGURE 6-1. The percentage of new computer models manufactured, 1944–1962. Source: Kenneth E. Knight, *A Study of Technological Innovation—The Evolution of Digital Computers,* doctoral dissertation, Carnegie Institute of Technology, November 1963, p. VII–13.

1965, include only general-purpose computers offered for sale commercially. Needless to say, the classification of a computer system as a "new" model is often arbitrary, so these data should be viewed with considerable suspicion. Nonetheless it is clear that new models have been introduced in substantial numbers since the early 1950's and that there is no indication that innovative activity is abating.

The March, 1967, Computer Census published by *Computers and Automation* lists twenty U.S. manufacturers of general-purpose digital computers, including small independent companies (e.g., Systems Engineering Laboratories), large, highly diversified corporations (e.g., General Electric), and of course the giant of the field, IBM. Two of these firms, the Philco division of Ford Motor Company and the Autonetics Division of North American Aviation Company, no longer offer computers for general sale. Also, some firms now maintain equipment originally developed by another company. There have been several notable acquisitions in the industry. As indicated earlier, Remington Rand (now Sperry Rand) entered the industry by acquiring the Eckert-Mauchly Corporation and Engineering Research Associates. The National Cash Register Company followed suit with the acquisition (in 1953) of the Computer Research Corporation. Burroughs purchased the ElectroData Corporation in 1956, and with it the popular E101 and E103 small-scale machines. Control Data bought the computer division of the Bendix Corporation in 1963 for $10 million, obtaining rights (and responsibility for maintenance) for the G-15 and G-20 computers. In 1964 Raytheon purchased the com-

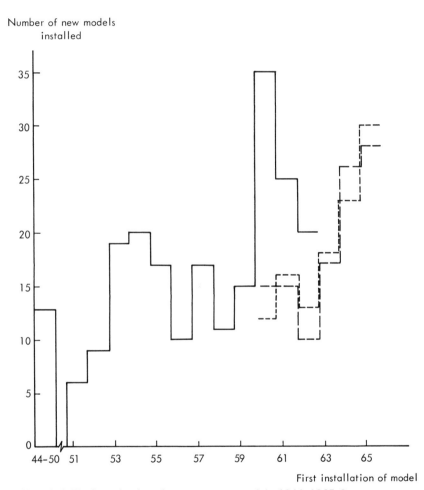

FIGURE 6-2. The introduction of new computer models, 1944–1965. Sources: ———— Knight, *op. cit.,* p. VI–30. – – General-purpose computers (Sec. 1), *Adams Computer Characteristics Quarterly,* October 1966. – – – *Computers and Automation,* March 1967, Census.

puter division of Packard-Bell for about $6 million, thus obtaining the model 250 and model 440 computers. In 1966, Honeywell acquired the Computer Control Company and its DDP series of machines. Abroad, General Electric acquired controlling interests in the Compagnie des Machines Bull of France (1964) and the computer division of Olivetti in Italy (1965).

Many other mergers, joint ventures, and outright sales have taken place in the industry. For example, in 1955 Raytheon and Honeywell set up a firm to manufacture the Datamatic 1000, a large-scale machine. Honeywell owned controlling interest (60%) and subsequently (in 1957) bought out Raytheon's minority share, incorporating the firm as an operating division. As another example, in 1965 Raytheon purchased the BIAX memory business of Philco's Aeronutronics Division. Clearly, change is common within the industry.

One overriding characteristic of the industry does not, however, appear to be subject to major change—IBM's commanding position. Despite Remington Rand's early lead, IBM was the leading manufacturer by mid-1956, having delivered 76 large machines with firm orders for 193 more (the figures for the UNIVAC division were 46 and 65, respectively).[5] Since that time, IBM has retained from 70% to 80% of the market.[6] Table 6–1 shows estimates of market share (by value) for the eight leading manufacturers at various points of time, with one set of predictions concerning their shares in 1970. While precise figures are open to some question, IBM's position is not. In 1965 the corporation received $2.75 billion from the rental and sale of electronic and punched-card data-processing machines and systems, constituting about 77% of its total gross income; this is particularly impressive since only 20% of all IBM equipment in use at the time had been purchased outright.[7] According to one estimate, in March, 1966, IBM had a backlog of orders for equipment with a gross sales value of $10.5

[5] Schussel, op. cit., May, 1965, p. 55.

[6] This represented a return to the company's long-standing position in the data-processing industry. According to one source, in the thirties, ". . . the company controlled over 80 percent of the tabulating machine market," and in 1952, IBM ". . . owned more than 90 percent of the tabulating machines in the United States. . . ." The company's success in selling to the federal government was even greater—in the early 1950's, Thomas J. Watson Sr. could claim that "95% of [the government's] punched card machines are IBM's." Source: Belden and Belden, op. cit., pp. 294–297.

[7] Source: IBM prospectus accompanying an offer of additional common stock shares to stockholders, May, 1966.

TABLE 6-1

Firm	Percent of Installed Value						Percent of Value on Order Feb. '67	Predicted Percent of Installed Value for 1970
	Aug. '62	Jan. '64	Sept. '64	Nov. '65	Dec. '65	Feb. '67		
IBM	71.1	76.3	74.2	71.4	73.7	69.9	75.3	60–70
GE	2.1	2.3	2.5	3.0	2.2	3.3	3.4	5–9
Sperry Rand	12.1	6.2	7.2	7.4	6.6	7.7	6.5	5–8
Honeywell	1.5	1.8	1.9	4.7	3.1	5.0	3.0	5–8
RCA	4.1	3.6	3.9	3.5	2.9	2.7	2.8	4–7
Control Data	3.1	3.1	3.5	4.4	4.5	5.0	4.0	3–6
Burroughs	2.1	2.2	2.1	2.8	3.1	2.2	1.8	2–3
NCR	1.5	2.3	2.5	1.6	2.3	2.2	1.9	1–2
Other	2.4	2.2	2.2	1.2	1.6	2.0	1.3	1–2
Source: *	(1)	(1)	(1)	(1)	(2)	(3)	(3)	(1)

* Sources: (1) Frederic G. Withington, *The Computer Industry — The Next Five Years,* Arthur D. Little, December, 1965, p. 27. (2) Based on the Computer Installation File of International Data Corporation, Newton, Mass.; reported in "The Computer Field and the IBM 360," by Patrick J. McGovern, *Computers and Automation,* January, 1967, p. 20. (3) Based on data given in *Computers and Automation,* March, 1967 (computer census).

billion.[8] Possible reasons for IBM's success will be discussed in subsequent chapters. Here we merely record the undisputed fact.

Questions often arise about the profitability of computer manufacturing for the other firms in the industry. Packard-Bell and Bendix might be presumed to have considered the area unprofitable, since they sold their computer divisions. Philco has essentially withdrawn from the general market, concentrating its attention on special-purpose systems, as have others. A number of firms, however, have remained in the industry for a considerable period. Are their computer sales profitable?

As indicated in Part I of this book, the economist's use of the word *profit* differs considerably from that of the accountant. The fact that income has not yet exceeded outflow (or outflow plus depreciation calculated with some rigid formula) does not necessarily make an activity unprofitable. Thus accounting profits or losses should be regarded with considerable skepticism. Unfortunately (or, perhaps, fortunately),

[8] *EDP Industry and Market Report,* Vol. 2, No. 4 (May 31, 1966), International Data Publishing Co., Newtonville, Mass.

even these figures are generally unavailable for computer sales per se, since most manufacturers report profits on a company-wide basis. Little is available other than general statements by various spokesmen concerning the profitability of some of the companies' computer divisions. By and large these statements suggest either (1) that computer operations have not yet "shown a profit," or (2) that only recently have such operations become "profitable." For example, James H. Binger, chairman of the board of Honeywell, stated that the firm "passed a major milestone in 1966 when its domestic computer business became profitable." [9] On the other hand, RCA reported a loss in 1966 on its EDP operations, attributable "largely to increased development costs and a 45% increase in the sales force." [10] In its 1966 annual report, General Electric warned its stockholders that the information systems business was ". . . still some time away from emerging from its loss position" [11] (according to one report, the company sustained "EDP losses in 1966 of 45¢ per sales dollar").[12] And Sperry Rand's UNIVAC Division, despite its continued hold on second position, is reported to have only recently "been able to enjoy even a small profit picture." [13]

Such statements clearly do not refer to profitability in the economic sense. More relevant questions are these: (1) if the firm had known in advance the success or failure of its systems, would it have produced them, and (2) taking its past activities as given, does the firm consider the future sufficiently hopeful to remain in the industry? Answers to the first question are probably impossible to obtain. It can be presumed, however, that the major firms have consistently answered the second question in the affirmative, since they have chosen to remain in the industry. Whether their current expectations will prove correct or not is difficult to predict, as is their continued participation in the computer field.

How large is the market for general-purpose digital computers? And how large can it be expected to become? Both questions are difficult to answer; Fig. 6–3 represents one attempt. These projections

[9] *EDP Weekly,* Jan. 16, 1967, p. 15.
[10] *Ibid.,* p. 13.
[11] *General Electric, 1966 Annual Report,* p. 7.
[12] *Datamation,* January, 1967, p. 17.
[13] "The Big Prize Is Second Place," Arnold E. Keller, *Business Automation,* February, 1967, p. 40.

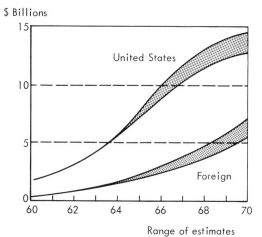

$ Billions

FIGURE 6–3. Cumulative value of business and government digital computers in use, 1960–1965 (actual) and 1966–1970 (estimated). Does not include process control or special military computers. Source: *Business Week,* Feb. 19, 1966, p. 113.

suggest that by 1970 the cumulative value of digital computers in use by business and government will equal $18 billion. Even under the most pessimistic assumptions the market for new machines can be expected to remain large. Assume, for example, that the total value of computers in use was to remain at $18 billion after 1970, with only 10% of all machines replaced annually. This would still require an annual output of $1.8 billion, a substantial figure by any standards.

Who uses computers? It is generally agreed that the U.S. government is the largest single user. Among industrial firms (excluding computer manufacturers themselves) those in the aerospace industry represent the most important group, according to one study.[14] Thus the influence of government, and especially of the Defense Department, is considerable. However, it appears to be declining in relative importance, as shown in Fig. 6–4.

What are computers used for? A classical dichotomy is made between commercial and scientific applications. The distinction has always been highly arbitrary, and data are difficult to obtain. However, in the early years of the mass market for computers it was possible

---

[14] *Computers and Automation,* April, 1967, p. 14.

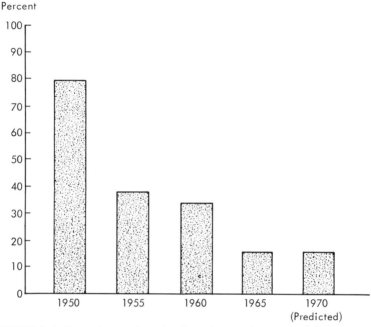

Percent

FIGURE 6-4. Percentages of total value of general-purpose digital computers installed in government agencies from 1950 to 1970 (predicted). Source: *An AFIPS Report: The State of the Information Processing Industry,* CEIR, 1966, p. 66.

to at least attempt rough answers, since computers were often classified as either commercial (business) or scientific. As shown in Chapter 9 the cost of logic circuitry relative to other components of computer systems has declined over time. This has led to a breakdown in the traditional dichotomy—computers now typically come with a set of operation codes capable of efficiently performing basic applications in both business and science, and additional sets of codes are available as special options.

Table 6–2 is an attempt to estimate the relative importance of commercial and scientific applications. Three qualifications are in order. First, few machines are used solely for commercial or scientific operations (as indicated by the quotations included in the table footnotes). Second, one or more machines may have been assigned to the wrong group. Finally, the equipment studied (IBM computers introduced between 1960 and 1964) and the time period covered (through February, 1967) may not be the most relevant for current applications.

Even when these limitations are recognized, the qualitative results are still of interest. Commercial computers accounted for 86% of machines sold. However, since the average monthly rental for a scientific machine was greater than that for a commercial machine (slightly

TABLE 6-2. IBM Computers Introduced Between 1960 and 1964 *

Computer	Monthly Rental ‡ ($/month)	Number § Produced	Total Value Produced ‖ ($/month rental)
Commercial †			
1401-G	2,300	1,620	3,726,000
1440	4,800	3,440	16,512,000
1401	6,600	7,650	50,490,000
1460	11,500	1,780	20,470,000
1410	14,200	808	11,473,600
7010	22,600	216	4,881,600
7080	55,000	75	4,125,000
		15,589	111,678,200
Scientific †			
1620	4,000	1,670	6,680,000
7040	22,000	120	2,640,000
7070/2/4	27,000	336	9,072,000
7044	32,000	130	4,160,000
7094	72,500	114	8,265,000
7094 II	78,500	132	10,362,000
7030	160,000	7	1,120,000
		18,098	153,977,200

* Date of introduction is defined as the date of first delivery shown in *Computers and Automation,* monthly censuses (various dates).

† Computers classified as "commercial" are character-oriented machines (i.e., word size = 1 alphanumeric character). Those classified as "scientific" use either decimal (1620, 7070/2/4) or binary storage (7040, 7044, 7094, 7094 II, 7030). These classifications are less than perfect, however, as the following descriptions from various IBM manuals indicate:

1401: "specifically designed and planned to make the transition . . . from unit record equipment to intermediate and large-scale data processing."
1410: designed for the "intermediate data-processing area."
1440: a "low-cost data-processing system."
1460: a "1401-compatible data-processing system."
7010: "adaptable to both commercial and scientific applications"; "handles problems and data volumes that characterize the large-scale data-processing area."
7080: "adaptable to both commercial and scientific applications."
1620: "designed for scientific and technological applications."
7040/44: "designed to handle business and scientific data."
7070/2/4: "for commercial and scientific applications."

‡ As shown in the February, 1967, census, *Computers and Automation,* March, 1967.

§ For computers in production as of February, 1967, the number installed at that time; for computers out of production in February, 1967, the number installed as of the first month in which the computer was listed as out of production. All data from *Computers and Automation,* monthly census.

‖ Equals monthly rental times number produced.

Number on order

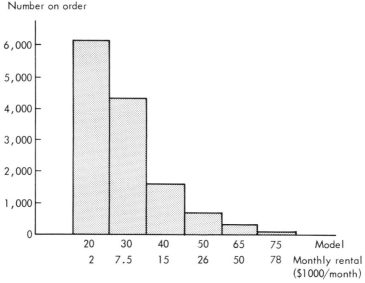

FIGURE 6-5. The number of computers ordered: six IBM machines. Source: *Computers and Automation,* Census as of March 1967 (in April 1967 issue).

under $17,000 as opposed to slightly over $7000), the proportion of total *value* represented by commercial computers was lower — about 72.5%. If these figures have any relevance at all, they suggest that commercial applications *are* more important than scientific, in terms of value of computers sold. Needless to say, this does not necessarily imply that they are more profitable to the seller.

Although currently offered computer systems cannot usefully be designated as commercial or scientific, they can be classified on the basis of expense. Figure 6–5 provides information concerning the orders for six machines in the IBM 360 line, as of March, 1967.[15] As might be expected, the number on order declines with cost. However, the total value on order does not, as Fig. 6–6 shows. Clearly medium-scale machines provide the greatest receipts to IBM, although this does not necessarily imply that they produce the largest profit.

[15] Models 25, 44, 67, 85, and 91 are omitted. Model 44 was introduced at a somewhat later date than the others, and it differs in several respects from the regular line. Model 67 is a time-sharing machine with unique properties; it too was introduced at a later date. Model 91 is no longer available for purchase. Models 25 and 85 were introduced in 1968.

Before concluding this survey of the computer-manufacturing industry, something must be said about the notion of computer generations. The concept is summarized well in the following quotation:

According to the cycle theory of the computer industry, significant economic and technological transitions occur in the industry approximately every five years, resulting in the appearance of a "new generation" of computer systems and the beginning of a new cycle. . . . The computers of the first generation were built with vacuum tubes operating at slow speeds and had limited memory capacity (2–4 thousand words) consisting of magnetic drums and slow cores. The computer lines of different manufacturers were isolated, unrelated machines and were applied primarily to scientific applications. The second generation of systems (1959–1964) saw the introduction of solid-state components on a large scale, increasing the speed of the computers to the microsecond range, and extending memory capacities to 32 thousand words. The computers of various manufacturers tended to be separated between business and scientific machines. . . . [Third-generation machines] incorporate some of the most recent advances in technology, including (1) micro-electronic cir-

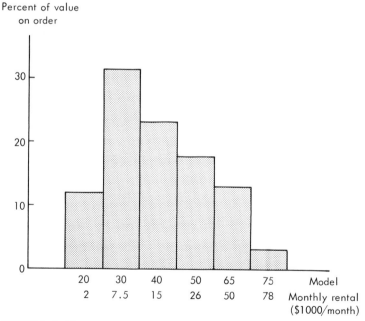

FIGURE 6–6. The percentage of value on order: six IBM machines. Source: *Computers and Automation*, Census as of March 1967 (in April 1967 issue).

cuits, (2) faster main-memory speeds, (3) expanded main-memory sizes, (4) more flexible mass random-access memories, (5) extensive equipment to handle data communications, (6) various remote terminal devices, and (7) improved programming languages.[16]

Not all authorities agree on the lengths of the cycles. It has been suggested that each cycle is twice as long as the previous one, because of the rather mysterious "principle of binary powers." [17] Thus there is some question about the date of introduction of "fourth-generation" machines. But whether they are expected to arrive in 1970 or 1973, many people find it useful to talk in terms of such machines. Indeed, one of the leading publications in the computer field devoted an entire issue to the subject.[18]

Not only is the pattern of the cycle subject to dispute; also, the generations are often defined differently by different authorities. One classificatory scheme relies primarily on the internal hardware of the processing unit. Thus first-generation machines used vacuum tubes; second-generation equipment, transistors; third-generation machines, integrated circuits; and fourth-generation machines will be characterized by batch fabrication—in particular, large-scale integration (LSI).[19] Such definitions make it possible to argue, for example, that some models of the IBM 360 series are not "true" third-generation systems, while the SDS Sigma series machines are.

Whatever may be the merits of such notions, they are widely held. Of more concern here is the question of improvements in the relationship of cost to overall effectiveness. Consider a graph relating cost per unit of performance (somehow defined) to time. The cycle theory could be interpreted to imply that new computers follow a pattern such as that shown in Fig. 6–7. If so, the periods during which major drops in cost/performance occurred could be used to delineate generations. As shown in Chapter 9, however, dramatic and isolated declines of this sort have not been experienced in the past. Instead the pattern is one of rapid but relatively continuous decreases over time. Thus, from an

[16] Patrick J. McGovern, "The Computer Field and the IBM 360," *Computers and Automation,* January, 1967, pp. 16, 17.
[17] G. M. Amdahl and L. D. Amdahl, "Fourth-generation Hardware," *Datamation,* January, 1967, pp. 25, 26.
[18] *Datamation,* January, 1967.
[19] Amdahl and Amdahl, *op. cit.,* pp. 25, 26.

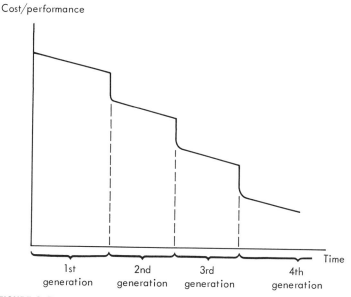

Cost/performance

Time

1st generation   2nd generation   3rd generation   4th generation

FIGURE 6-7. Hypothetical pattern of cost/performance over time.

economic point of view, the concept of computer generations is of limited value. This is not to deny the utility of the concept in other contexts. But its importance lies more in the realm of technology and, perhaps, market strategy.

Much more remains to be said about the computer manufacturing industry. Additional material will be presented throughout the book, in the context of specific issues and problems.

C. DATA SOURCES

Information is not a free good—its collection and dissemination cost money; in a free-enterprise economy information is typically provided only if its value exceeds its cost. The value of information about computers can be substantial, however, since these devices are both complex and expensive. Thus it is not surprising that a great many sources of information about the computer industry are available, ranging from monthly magazines distributed free of charge to people likely to buy the advertisers' products to a service providing detailed analyses of alternative systems for over $1000 per year.

The empirical information in this book comes from a number of sources, both original and secondary. To provide some indication of the type of data available, we will briefly describe some of the more important sources.

1. Computer Prices

For a number of years the General Services Administration, the agency charged with centralized procurement for the federal government, has negotiated annual contracts with each of the major computer manufacturers. Such contracts include detailed specifications of the terms offered by the manufacturers to U.S. government agencies for rental, purchase, and maintenance of computer equipment. Each manufacturer publishes the final version of the contract for his equipment. Officially such a document is an Authorized Federal Supply Schedule Price List; FSC Class 7440, Electronic Data Processing Machine Service. We adopt the common usage, referring, for example, to the IBM GSA Price List for July 1, 1967, through June 30, 1968.

A GSA price list includes detailed schedules of rental rates and purchase prices for virtually the entire line of the manufacturer's equipment, specified separately for each component, special feature, etc. The contractual arrangements tend to be similar among manufacturers, since they are, to some extent, negotiated by the GSA (although notable differences arise, as indicated in Chapter 7). The actual dollar figures, however, are specified by the manufacturer; the GSA has had little success to date with attempts to negotiate lower prices than those initially offered.

In signing a GSA contract, a manufacturer assumes an obligation to provide any federal government agency with equipment on the stated terms during the fiscal year covered (although revisions may be issued during the year, if desired). However, the manufacturer is not precluded from making a more attractive offer to win a contract with a particular agency. Thus GSA prices are not necessarily those paid even by federal government agencies. In practice, however, deviations are rather rare. IBM makes it a policy not to depart from the GSA contract terms, and other manufacturers deviate only under extenuating circumstances. Moreover, some government agencies follow the policy of strict adherence to the GSA terms. Deviations, when they do occur, tend to take the form of better service, lower surcharges for extra use, etc. Thus the GSA price lists provide a good, if not perfect, indication of terms offered to federal agencies. Moreover, they are publicly available and highly detailed.

Terms offered nongovernmental customers are very difficult to obtain. By and large they are similar to those specified in the GSA contracts, except that educational institutions are often given discounts. Typically there is more negotiation with nongovernmental customers, and all the terms are considered candidates for concessions. For obvious reasons the results are seldom made public. Thus the GSA price lists constitute the only consistent and available source of information on prices and contract terms; they are used for almost all the studies reported here—unless otherwise indicated, "price" should be interpreted henceforth as that shown in the relevant GSA price list.

The first GSA price lists for IBM equipment covered the fiscal year from July 1, 1957, through June 30, 1958. It is thus possible to trace IBM's terms over a full decade. Other manufacturers began issuing contracts at somewhat later dates, so that studies of changes over time are more difficult. However, the availability of such detailed information regarding prices and terms on an annual basis is a great aid to those studying the industry. Were it not for the General Services Administration, such data would be virtually impossible to obtain. For example, computer manufacturers outside the United States will not release detailed price information to the general public, and no other country requires the publication of price lists similar to the GSA schedules.

2. Computer Censuses

The popularity of particular computer systems and the overall acceptance of the products of a manufacturer are subjects of widespread interest. Computer manufacturers are obviously eager to obtain information about their competitors' sales. Investors in the securities of manufacturers have similar interests. But a much larger group also finds such data helpful—computer users.

Other things being equal, most users prefer popular computer systems and manufacturers, and want reliable information about the acceptance of alternative models. The preference for a widely accepted system is based partly on a suspicion that to depart from the crowd involves risk. If a popular system turns out badly, management may not blame the person who selected it, whereas a disaster associated with an unusual choice (i.e., an unpopular machine) may cause heads to roll. But there are other, better reasons for preferring widely used equipment. First, the system may well have superior capabilities relative to its cost. Second, experience with both the hardware and the software will accumulate at a faster rate, leading to early detection and, hopefully, removal of "bugs." And, finally, much more software will be written for such a system (by users, software companies, and perhaps the manufacturer), and such software will probably be available to other users at a lower price — some of it, through users' groups, for nothing.

Unquestionably, information on computer installations and orders is valuable. Unfortunately it is extremely difficult to obtain. Manufacturers almost uniformly refuse to release such data. IBM apparently prefers not to confirm the Justice Department's suspicion that it has a very large share of the market. Similarly, other manufacturers apparently prefer not to confirm customers' suspicions that they have a very small share. Thus any attempt to assess the market involves a painstaking collection of information obtained from users, and the results will at best be approximate.

Despite these formidable obstacles a monthly computer census is prepared by the International Data Corporation, Newtonville, Mass., for publication in its newsletter entitled *EDP Industry and Market Report.* The data are

developed through a continuing market survey. . . . This market research program compiles and maintains a worldwide computer installation locator file which identifies, by customer, the installation sites of electronic computers. The resulting census counts are submitted to the individual computer manufacturers for their review and voluntary confirmation.[20]

The census covers most of the computers in general use (with an indication if the machine is no longer being produced). Four key items are given: average monthly rental, date of first installation, number of installations, and number of unfilled orders. No explicit definition is given for the average monthly rental. At least one manufac-

[20] *Computers and Automation,* April, 1967, p. 54.

turer provides the figures directly, based on current customer contracts.[21]

From 1962 until late 1967 *Computers and Automation* published the International Data Corporation census figures monthly. Since then the magazine's staff has prepared its own census data. Machines manufactured outside the United States have been added. Most notably, however, many of the figures have been deleted or combined with others on the grounds of inadequate data. As the publisher regretfully noted,

From the start of our magazine in 1951, our policy has been to publish "factual, useful and understandable" information—with emphasis on "factual." It has become increasingly difficult to substantiate the research performed by *Computers and Automation* to confirm figures we desire to publish in our Monthly Computer Census. As soon as we have the necessary cooperation from certain manufacturers, we hope to return to publishing additional data on computer installations by type of computer.[22]

In compiling its census data, *Computers and Automation* divides manufacturers into two groups. As of October, 1967, they were as follows:

1. Manufacturers for whom "figures [are] derived in part from information released directly or indirectly by the manufacturer or from reports by other sources likely to be informed": Autonetics, Bunker-Ramo Corp., Burroughs, Control Data Corp., Digital Equipment Corp., Electronic Associates, EMR Computer Division, Honeywell, National Cash Register Co., Philco, RCA, Raytheon, Remington-Rand UNIVAC, Scientific Control Corp., Systems Engineering Laboratories, and Varian Data Machines.
2. "Manufacturer refuses to give any figures, and refused to comment in any way on the figures stated here beyond saying that they are not correct": General Electric, IBM, and Scientific Data Systems.

The *Computers and Automation* census figures on installations and unfilled orders are widely used (occasionally with no explicit

[21] "The updated average monthly rental figures are based on present customer contracts." From a letter written by J. F. Sand, RCA Electronic Data Processing, quoted in *Computers and Automation,* November, 1966, p. 8.
[22] *Computers and Automation,* October, 1967, p. 64.

acknowledgment). Several of the comparisons in this chapter are based on them. Throughout the book, unless indicated otherwise, data on installations and orders are derived from this source.

Business Automation publishes a semiannual census of U.S.-built computers. No data are given on unfilled orders, but the number of machines installed in foreign countries is indicated, as well as the total number installed. Average system costs (purchase price) are given, along with approximate monthly rentals. Both the first shipment date and the current delivery time in months are included. The magazine's editors indicate a healthy degree of realism concerning the accuracy of the data:

Installation figures are always subject to question. Few companies officially divulge order and shipment data. Much of the information is of the "leaked" variety and tends to reflect an optimistic viewpoint. Another factor is the lack of reliable figures on replacement shipments as opposed to new installations. Despite the "guesstimates" involved, the survey totals reflect a reasonably accurate picture of the industry.[23]

Perhaps the most-analyzed group of computer manufacturers is that in the United Kingdom. The magazine *Computer Survey* publishes detailed information on installations on a bimonthly basis. The objective is commendable:

Computer Survey aims to include details of user, location, type of machine, delivery date and application for all British and foreign-built machines in the U.K. [and] British-built machines installed and on order for overseas. . . . The Survey is necessarily incomplete, especially with regard to machines on order, for reasons of national or commercial security.[24]

The data are likely to be quite reliable, however, since installations are identified explicitly and publicly, with users enjoined to offer corrections or additions: "Users' letters continue to be the most valuable means of maintaining the accuracy of the Survey. If all details concerning your organization's machine are not correct, please inform the Editor." [25]

3. Technical Characteristics
The primary source for information about the technical characteristics of a computer system or component is, of course, its manufacturer's

---

[23] *Business Automation,* February, 1967, p. 41.
[24] *Computer Survey,* November, 1966, p. 11.
[25] *Ibid.*

reference manual. However, users often prefer summary information in a simple form that allows comparison of the products of several manufacturers. A number of secondary sources of this type are available, varying in both cost and sophistication. The two most widely used are the annual directory issue of *Computers and Automation* (published in June) and *Adams' Computer Characteristics Quarterly,* parts of which are reprinted from time to time in *Datamation.*

The *Computers and Automation* directory gives key characteristics for every general-purpose digital computer manufactured in the United States. The following characteristics have been included in the past:

Number system
  Base
  Bits per digit
  Bits per alphabetic character
  Word length
Memory
  Number of words
  Type (core, drum, etc.)
  Access time
Machine programming
  Number of instructions
  Addresses per instruction
  Number of index registers
  Indirect addressing? (yes or no)
  Floating-point arithmetic?
    (yes or no)

Magnetic tape
  Maximum number of units
  Tape density
  Tape speed
  Capacity (in words per reel)
Punched cards
  Reading speed
  Punching speed
Paper tape
  Reading speed
  Punching speed
Line printer
  Speed
Average monthly rental
Rental range
One-sum price range

Before 1967, *Adams' Computer Characteristics Quarterly* was also organized by computer system. Now the focus is on components. Extensive technical data have been provided in the past for the following components:

Central processors
Auxiliary storage units
Magnetic tape drives
Card readers and punches

Line printers
Paper tape equipment
Display units

In 1968, the subscription price for the *Quarterly* was $25 per year.

4. Personnel Salaries

The most widely publicized source of data on the salaries of personnel in data processing is the annual "Report on EDP Salaries," published every June by *Business Automation.* The survey has been conducted annually since 1959 by Philip H. Weber and Associates, with assistance from the Administrative Management Society. The data on which it is based are extensive; for example:

The 1966 survey was conducted among 2324 data processing users representing areas of business, government and education in the United States. Salaries of over 92,000 employees, working on over 25,000 jobs in 427 cities are reflected in the results, which cover 81 job titles.[26]

Summaries of the data, published in *Business Automation,* give salary ranges by position for various areas of the country and size of installation as well as distributions of other data collected.

Another survey ("National Salary Survey, Digital Computing Personnel") was conducted annually through 1966 by the Systems Development Corporation. Since 1967, the survey has been conducted by an independent firm, Industrial Relations Counselors Service, Inc., New York. Although based on information from fewer respondents, this survey provides considerably greater detail than the "Report on EDP Salaries." In 1965, for example, data were included for over 16,000 personnel from 267 organizations (48% of which classified their applications as primarily business, 29% as primarily scientific, and 23% as both). Since SDC conducted such surveys from 1958 through 1966, time trends constitute an important component of the analysis. Other factors influencing programmers' salaries on which data have been collected and analyzed include position, type of application, years since degree, and years of programming experience.

Since much detail is included, the reports are not made generally available. For example, the 1965 survey warned:

The salary data reported herein were provided by participating companies on a confidential basis. Accordingly, the contents may not be reproduced or further distributed without the express written permission of the System Development Corporation.

This policy was undoubtedly meant to encourage participation, since all participants received copies. As of 1968, participants were required

---

[26] *Business Automation,* June, 1966, p. 36.

to pay a minimum fee of $250 per year (plus $100 to exchange "maturity curve" data).[27]

5. Historical Surveys

A number of historical studies of various aspects of the computer industry have been made; many of them will be described in later chapters. However, two merit special mention here—the first because it represents a major source of data on computers installed between 1944 and 1967, the second because its title and sponsorship alone render it worthy of special attention.

"A Study of Technological Innovation—the Evolution of Digital Computers" was Kenneth E. Knight's doctoral dissertation, submitted at Carnegie Institute of Technology in November, 1963. It covered systems delivered before 1963. An abbreviated version, "Changes in Computer Performance,"[28] was published in 1966. The study was updated in 1968, and the new results were reported in a short paper, "Evolving Computer Performance, 1963–1967."[29] The methods of analysis used and the substantive findings will be discussed at length in later chapters. Here we simply describe the basic data.

Knight was able to obtain technological and cost information on 310 general-purpose computers introduced between 1944 and 1967. In addition to cost, measured in terms of monthly rental for one-shift operation, 17 basic technological measures were used (e.g., memory capacity, word size, times for several arithmetic operations, and primary and secondary input-output times). For each computer system, two summary measures of performance were computed from the basic technological measures: one for "commercial operations per second" and one for "scientific operations per second." Only these summary measures were reported by Knight, along with cost (expressed as seconds per dollar) and date of introduction. The appendices to the dissertation contain additional information on functional improvements, structural changes, and innovations, expressed both qualitatively and quantitatively, for systems introduced before 1963. The implications of Knight's data concerning technological change in the industry, economies of scale in computing, and the nature of the learning process in

[27] Letter from Industrial Relations Counselors Service, Inc., Dec. 5, 1967.
[28] *Datamation,* September, 1966.
[29] *Datamation,* January, 1968.

computer production are of major importance; we will discuss them in later chapters.

In 1965 the American Federation of Information Processing Societies (AFIPS) contracted with C-E-I-R, an independent consulting firm, to "compile data about the present status of the Information Processing Field and [make] authoritative projections of its growth five and ten years [hence]."[30] The study, *An AFIPS Report: The State of the Information Processing Industry,* was completed in late 1965 and updated early in 1966. In a sense it is a survey of surveys:

The study . . . involved an exhaustive search of existing literature, including books, magazines, abstracting services, professional journals and other published sources. In addition, many experts in the field were contacted and interviewed personally. The resulting full report represents, in AFIPS' opinion, the best available data on the subjects covered.[31]

The report covers a great many areas of interest. Trends in both employment and salaries are given for selected occupations; changes in performance relative to cost are indicated for both computer systems and certain components; the overall growth of the industry is considered; and past, present, and future application areas are also treated.

Unfortunately, sources for the data given in the AFIPS report are sometimes omitted; more often, several sources are given, with little or no indication of the manner in which they were combined (an omission due, in many cases, to restrictions on divulging company-confidential data). Thus it is difficult to assess the accuracy of much of the information concerning past and present values of key variables. The accuracy of predictions can, of course, be judged only after the fact. But this inherent uncertainty is increased, in the case of the AFIPS report, by possible errors in past and present data and a lack of information about the methods used to derive predictions from these data. However, the study was an ambitious undertaking; thus it is not surprising that it lacks some of the niceties of more scholarly research.

6. Financial Data
The size of the computer industry and its apparent glamor make it particularly appealing to investors: securities of computer manu-

[30] Preface, *An AFIPS Report: The State of the Information Processing Industry.*
[31] *Ibid.*

facturers, component manufacturers, leasing companies, and software firms command considerable attention. Information about past performance and predictions about the future of such firms are considered valuable by many investors. Hence it is not surprising to find a service devoted especially to meeting this demand.

Moody's Computer Industry Survey has been published quarterly since 1965 by Moody's Investors Service and Brandon Applied Systems; in 1966 the subscription rate was $95 per year. The service is intended to provide "an evaluation of developments in Electronic Data Processing" and to be "an informational and interpretive service covering the data processing field."

Much of the material is taken from other sources. Installation and order data are based on the International Data Corporation census figures. Financial data and security price trends are based, to some extent, on information published annually in Moody's manuals of security data. But much is unique, especially the extensive discussions of future prospects and the evaluations of the desirability of holding various securities. *Moody's Survey* thus provides a good source of data for industry observers of all types.

7. Government Publications

Computer systems constitute a major item in the budget of the federal government. Estimates for 1967 included: 2600 general-purpose computers in 1243 different organizations, with computer operations requiring 77,400 man-years — total annual cost: $1.136 billion.[32] The management of such a resource deserves, and has received, careful attention. The annual Index of Federal Publications typically lists a great many references under the heading "Electronic Data Processing Systems" (the term used to refer to computer systems in the federal government).

One of the most useful documents is the *Inventory of Automatic Data Processing Equipment in the Federal Government,* published annually by the Bureau of the Budget. Since 1966 this document has included detailed information on all unclassified computers used by government agencies and certain contractor-operated equipment. Each line in the report includes the following data:

---

[32] Bureau of the Budget, *Inventory of Automatic Data Processing Equipment in the Federal Government,* July, 1966, pp. 7, 9, 10, 13.

1. Department.
2. Bureau, office, command.
3. Unit number.
4. Location.
5. Contractor operated?
6. Current-year data (actual)
   a. Computer.
   b. Model.
   c. Cost range.
   d. Purchased or leased?
   e. Monthly average hours in service.
7. Next-year estimates (same categories as 6).
8. Following-year estimates (same categories as 6).

Three listings of the data for general-purpose computers are given: by department, by location, and by make and model. A separate listing shows special-purpose computers (by department). Summary charts provide historical data and projections for:

1. Number of computers.
2. Number of agencies using computers.
3. Number of organizational units.
4. Total costs.
5. Distribution of costs by agency.
6. Major elements of costs.
7. Man-years utilized.
8. Computers purchased versus leased.
9. Average hours per month in service.

The U.S. Congress has maintained a continuing interest in the management of computer systems. Two committees of the House of Representatives hold periodic hearings that provide particularly important information; they are (1) the Government Activities Subcommittee of the Committee on Government Operations and (2) the Subcommittee on Census and Statistics of the Committee on Post Office and Civil Service.

There are, of course, many other sources of data, both public and private, and new ones are constantly appearing. The discussion in this chapter is intended primarily to indicate the type of information readily available.

CHAPTER 7 **THE SALE AND RENTAL OF COMPUTERS**
TERMS AND CONDITIONS

A. INTRODUCTION

An understanding of the economics of computers presumes a knowledge of the terms and conditions under which they may be obtained from manufacturers. Unfortunately such knowledge is not easily obtained. The alternatives offered by a single manufacturer in a given year are many and complex. Moreover, the range is greatly expanded if several manufacturers are to be considered. Also, the variations that have been offered over the years are little short of bewildering.

The mere facts concerning terms and conditions offered at various times by individual manufacturers are, of course, of little importance per se. More interesting questions concern the terms that will be offered in the future and the reasons that certain terms have been offered in the past. Thus we must confront the factual data with economic theory (and vice versa).

To accomplish this purpose it is useful to present the material in two chapters. This chapter provides a reasonably detailed description of the terms and conditions offered by manufacturers in the period 1966–1967. Little historical information is included, and an attempt to analyze or "explain" the alternatives is made only for selected provisions. Legal constraints, historical trends, and the economics of some of the more complex terms will be covered in Chapter 8.

This chapter provides a summary of the terms and conditions offered by the major computer manufacturers to agencies of the federal government during the fiscal year from July 1, 1966, through June 30, 1967. With few exceptions, all information was taken directly from the applicable Federal Supply Schedules. Although terms offered to commercial customers do not always coincide with those offered the federal government, most differences are relatively minor.

In many important respects the terms offered by various manufacturers are quite similar. To some extent this is due to a conscious effort by the General Services Administration to impose uniformity (negotiations begin with a *pro forma* contract prepared by the GSA; thus even the wording of the final contracts may be very similar). On the other hand, the natural forces of competition can be expected to lead manufacturers to counter one another's offers. In view of the manner in which the GSA contracts are obtained, the diversity that remains is quite remarkable. It should be noted, however, that during the period covered here (before 1967), the General Services Administration viewed its role in the negotiating process as related more to qualitative than to quantitative aspects. Thus an attempt might be made to have each manufacturer offer a quantity discount, but the magnitude and even the form of the allowance would probably be left to the manufacturer and not considered a subject for negotiation. Of particular importance, the prices and rental charges for individual items of equipment were specified directly by the manufacturer in each instance.

The discussion that follows is organized by major items, with emphasis on the economic aspects of the overall contract. It follows closely the organization of an earlier study made by Paul E. Giese.[1] Giese's study provides a detailed comparison of the contracts covering the period 1965–1966; this chapter draws on his work more for organization and method of presentation than for actual data. However, some of Giese's results are directly applicable to the discussion of changes over time included in Chapter 8.

B. RENTAL TERMS–THE CONTRACTUAL PERIOD

As indicated earlier, more computers are rented than purchased outright. Within the computer industry the terms *rent* and *lease* are used almost interchangeably, since the most widely used lease contracts cover sufficiently short periods of time to be termed rental contracts.

The standard government rental contract is that offered by IBM:

Period of Rental–IBM shall honor orders for periods of one year or less. After IBM receives written notice from the Government, the Government may discontinue use and rental for:

---

[1] Paul E. Giese, *GSA Computer Contracts for Fiscal Year 1966,* June, 1966 (A research report submitted in partial fulfillment of the requirements for the degree of Master of Business Administration, University of Washington).

(1) A System 90 days thereafter.

(2) A Machine 30 days thereafter.[2]

All major manufacturers offer identical terms to federal government agencies.[3]

This standard contract follows, almost verbatim, the requirements imposed on IBM during the period 1956–1966 by a consent decree with the Justice Department:

IBM is hereby enjoined and restrained for a period of ten years after entry of this Final Judgment, from entering into any lease for a standard tabulating or electronic data processing machine for a period longer than one year, unless such lease is terminable after one year by the lessee upon not more than three months' notice to IBM.[4]

Although this restriction did not apply to other manufacturers, each has chosen to offer terms of the same kind for rental.

Government agencies cannot, in general, enter into contracts for periods covering more than one fiscal year. For this reason most computer manufacturers do not offer longer-term leases to the government. There is, however, one exception: Burroughs offers optional "extended rental period" contracts on some older machines. Examples of the reductions offered under this plan in 1966–1967 are shown in Table 7–1. In order to meet restrictions on government obligations, Burroughs requires simply that selection of one of these options indicates the government's "intent" to install or retain the system for the minimum period specified. The agency is permitted to cancel the contract at the end of any fiscal year during the period or upon 90 days' notice after the first year if "required by extreme operational or economic necessity." Moreover, no retroactive adjustment of rental charges is made if the equipment is discontinued prematurely.[5]

Although IBM did not offer leases for periods in excess of 1 year to commercial customers during the period 1956–1966 because of restrictions contained in the consent decree, other companies did. Whereas terms offered government agencies were essentially 90-day

[2] IBM GSA Contract, July 1, 1966, through June 30, 1967, p. A–1.

[3] With one important exception – Digital Equipment Corporation did not rent equipment at all in 1967.

[4] IBM Consent Decree, paragraph VII(a). For a full account of the circumstances leading to the consent decree see Chapter 8.

[5] Burroughs GSA Contract, July 1, 1966, through June 30, 1967, pp. A–6, A–7.

TABLE 7-1. Burrough's Extended Rental Period Terms, 1966–1967 *

Computer System	Minimum Period (months)	Reduction in Basic Monthly Rental (%)
B-5500	36	25
B-5500	60	30
B100/200/300	36	40 on central processor and core memory 25 on peripheral devices
B100/200/300	60	50 on central processor and core memory 25 on peripheral devices

* Source: Burrough's GSA Contract for July 1, 1966, through June 30, 1967, pp. A–6, A–7.

leases (since they might be for 1 year or less), commercial customers had to agree to retain equipment at least 1 year, and Burroughs once required a minimum term of 2 years.[6] Moreover, most companies (other than IBM) offer longer-term leases with appropriate discounts for the lower risk borne by the manufacturer.

Although no authoritative source is available for commercial terms, periodic announcements by manufacturers suggest the alternatives available. The following examples indicate the range of possibilities.

In November, 1965, Honeywell offered 5-year leases on its series 200 machines with considerable discounts from the terms applicable under the standard (1-year) lease. Within 64 days, approximately $50 million worth of equipment was converted to the new terms.[7] Honeywell subsequently sold some of these leases to finance companies in order to obtain needed cash.[8] Honeywell has also offered 3- and 4-year leases.[9]

In 1966 Scientific Data Systems offered a standard contract that was nominally a 4-year agreement but could be canceled after 1 year. Three possible long-term (guaranteed) contracts were also offered: [10]

[6] "Auerbach Special Report: How Computer Terms Look in 1965," Auerbach Information, Inc., 1965.
[7] *EDP Weekly,* Jan. 24, 1966.
[8] *EDP Weekly,* Mar. 7, 1966; the policy was discontinued in September, 1967 (*EDP Weekly,* Sept. 18, 1967, p. 4).
[9] *EDP Weekly,* Nov. 22, 1965.
[10] *EDP Weekly,* Apr. 25, 1966.

4-year: 90% of standard terms, 5-year: 85% of standard terms, and 6-year: 80% of standard terms.

In 1966 Control Data Corporation offered standard 1- and 3-year contracts. In addition, the company would arrange for a user to lease equipment from a separate company (LEASCO) for either 4 or 6 years.[11]

In 1965 Burroughs offered discounts on long-term leases for its B100/200 and 300 series equipment. The terms were as follows:[12] 2 years: 7.5% discount, 3 years: 15% discount, 4 years: 20% discount, and 5 years: 25% discount.

Needless to say, these provisions are not likely to be directly applicable at the present time. However, they illustrate the general availability of procedures for risk sharing. The longer the contractual period, the greater is the risk borne by the user and the less that assumed by the manufacturer. Since risk is generally an undesirable attribute, manufacturers are willing to pay users to assume it; conversely, users will typically not accept risk without some compensation. This relationship is obvious when rental contracts of differing durations are compared, since the payment appears explicitly as a discount. It is not as obvious when rental is contrasted with outright purchase (in which the user relieves the manufacturer of almost all risk), but it is present nonetheless.

C. RENTAL TERMS—OPERATIONAL USE TIME

Many computer rental contracts base actual monthly charges on the extent to which the equipment is used. The manner in which so-called billable time is measured varies considerably among manufacturers. For example, IBM equips all rented machines with meters at no cost to the user. Other companies allow the user to keep his own records in lieu of installing meters. In some cases the time logged on a central component is considered applicable to many (or all) of the other components in a system. In other cases the use of each peripheral device is measured separately. Several manufacturers allow the user to choose from among a number of options regarding the location and applicability of usage-measuring meters.

[11] *EDP Weekly,* June 27, 1966.
[12] *EDP Weekly,* Jan. 14, 1965.

The procedure followed by IBM illustrates the complexity of measuring operational use (billable) time. Time required for preventive and remedial maintenance is not billable. A separate meter is used during maintenance periods, and hence this time is not recorded on the primary meter(s). The user may manually record information concerning the time required to rerun programs when "the necessity for rerun is due to Equipment Failure." Such rerun time "between reasonable check points" can then be deducted from the billable time shown on the meter(s). During the first few months after installation, limited amounts of nonbillable time are also made available for program testing and compiling, debugging manufacturer-supplied software, and similar activities.

The primary meter is located on the central processing unit. It records

... time during which the processor is executing or completing program instructions, excluding:

        (a) programmed halts
        (b) manual halts
        (c) machine halts
        (d) time when maintenance meter is recording.[13]

Separate meters are located on assignable units such as control units, files, and drums. Such devices must be switched on to operate. Once the device is switched on manually, the meter begins to record as soon as the central processing unit performs an operation. It continues to record until the first central processor halt *after* the device is manually turned off (rendering it inoperative).

Peripheral units have separate meters to record the time during which the unit is either operating or available for operation. Typical specifications are as follows:

Card unit: From the first Read and/or Write Instruction until cards are run out of all feeds.
Printer: From the first Write Instruction until carriage "Space Key" or "Restore Key" is depressed.
Tape drive: From the first Read or Write Instruction until rewind or unload, as applicable.[14]

[13] IBM GSA Schedule, July 1, 1966, through June 30, 1967, p. G–43.
[14] *Ibid.*

It is important to note that several manufacturers offer selected components and even entire systems under terms in which rental charges are not related to utilization. Obviously operational use time is not measured for such equipment. UNIVAC and SDS apply this policy to their entire lines of equipment; hence operational use time is not even defined, let alone measured, for their systems.

D. RENTAL TERMS—EXTRA-USE CHARGES

The traditional terms for rental in the computer industry include the following:
1. A basic monthly rental (BMR)—the minimum charge for renting the equipment.
2. A basic utilization—the number of hours per month that the equipment can be used without incurring extra-use charges.
3. An extra-use charge—the additional cost per hour for utilization in excess of the specified basic utilization.

Some manufacturers have now dropped extra-use charges entirely. Others are applying them to fewer items of equipment and/or lowering these rates. Thus change is very much in evidence in this area. We will trace this change and discuss the important economic issues connected with it in the next chapter. Here we briefly summarize the terms offered during 1966–1967.

At this time IBM specified a basic utilization of 176 hours per month (the amount used if a system is run 8 hours per day for the 22 working days in a typical month). However, *any* 176 hours during the month qualified. Extra-use charges were expressed as a percentage of the average hourly rental that would be obtained if the equipment were run 176 hours per month (=BMR/176). For most System/360 equipment, the extra-use charge was 10% of this amount. Thus every hour in excess of 176 hours per month was charged at a rate equal to $0.1 \times (1/176) \times$ BMR. Second-generation systems (e.g., the 1400 and the 7000 series) were charged at a higher rate: 30%. Certain real-time systems and components, such as the 1800 series and various remote consoles, were offered for no extra-use charge.

Figure 7–1 illustrates the relationship between actual monthly rental and utilization for IBM equipment during 1966–1967. For convenience, utilization is shown in terms of both hours and "shifts," a shift

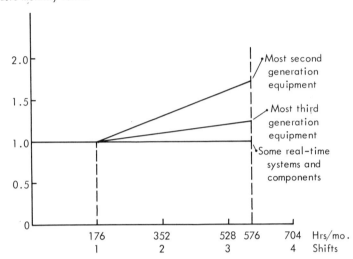

FIGURE 7-1. Monthly rental versus utilization: IBM equipment, 1966-1967.

being defined as 176 hours. The theoretical maximum utilization is 720 hours (30 × 24) per month — slightly over four "shifts." However, preventive and remedial maintenance requirements make the practical limit somewhat lower. The Bureau of the Budget considers 576 hours per month (shown in the figure) a representative amount, since it allows a 20% reserve for "workload contingencies" and preventive and remedial maintenance.[15]

For billing purposes, identical components may be pooled. For example, if an installation has 10 tape drives of the same model, extra-use charges apply only for the excess of total utilization over 1760 hours. However, averaging over a period of months is not allowed — if equipment is utilized for fewer than 176 hours in one month, the deficit may not be applied against an excess in some other month.

During the period IBM offered no options to the user. Each item of equipment and/or component carried a mandatory extra-use charge — either 30%, 10%, or 0%, as stated in the GSA Schedule.

Terms offered by other manufacturers differed significantly; more-

---

[15] *Inventory of ADP Equipment in the Federal Government,* July, 1966, p. 15.

over, several offered a wide range of options for certain machines. Basic utilization was typically either 176 hours or 200 hours per month. Table 7–2 indicates the availability of these two alternatives plus unlimited use during 1966–1967.

The options offered by Control Data Corporation were typical of those of several manufacturers. The standard terms for central processing units specified a basic utilization of 176 hours with extra-use charges approximately equal to 20% of $1/176$ of the basic monthly rental. However, the user might elect instead to pay 120% of the BMR and thereby be entitled to unlimited use. These options are illustrated in Fig. 7–2. Obviously the standard terms (shown by curve $ABCD$) are less expensive for utilization of less than 2 shifts, whereas the unlimited-use option (shown by curve XCY) is preferable for utilization in excess of this amount. The effective relationship between monthly cost and utilization would thus appear to be the lower envelope — curve

TABLE 7–2. Utilization Provisions, 1966–1967 *

	Equipment for Which:		
Manufacturer	Basic Utilization = 176 hr/month	Basic Utilization = 200 hr/month	Use is Unlimited
Burroughs	Most third-generation equipment	Most second-generation equipment	
CDC	Central processors, etc.		Peripheral equipment
GE		Available for most equipment	Available for most equipment
Honeywell		Most equipment	
IBM	Most equipment		Some real-time systems
NCR		NCR 304 systems	Most equipment
RCA	Most second-generation equipment		Most third-generation equipment
SDS			All equipment
UNIVAC			All equipment

* Source: applicable GSA Schedules.

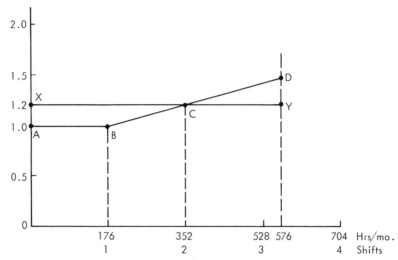

FIGURE 7–2. Monthly rental versus utilization: Control Data Corp. central processors, 1966–1967.

ABCY. However, this was not necessarily the case, since the user had to specify 60 days in advance which of the two options he would select. If he were uncertain about the actual level of utilization, and if the actual level fell on the "wrong" side of 2 shifts, his actual cost would be greater than that shown by curve *ABCY*. It is conceivable that the selection of the appropriate option could require a rather subtle analysis of the demand for computer services and the extent of uncertainty about its level.

Figures 7–3a through 7–3d show the terms offered for selected types of Burroughs equipment during 1966–1967. Note that the so-called measured-time option offered for the B200 and B300 systems completely dominated the standard terms; however, it was available only to those committing themselves to at least a 3-year contract.

During 1966–1967, Honeywell offered options giving unlimited use for 5, 6, or 7 days a week. If the 5-day option were selected, extra-use charges were incurred only for utilization on weekends; under the 6-day option charges were incurred only on Sundays. Figure 7–4 shows the total costs of some of these options, under the assumption that 90% of the total time covered by each option would be utilized.

General Electric offered options during 1966–1967 similar to those shown in Fig. 7–4. However, even more combinations were specified — the user could select the number of days per week (5, 6, or 7) and any of four daily utilization rates (9, 13, 18, or 24 hours). Table 7–3 shows the charges for the options.

It is difficult to draw any conclusions from the information just presented except the obvious one: the user who wishes to rent equipment should assess carefully each of the options offered by the alter-

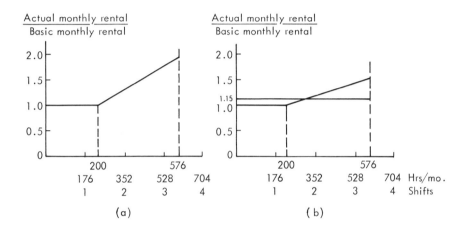

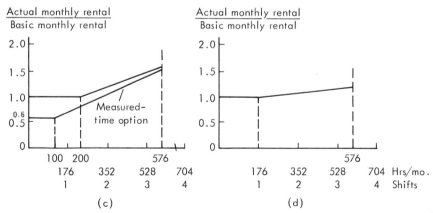

FIGURE 7–3. Monthly rental versus utilization: Burroughs equipment, 1966–1967. (a) Burroughs B100, 1966–1967. (b) Burroughs B5500, 1966–1967. (c) Burroughs B200 and B300, 1966–1967. *Note:* Measured-time option available only on contract of 36 months or more. (d) Burroughs B2500 and B3500, 1966–1967.

TABLE 7-3. General Electric Rental Charges: Option B — Extended Use, 1966–1967 *·†

Hours per Day Utilized	Number of Days per Week Utilized		
	5	6	7
Principal period of operation = 9 hr/day	100%	102%	103%
Principal period of operation plus 4 hr = 13 hr/day	103	104	105
Principal period of operation plus 9 hr = 18 hr/day	105	107	109
Unlimited use = 24 hr/day	108	110	112

* Source: General Electric GSA Schedule, July 1, 1966, through June 30, 1967, p. A–6.

† Figures in table show maintenance charge as a percentage of the basic monthly rental charge.

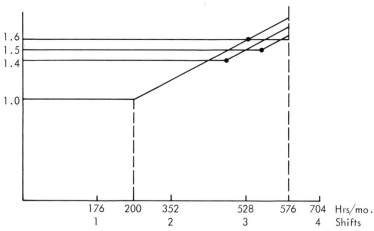

FIGURE 7-4. Monthly rental versus utilization: Honeywell equipment, 1966–1967. 400, 1400, 800, and 1800.

native manufacturers. However, Figs. 7–1 through 7–4, in conjunction with Tables 7–2 and 7–3, suggest that extra-use charges are far more likely to prove significant for second-generation equipment than for third-generation systems. The latter typically may be rented for unlimited use for either the basic monthly rental or a relatively small surcharge. Even in cases in which extra-use charges are required for third-generation equipment, the sums are likely to be relatively small. These observations are consistent with historical trends—extra-use charges have been falling (and even disappearing) over time. The reasons for such changes and their significance for the industry will be discussed in Chapter 8.

E. RENTAL TERMS—MAINTENANCE COSTS

To some extent the costs of maintaining a computer system are uncertain; risk must be borne by either the manufacturer or the user or shared between them. Moreover, the cost of maintenance depends to some extent on the time when it is performed, since maintenance personnel must be paid premiums to work at night or on weekends. Several manufacturers choose to provide users with an incentive to request maintenance during normal working hours whenever possible by increasing the monthly cost when maintenance is required outside normal hours. And several manufacturers allow the user the option of bearing more or less of the risk inherent in equipment maintenance.

Users are typically not given a choice with regard to three key components of maintenance: parts, preventive maintenance, and remedial maintenance performed during normal working hours. The costs of these services are typically included in the basic monthly rental and thus are provided without extra charge. There is one notable exception: Sperry Rand requires the UNIVAC user to contract for a separate maintenance coverage with these three basic components included in the coverage provided for the "basic monthly maintenance charge." Thus UNIVAC's BMR charge is purely a rental charge, whereas other manufacturers include both rental and basic maintenance costs in this item.

The manner in which the user pays for remedial (unscheduled) maintenance performed outside normal working hours varies from manufacturer to manufacturer. In some cases the cost is included in the extra-use charges required as part of the rental contract. Thus an IBM user incurs no additional charge for maintenance unless it is due to his own "fault or negligence" or unless he has made alterations or installed attachments that "substantially increase the cost of maintenance." Honeywell's policy is similar.

An alternative policy involves the selection by the user of a so-called "principal period of maintenance." The standard period covers 8 hours per day, Monday through Friday, and is usually restricted to fall between 7:00 A.M. and 6:00 P.M. Remedial maintenance performed outside the principal period incurs an extra charge, calculated in terms of man-hours required. The rate usually depends on the day of the week; typical values in 1966–1967 were $15 per man-hour for weekdays, $18 per man-hour for Saturdays, and $20–$30 per man-hour for Sundays and holidays. Such costs need not be incurred if the user is willing to wait until the next principal period of maintenance to repair equipment failing outside the principal period. Thus the user is given an incentive to economize on expensive maintenance time.

Some manufacturers allow the user to subtract the number of hours for which extra-use charges were paid from the maintenance man-hours used outside the principal period; the hourly maintenance cost then applies only to the difference (if any). Of course for systems for which no extra-use charge is levied, this method is not available.

Some manufacturers restrict the "covered" period of maintenance to the standard principal period of 8 hours per day on weekdays, requiring the user to pay for remedial maintenance man-hours outside the covered period. This imposes some of the risk associated with maintenance on the user, but it also provides him with appropriate incentives to reduce the overall cost. As an alternative, other manufacturers allow the user to contract for an extended "covered" period by paying an additional monthly charge. Some or all of the risk may thus be shifted to the manufacturer. UNIVAC offers a number of such alternatives, basing the additional monthly charge on the basic monthly maintenance charge. Similar options are available from SDS and NCR, the additional charge being based on the basic monthly rental. The additional cost for each of the twelve options offered by SDS in 1966–1967 is shown in Table 7–4.

Remedial maintenance is usually provided "on-call," with personnel dispatched as soon as possible. The wording of the IBM contract

TABLE 7-4. SDS Charges for Extended Maintenance
Coverage, 1966–1967 *·†

Consecutive Hours Per Day	Coverage (days/week)		
	5	6	7
8	100%	105%	110%
12	105	110	115
16	110	115	120
Around the clock	115	120	125

* Source: SDS GSA Contract, July 1, 1966, through June 30, 1967, p. A–3.
† Figures in table are percentage of basic monthly rental charge.

is typical: it guarantees that all remedial maintenance shall be performed "upon notification of Equipment becoming inoperative and IBM shall always be responsive to the maintenance requirements of the government." [16] In some cases "on-site" maintenance personnel are provided free of charge to the user during the normal working day. Generally on-site personnel are furnished "upon mutual agreement" between the manufacturer and the user, although some manufacturers specify that on-site personnel will be furnished if the value of equipment installed exceeds a specified amount (e.g., $35,000 per month basic monthly rental for CDC, $50,000 per month for General Electric 600 series equipment).

Two trends concerning maintenance charges appear to be associated with computer rental: (1) an increasing tendency to identify maintenance costs separately from rental charges, and (2) an increasing tendency to offer the user options concerning the amount of risk borne. Since terms are both diverse and complex, and since they are related to some extent to rental terms, the user must be careful to make a detailed comparison when considering alternative systems. Comparisons based solely on basic monthly rental values are fraught with hazard. For example, UNIVAC equipment is unduly favored by such a comparison, since an important required monthly cost (the basic monthly maintenance charge) is not included. The solution in this case is obvious – include both charges when evaluating UNIVAC equip-

[16] IBM GSA Contract, July 1, 1966, through June 30, 1967, p. A–9.

ment. Other instances involving discrepancies may be more complex. However, both absolute and relative costs (rental plus maintenance) of alternative systems are likely to depend on planned utilization; any comparison should somehow take this factor into account.

F. RENTAL TERMS — PURCHASE OPTIONS

Suppose that a user who has rented a computer system for a period of time decides that he prefers to purchase the equipment. Since the system is no longer new, he may feel that he should not have to pay the price charged by the manufacturer for comparable new equipment. On the other hand, since the cost of changing systems is undoubtedly considerable, the user may be willing to pay more for his system than other customers will pay for comparably used equipment. To protect himself against having a manufacturer subsequently take advantage of him, a rental customer usually prefers to be guaranteed specified prices at which he may later choose to buy his equipment. This preference provides one explanation for the purchase options offered by all manufacturers to rental customers.

Although the presumption "the older the machine the smaller its value" is not universally held at present, it clearly accounts for some purchase options. For example, in the period 1966–1967, NCR offered two options for its 315 series. One provided that a rental customer could purchase equipment for the current list price less $1/12$ of 10% times its age in months (except that he had to pay at least half the current list price). For equipment announced before October, 1963, IBM offered a similar arrangement; purchase prices were related to age, falling to a minimum of 25% of the list price after 60 months for systems such as the 650 and after only 36 months for some other systems (e.g., the 7080, 7090, and 7094).

This explanation for the existence of purchase options suggests that the purchase price should depend solely on the total age of the machine. It clearly should not depend on the period of time during which the equipment was installed in the last customer's facility or on the amount of rent he paid (unless the equipment was new when installed). Moreover, the presumption that the relevant price is smaller than that shown in the manufacturer's current price list assumes that the latter applies to new equipment.

Unfortunately current practice is generally inconsistent with this simple explanation. The basic assumption that used equipment is worth less than new equipment is violated in a number of cases. For example, during 1966–1967 neither IBM nor UNIVAC guaranteed to deliver new equipment when a purchase order was placed by a government agency. Thus the purchase prices listed in the IBM and UNIVAC price lists applied equally to new and used equipment. More relevant in this context is the fact that almost all purchase options are based on the length of time that a system has been rented by the *current* customer and/or the amount he has paid in rental charges. Obviously some purpose in addition to that previously suggested is being served by purchase options.

When a user chooses to rent a computer system, he avoids certain types of risk. Should the machine perform poorly, he may cancel his rental contract on reasonably short notice. If new equipment with a significantly smaller cost per unit of effectiveness becomes available, he can switch machines if the manufacturer does not lower the rental rate of his current equipment sufficiently.

On the other hand, a rental customer takes on certain risks. Rental charges may be increased. Moreover, if the user finds that the machine performs well, he may choose to invest heavily in software and systems specific to the machine and thus wish to retain it for a relatively long period of time; in this case rental payments may greatly exceed the original purchase price. A long-term lease allows the user to assume more of the risks of the first type with a consequent reduction of risks of the second type; outright purchase represents a more extreme strategy. Manufacturers offer all three alternatives (at appropriate costs) to satisfy the desires of customers with diverse attitudes and/or needs.

The purchase option represents a fourth alternative. In a sense it allows the user to "have his cake and eat it too," although this advantage is not obtained from the manufacturer at zero cost. In some instances the user may be required to pay this cost explicitly if he wishes to receive the purchase option. For example, before 1966, IBM required a deposit of 1% of the purchase price if a user wished to have a purchase option included in his rental contract. The deposit could be applied toward the purchase price but was not refunded if the equipment was not eventually purchased. This procedure, however, has fallen into disuse. Most manufacturers now include a purchase option as part of their standard rental contracts; the cost is presumably also included.

The usual purchase option is stated in terms of the list price of the equipment and the rental charge paid by the customer. Typically the equipment must have been under continuous rental by the customer throughout the applicable period (the federal government is usually considered a single customer, even though more than one agency may have rented the equipment). The list price is (1) that prevailing when the equipment was first rented, (2) that prevailing when the purchase option is exercised, or (3) the smaller of the two. The third alternative allows the renter both a hedge against price increases (e.g., those due to inflation) and an opportunity to benefit from price decreases, such as those required to keep older designs competitive with newer ones; obviously it is the best of the three options. The merit of the first option relative to the second depends primarily on expectations regarding the price at the time of purchase relative to that in force at the time the equipment is rented. Some alternatives offered during 1966–1967 were as follows:

1. Price when equipment first rented:
   SDS Sigma series.
2. Price when purchase option exercised:
   IBM 360 series, Honeywell 200 series (option 2), NCR 315 series (option 2), Burroughs 2500/3500.
3. Smaller of (1) and (2):
   CDC systems, UNIVAC systems, SDS 9 series, RCA Spectra 70, NCR 315 series (option 1), Burroughs 5500, Honeywell 200 series (option 1), GE systems.

The percentage of rental payments deductible from the list price may depend on the length of time during which the equipment has been rented by the customer. In some cases the applicable percentage decreases over time, in others it increases, and in still others it is constant. In every instance some lower bound is placed on the percentage of list price that must be paid. The credit may be based on total rental payments or only on the basic monthly rental.

Figures 7–5a through 7–5k illustrate some of the options offered during 1966–1967. Each shows the effective price as a percentage of the relevant list price under the assumption that the applicable monthly rental is $1/45$ of the list price (a typical proportion).

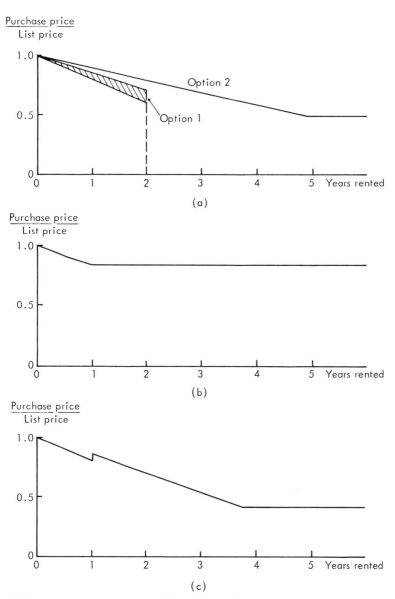

FIGURE 7-5. Purchase options, 1966–1967. (a) NCR 315 Series. (*Notes.* Percentage of rental applicable for option 1 depends on exact configuration; values range from 50% to 70%. Option 1 available only if equipment has been rented less than 24 months. Option 2 is based on total age; figure assumes that equipment was new when installed.) (b) Burroughs B2500 and B3500. (c) Burroughs B5500.

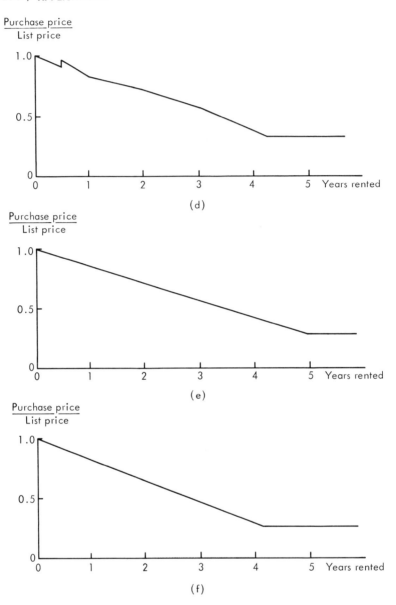

FIGURE 7-5 (continued). (d) SDS 9-Series. (e) SDS Sigma Series. (f) RCA Spectra/70 Equipment.

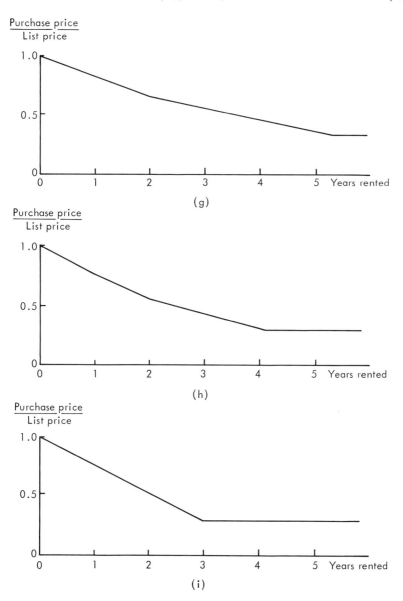

(g) CDC Equipment. (h) UNIVAC Equipment. (i) IBM 7080, 7090, and 7094. (*Note.* Years rented assumed to equal total age of equipment.)

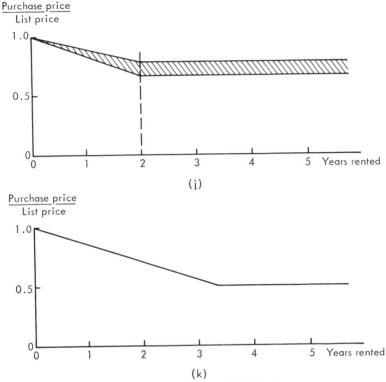

FIGURE 7–5 (concluded). (j) IBM 360 Series. (k) GE Systems.

In a sense the curves in these figures may be viewed as representing upper bounds on the prices of used equipment. Obviously a customer renting equipment will never pay more to a third party than the price for which he could purchase his equipment from the manufacturer. Also, a new customer desiring to purchase used equipment may very probably be able to find another user about to turn back a rented system. The current renter can clearly exercise his purchase option and then immediately sell the equipment to someone else who wants a used system. If the initial user rented the equipment from the time that it was new, the price to the final owner as a function of the equipment's age might be expected to be slightly higher than that shown in the appropriate diagram. There is, however, one possible qualification. If the purchase option price happens to fall considerably below the market value of the equipment, a renter choosing to change systems will actually profit from exercising the option and selling his old equipment. Thus the figures do not necessarily show upper bounds on used-equipment prices. However, as a practical matter, prices are not likely to exceed those shown.

Note that a manufacturer may have to sell equipment to new and/or old customers at considerably lower values than those indicated in the figures. Thus one can conclude, for example, not that the value of a Burroughs 2500 is expected to decrease less rapidly than that of an RCA Spectra 70, but only that the purchase option offered on the former is less attractive than that available on the latter.

G. PURCHASE TERMS

One would expect terms for purchase to be considerably simpler than those associated with rental, since the seller and buyer need not be associated as intimately with one another once the equipment is installed. This lack of necessary seller involvement (with the accompanying possibility of a lack of interest) is the great drawback associated with the purchase of equipment. The argument is often made that a manufacturer will provide inadequate hardware and software support for a purchased system, since he receives full payment at the outset; on the other hand, it is asserted that he will have major incentives to both maintain and improve the overall performance of a rented system, which may be returned on short notice at almost any time. The counterargument holds that most manufacturers hope to remain in the computer business, and that poor support of an installation will damage prospects for later sales not only to those in charge of the system in question but to others as well.

Whatever the merits of such arguments, attempts have been made to assure the purchaser of computer equipment that he will receive the same type of support offered those renting similar systems. The most important procedure is the offer by the manufacturer to provide maintenance service under a separate contract (described in Section H). The manufacturer also promises to provide generally available software developed after the equipment is purchased and to supply adequate training and technical services both before and after the equipment is installed. In spite of these provisions, however, the user's primary opportunity to hold the manufacturer to his promises comes during the first few months after the equipment is installed.

A relatively recent innovation is the inclusion of software specifications in purchase contracts with government agencies. The manufacturer typically provides a list of "programming aids," including "programs, routines, subroutines, translation compilers, etc.," to the prospective purchaser. Some or all may be included in the purchase order with specified delivery dates; however, the precise list must be agreed upon by both the manufacturer and the prospective purchaser. If any of the promised software is not delivered on the date specified, a penalty will be paid by the manufacturer. The penalty may be based solely on the number of days (up to 180) of the delay (e.g., $100 per day), or on the number of software items delayed (e.g., $100 per day per item). In some cases the daily amount is stated in dollars, in others as a proportion of the basic monthly rental, and in still others as the smaller of the two. The contracts are understandably vague about the meaning of "delivery" of software — no performance standards are specified.

Penalties are also provided for delays in installing equipment. If the delay exceeds 30 days, the customer is usually allowed to cancel the purchase order. If he does not cancel, the manufacturer pays an amount equal to, for example, $100 or $\frac{1}{30}$ of the basic monthly rental (whichever is larger) for each day of delay up to 180 days.

Final acceptance (and payment) is not required until the equipment performs satisfactorily for a period of 30 consecutive days. Such a period is termed a *performance period*. The provisions in Sperry Rand's UNIVAC contract for 1966–1967 are typical:

If the system operates in conformance with UNIVAC's technical specifications or as quoted in proposals at an average effectiveness level of 90 percent or more during the performance period of 30 consecutive days, it shall be deemed to have met the Government's Standard of Performance and payment in full shall be made. . . .

The average effectiveness level is a percentage figure determined by dividing the total productive operational use time by the total productive operational use time plus downtime. . . .

. . . downtime shall be measured by those intervals during the performance period between the time that UNIVAC is notified of equipment failure and the time that the equipment is returned to the Government in proper operating condition exclusive of actual travel time required by UNIVAC's maintenance personnel. . . .[17]

[17] UNIVAC GSA Contract, July 1, 1966, through June 30, 1967, pp. C–3, C–4.

The successful performance period is defined as the first period of 30 consecutive days after installation during which the specified effectiveness level is either met or exceeded. All the maintenance service and all the parts that are required up to the first day of the successful performance period are usually provided without charge by the manufacturer.

As indicated earlier, equipment provided for purchase need not be entirely new. During 1966–1967 UNIVAC, IBM, and GE did not guarantee to provide new equipment. Typical wording for other manufacturers' contracts was as follows: "____ shall install new equipment, ready for use, before an Installation Date agreed to by ____ and the Government." The adjective *new* was conspiciously absent, however, from the comparable sentence in the GE, IBM, and UNIVAC contracts. For example, IBM stated that "newly manufactured" equipment would be supplied if available, but that machines would "contain some used parts which are warranted equivalent to new in performance."

All manufacturers provide guarantees; however, the form of the guarantee is usually a commitment to provide maintenance service and parts for a specified number of days following the beginning of the successful performance period. The coverage usually extends for 90 days, although the period may be shorter (in 1966–1967, Honeywell specified 45 days and SDS 60 days). IBM provides free maintenance and parts for 90 days; in addition, parts are supplied during the first year if required to repair "defects in material and workmanship." The latter coverage, however, is typically not offered by other manufacturers.

Despite attempts to provide safeguards, the purchaser of computer equipment still bears considerable risk. Once the successful performance period is completed and the specified software "delivered," the purchaser is on his own. The manufacturer still has incentives to maintain and improve the performance of the system, but these incentives are based on long-term objectives, not the short-run and immediate goal of keeping a rented machine installed. Many users appear to feel that the level of manufacturer involvement required to keep a system operating efficiently is substantial, and that considerably more support (of both hardware and, more importantly, software) will be provided if equipment is rented. This opinion is reflected in the continuing preference for rental over purchase. It is far from clear, however, that the past performance of manufacturers is consistent with this view. Their future behavior is, of course, unknown.

H. MAINTENANCE CONTRACTS

All manufacturers offer maintenance contracts providing owners of computer systems with coverage similar to that available to users who rent equipment. The system must be "in good mechanical and operating condition" at the time that the maintenance contract goes into effect. The manufacturer will inspect the system (for no charge) to determine whether or not it qualifies. If defects are found, necessary repairs and alterations will be made at no charge if the equipment has been maintained previously by the manufacturer; otherwise the user must bear these costs. The terms of the IBM contract for 1966–1967 are typical:

If the Equipment was not under an IBM rental or maintenance contract, or was moved, immediately prior to the effective date of the maintenance order, all costs necessary to place the Equipment in good operating and mechanical condition and to make engineering changes necessary to bring the Equipment to the acceptable engineering level shall be borne by the Government.[18]

Maintenance contracts cover a period of up to 1 year; the user may cancel coverage upon 30–90 days' notice. The basic monthly maintenance charge entitles the user to all parts, scheduled preventive maintenance, and remedial maintenance during a principal period of 8 or 9 hours during the daytime, Monday through Friday, but the covered period may be extended by paying an amount expressed as a percentage of the basic monthly charge. Although IBM bases its charges not only on the period covered but also on the particular equipment installed, other manufacturers do not generally differentiate among types of equipment. A number of periods of coverage are normally offered. Table 7–5 gives some typical costs for around-the-clock coverage 7 days per week during 1966–1967.

Remedial maintenance performed outside the covered period is charged for on the basis of the man-hours required. If the user's installation is more than a stated distance from the manufacturer's nearest service center, there is an extra charge for travel time.

[18] IBM GSA Contract, July 1, 1966, through June 30, 1967.

TABLE 7-5. Maintenance Costs for Full Coverage (24 hours per day, 7 days per week), 1966–1967 *

Manufacturer	Total Maintenance Cost, Expressed as a Percentage of the Basic Monthly Maintenance Charge
Burroughs	235%
GE	220
Honeywell	175
IBM	151–193
RCA	130
SDS	215
UNIVAC	180

* Source: GSA Contract, July 1, 1966, through June 30, 1967.

Most manufacturers offer credit for equipment malfunction. Typical terms entitle the user to a reduction of $\frac{1}{2}$ of 1% of the basic monthly maintenance charge for each hour in excess of 12 consecutive hours; the credit applies to the machine that has malfunctioned and to all other components rendered useless as a result.[19]

Since maintenance contracts include the cost of all parts in the basic monthly charge for this service, it is difficult to assess the relative cost of parts vis-à-vis labor. However, some evidence is available. Under exceptional circumstances Burroughs will allow an overseas government user to perform maintenance on rented equipment; when this is done, the government's rental costs are reduced by an amount equal to 25% of the basic monthly maintenance charge. This suggests that 75% of the basic charge (and thus less than 75% of the total maintenance cost) is attributable to the cost of replacement parts, at least for Burroughs equipment.

Maintenance contracts formally cover at most one year. It has almost always been possible, however, to renew coverage at the end of every year. The user is thus virtually certain that he will be able to obtain the required maintenance services, although no guarantee is made concerning costs (which have usually increased over time) or, more importantly, the overall effectiveness of the installation.

---

[19] A similar provision is usually included in rental contracts.

I. EDUCATIONAL DISCOUNTS

Overt price discrimination is relatively rare in the computer-manufacturing industry—by and large, the same terms are offered to all customers. There is, however, one major exception. Most manufacturers offer equipment to certain educational institutions at lower prices than those charged other users. This procedure is often justified on charitable grounds. A somewhat more cynical interpretation holds that a manufacturer's interests are served if students associate computing with his equipment, since they may later have some influence on choices among competing manufacturers. Even if students do not pay particular attention to the brand of machine they use, they are likely to contribute later to the overall demand for computers, and the manufacturer may expect to share in the overall result. Other advantages are associated with having equipment in an educational institution, particularly one with an active program in computer science. Some of the best software has been developed by students, faculty, and staff at such institutions and is usually distributed without charge. To the extent that such software is specific to the machine for which it was developed, it benefits the manufacturer by adding to prospective sales.

An alternative interpretation of educational discounts rests on the simple model of price discrimination presented in Part I. It is entirely possible that educational institutions have more elastic demand curves than most other users. If this is the case, and if the manufacturer sets prices so that marginal revenue in each sector equals marginal cost, the price charged educational institutions will be lower than that charged other users.

Some manufacturers offer educational discounts to users renting equipment, others to those purchasing systems, and still others to both. Discounts on maintenance contracts are rare (during 1966–1967, only IBM offered such a discount). And some manufacturers (e.g., Burroughs in 1966–1967) offer no discounts at all. In some cases a standard discount applies to the manufacturer's entire line of equipment; in others different items are given different discounts.

Each manufacturer reserves the right to select the particular institutions to which discounts are to be offered. Contracts usually state that a "limited number" of such "grants" will be given to "selected institutions." However, certain qualifications that must be met by such institutions are usually specified. In some cases the statement is simple:

SDS, 1966–1967: "To qualify for this grant the educational institution must have an exempt standing with the Internal Revenue Service. . . ." [20]

Honeywell, 1966–1967: "Criteria to qualify will be governed by Honeywell's educational allowance program in effect at that time. . . ." [21]

In others it is more complex. The following phrase appeared in several contracts (NCR, UNIVAC, CDC) for 1966–1967:

The institution must have one accredited course per semester in computers or conduct seminars, lectures, etc., for educational purposes, or provide laboratory and library facilities for candidates for Master's and Doctorate degrees to perform scientific experiments and investigations and prepare their theses.[22]

In addition, NCR specified that the institution must be accredited and "must maintain a regular faculty and curriculum and have a regular enrolled body of students or pupils in attendance at the place where the educational activities are conducted. . . ." [23] IBM merely specified the types of institutions that might meet its qualifications:

(1) Universities and colleges
(2) Hospitals and clinics that are a corporate part of an accredited university . . .
(3) Junior colleges
(4) Secondary schools
(5) Post-high school technical-vocational training institutions [24]

The company also provided a statement of the purpose of the discount: "The educational allowance granted is to assist the educational institution in instruction, academic research and the administration of its internal affairs." [25]

Table 7–6 indicates the discounts offered during 1966–1967 by several manufacturers. Peripheral equipment was normally given the

[20] SDS GSA Contract, July 1, 1966, through June 30, 1967, p. C–4.
[21] Honeywell GSA Contract, July 1, 1966, through June 30, 1967, p. 12.
[22] NCR GSA Contract, July 1, 1966, through June 30, 1967, p. 7.
[23] *Ibid.*
[24] IBM GSA Contract, July 1, 1966, through June 30, 1967, p. A–7.
[25] *Ibid.*

TABLE 7-6. Educational Discounts, 1966–1967 *

| Manufacturer | Educational Discounts for | | |
	Rental	Purchase	Maintenance
Burroughs	None	None	None
CDC	20%	20%	None
	50% on GE 215 computers installed before June 30, 1965	None	None
Honeywell	10–50%, depending on system	10–50%, depending on system	None
IBM	20–45%, depending on system	20–45%, depending on system	20%
NCR	20% on 315 series	20% on 315 series	None
RCA	20–40%, depending on system	20–50%, depending on system	None
SDS	None	10–25%, depending on system	None
UNIVAC	20%	None	None

* Source: GSA Contracts, July 1, 1966, through June 30, 1967.

smallest discount; larger discounts were typically reserved for more expensive components, such as central processors, and/or certain obsolete systems.

In any case of price discrimination it is important that members of the group receiving lower prices be clearly identified and precluded from reselling either the equipment or services to others at their (lower) costs. The first condition is clearly met in the case of educational institutions, but the second is more difficult to enforce.

No manufacturer attempts completely to prevent educational institutions from reselling equipment or (more important) from selling time on installed equipment to users unable to qualify for educational discounts. However, for a number of reasons such practices do not represent a major threat. First, contractual arrangements may be used to impose explicit penalties for activities of this type. Second, educational institutions are generally nonprofit institutions; therefore incentives to gain from such operations are somewhat reduced. Third, the disparity in costs is typically rather small (usually about 20%) so that the gains to be made are not substantial. And, finally, since no manufacturer agrees to grant discounts automatically to any educational institution, a recipient must beware of actions that may diminish his prospects for receiving additional discounts in the future.

Even when equipment obtained under discount is rented rather than purchased, few manufacturers impose explicit constraints on its use. However, both IBM and Honeywell require the user to make extra payments if a rented system is used for "external purposes."

IBM allows an educational institution to rent equipment for the basic monthly rental less the applicable discount; this entitles the institution to unlimited use (i.e., there is no extra-use charge) for "internal purposes." Such purposes include "use by the faculty, staff, students or employees of the educational institution in instruction, academic research and the administration of its internal affairs."[26] "Academic research" is further defined at length to preclude consulting work and classified research. "External use" is defined as all other activity, for example, "commercial research, service bureau business, sale of block time or any work by other than faculty, staff, students or employees of the educational institution."[27]

The educational institution renting equipment from IBM must pay a surcharge equal to $1/176$ of the basic monthly rental for each hour of external use up to 176 hours per month. Additional hours are charged at the normal extra-use rate. Obviously an institution operating under these restrictions will not provide serious competition for nearby service bureaus or other users with similar equipment.

Honeywell's provisions for external use are similar, except that a base of 200 hours is used for the computations instead of 176 hours. "Internal use" is not defined explicitly, but presumably the interpretation of the term is similar to that given by IBM.

IBM also imposes penalties if equipment purchased by an educational institution and covered by an IBM maintenance contract is used for external purposes. The 20% discount on maintenance charges must be forfeited on any day during which the computer is put to such use.

An interesting question concerns the reductions that have occurred in educational discounts over time. For years IBM's policy was to grant a 60% discount subject to the requirement that equipment be utilized at least 88 hours per month for instruction and academic research (administrative use could not be counted toward the total). The

[26] *Ibid.*   [27] *Ibid.*

policy was changed in 1964; the discount was lowered to 20%, but no restrictions were placed on the internal use of the equipment (as before, payments to IBM were required for external use). Although in certain instances the change proved beneficial to the customer, in most cases the result was to double the effective cost of newly acquired equipment to educational institutions. Since 1964, discounts on selected types of equipment have been further reduced (e.g., to 10%) or removed entirely.

One explanation attributes such changes to the maturation of the industry. In the early years IBM may have felt it worthwhile to promote the use of computers by offering substantial educational discounts, but now that the campaign has been successful, at least part of the advertising budget can perhaps better be spent elsewhere. An alternative explanation begins with the assertion that IBM is willing to provide equipment to educational institutions as long as the marginal cost of producing it is covered. Most first- and second-generation machines were produced in relatively small quantities; thus marginal cost was probably substantially lower than average cost and, a fortiori, considerably below list price. But most models in IBM's current line are being produced in rather large quantities; marginal cost may now be closer to average cost and thus to list price.[28] This argument provides at least a plausible explanation for the reduction in educational discounts.

J. QUANTITY DISCOUNTS

In recent years considerable pressure has been exerted on computer manufacturers to provide quantity discounts to the federal government. The argument is usually made on the grounds of equity: the federal government is the largest single user of computer equipment; thus it should not have to pay prices equal to those paid by the user of only one or two systems.

Whether equitable or not, under certain conditions manufacturers may find it profitable to offer quantity discounts. Certain types of quantity purchases will reduce a manufacturer's overall costs below

---

[28] The gap between marginal and average cost may still be substantial; the former includes primarily hardware costs, while the latter includes the costs of hardware, software and development.

those associated with a comparable series of separate sales. Usually a rather substantial fixed cost is associated with administering a rental or even a purchase order; the larger the number of machines covered by an order, the lower will be the administrative cost per machine. Moreover, an order for many machines reduces uncertainty and allows the manufacturer to arrange a low-cost production schedule. This is the reason given by SDS for its discounts: "SDS offers a quantity discount plan which recognizes the economies that can be realized by dealing with well-scheduled quantity orders." [29]

If many machines are ordered to perform the same function at a number of locations, the required software and systems support per machine will be reduced. To the extent that the manufacturer is expected to provide some of this support, such an order carries lower costs per machine. Several manufacturers offer quantity discounts for orders involving a single type of machine if (and only if) "the project or program for which systems are acquired [is] comprised of a common, standard application." [30]

Another type of quantity discount is, of course, possible—one completely unrelated to costs. As shown in Part I, any given customer's demand curve for a particular type of equipment will generally be downward-sloping. If the manufacturer has a reasonably good idea of the location of such a curve, and if he can tailor his terms appropriately, it will pay him to engage in multipart pricing. Quantity discounts are one form that such a strategy may take. A manufacturer engaging in this type of activity would presumably relate his discount to the total quantity and/or dollar volume purchased rather than to the number of systems of a particular type. Moreover, no constraints would be placed on the applications. Some discounts offered by CDC and SDS during 1966–1967 conform to this pattern, and the Digital Equipment Corporation has offered discounts based on the dollar volume of purchases by a single customer (broadly construed) over an extended period of time.

Table 7–7 summarizes some of the quantity discounts available during 1966–1967. Several reflect commitments made in earlier years to obtain particular multi-installation contracts. Others represent

[29] SDS GSA Contract, July 1, 1966, through June 30, 1967, p. C–4.
[30] UNIVAC GSA Contract, July 1, 1966, through June 30, 1967, p. ix.

attempts to lower the prices of obsolete equipment. Some manufacturers (most notably, IBM) offered no quantity discounts at the time. The discounts shown in Table 7–7 should simply be considered illustrative of alternative policies, since this is an area in which there is neither standardization nor consistency over time.

Our survey of current terms and conditions has of necessity been long and detailed. Some cannot be fully understood without an additional excursion into legal constraints and historical trends. The next chapter attempts to provide the relevant additional information and then to cope with some of the more vexing issues concerning the purchase and rental of computer equipment.

TABLE 7–7. Quantity Discounts, 1966–1967

UNIVAC 1004 systems (applies for purchase or rental contracts)

Number of Proc- essors Used for a Common Application	Total Discount
20–29	5%
30–39	10
Over 40	15

UNIVAC 1005 systems (applies only to rental contracts)

Number of Proc- essors Used for a Common Application	Total Discount
20–29	2%
30–39	5
Over 40	10

RCA 301
  If 12 or more systems are used for a common application and more than 2 are installed at each location, rental charges will be reduced by 7%.
Burroughs B475 disk file storage modules
  If more than 25 are installed on a single B-5500 system, the net monthly rental rate for each will be $500, instead of the regular rate of $990.
Burroughs B200/300 systems
  If 10 or more systems of the same type are ordered by the same government headquarters agency for a common application, the purchase price and/or basic monthly rental rate will be reduced 5%.

TABLE 7–7. (continued)

CDC central processors, core storage, controllers, printers, card readers and punches, drums, etc. (applies to purchase orders only)

Quantity Ordered	Total Discount
0–4	0 %
4–9	7½
10–19	15
Over 20	20

CDC data channels and magnetic tape transports (applies to purchase orders only)

Quantity Ordered	Total Discount
0–16	0 %
16–25	7½
26–49	15
Over 50	20

CDC disk storage (applies to purchase orders only)

Quantity Ordered	Total Discount
0–9	0 %
10–19	7½
20–39	15
Over 40	20

SDS Sigma series quantity discount plan

Total Sales Price (millions of dollars)	Total Discount
Less than 1	0%
1–3	5
3–5	7
5–10	9
Over 10	10

□ □

CHAPTER **8** **THE SALE AND RENTAL OF COMPUTERS**

□ □ LEGAL CONSTRAINTS AND ECONOMIC ISSUES

□

□
□ **A. ANTITRUST LEGISLATION**

Laws of all kinds impinge on the computer industry. Restrictions are placed on the exports of U.S. computers to certain countries; communications, a vital factor for computer utilities, are heavily regulated; most countries restrict or penalize imports of computer equipment; and a host of laws constrains the activities of sellers of all types of systems and services. We will deal with some of these constraints in subsequent chapters. Here we concentrate on antitrust legislation in general and, in particular, the legal constraints placed upon IBM, the leading computer manufacturer.

Two major acts constitute the basic antitrust legislation of the United States. The Sherman Act of 1890 prohibits "contracts, combinations or conspiracies in restraint of trade" and makes it "unlawful to monopolize trade, attempt to monopolize trade or combine or conspire to monopolize trade." The Clayton Act of 1914 makes it unlawful for a seller to discriminate in price between different customers when the effect might be to "substantially lessen competition or tend to create a monopoly"; such discrimination now includes quantity discounts not based on actual cost savings to the seller. The Clayton Act also prohibits tie-in sales or contracts under which commodities are made available only upon the condition that other, different commodities are taken.[1]

As with other legislation of such broad intent, the effective antitrust law has depended heavily on court decisions, the actions of the Justice Department (charged with bringing suit against presumed offenders), and subsequent legislation. Over the course of the years the courts have increasingly held that continuing dominance of an important market is, in itself, grounds for antitrust action. The term *restraint of trade* has been interpreted to mean "unreasonable" restraint of trade

[1] *Commerce Clearing House Trade Regulation Reports,* Vol. 1, pp. 1017–1020.

(but the latter expression remains undefined). Monopoly power has been defined as "the power or ability to fix or control prices in a market or the power or ability to exclude competition from a market,"[2] but the relevant definition of market has not been specified and no simple tests for monopoly power (e.g., percentage of a market held) have been prescribed.

The action taken against a firm found guilty of violating the antitrust laws may take many forms, but the intent is usually to force the creation and/or strengthening of competing firms, even though this may be inefficient in terms of production and/or distribution costs. Unfortunately there are no standard procedures; therefore a firm seldom can predict the penalties that may be incurred if certain (possibly illegal) activities are pursued.

B. THE 1936 IBM DECISION

As indicated earlier, IBM has been the dominant firm in the tabulating machine industry for decades. It also became the giant in the computer manufacturing field shortly after the industry became truly commercial and has retained this position to the present time. Not surprisingly, the Justice Department has shown a continuing interest in the firm's activities.

The first confrontation came in the 1930's, when IBM operated under two policies which together were held to violate the Clayton Act's provisions against tie-in sales. First, customers were allowed not to buy machines but only to rent them; and second, only cards manufactured by IBM could be used in the machines.[3] The Justice Department charged that the net effect was to tie the purchase of IBM cards to the use of IBM equipment, and brought suit. The company fought the case to the U.S. Supreme Court, where it lost (in 1936), the court holding that the practice "substantially lessened competition in the sale of tabulating cards and tended to create a monopoly."[4]

Actually, however, the Justice Department's victory proved hol-

[2] *Ibid.*, p. 1087.
[3] If a customer used a card made by another firm, the rental contract was terminated and all rent payments became immediately due and payable (*Commerce Clearing House Trade Regulation Reports,* Vol. 1, p. 4058).
[4] *Ibid.*, p. 4058.

low. IBM was allowed to continue its policy of not selling equipment; and although customers were allowed to use cards manufactured by other firms, IBM was given the right to require that the cards meet certain minimum specifications (so as not to damage the equipment, according to IBM spokesmen). Since the company held the patents on a superior automatic rotary card press (producing 81% of the cards sold at the time [5]), no other firm could, in fact, produce cards meeting the specifications subsequently laid down by IBM. Thus in practical terms the Supreme Court decision had no effect whatever. According to one estimate, as much as 25% of IBM's profits between 1930 and 1950 was attributable to card sales.[6]

C. THE IBM CONSENT DECREE

In 1947 the Justice Department began a new investigation of IBM.[7] Three years later the Department was apparently willing to accept an agreement that IBM would license its patents for reasonable charges, but the company refused to comply with the request.[8] Hence the Justice Department continued its investigation and in January, 1952, filed charges against IBM under the antitrust laws.

Since the processing of an antitrust case through the courts is both time-consuming and costly, there are real incentives for the parties to settle out of court. The formal procedure used in antitrust cases for this purpose is the consent decree, in which the accused firm consents to certain provisions without any admission of guilt with regard to the original charges. No testimony is taken, and no judgment (other than the decree itself) is rendered. The plaintiff (the Justice Department) withdraws its original suit on the grounds that the decree issued and enforced by the court constitutes a satisfactory settlement. Obviously considerable negotiation must take place before terms for such a decree can be agreed upon by both parties, and in some instances only a full court case can resolve the issues.

Even after the Justice Department filed suit in 1952, negotiations continued in the effort to settle the issues out of court. During the next

[5] Ibid.
[6] T. G. Belden and M. R. Belden, The Lengthening Shadow, The Life of Thomas J. Watson, Little, Brown, Boston, p. 309.
[7] Ibid., p. 298.   [8] Ibid.

few years IBM is said to have spent as much as $3 million annually in the preparation of its case.[9]

At approximately the same time a markedly similar case was being argued in the courts. The United Shoe Company, like IBM, refused to sell its equipment and required users to pay a rental based on utilization (a stated amount per shoe manufactured). This company also controlled a major share of the market. The Justice Department won its case against United Shoe in 1953 in the Massachusetts courts, and the decision was upheld by the U.S. Supreme Court in 1954. United Shoe was required to sell its equipment, to offer only short-term rentals, to avoid the purchase of second-hand equipment, and to license all its patents at reasonable royalties.

In 1956 IBM entered into a consent decree with the Justice Department. Many of the terms were virtually identical to those specified in the United Shoe case. The consent decree covered a number of subjects; the more important will be summarized briefly.

1. The Sale of Equipment

IBM was ordered to offer new equipment for sale "at prices and upon terms and conditions . . . not substantially more advantageous to IBM than the lease charges, terms and conditions for such machines." [10] The sales prices must "have a commercially reasonable relationship to the lease charges." [11]

The decree also specified that each user leasing equipment at the time be given an option to purchase his system at specified terms—the current sales price less 10% for each year of age, down to a minimum of 25% of the current price.

The purchase option terms were mandatory only for a period of 18 months, but the requirement that new equipment be sold was not limited in any way. However, the decree stated that from 1956 to 1966 (only) the burden of proof that sales prices were not "substantially more advantageous to IBM" would be on the company. In this respect IBM presumably has more freedom now than it did from 1956 through 1966, but the extent of the difference is uncertain.

[9] *Ibid.,* p. 304.
[10] IBM Consent Decree, Section IVa.
[11] *Ibid.,* Section IVc–2.

2. Used Equipment

The company was ordered to avoid purchasing used IBM machines except as trade-ins for other systems. Moreover, such equipment, when acquired, must be offered to second-hand dealers at 85% of the price computed by applying the purchase option formula described above.[12]

3. Service and Parts

The company was ordered to "offer to render, without separate charge, to purchasers . . . the same types of services other than maintenance and repair services, which it renders without separate charges to lessees of the same types of machines." [13] As for maintenance services, the company was required to "maintain and repair at reasonable and non-discriminatory prices and terms . . . [IBM] machines for the owners of such machines." [14] Finally, parts must be sold to all "at reasonable and non-discriminatory prices and terms." [15]

4. Lease Terms

From 1956 to 1966, IBM was "enjoined and restrained . . . from entering into any lease . . . for a period longer than one year, unless . . . terminable after one year by the lessee upon not more than three months' notice." [16] A lessee or purchaser may not be required to disclose the use to be made of the machine.[17] No user may be required to purchase IBM cards, but IBM may include in leases "provisions reasonably designed to prevent such interference with the normal and satisfactory operation and maintenance of such machines as will substantially increase the cost of maintenance thereof." [18] This latter provision is similar to that of the 1936 decision, but its value to IBM is considerably smaller, since the company's monopoly on high-quality card production has been broken (see item 6 below).

5. Service Bureau Business

By the terms of the consent decree IBM was required to maintain a separate (though wholly owned) company for service bureau business. This company (the Service Bureau Corporation) must keep separate books and set prices and rates based on its full costs. Moreover, IBM may not favor SBC over any other customer—in particular, another

[12] *Ibid.*, Section V. [13] *Ibid.*, Section VIa. [14] *Ibid.*, Section VIb.
[15] *Ibid.*, Section VIc. [16] *Ibid.*, Section VIIa. [17] *Ibid.*, Section VIIb.
[18] *Ibid.*, Section VIId.

service bureau — with regard to prices, conditions, or delivery schedules.[19]

6. Tabulating Cards

One of the goals of the Justice Department was to break IBM's monopoly power in the tabulating card business. According to one authority, the provisions designed to achieve this end were the most difficult for the company to accept.[20] There were three requirements. The company had to prove that any differentials in the price of cards were based only on "differences in the cost of manufacture, sale or delivery" or were "made to meet an equally low price of a competitor."[21] From 1956 through 1961 the company was required to sell up to thirty of its rotary presses each year on reasonable terms,[22] as well as any excess paper suitable for card manufacture.[23] Finally, a test was set. If IBM could not convince the court that "substantial competitive conditions existed in the manufacture, sale and distribution of tabulating cards," the company was to divest itself of any manufacturing capacity in excess of 50% of the total U.S. capacity before 1962.[24]

The provisions were effective. By the mid-1960's IBM was by no means a monopolist in the manufacture of tabulating cards. Moreover, the company has shown few signs of attempting to regain its former dominant status in this market.

7. Patents

IBM was required to offer patents under unrestricted, nonexclusive license to any applicant, subject only to the payment of a "reasonable" royalty. If an applicant and IBM disagree on the latter point, the court may be asked to determine the appropriate royalty, but the "burden of proof shall be on IBM to establish the reasonableness of the royalty requested by it."[25]

8. Duration

With the exceptions noted, the terms of the consent decree presumably apply permanently. However, a careful reading suggests that the first 10 years were considered the most crucial: some provisions reflect this directly, others by implication (e.g., the company was required to furnish detailed reports on sales, leases, and trade-ins for only 10 years).

---

[19] *Ibid.*, Section VIII.   [20] Belden and Belden, op. cit., p. 309.
[21] IBM Consent Decree, Section Xa–2.   [22] *Ibid.*, Section Xb.
[23] *Ibid.*, Section Xc.   [24] *Ibid.*, Section Xd.   [25] *Ibid.*, Section XIc.

Apparently the Justice Department felt that after a decade the situation should be re-examined. Whether or not this was originally intended, a new investigation was, in fact, begun in 1967. If the previous case is at all relevant, any final action (or a decision to take no action) is likely to come only after several years. Meanwhile, many of the provisions of the 1956 decree still apply, and IBM continues to show signs of an acute awareness of the Justice Department and the ever-present threat of new constraints.

D. THE ECONOMICS OF TIE-IN SALES

One of the major issues in the proceedings against IBM was the use of tie-in sales. Such procedures are illegal under the Clayton Act if they serve to substantially lessen competition. The general thesis holds that a seller with monopoly power over good A will attempt to obtain monopoly power over good B by requiring its purchase as a pre-requisite for the purchase of A. The tie-in sale is thus viewed as an attempt to extend monopoly power to more goods. Such an interpretation was given explicitly in the 1936 IBM case: the company was held to be taking advantage of its monopoly in the tabulating machine market to lessen competition in the market for tabulating cards.

Like many simple theses, this one contains some elements of truth. It is true that a seller with monopoly power over one good may find it highly advantageous to use tie-in sales. The actual advantage, however, lies in the ability to use the purchases of the secondary product as a device for metering the benefits that the user derives from the primary (monopolized) product.

A seller enjoying a substantial monopoly position will find it quite profitable to discriminate among buyers, charging each as much as he is willing to pay, if possible. But the antitrust laws make explicit price discrimination an exceedingly hazardous practice, and the danger increases with the seller's monopoly power. Hence monopolists often attempt to obtain the same effect in more subtle ways. In particular, they may engage in multipart pricing, offering the same *terms* to all, even though the actual *amounts* paid by customers will vary in ways not entirely related to costs. Such practices are also illegal, but their use is far more difficult to prove than outright discrimination.

As indicated earlier, before 1956 IBM in effect employed multipart pricing. Equipment was not sold—obviously an essential condition if users must pay amounts differing significantly from the relevant costs. Also, users were required to buy cards from IBM at (admittedly) highly profitable prices. Requirements for cards are presumably well correlated with the value received from equipment; thus IBM appears to have been using cards as a rough metering device in order to charge users partly on the basis of value received instead of purely on the basis of costs incurred.

This view suggests that, even if cards accounted for 25% of the company's profits, and even if IBM sold the majority of cards produced, equipment was still the important part of the company's business, since it was responsible indirectly for these results. Therefore the damage that would result from the Justice Department's victory in 1956 would depend essentially on subsequent answers to two questions: (1) how "commercially reasonable" must purchase prices be, and (2) could some other form of multipart pricing be as effective as the tie-in sales of cards?

It is interesting to note, in passing, that United Shoe's policy was similar in intent to that of IBM, although tie-in sales were not an essential component. Both firms used two-part pricing policies, with the user required to pay a fixed monthly fee plus a surcharge based on utilization. United Shoe charged for utilization explicitly by means of a fixed royalty per shoe, whereas IBM did so indirectly, in the form of a surcharge (high price) per card utilized.

Economic theory suggests that a seller's use of tie-in sales is a symptom of monopoly power over the primary product, not an attempt to extend this power to another product. The prohibition of such practices is thus consistent with the intent of antitrust legislation, although the rationale is at least partly faulty. However, the prohibition may not serve to reduce the seller's monopoly power at all, even though the supposed extension of this power to a second good is precluded. Thus the IBM consent decree apparently had little effect on the company's position in the computer industry. More important, it did not seem to hamper the company seriously in the exercise of the monopoly power that it already had. As shown in the next section, extra-use charges proved a convenient alternative to tie-in sales.

E. EXTRA-USE CHARGES AS A FORM OF MULTIPART PRICING

Shortly after the consent decree became final, IBM began to offer equipment for outright sale. Rental customers were allowed to use equipment during a designated "prime shift" for the basic monthly rental charge, with all maintenance performed when and as needed without extra charge. However, for each hour of use outside the prime shift a payment of 40% of $1/176$ of the basic monthly rental was required (this surcharge included the cost of any additional remedial maintenance needed).

Initially the prime shift was restricted to 8 hours out of no more than 9 consecutive hours on each of 5 designated days each week. In 1958 the terms were broadened slightly to allow 40 hours over 6 days per week, and beginning in 1959 equipment could be used during any 176 hours per month without incurring extra-use charges.

The surcharge remained at 40% of $1/176$ of the basic monthly rental charge until 1964. Early in that year General Electric announced that its new family of computers (the 600 series) would be made available under a "one-class" rental plan—for a basic monthly charge the user would be entitled to unlimited use, extra charges being incurred only for maintenance.

Shortly after the GE announcement, IBM dropped its extra-use rate from 40% to 30%. The new policy was supposed to apply to all equipment, including models not yet being delivered. However, in October, 1964, the company announced that the surcharge for third-generation equipment (the 360 series) would be even lower than previously indicated—only 10% of the average cost at 176 hours. The reasons given were somewhat vague:

When the 360 was announced on April 7 there was little information on the expected customer usage patterns and applications. Analysis of the growing System/360 backlog on planned customer use now makes it possible to set additional use rates which reflect the improved price performance achieved by advances in system design and technology.[26]

Clearly IBM's extra-use charges have fallen. But why were they imposed in the first place? And what accounts for their decline?

One explanation attributes extra-use charges to the increased main-

[26] *EDP Weekly*, Dec. 7, 1964, p. 11.

tenance costs associated with high utilization. Since maintenance has traditionally been included in IBM rental contracts, rental costs include two components: maintenance and "pure rent." It is not surprising that total rental costs are greater for high-utilization installations than for others. The more important question concerns the relationship between "pure rent" and utilization.

Table 8–1 provides evidence on this point. It shows the ratio of "pure rent" for three-shift operation to that for one-shift operation for each of several types of equipment over the period 1958–1967 (the details of the calculations are given in the footnotes).[27] The conclusion is obvious: during the period from 1957 through 1965, high-utilization customers were required to pay considerably greater rents than low-utilization customers, and these differences were substantially greater than any differences attributable directly to maintenance costs.

Of course the discrepancies might have reflected a higher rate of depreciation for equipment subjected to heavy use. Note, however, that the rate at which equipment depreciates can be decreased, at least within bounds, by greater maintenance effort. For example, periodic replacement of assemblies with new components, either as part of a preventive maintenance plan or upon failure, can serve to keep a system almost as good as new (a great many DC-3 aircraft are still flying after 30 years in service). Beginning in October, 1965, IBM explicitly stated that its maintenance procedures would be designed to keep equipment equivalent to new, and charges were simultaneously increased. This suggests that previously machines had been allowed to depreciate relative to equivalent ones newly manufactured. Even so, was the depreciation a function of usage or age? IBM's own maintenance rates at the time for customer-owned equipment were based on the age, not the past use of machines. However, this may have been due simply to the fact that accurate and unbiased data on past usage cannot always be obtained for customer-owned equipment. The situa-

---

[27] The ratios shown for peripheral units tend to be smaller than those for other units. This is easily explained. The ratio of total rental for three-shift relative to one-shift operation is the same for all types of equipment (it is apparently not worthwhile to adopt a more selective policy). But the ratio of three-shift to one-shift maintenance coverage is typically higher for peripherals than for other units, since maintenance is more labor-intensive and is affected more by usage. Thus the ratio of pure rental for three-shift versus one-shift operation is smaller for such devices.

TABLE 8–1. 'Pure Rental'': Three-Shift versus One-Shift Operation Selected IBM Systems, 1958–1967 *

Period and System	Ratio †,1	Period and System	Ratio †,1
1958–1959		**1962–1963**	
709 System [2,5,6]		*7074 System* [2,5,9]	
Central processor (709/1)	1.80	Central processor	
Core storage (738)	1.80	(7104/1)	1.80
Power supply (741/2)	1.80	Core storage (7301/4)	1.80
Data synchronizer (766/1)	1.80	Tape drive (729/6)	1.60
Tape controller (755/1)	1.80	**1963–1964**	
Drum (733/1)	1.80		
Tape drive (729/1)	1.31	*7010 System* [2,5,10]	
Card reader (711/2)	1.57	Processing unit (7114/1)	1.80
Card punch (721/1)	1.49	Console (1415/1)	1.80
Printer (716/1)	1.49	Disk (1405/1)	1.82
1959–1960		**1964–1965**	
7070 System [2,5,6]		*1401 System* [3,5,11]	
Central processor		Complete system	
(7601/1)	1.79	(actual configuration)	1.60
Core storage (7301/1)	1.81	*7040/7044 Systems* [3,5,11]	
Disk (7300/1)	1.51	Complete system (actual	
Tape drive (729/2)	1.31	configuration;	
Card reader (7500/1)	1.65	1–7040 plus 1–7044)	1.62
Card punch (7550/1)	1.73	**1965–1966**	
Printer (7400/1)	1.74		
1960–1961		*1130 System* [4,5,12]	
		1130 computer	
1620 System [2,5,7]		(1131/2B)	1.18
1620 computer		**1966–1967**	
(1620/1)	1.73		
1961–1962		*360/50 System* [4,13]	
		Central processor and	
1410 System [2,5,8]		core (2050H)	1.12
Central processor		Disk drive (2311)	1.16
(1411/3)	1.79	Tape drive (2403/1)	1.04
Disk (1301/2)	1.72	Card read-punch (2540)	1.12
Tape drive (729/4)	1.60		
Card read-punch			
(1402/2)	1.65		
Printer (1403/1)	1.43		

* Source: IBM GSA Schedules, 1957–1967.
† Notes:
[1] Ratio shown is PR_3/PR_1, where PR_3 = pure rent, 3-shift operation = $R_3 - M_3$; PR_1 = pure rent, 1-shift operation = $R_1 - M_1$; R_3 = total rental charges at 528 hours/month (=3 × 176); R_1 = total

tion would naturally be different for IBM-owned machines. The company would know the previous history of utilization, and additional (future) maintenance costs attributable to high (past) utilization would be borne by IBM, as long as the equipment continued on rental. For pre-1965 maintenance policies this relationship may have been of some importance, and differences in "pure rent" based on utilization may have been justified as a reflection of future maintenance costs for equipment that IBM intended to continue to rent out. This situation would not prevail, however, for equipment that the company intended to sell in the near future.

We are left with an ambiguous situation. Some differences in "pure rent" during the period 1956–1965 could have been cost-based. It seems most unlikely, however, that differences of 80% could be attributed entirely to accelerated depreciation resulting from high utilization. Moreover, the dramatic decreases in apparent response to a competitive threat are difficult to explain on this basis. But IBM's policies are highly consistent with a relatively simple economic explanation: extra-use charges were employed as a form of multipart pricing, replacing the previous strategy in which card use provided a surrogate for value received.

There is no need to repeat here the discussion in Chapter 3 of this type of three-part pricing policy. It is interesting to note, however, that the leading producer of copier machines uses a similar policy, although it is stated in different terms. A customer renting a copier pays a given amount per copy made, subject to a minimum monthly payment. This policy is shown in Fig. 8–1a; note that it is a three-part policy of the same type as that used by IBM, shown in Fig. 8–1b.

Notes to Table 8–1. (continued)

rental charges at 176 hours/month (= basic monthly rental); M_3 = total maintenance charges for 3-shift operation; and M_1 = maintenance cost for 1-shift operation (= basic monthly maintenance).

[2] $R_3 = 1.8R_1$.   [3] $R_3 = 1.6R_1$.   [4] $R_3 = 1.2R_1$.

[5] Maintenance charges are for equipment 0–36 months old.

[6] M_3 = basic monthly charge plus twice the charge for an additional 40-hour work week.

[7] M_3 = charge for first 176 hours of use plus twice the charge for each additional 176 hours of use.

[8] $M_3 = 1.8M_1$ for central processor and core storage and = $3M_1$ for tape drive.

[9] $M_3 = 3M_1$.   [10] $M_3 = 1.6M_1$.

[11] Configurations used were those installed at the RAND Corporation.

[12] $M_3 = 1.45M_1$.

[13] $M_3 = 1.3M_1$ for central processor and core and = $1.6M_1$ for other components shown.

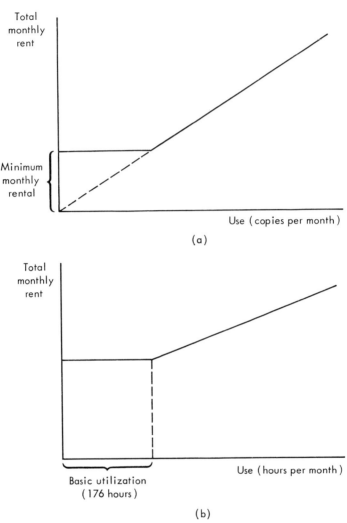

FIGURE 8-1. Three part pricing policy used by (a) manufacturer of copiers and (b) IBM.

The extra-use charges imposed by IBM in the period 1956–1965 provide strong evidence that the company enjoyed considerable monopoly power in the computer industry and took advantage of it in spite of the consent decree. But the decrease in surcharges since 1965 constitutes equally strong evidence of increased competition in the industry (in fact, this may be the only clear evidence of such change). Despite IBM's major share of the market, the computer-manufacturing industry appears to be far more competitive than it was in 1956. This development may be attributable to some of the provisions of the consent decree, in particular, those concerning the licensing of patents. It must be emphasized, however, that the effort directed against tie-in sales was primarily misdirected; extra-use charges appear to have accomplished the same purpose adequately.

F. PURCHASE PRICES AND EXTRA-USE CHARGES

As indicated earlier, IBM's reluctance to sell equipment before 1956 can be considered a reflection of its monopoly position at the time — a position best exploited by renting equipment and engaging in multipart pricing. In the consent decree the company was required to sell its equipment at prices "commercially reasonable" in relation to rental charges. But which rental charges, those paid by low-utilization customers or high-utilization customers? And what relationship is, in fact, commercially reasonable? The complexity of the issue suggests that IBM may have enjoyed considerable latitude in meeting the terms imposed. It is thus interesting to consider the most profitable strategy for the company in the absence of any constraint at all.

As shown in Chapter 3, the most desirable arrangement would use the purchase price as a fourth component of the multipart pricing policy. This is illustrated in Figs. 8–2a and b, in which the purchase price is stated as an equivalent monthly cost (we defer for now a discussion of such an equivalence). As shown earlier, the optimal policy would involve a purchase price equivalent to the rental paid by high-utilization customers; and only they would find it clearly advantageous to buy equipment. Rental would thus be preferable for the majority of customers. Note that in this situation there is an intimate relationship between extra-use charges and the relative desirability of rent over purchase for low-utilization customers. In the case shown in Fig. 8–2b extra-use charges are lower, and purchase is relatively more attractive for the low-utilization (e.g., one-shift) user than in the situation illustrated in Fig. 8–2a.

The evidence appears to be consistent with this explanation. During the period 1956–1965 the majority of users continued to rent equip-

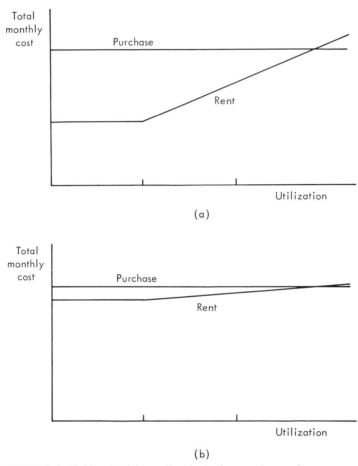

FIGURE 8-2. Multipart pricing policy, including purchase price as a component.

ment. Also, there is some indication that those purchasing equipment were in fact high-utilization customers. Utilization and system cost are usually positively correlated (in the fiscal year 1966, use by federal government agencies averaged 495 hours per month for systems costing over $3 million but only 248 hours per month for those costing less than $250,000).[28] And at least one set of data indicates that a relatively high proportion of large-scale systems are eventually pur-

[28] Inventory of Automatic Data Processing Equipment in the Federal Government, July, 1966, p. 15.

chased. Estimates for six IBM systems first delivered between 1960 and 1961 are as follows: [29]

System	Percentage Purchased by 1965
Small-scale	
1401	16%
1410	17
1620	22
Medium-scale	
7070	45
Large-scale	
7080	55
7090	58

There is relatively little evidence to support a corollary of this analysis. As indicated, a diminution of extra-use charges should be accompanied by a higher proportion of purchased systems relative to those rented, *ceteris paribus*. However, except for federal government agencies, there was no clear evidence of such a change from 1965 to 1967. To some extent this may be attributed to a counteracting influence. One of the advantages of rental is the accompanying pressure on the manufacturer to maintain and improve both hardware and software. This pressure is more important for newly developed systems than for older, well-tested ones. The decline in extra-use charges was concurrent with the introduction of new, third-generation equipment, and many users (quite correctly) believed that much of the new hardware and software might require a great deal of attention before performance levels promised by manufacturers would be reached. Thus a force leading to increased purchase (the decline in extra-use charges) was accompanied by a counterforce leading to decreased purchase (the problems associated with third-generation hardware and software).

Figure 8–3 shows the percentage purchased by 1965 for sixteen IBM systems delivered between 1955 and 1965. The hypothesized relationship is clearly present.[30] If the analysis given here is correct,

[29] *EDP Industry and Market Report*, Oct. 8, 1965, p. 3.
[30] There is, however, an alternative (and perhaps more persuasive) explanation for the results; it is discussed in Section G.

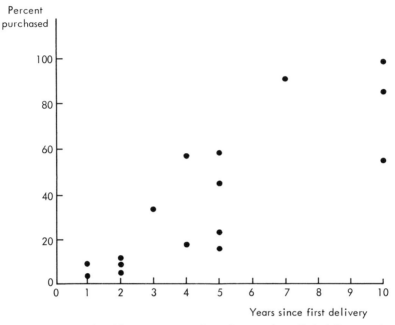

FIGURE 8–3. Relationship between number of years since first delivery and percentage of machines purchased, for sixteen IBM systems. Source: *EDP Industry and Market Report,* Oct. 8, 1965, p. 3.

there should be a similar relationship for third-generation equipment, but the percentage purchased for any given number of years since first delivery should be greater than that implied by the rough relationship in Fig. 8–3.

G. CHANGES IN PRICES AND RENTAL CHARGES

As described in detail in Chapter 9, the computer industry has been marked by rapid technological change: the cost of producing a computer with given hardware capability has fallen between 20% and 25% per year. This suggests that the rental charged for older equipment should decrease over time in order to keep such equipment competitive with newer systems. If no costs were associated with the substitution of one computer for another, systems of comparable effectiveness would command equal monthly rentals (unless a manufacturer chose to have no rental customers at all for some of his systems).

The facts are greatly at odds with this simple view. By and large the monthly rental charged for a given piece of equipment remains the same throughout the period over which it is offered for lease. The relationship has been most dramatic for IBM equipment. A comparison of the basic monthly rental charge for a specified piece of equipment shown in one GSA schedule with that in the following year's schedule provides one observation of a price change or lack thereof. A total of 360 observations of this type was collected for IBM equipment rented during the period 1957–1967; [31] 207 of these observations pertained to equipment no longer being produced. In only 12 cases were there changes (9 increases and 3 decreases) in the basic monthly rental charged, and all of these occurred early in the period during which the equipment was being produced.

Although other manufacturers have altered rental charges, most changes have been one-time adjustments to competitive conditions, not gradual reductions over time. Some particularly striking examples occurred in 1965 and 1966, when rental charges for General Electric's 400 series, 600 series, and Datanet-30 systems were reduced. Some of the major changes were the following:

Item	Percentage Reduction
415 central processor with 4K memory	17%
425 central processor with 8K memory	17
435 central processor with 16K memory	10
600 series single processor	37
600 series dual processor	28
600 series 2-microsecond memory module	10
600 series 1-microsecond memory module	32
Datanet-30 with 4K memory	47

The reductions in 600-series charges were admittedly designed to meet a competitive threat. According to a company source, the rates were lowered ". . . to meet the substantial price reductions represented

[31] The items included model 729 tape drives, model 1405 disk drives, and components of the 650, 705, 1401, 1620, and 7090 computer systems.

in IBM's new System/360 Model 65." [32] This statement also illustrates the difficulty of identifying effective price changes. Any manufacturer can avoid explicit changes by simply introducing "new" models that differ from old ones primarily in price (and model number). More subtle changes involve, for example, improved performance for given models or better software support.

All that can be said categorically is that IBM appears to avoid *explicit* price and rental changes whenever possible. Several explanations for this phenomenon appear to be plausible. First, increased reliability and software support may make older equipment as effective overall as newly designed models of comparable cost. Second, IBM may be particularly wary of Justice Department disapproval of price cuts, preferring to eventually scrap its used systems rather than to reduce prices to keep the equipment competitive. Alternatively, the maximum-profit position may involve prices at which some of the used systems are not rented. Finally, the actual policy may reflect attempts to engage in discriminatory pricing.

In this connection IBM did not significantly reduce the rental charges on second-generation equipment after third-generation machines had been widely installed. A new customer had little reason to pay more for a second-generation computer than for a third-generation machine of comparable power (taking into account hardware, software, reliability, etc.). But customers already renting second-generation machines were often willing to pay more in order to avoid (at least for a while) the substantial costs associated with the conversion of their programs to a radically different system. The demand for second-generation equipment was thus probably rather inelastic over a range of prices above that of comparable third-generation equipment.

There are also differences between the domestic and foreign markets for computers. The U.S. government imposes restrictions on the sales of third-generation computers to countries in the Soviet bloc (and, from time to time, to other countries). Within this particular part of the foreign market there is no competition from newly designed U.S. systems, leading to a demand for used equipment differing from that in this country. The optimal policy for a manufacturer may thus be to keep up the price of used equipment, eventually selling much of it

---

[32] *EDP Weekly,* June 21, 1965, p. 14.

to customers precluded from purchasing third-generation U.S. systems. Another factor may be relevant—some argue that many foreign users do not have the experience and sophistication to benefit fully from third-generation systems, so that the value of an older system relative to that of a newer one is greater for these customers than for their more experienced counterparts here. It is thus widely believed that IBM will concentrate its marketing effort for returned second-generation machines on foreign customers.

For the computer industry in general, the first set of across-the-board changes in terms came in late 1966 and early 1967. Most manufacturers increased rental charges from 2% to 5%, but there was no consistent pattern with regard to purchase prices. Some of the changes made were as follows: [33]

Equipment	Percentage Change in Purchase Price	Percentage Change in Basic Monthly Rental
IBM third-generation equipment	−3%	+3%
IBM second-generation equipment	None	None
GE 400/600 series	None	+4
Honeywell series 200	+2 to 4	+2 to 4
SDS 9 series	+5	+5
SDS Sigma-7 series	+3 to 5	+3 to 5
SDS Sigma-2 series	None	+5
UNIVAC central processors and memories	None	+5
UNIVAC peripheral devices	−2	+3

The reasons given by company spokesmen for changes in prices and/or rental charges vary considerably, as the following quotations indicate:

The reductions were made possible by improvements in the design of modular solid-state elements and circuitry and by advances in automated inspection and test techniques. . . .[34]

The changes resulted as part of a periodic review of the company's pricing structure. . . .[35]

Increased software expenditures . . . combined with the increasing costs

---

[33] Source: *EDP Weekly*, various dates.

[34] Bunker-Ramo Corp., explaining major reductions in purchase and rental terms for series 200 input/output equipment, *EDP Weekly*, June 21, 1965.

[35] UNIVAC, explaining its changes in rental and purchase terms, *EDP Weekly*, Apr. 17, 1967, p. 6.

of obtaining money to finance the rapid growth of our deferred-income business, has necessitated the selected price increases.[36]

The decrease resulted from substantial reduction in calibration and testing times . . . and the introduction of automated manufacturing processes. . . .[37]

The decrease is a result of lower manufacturing costs, and the company's desire to broaden the product's market.[38]

The decrease was made possible by continuing economies in production.[39]

Can any sense be made of these changes and the justifications given? To some extent the rise in rental charges reflected increased maintenance costs due to both higher wages per man-hour and the higher level of maintenance support required to keep equipment "as good as new." Variations in purchase prices are harder to explain, and the statements made by company spokesmen provide little help. Again it is clear that IBM does not like to change terms explicitly, either individually or collectively. Apparently many of the other companies follow IBM's lead. The October, 1966, changes made by IBM may thus have opened the door for adjustments by other companies — adjustments based on a variety of causes, some of them unique to a given manufacturer or system.

It is difficult to tell whether or not the events of 1966 represent a change in the industry's behavior. The answer depends to some extent on IBM's perception of the attitude of the Justice Department. The company appears to believe that explicit price changes (especially reductions) may be interpreted as unfairly competitive behavior; thus such changes are avoided. Since other companies tend to adopt IBM's policies in these matters, a pattern of relative stability in regard to explicit prices has become predominant in the industry. In any event, as suggested earlier, variations in the actual cost of equipment relative to its effectiveness are many and frequent. The performance of a system is typically increased during its life, often by expanding the number and types of devices that can be attached to it. Model

[36] Honeywell, explaining increases in both prices and rental charges for series 200 equipment, *EDP Weekly,* Oct. 10, 1966, p. 13.

[37] Adage, Inc., explaining a one-third reduction in the prices of analog-to-digital converters, *EDP Weekly,* Oct. 10, 1966, p. 6.

[38] Honeywell, explaining a 30% decrease in price for some of its special-purpose computers, *Data Processing Magazine.*

[39] Scientific Data Systems, explaining a 35% decrease in the price of its model 92, *EDP Weekly,* Feb. 7, 1966, p. 8.

number changes, extra types of support, and "special arrangements" with regard to, for example, extra-use charges, provide other methods for adjusting prices indirectly.

The behavior of purchase prices over time differs somewhat from that typical of rental values. Nominal prices of equipment typically remain constant from year to year, but purchase options provide a method for buying machines at prices that fall over time. This was especially true for second-generation systems, since the purchase option discount often depended on the age of the machine, not the number of months that it had been rented by the current user. Thus the effective purchase prices of such systems decreased with age while rental charges remained roughly constant; as a result, users tended to purchase an increasing number of systems over time. This provides an additional explanation for the data shown in Fig. 8-3.

The general pricing pattern in the computer industry before 1965 thus involved relatively constant rental charges accompanied by decreasing effective purchase prices via options to buy. This strategy induced users to buy older equipment, leaving mostly newer machines in the manufacturer's inventory of rental equipment. As described in Section E, however, IBM announced in October, 1965, a major policy change designed to substantially alter the traditional pattern. Henceforth all equipment was to be maintained in such a way that it would be "as good as new." Maintenance charges for customer-owned equipment were increased substantially (having doubled since 1963, according to one source [40]), although rental charges were unaffected. Moreover, the purchase option was revised to allow the customer to apply only 40–60% of first-year rental payments toward the purchase price.

The change was generally interpreted as a move on IBM's part to encourage rental. One authority felt that, as a result, 80–85% of System/360 users would rent equipment "for the long haul." [41] An alternative explanation attributes the change to a prediction of reduced technological change. Before 1965 it seldom paid to maintain equipment for a really long life, since technological obsolescence could be expected to reduce its value rapidly. If the pace of such change seems

---

[40] *Computers and Automation,* December, 1965, p. 8.
[41] *Ibid.*

likely to decrease, it makes more sense to minimize physical deprecia-tion.[42] Moreover, the net value of the equipment may remain relatively constant, with software improvements offsetting almost all the advan-tages associated with competitive hardware of improved design.[43] The revised purchase option policy adopted by IBM seems to reflect such an expectation, although it is important to note that the company has not assumed any long-term obligations in this connection: the actual purchase price for installed equipment can be set at any level the company chooses upon no more than 30 days' notice.

H. PURCHASE PRICES, RENTAL CHARGES, AND MAINTENANCE COSTS

As indicated earlier, according to economic theory a manufacturer will offer a component or system for purchase at a price equal to the present value of expected future net rental charges, calculated by using a dis-count rate appropriate for the risk involved. This is illustrated in Figs. 8–4a and b (for convenience we ignore temporarily the effect of utili-zation on rent and/or maintenance costs). The maximum total rent that can be charged at any point of time will depend on the cost of competi-tive equipment. This amount, shown by curve TR, will probably de-cline over time as indicated in Fig. 8–4a, unless software unique to such systems is increased substantially to offset the technological advances reflected in the price and capabilities of new equipment. Maintenance costs may or may not increase over time. In any event, at some point the pure rent (total rent less maintenance and other costs), shown by curve PR, will equal zero (at $t = t^*$); this is the end of the economic life of the system, although its physical life may be much longer. Figure 8–4b illustrates a situation in which the manufacturer maintains the total rental value of the system by increasing expenditures on mainte-nance and other types of support. Here too the economic life of the system terminates at time t^*.

---

[42] Assume, for example, that a given dollar cost is required to keep a machine 95% ef-fective instead of letting it depreciate to the point at which it is 90% effective. If tech-nological obsolescence is rapid, the value of the equipment will decline, and the fixed maintenance cost may exceed the value of the improvement. If, on the other hand, the value of the equipment remains high, the maintenance cost may be justified.

[43] An alternative assertion involves an expectation of technological improvements pro-ceeding at a constant rate but holds that proven software is more important (and hence more valuable) for the more complex third-generation equipment.

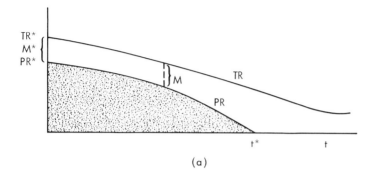

(a)

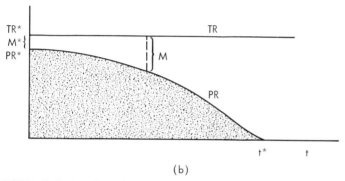

(b)

FIGURE 8-4. Relationships between purchase price, rental charges, and maintenance costs.

According to this view, the purchase price should equal the present value of the pure rental figures. If a zero discount rate is utilized, price will equal the shaded area under the pure rent curve; if a positive rate is used, the present value will be smaller — in general, the higher the relevant discount rate (i.e., the greater the risk), the smaller will be the present value and hence the appropriate price.

At any point of time it is possible to observe directly only the current values of TR, M, and PR (e.g., TR^*, M^*, and PR^* for $t = 0$ in Figs. 8-4a and b), plus the current purchase price. Needless to say, this is not enough information to impute the shape of the PR curve, let alone that of the TR curve. The area under the PR curve will be related not only to the purchase price, which is known, but also to the degree of risk assumed by the manufacturer, which is unknown. Even if the risk (discount rate) were known, the economic life (t^*) could not be determined, since many curves with different horizontal intercepts can enclose equal areas.

Despite these objections, it is common practice to divide current purchase price by monthly rental. The result is sometimes termed the equipment's "economic life," "breakeven point," or "payout period," but we will use the more satisfactory designation *purchase/rent ratio*. The almost universal practice is to use the basic monthly rental charge (i.e., TR, not PR) when computing the ratio.

To investigate the relationships among purchase price, rental charges, and maintenance costs, a sample of 483 devices in production during 1967 was analyzed.[44] For each device the following information was obtained:

TR_1 = total rental charge per month, including full maintenance coverage, for one-shift (176-hour) operation;

TR_3 = total rental charge per month, including full maintenance coverage, for three-shift (528-hour) operation;

M_1 = charge for full maintenance coverage for 1 month at one-shift (176-hour) operation;

M_3 = charge for full maintenance coverage for 1 month at three-shift (528-hour) operation;

PR_1 = pure rental cost for one-shift operation,

    = $TR_1 - M_1$;

PR_3 = pure rental cost for three-shift operation,

    = $TR_3 - M_3$; and

P = purchase price.

All data were based on figures given in GSA price schedules for the period July 1, 1966, through June 30, 1967. For all equipment but that produced by Sperry Rand (UNIVAC), pure rental costs were computed from quoted (total) rental and maintenance costs. For UNIVAC equipment, total rental costs were computed by adding maintenance charges to the quoted (pure) rental costs.[45]

Table 8–2 shows the composition of the sample. Note that in many

---

[44] The analysis was performed by Nancy Jacob of the University of California, Irvine. Any errors in the interpretation of the results are, of course, the responsibility of the present author.

[45] Needless to say, some unusual figures were obtained. For example, CDC does not require extra-use charges for peripheral devices, presumably on the grounds that their use is correlated with that of the central processor, for which there is a substantial extra-use charge. But maintenance costs for such devices are related to utilization. This im-

TABLE 8–2. Number of Devices, by Manufacturer

Device *	Bur.	CDC	GE	Hon.	IBM	NCR	RCA	SDS	UNV	All Manufac- turers
CPU/wc	0	7	13	25	43	1	17	0	10	116
CPU/nc	3	5	7	0	9	4	0	14	5	47
Core	7	8	13	0	5	5	0	6	12	56
Ctrlr	2	7	8	3	14	4	13	3	17	71
Tape	5	4	8	7	27	6	8	2	9	76
Card	5	1	7	4	11	3	7	3	6	47
Print	4	2	3	3	2	5	6	2	2	29
Drum	0	1	4	2	2	0	2	0	5	16
Disk	5	4	2	0	5	0	0	2	0	18
Mass st	0	0	2	0	1	3	1	0	0	7
All devices	31	39	67	44	119	31	54	32	66	483

* Key:
CPU/wc: central processor with core storage.
CPU/nc: central processor with no core storage.
Core: core storage unit.
Ctrlr: controller unit.
Tape: tape drive.
Card: card reader, punch, or reader-punch.
Print: line printer.
Drum: magnetic drum unit.
Disk: Magnetic disk drive.
Mass st: mass storage unit (e.g., data cell or CRAM).

categories the number of devices was extremely small or even zero. Note also the disparities in the distributions (1) of devices among manufacturers and (2) of manufacturers by device. These disparities suggest that some of the apparent differences among manufacturers may be attributable to differences among devices, and vice versa.

Table 8–3 shows the average ratio of price to total one-shift rental (i.e., P/TR_1) for each category studied (an asterisk signifies that no device was included). Table 8–4 indicates the average ratio of price to pure one-shift rental (i.e., P/PR_1) for each category. In each table

plies that the pure rental cost for three-shift operation is lower than that for one-shift operation. The result is correct, but it suggests that, for some purposes, to consider components rather than overall systems may be dangerous. Similar complications arise with other measures. Thus the results in this section should be considered as primarily presumptive evidence for or against the hypotheses tested.

TABLE 8-3. Average values of P/TR_1

Device	Bur.	CDC	GE	Hon.	IBM	NCR	RCA	SDS	UNV	All Manufacturers
CPU/wc	*	37.87	50.39	44.88	42.99	45.00	50.00	*	38.19	44.55
CPU/nc	48.00	35.96	44.05	*	41.97	62.06	*	31.57	38.95	40.32
Core	48.00	38.37	43.15	*	46.18	46.73	*	33.98	42.66	42.57
Ctrlr	48.00	43.06	42.40	44.30	49.20	45.53	50.03	35.86	39.33	44.61
Tape	48.00	45.86	40.90	44.70	48.67	41.35	47.01	37.50	37.05	44.87
Card	49.73	32.84	42.27	44.00	53.46	55.55	50.03	36.00	33.42	46.10
Print	56.29	44.60	45.33	44.20	45.05	47.60	50.00	36.06	31.18	46.40
Drum	*	50.91	44.45	43.98	43.33	*	50.00	*	42.00	44.59
Disk	50.35	38.96	47.56	*	41.21	*	*	36.30	*	43.41
Mass st	*	*	46.53	*	48.75	42.25	50.43	*	*	45.57
All devices	49.73	40.14	44.61	44.64	46.05	48.02	49.57	33.79	38.84	44.20

* No device included in this category.

overall averages by manufacturer and by device are indicated, as is the average value for the sample as a whole.[46]

The average ratio of price to total rental for the sample was 44.20; this is somewhat higher than the value of 40.82 obtained by Knight [47]

---

[46] The summary columns show weighted averages. Let R_{ij} be the ratio in row i, column j, of either Table 8-3 or Table 8-4, and N_{ij} the number in row i, column j, of Table 8-2. Then the row sums are:

$$S_i = \sum_j N_{ij}R_{ij} \Big/ \sum_j N_{ij}$$

the column sums are

$$S_j = \sum_i N_{ij}R_{ij} \Big/ \sum_i N_{ij}$$

and the overall average is

$$A = \sum_i \sum_j N_{ij}R_{ij} \Big/ \sum_i \sum_j N_{ij}$$

[47] Kenneth E. Knight, "A Study of Technological Innovation—The Evolution of Digital Computers," doctoral dissertation, Carnegie Institute of Technology, November, 1963, p. IV–17. The slight discrepancy between the results is hardly surprising, since Knight's data weighted components differently.

TABLE 8-4. Average Values of P/PR_1

Device	Bur.	CDC	GE	Hon.	IBM	NCR	RCA	SDS	UNV	All Manufac- turers
			Manufacturer							All
CPU/wc	*	42.24	56.85	48.16	45.00	46.71	52.08	*	46.17	47.99
CPU/nc	58.17	39.06	46.22	*	43.29	70.86	*	37.72	46.00	45.20
Core	49.40	42.03	45.50	*	49.06	47.39	*	41.08	46.00	45.61
Ctrlr	52.90	49.51	44.87	49.08	51.06	49.46	52.11	41.96	45.97	48.68
Tape	59.89	58.90	46.60	55.47	55.78	52.31	54.67	50.47	46.08	53.54
Card	67.28	39.29	52.88	57.95	64.14	65.40	58.17	46.68	46.08	57.51
Print	71.40	62.56	58.79	58.34	51.12	56.15	58.14	47.04	46.09	57.94
Drum	*	59.57	50.01	51.45	52.64	*	58.14	*	45.98	50.88
Disk	60.19	43.69	61.47	*	45.46	*	*	44.50	*	50.83
Mass st	*	*	55.24	*	58.71	51.11	54.82	*	*	53.91
All devices	59.63	46.36	50.24	51.12	50.33	55.13	54.21	41.39	46.04	50.23

* No device included in this category.

for a group of 51 computer systems introduced between 1950 and 1963, although it is consistent with his finding that the ratio appeared to be increasing over time.[48] The average ratio of price to pure rental for this sample was, of course, considerably higher than that of price to total rental—50.23 compared with 44.20.

Tables 8-3 and 8-4 show that there are considerable differences among manufacturers. UNIVAC separates maintenance from rental charges and prices virtually all equipment at 46 times the pure rental charge. Honeywell and RCA generally price their equipment at a constant multiple of the total rental charge. Other manufacturers seem to use more complex rules.

The range of values is considerable. The average purchase/rent ratio for Burroughs equipment, at one end of the spectrum, is approximately 45% greater than that for SDS equipment, at the other end. The firms can be classified roughly into three groups:

1. Low purchase/rent ratios: SDS, UNIVAC, and CDC.
2. Average purchase/rent ratios: GE, Honeywell, and IBM.
3. High purchase/rent ratios: NCR, RCA, and Burroughs.

The differences among manufacturers may be an artifact of this particular sample. On the other hand, they may be due to real differ-

[48] However, the increase was not statistically significant.

ences in attitudes regarding equipment depreciation. The relationship between financial position and purchase/rent ratios is not clear: the two largest companies in the industry (GE and IBM) fall in the middle group, whereas the two smallest (SDS and CDC) accept lower-than-average purchase/rent ratios. There is a widely held belief that IBM has consciously encouraged users to lease equipment rather than purchase it outright in order to take advantage of this company's low cost of capital. This strategy is supposed to work to the detriment of small firms (such as SDS, whose president is a strong believer in the hypothesis), which often must pay a high cost for capital.[49] The argument has some merit, but it confuses cause with effect. If market mechanisms are working reasonably well, a firm's cost of capital will depend on the prospects of the investment for which the capital is to be used. The riskier these prospects, the greater will be the capital's (nominal) cost. If SDS must pay more for capital than IBM, the reason is that investors consider it more risky to put their money in SDS equipment than in IBM equipment. And if the investors are right, then SDS should be willing to sell equipment at a price that is lower relative to current rental charges than that set by IBM.[50]

Officers of both SDS and CDC have complained periodically that outright sales are too rare in relation to leases. As these data show, both companies appear to have attempted to correct the situation in part by offering low purchase prices relative to rental charges. On the other hand, Sperry Rand (UNIVAC) has apparently not been beset with critical cash-flow problems; and, at the other end of the spectrum, few complaints of excessive outright sales have been made by officers of NCR, RCA, and Burroughs.

Differences in purchase/rent ratios among devices appear to be much smaller than those among manufacturers. In general, the ratio of price to pure rent is higher for mechanical devices than for elec-

---

[49] In a speech given in 1965, Max Palevsky, the president of SDS, asserted, "IBM's main strength is their cash flow, which is approximately $600 million a year. With this financial edge, IBM has structured the business so that leasing is the preferred method of acquiring computers, and they have made the leasing business one in which the terms are more difficult for the leaser of equipment than anywhere in American enterprise" (*EDP Weekly,* June 14, 1965, p. 8).

[50] Of course investors may be wrong: prospects for a particular company may be better than they suppose. This misapprehension may reflect a lack of communication between investors and the company's officers. In any event, such a situation (if it really exists) poses difficult problems for the executives of a firm.

tronic components. This is consistent with the historical pattern of technological development in the industry: advances have come more slowly in the areas upon which peripheral devices are primarily dependent than in the area of electronic circuitry. However, another explanation must be considered. Differences in the ratios of price to total rent, though present, are relatively small. But the proportion of total rent attributable to maintenance differs widely – the more mechanical (relative to electronic) components in the device, the larger is the ratio. The values for the components in this sample were as follows:

Category	Maintenance Cost as a Percentage of Total Rental [51]
Core storage	6.7%
Central processors with core storage	7.2
Controllers	8.4
Central processors with no core storage	10.8
Drums	12.4
Disks	14.6
Mass storage devices	15.5
Tape drives	16.2
Card readers and punches	19.8
Printers	20.0

In general, prices appear to be related more closely to total rental charges than to pure rent. Table 8–5 shows the means and standard deviations of the two ratios. Even more relevant for this comparison are the values of the coefficient of variation,[52] a measure that indicates the relative dispersion around the mean. As the table shows, there is less relative variation in the ratio of price to TR_1 than in the ratio of

[51] Based on the average ratios shown in Tables 8–3 and 8–4, using the following ratio:

$$\frac{P/PR_1 - P/TR_1}{P/PR_1}$$

The equivalence is easily shown:

$$\frac{P/PR_1 - P/TR_1}{P/PR_1} = 1 - \frac{PR_1}{TR_1} = \frac{TR_1 - PR_1}{TR_1} = \frac{M_1}{TR_1}$$

[52] That is, the standard deviation divided by the mean.

price to PR_1: for the sample as a whole, the coefficient of variation for the former was .147, compared to .162 for the latter. Similar results are obtained in most cases when a manufacturer's equipment is considered separately. UNIVAC is a clear exception—its purchase/rent policy differs from that of other manufacturers in more than form: not only is pure rental quoted explicitly, but also it apparently constitutes the major determinant of purchase price.

Table 8–5 illustrates another difference among manufacturers. Note that the coefficients of variation for Honeywell and RCA equipment are quite small. This suggests that these two companies have relatively simple policies concerning the relationship between purchase price and rental charges, whereas some others follow complex rules that result in substantial differences in purchase/rent ratios for different devices. This difference is shown in Fig. 8–5, which relates the ratio (P/TR_1) to purchase price (P) for several IBM central processors. Each set of connected points consists of processors differing only in the amount of core storage included. Note that within a family of processors the ratios differ, and that neither the magnitude nor the direction of the difference is the same for various families. This contrasts sharply with Honeywell's practice. For example, for the processors in the 120, 1200, and 2200 series the P/TR_1 ratios are virtually the same (slightly less than

TABLE 8–5. Means, Standard Deviations, and Coefficients of Variation for P/TR, and P/PR_1

	P/TR_1			P/PR_1		
Manufacturer	Mean	Standard Deviation	Coefficient of Variation	Mean	Standard Deviation	Coefficient of Variation
Burroughs	49.73	2.88	.058	59.63	7.96	.134
CDC	40.14	4.79	.119	46.36	8.31	.179
GE	44.61	6.10	.137	50.24	9.23	.184
Honeywell	44.64	1.26	.028	51.12	4.26	.083
IBM	46.05	5.72	.124	50.33	8.11	.161
NCR	48.02	7.81	.163	55.13	9.89	.179
RCA	49.57	1.07	.022	54.21	2.62	.048
SDS	33.79	4.10	.121	41.39	5.72	.138
UNIVAC	38.84	3.67	.095	46.04	0.74	.016
All manufacturers	44.20	6.50	.147	50.23	8.16	.162

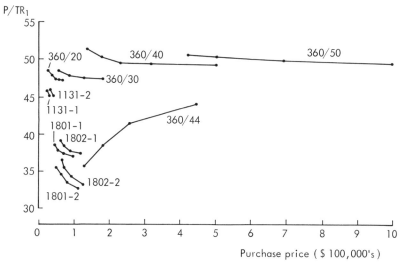

FIGURE 8-5. Relationship between P/TR ratio and purchase price for several IBM central processors.

44.0); for the processors in the 4200 series all the ratios are slightly over 46.5; and for those in the 8200 series all the ratios are approximately 47.3.

As shown by the example in Fig. 8-5, purchase/rent ratios are not related to price in any simple way. One might hypothesize that large systems are particularly risky and thus that their prices would be low relative to rental charges. However, the data are not consistent with this hypothesis: for the sample as a whole, price is virtually uncorrelated with the ratio of P to TR_1, and only slightly (negatively) correlated with the ratio of P to PR_1.[53]

I. PURCHASE VERSUS RENT

We have discussed the relationship between purchase price and rental charges at length, often from the seller's point of view. For the sake of emphasis, we conclude this chapter by posing once again the problem faced by most computer center managers at one time or another: should equipment be purchased or rented? Much has been written on the sub-

---

[53] The correlation coefficient between P and P/TR_1 was $-.02$; that between P and P/PR_1 was $-.15$.

ject; the manager is usually advised to consider all costs, contingencies, and risks and then to choose the cheaper alternative (sometimes expressed in present-value terms, sometimes not). It goes without saying that this is a sensible procedure. But what conclusion is the manager likely to reach when the exercise is completed? We have attempted to go beyond the usual discussion of the problem by considering the manner in which the seller may set price relative to rental charges. This view suggests, for example, that a high purchase/rent ratio does not necessarily indicate that a component is overpriced and clearly should be rented; it is more likely to indicate that the manufacturer expects the component to have a relatively long economic life.

Needless to say, none of this implies that managers should avoid calculating the total (present-value) cost of each alternative approach (e.g., purchase, rent, or lease from a third party). The discussion does imply, however, that if one alternative appears, after such careful consideration, to be considerably more desirable than another, the result (if correct) is probably due to significant differences between the situation of the installation in question and that of the typical user. Hence it behooves the manager to attempt to explicitly identify such differences in order to ensure that they exist and are, in fact, significant.

A. COMPUTER SELECTION

1. The Problem

The correct approach to computer selection is as simple in theory as it is difficult to implement in practice. Assume that a selection must be made among M alternative computer configurations. Let there be N possible uses. For configuration i, devoted to use j, let

$$NV_{ij} \equiv TV_j - TC_{ij}$$

where TV_j = the total value of use j,

TC_{ij} = the total cost of configuration i devoted to use j, and

NV_{ij} = the net value obtained when computer i is devoted to use j.

For completeness, assume that these values are defined for all $M \times N$ combinations (in any case in which it is completely infeasible to perform some or all of the tasks included in use j with configuration i, TC_{ij} can be considered infinite, giving a net value, NV_{ij}, of minus infinity).

Configurations may be defined either narrowly (e.g., "IBM 360/50 with 6 tape drives") or broadly (e.g., "an RCA Spectra/70 System"), as may uses. A narrowly defined use would indicate precisely the jobs to be performed, the time each is to be submitted and completed, etc. Examples of very broad definitions would be "batch processing only" and "batch processing plus conversational computing." Obviously the broader the definition of configuration i and/or use j, the greater will be the analysis required to find the largest possible value of NV_{ij}. In any event, we assume that the required analyses have been performed and that each NV_{ij} represents such a value.

The computer selection problem is completely trivial once the set of net values has been obtained. The optimal configuration will be i^*, and its optimal use will be j^*, where

$$NV_{i^*j^*} \geqq NV_{ij} \quad \text{for all } i \text{ and } j$$

In theory the optimal configuration and use cannot be obtained without explicit consideration of all possible alternatives (i.e., NV_{ij}'s). However, the choice can be made by using either of two stepwise procedures. One involves a selection among configurations on the basis of the maximal net value obtainable from each. Let

$$NV_i^{\max} = \max_j (NV_{ij})$$

Then select configuration i^*, where

$$NV_{i^*}^{\max} \geqq NV_i^{\max} \quad \text{for all } i$$

An alternative approach selects the best use on the basis of the maximal net value (or, equivalently, gross value less minimal cost) for each use. Let

$$NV_j^{\max} \equiv \max_i (NV_{ij})$$

$$= TV_j - \min_i (TC_{ij})$$

Then select use j^*, where

$$NV_{j^*}^{\max} \geqq NV_j^{\max} \quad \text{for all } j$$

Once the optimal computer configuration is known, the appropriate use is clearly the one giving the maximum net value. And once the optimal use is known, the appropriate configuration is clearly the one that will do the job(s) at lowest cost. But neither the optimal use nor the optimal configuration can, in theory, be determined without explicit consideration of all possible combinations.[1]

Users attempting to make explicit and quantitative analyses on which to base computer selection often evaluate alternative systems on the basis of the cost of performing a specified set of tasks. In our terms, given use j', select configuration i', where

$$NV_{i'j'} \geqq NV_{ij'} \quad \text{for all } i$$

or, equivalently,

$$TV_{j'} - TC_{i'j'} \geqq TV_{j'} - TC_{ij'} \quad \text{for all } i$$

$$TC_{i'j'} \leqq TC_{ij'} \qquad\qquad \text{for all } i$$

---

[1] In other words, one must guard against procedures that may lead only to a local optimum instead of the global optimum.

If (by chance) the selected use is indeed optimal, this procedure will clearly give the optimal configuration. But if it is not, the result may be worse (i.e., give a lower value of NV_{ij}) than random selection of *both* a configuration and a use. In practice the selected tasks are often those performed by a currently installed system. Even if the tasks are optimal for that system, it is unlikely that they constitute the best use, given new types of configurations. Obviously the greater the differences between currently available equipment and the equipment available when the present system was selected, the less satisfactory will be selection based on current use.

This discussion suggests that the objectivity of selection based on competitive bids in response to a set of "requirements" may be expensive, in the sense that it may result in a clearly suboptimal computer configuration. A less objective approach, in which each of several alternative configurations is rated on the basis of its overall value and cost if used in the best manner (i.e., best for the configuration in question), may give far better results. Of course the latter approach provides greater opportunity for malfeasance. If the interests of the person selecting a system diverge from those of the people to whom he is responsible, the problem becomes considerably more complex. An extreme example would include actual bribery by a manufacturer. However, more subtle but nonetheless damaging biases may affect the decision. If the maximum net value obtainable with computer A is 10% less than that obtainable with computer B, but computer A is more prestigious (e.g., costs more, has more impressive peripheral devices, or is made by a better-known manufacturer), the person charged with the task may be strongly tempted to select computer A. Although he may be able to accomplish this even under competitive bidding (by the appropriate definition of the required tasks), it may be more difficult than in the freer environment of a selection among alternative (and, in a sense, "incomparable") systems.

2. Competitive Bidding
Competitive bidding is widely used for procurement by federal government agencies. Since the prices of individual components are essentially fixed by the Federal Supply Schedule Price List, competitors bid against one another by offering configurations that meet a particular agency's requirements at the lowest possible cost (i.e., Fed-

eral Supply Schedule price). The Department of the Air Force, one of the largest users of computer equipment, has set up an agency charged solely with technical assistance in the selection procedure. The Electronic Data Processing Equipment Office, Electronic Systems Division, located at L. G. Hanscom Field, is

the Air Force's centralized agency for the competitive evaluation and selection of commercially available computer systems for Air Force users worldwide. . . . [Its] job is to solicit proposals and to evaluate vendors' proposals, and to recommend a source from which the selected computer is to be acquired.[2]

The Air Force procedure involves a number of subjective evaluations and is in no sense based simply on minimizing cost for a specified level of performance. However, selection typically involves a request for proposal (RFP) stating a set of mandatory requirements; only vendors of configurations meeting these requirements are judged to be "responsive" and thus are considered further. Some of the implications of such a policy commanded considerable attention during 1967. The issue concerned an initial award to IBM of a contract for 135 computers for the Air Force Phase II Base Level Data Automation Standardization Program. The contract, involving a purchase cost of approximately $146 million, was reported to be the largest single order for computers ever placed.[3] It also turned out to be the most controversial.

The controversy centered on the fact that only the three alternative configurations submitted by IBM were judged "responsive" to the RFP; moreover, none of the other bidders (Honeywell, RCA, and Burroughs) was allowed to revise its proposal for re-evaluation. The problem involved the time required to process each of the two sets of benchmark problems. The RFP stated that each set must be completed within 200 hours of operational use time. Actual tests showed that only IBM's configurations met the requirement; Honeywell's equipment, for example, required 266.7 and 260.8 hours for the two prescribed workload levels.[4] But Honeywell's proposed equipment in-

---

[2] Interview with Col. Sylvester P. Steffes, reported in *Business Automation,* August, 1967, p. 31.
[3] *Business Automation,* August, 1967, p. 58.
[4] *Ibid.*

volved an initial cost approximately $65 to $70 million lower than that of IBM. Moreover, company spokesmen claimed that, had a revised proposal been allowed, Honeywell could have provided a configuration that would have met the mandatory requirement at a cost only slightly above that originally proposed.[5]

The Air Force maintained that, considering maintenance costs, projected growth in workload levels, and similar factors, the overall cost of the Honeywell proposal would not have differed from that of IBM by more than a "very few" million dollars.[6] Moreover, a process of iteration to obtain a responsive system was regarded by Air Force spokesmen as undesirable in such circumstances:

We are talking about equipment that is available off-the-shelf. . . . We believe that it would be patently unfair to allow vendors to repair a proposal after live test demonstrations since the very purpose of these demonstrations is to prove that the system proposed meets the conditions of the request for proposal.[7]

Whatever the merits of the Air Force position as a general policy, the decision in this case was revoked. Honeywell filed an official protest with the Comptroller General (the head of the General Accounting Office). The resulting decision [8] was that "further written or oral discussions should be held with Honeywell as well as with other offerors. . . ." Although the overall source selection procedure used by the Air Force was held to be "reasonable," the selection of IBM in this case was considered unreasonable because of the failure to conduct further discussions with Honeywell well after the benchmark tests. The Air Force thus canceled the original award and reopened negotiations with the four bidders. The final contract was awarded to Burroughs, at a saving of $36 million compared to the original award, according to one source.[9]

This case provided a dramatic illustration of the conflict between efficiency and other goals such as equity, and objectivity. The imposition of any sort of rigid measure of performance and/or requirement for

---

[5] The increase was reported to have been approximately $1.25 million (*ibid.*).
[6] *EDP Industry and Market Report,* May 31, 1967, p. 2.
[7] *Ibid.*
[8] Comptroller-General Decision B161483.
[9] *EDP Industry and Market Report,* Dec. 29, 1967, p. 2.

performance is almost certain to lead to a less-than-optimal result. If all parties are willing to assume that selection is in the hands of unbiased and highly knowledgeable individuals with the time, resources, and interest required to consider all relevant alternatives, a thoroughly subjective selection procedure is obviously preferable. In the real world, where these conditions are virtually never met, procedures such as that used by the Air Force, although less than optimal, may be far better than any realistic alternative.

3. Cost Minimization for Given Performance

Some writers have proposed that virtually all subjective elements be removed from the computer selection process and that the goal be to select the cheapest configuration capable of meeting a clearly specified set of requirements. The most explicit statement of such an approach is that given by Norman Schneidewind,[10] who advocates a mathematical programming formulation. The decision variables would be the numbers of various types of devices, such as tape drives, printers, and processors; the constraints would indicate the elapsed time within which each of several jobs must be run; and the objective would be to minimize cost. Schneidewind shows that an analyst with thorough knowledge of both equipment and the tasks to be performed can in some cases formulate the selection process as an integer linear programming problem. However, even in simple cases it is a far from trivial exercise to prepare coefficients that capture all the intricate interrelationships involved. The prospects for general use of such methods do not appear particularly good.

4. Scoring Systems

Frequently those charged with computer selection attempt to combine objectivity with the consideration of apparently nonquantifiable factors. Relevant considerations are enumerated and assigned weights. Then each competing system is subjectively rated (e.g., given a score from 0 to 10) with respect to each attribute by one or more judges. The scores for each system are averaged (using the assigned weights), and the best system is selected on the basis of the overall scores.

---

[10] Norman Schneidewind, "Analytic Model for the Design and Selection of Electronic Digital Computers," doctoral dissertation, University of Southern California, January, 1966.

Cost is seldom included as one of the factors in a scoring system. A common approach is to consider only configurations of comparable cost, selecting the one with the best overall score. Often the cost level chosen is that of the currently installed system, on the (often implicit) grounds that (1) no more money can be obtained for computing and (2) the optimal amount is at least this great (and probably greater).

One study of several equal-cost systems [11] considered 123 separate items, organized into the following seven major divisions:

Division	Number of Items	Weight
Hardware	38	0.27
Supervisor	18	.27
Data management	8	.08
Language processors	31	.16
General programming support	4	.02
Conversion considerations	8	.12
Vendor reliability and support	16	.08

Another study,[12] designed to choose among competing families of equipment (with detailed configurations to be selected later), utilized a stepwise procedure to arrive at a final set of relevant weights. As a first step, a set of high-level goals was defined and weighted:

Goal	Weight
1. Increase employee productivity	0.20
2. Improve the availability, relevance, and timeliness of information used by administrators at all levels	.25
3. Reduce current and future corporate operating costs	.20
4. Improve the company's responsiveness	.25
5. Maximize the capacity to cope with change	.10
	1.00

Next a set of six characteristics was defined, and a matrix relating characteristics to goals specified in such a manner that all column sums were equal to 1:

[11] Performed at the RAND Corporation in 1966.
[12] Performed at North American Aviation; see Alan C. Bromley, "Choosing a Set of Computers," *Datamation,* August, 1965, pp. 37–40.

		Goal			
Characteristic	1	2	3	4	5
1. Low data-processing costs	0.20	0.20	0.30	0.10	0.15
2. Interchangeability	.10	.25	.25	.25	.30
3. Capability to exploit technological advances	.25	.30	.10	.30	.05
4. Adaptability	.10	.05	.10	.05	.40
5. Low risk	.15	.10	.15	.10	.05
6. Good support from supplier	.20	.10	.10	.20	.05

Multiplication of this matrix by the vector of goal weights provided the following set of characteristic weights:

Characteristic	Weight
1. Low data-processing costs	0.19
2. Interchangeability	.22
3. Capability to exploit technological advances	.22
4. Adaptability	.11
5. Low risk	.12
6. Good support from supplier	.14

Next a matrix relating each of forty-one attributes (rows) to each of the six characteristics (columns) was defined, again with each column sum equal to 1. Multiplication by the vector of characteristic weights gave a set of attribute weights. Then a matrix relating each of the four competing systems (rows) to each of the forty-one attributes (columns) was defined, with each column sum equal to 1. Finally, this matrix was multiplied by the vector of attribute weights to obtain the weight (score) for each of the four systems.

Weighting schemes must be used with considerable care. It is interesting to note that, as part of the latter study, sensitivity analyses were performed to investigate the impact of different assumptions regarding the appropriate weights. According to the author, "We were especially concerned with the sensitivity of the end score to changes in goal ratings . . . [but] we found that supplier scores were almost completely insensitive to even severe changes in goal weights."[13] Such a result may be cause for concern, not complacency, but analyses of this type are certainly desirable.

[13] Bromley, *op. cit.*, p. 40.

The usual weighting scheme assumes that the user's objective function is cardinal and linear. Letting S_i be the score for factor i and W_i its weight, the overall score is given by

$$S^* \equiv \sum_{i=1}^{N} W_i S_i \quad \text{with} \sum_{i=1}^{N} W_i = 1$$

Such a function is inconsistent with the usual assumptions of economic theory, since it asserts that the marginal rate of substitution of factor i for factor j is independent of the amounts (scores) of the two factors — that is, an equally desirable system can be obtained by substituting factor j for factor i at a rate equal to W_i/W_j. This is illustrated in Fig. 9–1 for a case involving only two factors, with weights $W_1 = 2/3$ and $W_2 = 1/3$. The indifference curves for $S^* = 2.5$ and $S^* = 5$, as shown, are linear. This implies, for example, that computer A will receive the same score as computer B, even though the former's superior hardware performance may never be available because of the complete lack of "vendor support" (i.e., $S_2 = 0$).

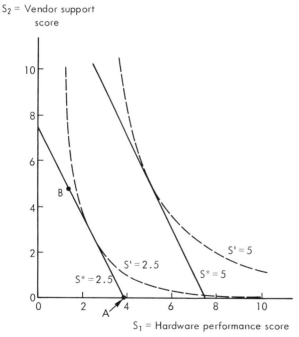

FIGURE 9–1. Isoquants based on two scoring schemes.

Economic theory usually assumes that indifference (iso-objective) curves are convex to the origin. A simple modification of the typical weighting scheme provides a function with such characteristics. Let

$$S' \equiv S_1^{W_i} \cdot S_2^{W_2} \cdots \cdots S_N^{W_N}$$

or, equivalently

$$\ln S' = \sum_{i=1}^{N} W_i \ln S_i \quad \text{with} \sum_{i=1}^{N} W_i = 1$$

S' is simply the weighted geometric average of the factor scores, while S^* is the weighted arithmetic average. In each case the weights are assigned to sum to 1. But note that S' will take on a value of 0 whenever any factor score is 0. Moreover, it does display the charactersitics expected of such functions, as shown in Fig. 9–1 by the curves for $S' = 2.5$ and $S' = 5$ based on the original weights ($W_1 = 2/3$ and $W_2 = 1/3$).

Nothing that has been said here implies that linear weightings are necessarily inappropriate, especially for "well-balanced" systems. Note, for example, that when all factors are given the same score, $S' = S^*$ and the curves are tangent. In practice the two measures are likely to be very close, as shown by the values obtained for five computer systems evaluated in one study: [14]

System	S^*	S'
A	4.44	4.27
B	5.51	5.42
C	5.64	5.57
D	6.27	6.19
E	6.44	6.40

Economic theory cannot provide a "correct" form for an objective function for this (or any other) purpose. However, a linear function

---

[14] The RAND study referred to in footnote 11. The score for each of the major factors was computed by taking a weighted arithmetic average of the scores assigned to the relevant subcategories. Thus S' is not the geometric mean of all 132 scores. In fact, the geometric mean is likely to be inappropriate for a detailed breakdown of factors, since a score of zero on one or more relatively minor items may not really be disastrous.

is not likely to prove applicable over a wide range of alternatives. In general, the function should reflect a willingness to give up less and less of A to obtain a unit of B as the amount of B is increased and the amount of A decreased. The geometric mean is one function meeting this criterion,[15] although it is only one of many that do.

Before leaving the subject of weighted scores, the treatment of cost deserves attention. It is perfectly consistent with economic theory to use a weighting scheme to measure performance, considering only equal-cost systems or, better yet, considering alternative levels of cost, with the final solution based on the best performance (score) obtainable for each cost. In either case no assumption about the relative importance of performance vis-à-vis cost is implicit in the procedure. However, some have advocated that cost be included directly in the overall score. This clearly involves a more heroic set of specifications.

Consider a case in which cost is the Nth factor and its score is determined as follows:

$$S_N = \frac{K}{TC}$$

[15] Let $S' = S_1^{W_1} \cdot S_2^{W_2} \cdot \cdots \cdot S_A^{W_A} \cdot S_B^{W_B} \cdot \cdots \cdot S_N^{W_N}$. For given values of all S_i except S_A and S_B,

$$S' = K S_A^{W_A} S_B^{W_B}$$

and

$$S_A = \left(\frac{S' S_B^{-W_B}}{K}\right)^{1/W_A}$$
$$= \left(\frac{S'}{K}\right)^{1/W_A} (S_B)^{-W_B/W_A}$$
$$= K'(S_B^{-W_B/W_A})$$

where

$$K' = \left(\frac{S'}{K}\right)^{1/W_A}$$

Now, for constant S',

$$\frac{dS_A}{dS_B} = \left(\frac{-W_B K'}{W_A}\right)(S_B^{-W_B/W_A - 1})$$
$$= -\left[\frac{C}{S_B^{1+(W_B/W_A)}}\right]$$

where C is a positive constant, since W_A, W_B, S', and K are all positive.
The formula thus has the desired characteristic: as S_B increases, dS_A/dS_B becomes less and less negative.

where K is a constant chosen so that $0 \leqq S_N \leqq 10$ for all systems, and TC is the total cost of the system. Assume that a linear scoring scheme is to be used. Then

$$S^* = \sum_{i=1}^{N} S_i W_i$$

$$= \sum_{i=1}^{N-1} S_i W_i + S_N W_N$$

Now, define a measure of performance based on the scores for all factors other than cost with all weights rescaled to sum to 1:

$$P^* \equiv \sum_{i=1}^{N-1} \left(\frac{W_i}{1 - W_N} \right) S_i$$

Obviously,

$$S^* = \left[P^* + \frac{W_N K}{1 - W_N} \left(\frac{1}{TC} \right) \right] [1 - W_N]$$

As shown in Fig. 9–2 (for a case in which $W_N = 0.2$ and $K = 10$), this type of scoring system assumes that the greater the total cost of a computer system, the greater is the additional expense that should be incurred to obtain a given increase in performance. This assumption is hardly likely to be consistent with the user's true objective function. Note that the weight assigned to the cost factor (W_N) will change the positions and slopes of curves such as those shown in Fig. 9–2, but not their general shape.

The effect of including cost in a geometric-average scoring system depends more heavily on the weight assigned. As before, let

$$S_N = \frac{K}{TC}$$

The overall score S' will be

$$S' = S_1^{W_1} S_2^{W_2} \cdots \cdot S_N^{W_N}$$

Let P' be the measure of performance, with weights rescaled to sum to 1:

$$P' \equiv S_1^{W_1/1-W_N} \cdot S_2^{W_2/1-W_N} \cdots \cdot S_{N-1}^{W_{N-1}/1-W_N}$$

Then

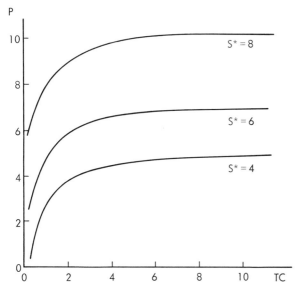

FIGURE 9–2. Performance and cost combinations with equal overall scores using a system in which cost is included.

$$S' = K^{W_N} \left(\frac{P'}{TC^{W_N/1-W_N}} \right)^{1-W_N}$$

For given S':

$$\frac{P'}{TC^{W_N/1-W_N}} = K$$

where K is a constant. This formula, which defines an iso-objective curve, shows the importance of the weight assigned to the cost factor. If $W_N < 0.5$, the curves become flatter as TC increases. If $W_N = 0.5$, the curves are all linear through the origin: maximizing S' is equivalent to maximizing the performance/cost ratio (P'/TC). Finally, if $W_N > 0.5$, the curves become steeper as TC increases.

This discussion suggests that, if cost is to be included in a scoring system, the geometric average is to be preferred, since it can be made to have reasonable characteristics by selecting a value of $W_N \geq 0.5$. However, the assumptions required are still substantial and, perhaps most important, far from obvious to the casual observer (and possibly to the eventual decision-maker). Assuming that an appropriate measure of performance can be obtained by weighting factor scores, it is far better to find the system giving maximum performance for each of several levels of cost and then choose the preferred cost and performance level explicitly.

5. Simulation Methods

One of the key tasks in computer selection is to estimate the manner in which each of several configurations will behave with one or more workloads. Some techniques use relatively simple formulas to obtain a single measure of performance; they will be discussed in Section B. Here we briefly consider methods designed to obtain relatively detailed estimates of performance, usually characterized by many measures, such as elapsed time for a task, percentage of idle time, percentage of time compute-bound, percentage of time input-output-bound, and probability of response time $\geqq 3$ seconds.

Perhaps the most popular system of this type is SCERT (Systems and Computer Evaluation and Review Technique), developed by Comress, Inc., and offered as a commercial service. The system includes a substantial file of information on computer components (e.g., timings, rental costs, and purchase prices). Instead of detailed simulation, SCERT uses "table-look-up and a series of empirically determined equations to estimate a computer system's behaviour under a given job mix." [16] It is designed to be used for many purposes. According to a Comress spokesman, for hardware selection it serves to facilitate the choice of "that particular configuration which will process the defined workload in acceptable time-frames and which achieves the best cost/performance ratio." [17] Figure 9–3 summarizes the system.

Other approaches utilize true simulation: tasks are created and then processed by various units in the proper sequence, and detailed statistics gathered on the overall operation. Usually a number of values are drawn randomly from prespecified probability distributions. Such simulations often are designed primarily to help select a preferred operating system or scheduling algorithm, or simply to predict the behavior of a given system under as-yet unencountered loads. How-

[16] L. R. Huesmann and R. P. Goldberg, "Evaluating Computer Systems through Simulation," *Computer Journal,* August, 1967, p. 150.
[17] F. C. Ihrer, "Computer Performance Projected through Simulation," *Computers and Automation,* April, 1967, p. 27.

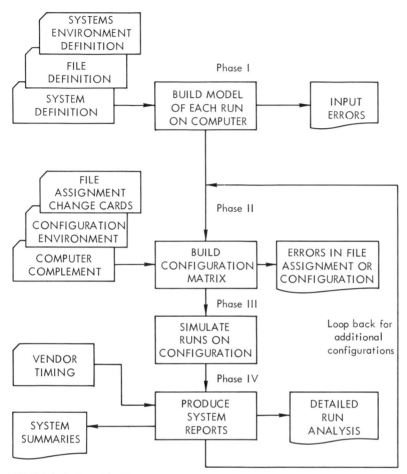

FIGURE 9–3. The SCERT system. Source: "Evaluating Computer Systems through Simulation," L. R. Huesmann and R. P. Goldberg, *Computer Journal,* August 1967, p. 151.

ever, they have been used to evaluate alternative configurations as well.

Three general methods have been employed. Some investigators utilize special languages or routines in conjunction with a standard algebraic language.[18] Others use a general-purpose simulation lan-

---

[18] For example, the SDC system based on JOVIAL, Neilsen's system based on FOR-TRAN-IV, and Scherr's CTSS system based on MAD. See Huesmann and Goldberg, *op. cit.*

guage.[19] And at least two groups have developed special languages designed specifically for simulating computer system operation.[20] Whatever the method used, studies of this type attempt to obtain many highly detailed estimates of performance; rarely is an effort made to obtain a single overall measure of "effectiveness."

6. Computer Selection in Practice

A survey of 69 installations drawn randomly from the readers of *Datamation* was made in 1966 to determine the way in which computer selection was performed in practice.[21] Five major techniques were described; the percentage using each is as follows:

1. Evaluation of benchmark problems   60.9%
2. Published hardware and software evaluation reports   63.8
3. Programming and executing test problems   52.2
4. Computer simulation   15.9
5. Mathematical modeling   7.2

Note that the sum exceeds 100%, since some readers reported two or more techniques.

Respondents were also asked to rank each of eight selection criteria in order of significance, with the most important given a rank of 1 and the least important a rank of 8. The average ranks were as follows:

Item	Average Rank
1. Hardware performance	2.63
2. Software performance	2.69
3. Cost	4.10
4. Support provided by manufacturer	4.15
5. Compatability with present hardware and software	4.54
6. Potential for growth (modularity)	4.63
7. Delivery date	6.40
8. Availability of application programs	6.85

---

[19] For example, GPSS, SIMSCRIPT, and SIMTRAN. See Huesmann and Goldberg, *op. cit.*

[20] IBM's CSS (Computer Systems Simulator) and Lockheed's LOMUSS II (Lockheed Multipurpose Simulation System). See Huesmann and Goldberg, *op. cit.*

[21] Norman F. Schneidewind, "The Practice of Computer Selection," *Datamation,* February, 1967, pp. 22–25.

Not surprisingly, installations with large complements of equipment made greater-than-average use of more sophisticated techniques. However, the relative importance attributed to the selection criteria varied little among major groupings of users. The author of the article describing the survey found the emphasis on "objective" (hardware and software) criteria relative to the other criteria surprising: "This result is the most significant one of the survey. It was anticipated that subjective criteria would play a greater role." [22]

When considering these results (or, for that matter, the results of any survey of this type), it is useful to be skeptical. As the author states, the finding in regard to the importance of objective criteria

is based on the assumption that the rankings provided by the respondents are truly indicative of the weight given the various criteria in the actual selection of a computer. It is possible that some users do not want to admit that a selection is made on other than a rational basis.[23]

Note also that the importance of each of the selection criteria was evaluated on the basis of ordinal rankings—no method was provided for a respondent to indicate, for example, that the first four criteria differed little in importance but that each was a great deal more important than criteria 5–8 taken together. Averages of such rankings are particularly deceptive, the more so because they appear to be cardinal measures.

B. MEASURES OF COMPUTER EFFECTIVENESS

1. Measuring Effectiveness

For some purposes any attempt to obtain a single cardinal measure of computer effectiveness ("performance," "throughput") would be ludicrous. But for other purposes it may be most sensible. Among the questions that may be answered reasonably well with such a measure are the following:

   a. What has been the rate of technological progress (i.e., improvement in cost/effectiveness) for (1) computer systems and (2) particular components?

[22] *Ibid.*, p. 24.   [23] *Ibid.*

    b. Are there economies of scale in computing, and, if so, of what magnitude?

    c. To what extent is the technological progress achieved by one manufacturer dispersed among all manufacturers?

    d. What is the relative (not absolute) effectiveness of computer 1 compared to that of computer 2?

The value of such measures for computer selection is subject to considerable dispute. It is obvious that the simpler the measure, the less "complete," "realistic," and "correct" it will be. However, it is usually also true that simpler measures are less expensive (and time-consuming) to use. It may thus be best to use a relatively simple measure after all. Only in a world in which information and analysis are free goods can it be stated categorically that the most realistic and complete method is the best.

A number of terms have been used to denote computer effectiveness. *Response* usually refers to the capacity of a system to react to some type of request; it is typically measured by the average or maximum time required for a response. Terms such as *throughput, performance,* and *capacity* usually deal with the system's capability in a steady-state operation. The measure may be the number of hours required to perform some specified set of tasks or the number of such sets of tasks that can be performed in a specified time period. The goal is usually to measure performance for a "typical" set of tasks. The importance of selecting an appropriate set cannot be minimized. Market forces should ensure that no computer dominates another, that is, provides better performance per dollar for every type of job. Any given system should perform some type of task more cheaply, or at least as cheaply, as any other system; if not, no sales will be made until its price is lowered. But no market mechanism guarantees uniformity of cost/effectiveness among systems for any single task. For some types of analysis it may be convenient to deal with "the" effectiveness of a system, but in general one must consider effectiveness for task A, effectiveness for task B, etc.

In this section we consider some important measures of effectiveness that have been used in the past. Several were designed for studies of technological change and/or economies of scale; we defer an extended discussion of such studies, which are covered in subsequent sections.

2. Simple Formulas

Some investigators have used extremely simple formulas for measuring the effectiveness of at least a portion of a computer system. The reciprocal of the time required to perform some rudimentary operation has been proposed as a measure of central processor effectiveness. Bourne and Ford found that the use of a single attribute, such as add time or internal clock time, as a measure implied that the effectiveness per dollar cost of 1960 computers was only slightly higher than that of computers of the early 1950's.[24] Since it is generally believed that major improvements took place during this period, such results suggest that these measures are not very satisfactory. Somewhat more useful results were obtained by Hillegass, who measured central processor effectiveness by the reciprocal of the time needed to add two numbers and store the result.[25] The record shows substantial improvement in effectiveness per dollar cost in the mid-1960's, with post-1964 computers giving almost three to four times the ratio obtained with pre-1964 equipment.

Since so-called central processors often include both processing units and high-speed storage (although not as commonly as at one time), several investigators have attempted to include estimates of the capabilities of both units in a single measure of performance. Schneidewind[26] and, later, Skattum[27] used a simple measure of this type:

$$E_{cpu}^s \equiv M \cdot N_c$$

where E_{cpu}^s = effectiveness,

M = high-speed memory storage capacity (in thousands of characters),

[24] Charles P. Bourne and Donald F. Ford, "The Historical Development and Predicted State-of-the-Art of the General Purpose Digital Computer," *Proceedings of the Western Joint Computer Conference* (May 3–5, 1960), pp. 1–21.

[25] John R. Hillegass, "Hardware Evaluation," *DPMA Proceedings,* Vol. VIII, 1965, pp. 391–392; the measure used is "the time to access the contents of storage locations A and B, add them together, and store the results in location C. This eliminates the usual bias in favor of single-address computers when add times are quoted. Furthermore, all operations are at least five decimal digits in length to eliminate bias in favor of computers with very short word-lengths."

[26] Norman F. Schneidewind, "Analytic Model for the Design and Selection of Electronic Digital Computing Systems," *op. cit.,* pp. 204, 205.

[27] Stein Skattum, "Changes in Performance of Components for Computer Systems" (unpublished). This paper was written as a term project for a seminar given by the author at the University of Washington in 1967.

N_c = cycles per second = $1/t_{\text{cycle}}$, and

t_{cycle} = time required to read a word from memory and regenerate it (if required).

The number of storage cycles per second (N_c) may measure processor speed imperfectly, but it has the virtue of relative ease of measurement. Multiplication of M by N_c, while essentially an arbitrary choice, at least provides an index with expected properties; in particular, each curve connecting equal-effectiveness combinations of M and N_c is convex to the origin.

Schneidewind and Skattum used even simpler measures for the performance of other components:

for tape drives:

E^s_{tape} ≡ maximum transfer rate (in thousands of characters per second);

for line printers:

E^s_{printer} ≡ maximum number of lines printed per minute;

for card readers:

E^s_{reader} ≡ maximum number of cards read per minute; and

for card punches: [28]

E^s_{punch} ≡ maximum number of cards punched per minute.

A more complicated formula, proposed by Gruenberger,[29] attempts to take into account a computer's speed in arithmetic processing and other factors:

$$E^G = \frac{M(N_a + N_m)}{L}$$

where M = high-speed memory storage capacity (in bits),

N_a = the number of additions per second = $1/t_a$,

t_a = the time required to perform an addition (in seconds),

---

[28] Schneidewind did not consider card punches; the definition is that given by Skattum. In Skattum's study, combination units (reader-punches) were considered to be two units, each costing half the total cost.

[29] Fred Gruenberger, "Are Small, Free-standing Computers Here to Stay?" *Datamation,* April, 1966, pp. 67–68.

N_m = the number of multiplications per second = $1/t_m$,

t_m = the time required to perform a multiplication (in seconds), and

L = the instruction length (in bits).

The inclusion of the instruction length may seem unusual; according to Gruenberger, "L attempts to measure inefficiencies due, for example, to decimal capability." [30] None of the elements is specified completely enough to be measured directly. For example, do t_a and t_m refer to fixed-point or floating-point, decimal or binary, operations? If instructions are of variable length, how is L to be measured? As Gruenberger indicates, "None of the . . . factors is wholly objective . . . and some are extremely difficult even to estimate for some machines." [31]

3. Instruction Mixes

Solomon [32] has proposed the following technique for comparing two processors with similar sets of instructions. Let C_j be the cost per unit time (e.g., microsecond) of processor j and T_{ij} the time (e.g., in microseconds) required to execute instruction i on processor j; [33] then the cost of executing instruction i on processor j is

$$C_{ij}^s = T_{ij} \cdot C_j$$

Processor $j*$ can obviously be said to cost less per unit of effectiveness than processor j if

$$C_{ij*}^s \leqq C_{ij}^s \quad \text{for all } i$$

and

$$C_{ij*}^s < C_{ij}^s \quad \text{for at least one } i$$

Unfortunately, such cases are rare. Typically one processor will be better (i.e., give a lower value of C_{ij}^s) for some instructions and poorer (i.e., give a higher value of C_{ij}^s) for others. In such instances some weighting scheme must be invoked. Let W_i be the weight assigned to

---

[30] *Ibid.*
[31] *Ibid.*
[32] Martin B. Solomon, Jr., "Economies of Scale and the IBM System/360," *Communications of the ACM*, June, 1966, pp. 435–440.
[33] In some advanced systems, T_{ij} may not be a constant—the time may depend on other activities taking place concurrently. Such complications are ignored here.

instruction i, and let there be N instructions in all. For convenience, assume that $\sum_{i=1}^{N} W_i = 1$, so that W_i can be interpreted directly as the relative importance (or frequency) of instruction i.

Processor j^* can be said to cost less per unit of effectiveness than processor j if

$$\sum_{i=1}^{N} W_i C_{ij^*}^s < \sum_{i=1}^{N} W_i C_{ij}^s$$

or, equivalently,

$$\sum_{i=1}^{N} W_i T_{ij^*} C_{j^*} < \sum_{i=1}^{N} W_i T_{ij} C_j$$

This can be rewritten as

$$\frac{C_{j^*}}{E_{j^*}^{IM}} < \frac{C_j}{E_j^{IM}}$$

where

$$E_j^{IM} = \frac{1}{T_j^{IM}} \quad \text{and} \quad T_j^{IM} = \sum_{i=1}^{N} W_i T_{ij}$$

T_j^{IM} can be interpreted as the time required by processor j to execute a "typical" instruction, while its reciprocal (E_j^{IM}) measures the effectiveness of the processor in terms of the number of "typical" instructions performed per unit time. The superscript indicates that the measures are based on an "instruction mix," defined by the weights W_i.

Obviously E^{IM} is appropriate only for measuring the effectiveness of a central processor. Moreover, its usefulness depends critically on the selection of relevant weights. In practice, instructions are normally grouped into relatively broad classes for this purpose; the more diverse the central processors to be considered, the broader are the classes (and, perhaps, the less relevant the results). Two approaches have been taken to obtain weights. The first uses the actual frequencies of execution for a "typical" mix of tasks, based on dynamic traces taken during the operation of an actual system. The second approach uses estimates of the relative frequencies that would be encountered if particular codes were executed.

Table 9–1 shows two sets of weights obtained by Knight from dy-

TABLE 9-1. Weights for a Scientific Mix and a Commercial Mix *

Instruction Category †	Scientific Weight	Commercial Weight
1. Fixed add (subtract) and compare instructions	0.10	0.25
2. Floating add (subtract) instructions	.10	0
3. Multiply instructions	.06	.01
4. Divide instructions	.02	0
5. Other manipulation and logic instructions	.72	.74
	1.00	1.00

* Source: Kenneth E. Knight, "A Study of Technological Innovation — The Evolution of Digital Computers," doctoral dissertation, Carnegie Institute of Technology, November, 1963, pp. IV–5, IV–6, IV–7.

† Category descriptions:
1. "These instructions are the fixed additions, subtractions and compare operations performed. We may obtain the fixed add time for each system from the computing literature."
2. "The floating add time is given in the computing literature for machines with built-in floating-point arithmetic. For other machines the figure can be approximated by multiplying the fixed-point add time by 10 . . . (the mean value for six computing systems considered)."
3. "We have included only one multiply category since the operating times for these two operations on systems capable of both floating- and fixed-point arithmetic are approximately equal. The multiplication time is a characteristic available in the computing literature."
4. "The fixed- and floating-point operations were combined . . . the divide time represents a characteristic of each system published in the computing literature."
5. "This category combines a large number of branch, shift, logic and load-register instructions. . . . For computers with parallel arithmetic, the time . . . is the shortest of . . . add time or . . . 2 [times] the memory access time for one word. . . . For computers with serial arithmetic, the . . . time equals the shortest of (1) add time or (2) [the time required to access an instruction, slightly modified]."

namic traces. The "scientific" weights are based on approximately 15 million operations of an IBM 704 and an IBM 7090 performed on a set of more than 100 problems. The "commercial" weights are based on approximately 1 million operations of an IBM 705 performed on a set of nine programs (two inventory control, three general accounting, one billing, one payroll, and two production planning). Another set of weights, obtained by Arbuckle using a dynamic trace, is shown in Table 9–2; according to the author, it "represents a composite of a number of scientific and engineering applications." [34] Although Ar-

[34] R. A. Arbuckle, "Computer Analysis and Thruput Evaluation," *Computers and Automation*, January, 1966, p. 13.

TABLE 9-2. Weights for a Scientific
Instruction Mix *

Instruction Category	Weight
Floating-point add/subtract	0.095
Floating-point multiply	.056
Floating-point divide	.020
Load/store	.285
Indexing	.225
Conditional branch	.132
Miscellaneous	.187
	1.000

* Source: R. A. Arbuckle, "Computer Analysis and
Thruput Evaluation," *Computers and Automation,*
January, 1966, p. 13.

buckle's mix is not directly comparable with Knight's scientific mix,
the two appear to be reasonably consistent.

Table 9-3 shows weights based on three programs analyzed by
Solomon:

The first is highly scientific, a matrix multiplication problem; the second [a
floating square root program] is also scientific but utilizes arithmetic capabilities less heavily; the third . . . is perhaps more closely related to data processing (and compiling) applications. It is a field scan of a card for control options.[35]

For purposes of comparison, the weights are also summarized by major
instruction category.

The differences among the three sets of weights given by Solomon
suggest that the selection of an instruction mix may greatly influence
the results of any comparison. And the contrast between Solomon's
detailed instruction weights and the much broader classes used by
Knight and Arbuckle suggests the dangers associated with using any
single set of weights when comparing systems with radically different
instruction sets. Calingaert provides an example of the problem:

The members [of a group of experienced system engineers] were asked to
specify the time in microseconds on System/360 Model 40 for the compare
class of instructions, given only the fact that the original mix was based on the

[35] Solomon, *op. cit.*, pp. 437, 438.

TABLE 9–3. Instruction Weights for Three Programs *

		Weight		
Instruction	Operation †	Matrix Multiplication	Floating Square Root	Field Scan

Fixed-point 32-bit operations

A RX	C(storage) + C(reg) → reg			0.0015
AR RR	C(reg 1) + C(reg 2) → reg 2	0.1559		.1773
L RX	C(storage) → reg	.1753	0.0634	
LM RS	{C(storage) → reg} 4 times	.0002		.0015
LR RR	C(reg 1) → reg 2	.0368		.0443
LTR RR	{ C(reg 1) → reg 2 / set condition code}			.0443
ST RX	C(reg) → storage			.0015

Floating-point 32-bit operations

AE RX	C(storage) + C(reg) → reg	.0421		
AER RR	C(reg 1) + C(reg 2) → reg 2	.1559	.1745	
DER RR	C(reg 1)/C(reg 2) → reg 1		.1429	
HER RR	C(reg 2)/2 → reg 1		.1587	
LER RR	C(reg 1) → reg 2		.1429	
ME RX	C(storage) · C(reg) → reg	.1559		
STE RX	C(reg) → storage	.0597	.0159	

Logical operations

CLC SS	{C(storage 1) : C(storage 2) (4 bytes)}			.1773
CLR RR	C(reg 1) : C(reg 2)			.0443
LA RX	{C(storage) → reg (24 bits)}	.0002		
STC RX	{C(reg) → storage (8 bits)}			.0044

Branching

BALR RR	PSW → reg	.0002	.1429	.0015
BC RX	Branch on condition to address in register			.2792
BCR RR	Branch on condition to address in register modified	.0002		
BCT RX	[C(reg) − 1] → reg / Branch if C(reg) = 0		.1429	
BCTR RR	[C(reg) − 1] → reg			.0443
BXH RS	Branch on index high	.2174		.1328
EX RX	Modify instruction and execute			.0443

TABLE 9–3. (continued)

		Weight		
Instruction	Operation †	Matrix Multipli- cation	Floating Square Root	Field Scan
Status switching				
SVC RR	Supervisor call	.0002	.0159	.0015
		1.0000	1.0000	1.0000
Summary by Major Instruction Category				
	Fixed-point operations	0.3682	0.0634	0.2704
	Floating-point operations	.4136	.6349	0
	Logical operations	.0002	0	.2260
	Branching	.2178	.2858	.5021
	Status switching	.0002	.0159	.0015
		1.0000	1.0000	1.0000

* Sources: Weights are based on frequencies given in Martin B. Solomon, "Economies of Scale and the IBM System/360," *Communications of the ACM,* June, 1966, pp. 435–440. In-struction descriptions and classifications are based on *IBM System/360 Principles of Opera-tion,* IBM Form A22–6821–1.
† C(x) stands for the contents of x.
Reg, reg 1, and reg 2 signify (arbitrary) registers.
Storage, storage 1, and storage 2 signify (arbitrary) locations in storage.
PSW represents the program status word.
a:b indicates that a is compared to b, and the condition code set on the basis of the result.

7090. . . . The ten answers ranged from 11.88 to 30.66 with a mean of 21.5 and standard deviation of 7.0.[36]

4. Kernel Timing Estimates
One way to deal with differences among processors is to compare the times (and costs) required to perform a specified task, called a *kernel,* assuming efficient coding for each machine analyzed. According to Calingaert, a kernel is "the central processor coding required to exe-cute a task of the order of magnitude of calculating a social security tax, or inverting a matrix, or evaluating a polynomial." [37] An attempt is generally made to have the problem "coded with equal levels of sophistication by experienced programmers in assembly language." [38]

[36] Peter Calingaert, "System Performance Evaluation: Survey and Appraisal," *Com-munications of the ACM,* January, 1967, p. 15.
[37] *Ibid.*
[38] *IBM System/360 Model 67 Time-sharing System, Technical Summary,* Aug. 18, 1965, p. E–1.

The three programs that Solomon used are typical kernels, and he identified them as such. However, since he wished to compare only processors with the same instruction set, each problem was coded only once. In this special case, the kernel approach degenerates to an instruction-mix comparison.

Table 9–4 describes seven kernels used to compare an IBM 360/67 with an IBM 7094–I. As shown in Table 9–5, the power of the 360/67 relative to that of the 7094–I varies considerably among the seven kernels; the appropriate overall ratio depends, of course, on the relative importance of each kernel. According to the study, "Estimation of computing center workload indicates that it may be represented by the distributions [shown in Table 9–5] between compiling and object code execution." [39] By using these weights, the ratio of the performance of the 360/67 processor to that of the 7094–I was estimated to be 3.991 for compilation and 3.157 for execution. No weights were given for combining the two ratios into a single result.

Note that some set of weights is required if a single figure of merit is to be obtained from timing estimates for several kernels. Needless to say, the collection and use of such weights involve problems similar to those associated with instruction mix comparisons. Moreover, both methods assume suboptimization at some level. Consider matrix multiplication and BCD arithmetic. The cost of the latter, in terms of the amount of the former sacrificed, is clearly lower for the 360/67 than for the 7094–I. Truly optimal use of the 360/67 would almost certainly involve more BCD arithmetic relative to matrix multiplication than would optimal use of the 7094–I. Any single set of weights must thus represent suboptimal use of one (or both) systems. Note, however, that the weighted-kernel approach at least allows optimal use of each system's instruction set; the suboptimization thus occurs at a higher level than in an instruction-mix comparison.

The importance of selecting appropriate weights has been emphasized by Calingaert: "In one study comparing the performance of one CPU relative to another, different kernels yielded performance ratios as high as 9.5 and as low as 3.3. I am aware of no rational technique for weighting kernels." [40] Although the situation may not be

[39] *Ibid.,* p. E–5.
[40] Calingaert, *op. cit.,* pp. 15, 16.

TABLE 9–4. Seven Kernels *

1. Matrix multiplication

    This is a matrix multiplication subroutine. Two 10×10 matrices were generated with single-precision floating-point elements. The matrix multiplication subroutine was then entered, and, using the standard formula below, the product was generated:

$$C_{i,j} = \sum_{K=1}^{n} a_{iK} b_{Kj} \quad \begin{cases} i = 1, 2, 3, \ldots, n \\ j = 1, 2, 3, \ldots, n \end{cases}$$

2. Square root approximation

    This kernel is indicative of the type of functional subroutine used often in a scientific program. In this case,

$$X = N^{1/2}$$

    is computed to the accuracy of the floating-point word or to 10 approximations, using the formula

$$X_{n+1} = \frac{1}{2} \left[X_n + \frac{N}{X_n} \right]$$

    It is assumed that N is in storage; the result is left in storage at X.

    For the first approximation, $X_1 = N$ is used. No test for negative or zero X is required. For timing purposes, it was assumed that 10 iterations are performed.

3. Field manipulation

    Control card scans, which this kernel represents, are similar to source statement scans found in FORTRAN and COBOL; consequently, this kernel is somewhat representative of both control card scans and source statement scans. Here, a variable field is scanned, starting in column 16 and ending with either the first blank or column 72, whichever comes first. The field that is scanned will have options delimited by commas (or a comma and a blank). Each option, 1–6 characters in length, is matched against an option dictionary of 8 items; an indicator is set if a match is found. For timing purposes, 30 columns were scanned in which 5 options (separated by 4 commas) are found.

4. Editing

    A common problem in commercial programs is to edit a field of decimal digits— supressing or leaving leading zeros, inserting commas and a decimal point, etc. In this kernel, a field of 10 decimal digits is edited in the following manner: leading zeros in the field are supressed; a decimal point is inserted between the second and third digits from the right; commas are inserted between the fifth and sixth digits and between the eighth and ninth digits (but, in each case, only if the high-order digit is nonzero); and a dollar sign is "floated," i.e., it precedes and is in juxtaposition to the first significant digit or the decimal point, whichever comes first. A field of 10 zeros should appear as $.00. A minus sign is carried in machine notation, and, if it appears in the original number, it should

TABLE 9-4. (continued)

appear after the edited field. For timing purposes, the number 0007777512 was edited. (It would appear as $77,775.23 after editing.)

5. Field comparison

This kernel is often found in programs when a decision is to be made on the basis of whether one number is greater than, equal to, or less than another number. A field consisting of N consecutive characters is compared to another field of N consecutive characters. An indication of whether the first field is less than, equal to, or greater than the second field should be made so that it can be interrogated later (this indication is normally made automatically by the machine). For timing purposes, two fields of 10 digits were compared.

6. BCD arithmetic

This kernel shows an execution time for a typical decimal addition if both addend and augend must be preserved. One field is moved to a work area, and the other field is added to it in the work area. For timing purposes, two fields of 10 decimal digits were added after moving the first field to a work area.

7. Character manipulation

This kernel represents a typical data movement. A source field of N bytes of alphanumeric information is moved (and left justified) into a target field at least 2 bytes longer than the source field. The timings were made for a 12-character source field and a 16-character target field.

* Source: *IBM System/360 Model 67 Time-sharing System, Technical Summary,* Aug. 18, 1965, pp. E-1, E-2, E-3.

TABLE 9-5. Relative Power: The IBM 360/67 versus the IBM 7094-I *

	Relative Power †	Weight	
Kernel	360/67 : 7094-I	Compilation	Execution
Matrix multiplication	2.29	0	0.30
Square root approximation	3.15	0	.35
Field manipulation	2.37	0.35	.07
Editing	5.09	.20	.05
Field comparison	4.00	.20	.11
BCD arithmetic	7.10	.10	0
Character manipulation	4.22	.15	.12
		1.00	1.00

* Source: *IBM System/360 Model 67 Time-sharing System, Technical Summary,* Aug. 18, 1965, pp. E-4, E-5.

† Relative power = $\dfrac{\text{processor time for 7094-I}}{\text{processor time for 360/67}}$

quite that hopeless, results based solely on kernel timing estimates clearly must be used only after careful analysis.

5. Benchmark Problem Times

One of the major drawbacks of the kernel approach is its concentration on processor performance. The point is often made that, to evaluate an entire computer system, much more must be taken into account— in particular, nonoverlapped input-output operations. Knight has proposed a general formula for accomplishing this; it is discussed in Section B–6. Here we deal briefly with an alternative approach: the estimation of the total time required to complete certain "benchmark" tasks.

Perhaps the most extensive set of estimates of this type is that prepared by Auerbach Info, Inc., for inclusion in the company's *Standard EDP Reports*.[41] Six major benchmark problems are utilized; however, the definition of a given problem may include one or more parameters, giving rise to a range of subproblems. Thus the standard file-updating problem is defined in terms of the average number of detail records per master record (among other things), and estimated times are given for values of this ratio from 0 to 1.0.[42]

The six benchmark problems used by Auerbach are as follows: [43]

Updating sequential files.

Updating files on random-access storage.

Sorting.

Matrix inversion.

Evaluation of complex equations.

Statistical computations.

Times are estimated, not obtained directly. The following quotation outlines the general approach:

> To help insure objective comparisons, the standard problems are rigidly specified in terms of available input data, computations to be performed, and results to be produced. On the other hand, factors such as master file arrange-

---

[41] *Auerbach Standard EDP Reports*, Auerbach Info, Inc., Philadelphia, Pa.; subscription rates (1967): $900 for one year, $695 per year thereafter.

[42] John R. Hillegass, "Standardized Benchmark Problems Measure Computer Performance," *Computers and Automation*, January, 1966, pp. 16–19.

[43] J. B. Totaro, "Real-time Processing Power: A Standardized Evaluation," *Computers and Automation*, April, 1967, and Hillegass, "Hardware Evaluation," *DPMA Proceedings*, Vol. VIII, 1965, p. 405.

ment and detailed coding methods are left flexible to permit maximum utilization of the distinctive capabilities of each computer.

To assure realistic comparisons between competitive systems, the equipment configurations, as well as the problems, must be standardized. For example, one configuration includes six magnetic tape units on a single channel and an on-line card reader, card punch and printer.

The execution time for each standard problem on each standard configuration is determined by computing all input-output times and central processor times, and then combining them with due regard for the system's capabilities for simultaneous operations. The problems are coded and timed in detail, and submitted to the computer manufacturers for checking to help assure their validity. The results are presented in the form of graphs that show the computer system's performance over a wide range of problem parameters and equipment configurations.[44]

Since many installations rely heavily on higher-level programming languages, evaluation of computer hardware alone may not suffice. To assess the capabilities of both hardware and software, estimates of the times required to compile and execute benchmark programs written in appropriate problem-oriented languages may be used. Such estimates are extremely difficult to obtain without actual runs on equipment that is at least similar to that being evaluated. However, even such a seemingly straightforward approach is likely to prove difficult in practice, as shown by the results of one study.[45]

Seven benchmark problems coded in FORTRAN were prepared; Table 9–6 summarizes their characteristics. Each was compiled and executed on the "old" computer system. The goal was to compile and execute each program on each of four new systems under consideration. However, this proved impossible. One program (number 6), could not be compiled on one of the computer systems. Execution times for another (number 3) proved incomparable because the execution path was dependent on the sequence of pseudo-random numbers generated and each system generated a different sequence. Execution times for yet another (number 4) could not be compared because "one manufacturer ran the problem in a multi-programmed mode and obtained an elapsed processor time of nearly zero. Another simulated tapes on a magnetic drum. Another used much smaller physical records." Finally,

---

[44] Hillegass, *op. cit.*, pp. 405, 406.
[45] Performed at the RAND Corporation in 1966.

TABLE 9-6. FORTRAN Benchmark Problems

Description	Size (cards)	Subpro- No. of grams	Input (cards)	Output (pages)
1. Evaluates a set of formulas to study blood and oxygen transfer between a pregnant ewe and her fetus.	85	3	36	14
2. Computes performance characteristics of rocket vehicles in simulated trajectories. 34 of the 68 subprograms were null; all but 4 of the remaining contained an identical set of 57 specification cards.	3868	68	96	5
3. Evaluates a mass-accretion hypothesis on the evolution of the solar system. Contains a relatively large number of CALL and IF statements. 11 subprograms contain 6 or fewer statements.	1188	25	5	84
4. Writes and rewinds two utility units n times.	26	1	1	1
5. Given the number of fragments and total weight of a fragmented object, applies Mott's law to compute the distribution of fragments by weight.	100	1	11	5
6. Simulates adaptive routing techniques for a distributed communications network. Contains essentially no floating-point arithmetic.	728	5	332	3
7. Computes the trajectories of two missiles in a simulated interception.	3208	44	723	99

the last program (number 7) could not be executed on two of the four systems "because of problems in random number generation."

Even the times that were obtained proved in most instances to be estimates. The figures given for the first system were obtained by doubling the actual times required on a faster system from the same family. Those for the second system were derived by multiplying the actual times required on a slower system by 0.6. In the case of the third system, actual times were adjusted to reflect improvements expected from extensive system modifications (e.g., a new loader and replacement of a disk system with a drum); these adjustments were substantial: compilation times were reduced to one-sixth and execution times to one-third of the actual amount. Of the four systems considered, actual times could be used without modification for only one.

In spite of all these problems, some comparisons were possible. For example, Table 9–7 shows the ratio of the time required to perform each of several tasks on the "old" system to that required on one of the new systems: Note the variation. How should these results be summarized? The ratio of total time required to compile all seven programs on the old system versus a new one is approximately 18 to 1. But the ratio of the time required to execute the four that could be executed is only 4.6 to 1. Since compilation is more time-consuming in this instance than is execution, the ratio of total time is far above the mean of the compile and execute ratios (approximately 14.6 instead of 11.3). However, all these ratios fall below the figures obtained if the

TABLE 9–7. Comparison of System Times

Problem	Compile or Execute	Time Required on Old System (minutes)	Time Required on New System (minutes)	Ratio of Old to New
1	compile	0.717	0.017	42.18
2	compile	22.5	1.357	16.58
3	compile	6.683	0.177	37.76
4	compile	0.183	0.007	26.14
5	compile	0.483	0.02	24.15
6	compile	1.783	0.16	11.14
7	compile	13.05	0.75	17.40
1	execute	0.317	0.077	4.12
2	execute	0.85	0.043	19.77
5	execute	0.183	0.003	61.00
6	execute	2.733	0.767	3.56
Total compile time:		45.399	2.488	18.25
Total execute time:		4.083	0.890	4.59
Total time:		49.482	3.378	14.65
	Average Ratio			
	Compile times:			25.05
	Execute times:			22.11
	Total time:			23.98

ratios for individual tasks are averaged, as shown in Table 9–7, the latter values all exceed 20 to 1. Clearly the problem of selecting appropriate weights is as difficult and important in this case as it is in any other.

One final problem deserves mention. Even if accurate benchmark problem times can be obtained, in general they may not be considered additive. If T_i is the time required to perform task i alone, how long will it take to perform N different tasks? All that can be said with certainty is that the total time will lie within the following range:

$$\max_i (T_i) \leqq \text{total time} \leqq \sum_{i=1}^{N} T_i$$

Clearly the possibility of substantial overlapping through multiprogramming and/or multiprocessing makes even more difficult the already impossible task of specifying for each system a set of benchmark problem weights that will give an overall indication of its effectiveness if used optimally.

6. Knight's Formula

We conclude this section with a description of the formula used by Knight to measure the "computing power" of an entire system: [46]

$$\text{Computing power} = \text{memory factor} \times \text{operations per second}$$

Considering first the latter term, we have

$$\text{Operations per second} \equiv \frac{10^{12}}{t_c + t_{I/O}}$$

where t_c = the time (in microseconds) required to perform one million operations, and $t_{I/O}$ = the nonoverlapped input-output time (in microseconds) necessary to perform one million operations.

The computing time (t_c) is based on the weights given in Table 9–1. Knight measures two kinds of computing power—commercial and scientific; the weights obtained from the appropriate mix are thus used to compute t_c.

The estimation of nonoverlapped input-output time is rather com-

[46] Kenneth E. Knight, "A Study of Technological Innovation—The Evolution of Digital Computers," doctoral dissertation, Carnegie Institute of Technology, November, 1963, pp. IV–1 through IV–16 and A–2 through A–5.

plex. It is based on the channel width, transfer rate, and start, stop, and rewind times for both primary and secondary input-output devices, plus estimates of the extent of possible overlaps and the utilization of primary and secondary input-output systems. Several of the required coefficients are specified by Knight, often with one value for commercial computation and another for scientific.

The other component in computing power is defined as follows:

$$\text{Memory factor} \equiv \frac{[(L-7)N(WF)]^P}{K}$$

where K = a constant,

L = word length (in bits),

N = the total number of words in high-speed memory,

$WF = \begin{cases} 1 \text{ for fixed word length memory,} \\ 2 \text{ for variable word length memory,} \end{cases}$

$P = \begin{cases} 0.5 \text{ for scientific computation,} \\ 0.333 \text{ for commercial computation.} \end{cases}$

This formula is based primarily on opinions:

A total of 43 engineers, programmers and other knowledgeable people were contacted and asked to evaluate the influence of computing memory upon performance.[47]

Authorities estimate that variable word length memories are twice as valuable as fixed word length . . . with an equivalent bit capacity.[48]

We also found that if word length is very short, the system encounters difficulties in carrying out many scientific and commercial calculations. For this reason we decided, upon the advice of the experts, to subtract seven binary digits from the actual word length, thus serving to penalize the short words.[49]

From the opinions of the experts the following approximations were made: (1) for scientific problems the computing power increases as the square root of the bit value of memory; (2) for commercial problems the computing power increases as the cube root of the bit value of memory.[50]

Knight's approach is certainly subject to criticism. However, it has advantages: it is relatively straightforward and can be applied without excessive effort. Perhaps most important, Knight has used it to obtain estimates of both the commercial and scientific computing

[47] *Ibid.*, p. IV–12.　[48] *Ibid.*, p. IV–13.　[49] *Ibid.*　[50] *Ibid.*

power of more than 300 systems. No other measure has been applied consistently to such a wide range of computers.

C. ECONOMIES OF SCALE IN COMPUTING

According to economic theory, average cost will be inversely related to output volume (given rate of output) and directly related to rate (given volume). Moreover, the strength of the volume effect is purported to decrease with volume and that of the rate effect to increase with rate. As shown in Chapter 5, this implies a U-shaped average cost curve for proportional changes in rate and volume.

Consider computers of different sizes. A "larger" system can produce computation at a faster rate; over any given period it can also produce a larger volume. For simplicity, consider a period of one month, with the manufacturer's rental charge (including maintenance) as total cost. Then rate (computation per month) equals volume (total computation during the month), and any system can be represented by a point on a (presumably U-shaped) average cost curve.

On the assumption that many system designs are available, and that each gives a point along a U-shaped average cost curve, which systems will be placed in production? One might expect that only those giving the minimum attainable cost per unit of effectiveness would be produced, the market being limited to machines that were neither too large nor too small, but "just right." However, this would occur only under very special circumstances. For many users a small machine may in fact be cheaper overall than a larger one, even though the latter can give a lower cost per unit of effectiveness if utilized to capacity. A larger system used only to perform tasks that could be completed with a smaller computer will clearly give a higher cost per unit of computation, since (by assumption), the two provide equal effectiveness and the larger has a greater cost. If computer sharing were cost-free, of course, any system could be used to capacity and a part-time user would pay only a proportional share of the total cost of the equipment, thus obtaining computation at the machine's optimal cost per unit of effectiveness. But sharing is not free: there are overhead costs, communications costs, and political problems (e.g., who gets top priority?). Thus small systems with nonoptimal cost/effectiveness are likely to be found on the market.

The case for larger-than-optimal systems is not as strong. Assume that the optimal system costs C^* and gives a total effectiveness (computation) of E^*. A system twice as large (i.e., giving $2E^*$ units of effectiveness) will cost more than twice as much. But two optimally sized computers will give $2E^*$ units of effectiveness at a cost of precisely $2C^*$. Why, then, would anyone buy one giant system instead of two or more optimal systems? Presumably because the former can do things that the latter cannot — things not adequately reflected in the measure of effectiveness. For example, assume that the giant computer processes jobs twice as fast as the optimal machine. Obviously any processor-bound job that must be performed sequentially can be completed in half the time with the giant machine. For certain applications (e.g., real-time control of a complex missile system) rapid response may be worth the higher cost.

In summary, economic theory implies a U-shaped average cost curve (although it may be very flat over a wide range), but only a portion of such a curve may actually be observed. There are reasons to expect that for computers much of the downward-sloping portion of the curve, and perhaps some of the upward-sloping portion, may be observed, although the question is essentially an empirical one.

In the 1940's, Herbert R. Grosch asserted that for computer equipment average cost decreases substantially as size increases.[51] This assertion, known as Grosch's law, is generally stated as follows:

$$C = K\sqrt{E} \quad \text{or} \quad E = \left(\frac{1}{K^2}\right) C^2$$

where $C =$ the cost of a computer system,

$\quad E =$ the effectiveness (performance, speed, throughput) of the system, and

$\quad K =$ some constant.

Concerning average cost (C/E), the law asserts:

$$\frac{C}{E} = \frac{K^2}{C} \quad \text{or} \quad \frac{C}{E} = \frac{K}{\sqrt{E}}$$

where K is some constant.

[51] Apparently Grosch did not publish this assertion at the time. It was part of the profession's early oral tradition, although it has since been cited in a number of articles, among them that by Solomon (*op. cit.*).

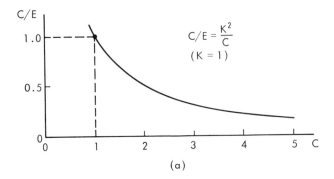

$$C/E = \frac{K^2}{C}$$
$$(K = 1)$$

(a)

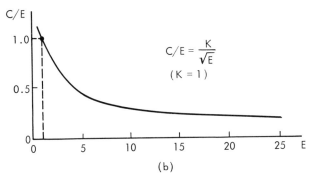

$$C/E = \frac{K}{\sqrt{E}}$$
$$(K = 1)$$

(b)

FIGURE 9-4. Cost per unit of effectiveness versus (a) cost and (b) effectiveness of system.

These relationships are shown in Figs. 9–4a and b for systems with cost and effectiveness normalized so that $C = 1$ when $E = 1$ Economic theory usually relates average cost to output, as does Fig. 9–4b; however, it is often convenient to use cost as the independent variable, as in Fig. 9–4a (e.g., when comparing results based on different measures of effectiveness).

One of the most important studies of economies of scale in computing was made by Solomon.[52] Five compatible models (30, 40, 50, 65, and 75) of the IBM 360 line were compared. Since all were introduced within a relatively short period of time, any differences in cost/effectiveness should be attributable primarily to scale effects and not to technological progress. Four instruction mixes were used to measure

[52] Solomon, *op. cit.*

TABLE 9-8. Relative Costs of Computer Systems *

Relative Cost

Model	Solomon's Average System [a]	Knight's Typical System [b]	Processor Rental Cost [c]
360/75	1.000	1.000	1.000
360/65	0.625	0.852	0.717
360/50	.400	.430	.433
360/40	.213	.218	.321
360/30	.100	.162	.292

* Sources:
[a] Solomon, "Economies of Scale and the IBM System/360," *Communications of the ACM,* June, 1966, p. 436.
[b] Kenneth Knight, "Evolving Computer Performance, 1962–1967," *Datamation,* January, 1968, pp. 31–35.
[c] Based on IBM GSA Price List, July 1, 1966 through June 30, 1967.

processor performance—three based on the kernels shown in Table 9–3 and one based on Arbuckle's scientific mix (shown in Table 9–2). Although only processor performance was measured, the average system rental given by Adams [53] was used for the cost of each model. In this connection Solomon asserts, "When comparing small machines with large ones, the large computers must necessarily be complemented with more devices or else the economies of scale are meaningless." [54] Table 9–8 shows the relative costs of the models (in terms of the rental cost of a model 75 system) calculated in three ways. The first is based on Solomon's (i.e., Adams's) figures for an "average" system, the second on Knight's figures for a "typical" configuration,[55] and the last on the monthly rental for the processor alone.[56] Although the figures differ, they suggest that overall results are not likely to be radically affected by the choice of one set rather than another.

[53] Charles Adams Associates, *Computer Characteristics Quarterly.* Solomon's figures are based on those given in the March, 1965, issue.
[54] Solomon, *op. cit.,* p. 436.
[55] Kenneth Knight, "Evolving Computer Performance, 1962–1967," *Datamation,* January, 1968, pp. 31–35.
[56] Source: IBM GSA Price List, July 1, 1966, through June 30, 1967. All figures are based on a processor with 256K bytes of storage (level H). Since the model 30 processor cannot be obtained with more than 65K bytes, the rental of a 30H was estimated by adding to the cost of a 30F the cost difference required to upgrade a model 40F to a model 40H.

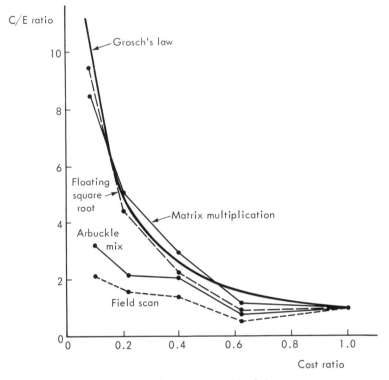

FIGURE 9–5. Economies of scale as measured by Solomon.

Model	Cost ratio	C/E Matrix Mult.	C/E Fltg. Sq. Root	C/E Arbuckle Mix	C/E Field Scan
75	1.000	1.000	1.000	1.000	1.000
65	.625	1.127	0.999	0.975	0.687
50	.400	2.879	2.162	2.250	1.426
40	.213	4.880	4.628	2.248	1.663
30	.100	8.595	9.597	3.238	2.143

Source: Based on data in Solomon, "Economies of Scale and the IBM System/360," *Communications of the ACM*, June 1966.

Figure 9–5 shows the results for Solomon's four measures of effectiveness as well as the relationship predicted by Grosch's law. Both cost and cost/effectiveness are expressed as ratios of the values obtained with model 75 (i.e., $C = E = C/E = 1$ for model 75). Clearly, the predicted economies of scale are obtained for Solomon's two scientific kernels. Somewhat smaller economies of scale appear to exist for Arbuckle's scientific mix. And the commercial mix (i.e., field-scan kernel) shows even more modest economies of scale. It is interesting to note also that, except for matrix multiplication, model 65 appears to be slightly more efficient than model 75, suggesting that the latter may lie at a point on the upward-sloping portion of the average cost curve.

To estimate the economies of scale for each of the four mixes, Solomon regressed the logarithm of system cost on the logarithm of the time required to perform a typical operation. The resulting (linear) equation

$$\log C = a + b (\log T)$$

is, of course, equivalent to

$$C = AT^b$$

where $A = 10^a$; and since $E = 1/T$, it is also equivalent to

$$\frac{C}{E} = KC^{1+(1/b)}$$

where K is a constant. According to Grosch's law, $b = -0.5$ and $C/E = KC^{-1}$. The actual results were as follows:

Instruction Mix	b	Equation
Matrix multiplication	−0.4935	$C/E = KC^{-1.026}$
Floating square root	− .4783	$C/E = KC^{-1.091}$
Arbuckle's scientific mix	− .6319	$C/E = KC^{-0.582}$
Field scan	− .6817	$C/E = KC^{-0.466}$

Thus Grosch's law held almost precisely for Solomon's two scientific mixes. But economies of scale, though present, were less pronounced for the other two mixes.

Knight's measures of effectiveness (and cost) for the five models suggest substantially greater economies of scale. Figure 9–6 shows the results obtained with Knight's data; again all figures are normalized so that $C = E = C/E = 1$ for model 75. Both curves lie well above that implied by Grosch's law, and both are monotonic throughout the

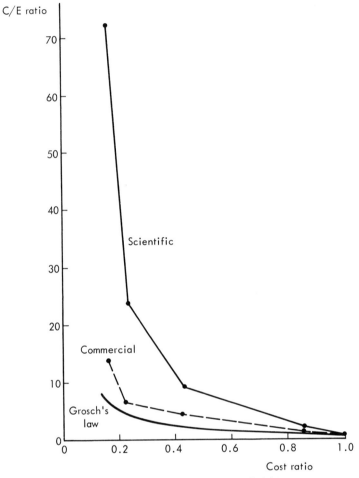

FIGURE 9-6. Economies of scale as measured by Knight.

range. These results differ somewhat from those of Solomon, but the two are similar in one respect: greater economies of scale appear to be available for scientific than for commercial computing.

Another study, by Allerdice, Carl, and Chartrand,[57] used the times given by Auerbach for each of six tasks. A system's effectiveness for a given job was measured by the reciprocal of the required time to

[57] Susan Allerdice, Bob Carl, and Richard Chartrand, "Computer Performance and Economies of Scale," December, 1965 (unpublished). This paper was written as a term project for a seminar given by the author at the University of Washington.

TABLE 9-9. Cost Effectiveness Equations for Six Tasks *

Task	Number in Sample	Correlation Coefficient	b	Alternative Form of Equation
Matrix inversion	22	.74	0.264	$C/E = KC^{-2.788}$
100% file update	72	.86	.464	$C/E = KC^{-1.155}$
Statistical computations	9	.88	.465	$C/E = KC^{-1.150}$
Mathematical computations	27	.86	.498	$C/E = KC^{-1.008}$
10% file update	77	.84	.667	$C/E = KC^{-0.499}$
Sorting	67	.85	.695	$C/E = KC^{-0.439}$

* Source: Susan Allerdice, Bob Carl, and Richard Chartrand, "Computer Performance and Economies of Scale," December, 1965 (unpublished).

complete it. Several equations were considered, but the best fit was obtained with a log-linear form:

$$\log C = a + b (\log E)$$

This is, of course, equivalent to the equation used by Solomon.[58]

The study was limited to equipment (a) covered in *Auerbach Standard EDP Reports*[59] in 1965 and (b) first installed during or after 1964. For each computer model, the configuration giving the lowest cost for a specified level of performance was selected. The results are shown in Table 9-9. The correlation coefficients indicate the predictive ability (fit) of the equation relating the logarithm of cost to that of effectiveness. It is not surprising that the results are significant — the implicit alternative hypothesis is that cost is unrelated to effectiveness. The final column shows the equations transformed to relate cost/effectiveness to cost. The results are roughly consistent with those obtained in the other studies. Grosch's law holds almost precisely for three tasks (100% file update, mathematical computation, and statistical computation), each of which utilizes the central processor relatively heavily. Far greater economies of scale are present for matrix inversion, which relies greatly on central processor capability. Finally, economies of scale are obtained for data-processing jobs (10% file update and sorting), but they are of smaller magnitude.

[58] Since $E = 1/T$, only the sign of the b coefficient differs.
[59] *Auerbach Standard EDP Reports, op. cit.*

Whatever drawbacks these studies might have, it seems clear that economies of scale have been present over the range of equipment offered for sale by manufacturers in the past. Furthermore, the extent of such economies is, on the average, similar to that predicted by Grosch's law, although typically greater for scientific than for commercial (data-processing) tasks.

Knight's important study bears directly on the issue of economies of scale; it is treated in detail in Section E.

D. TECHNOLOGICAL PROGRESS

The phenomenon of technological progress is only partly understood by economists (among others). It is said to occur when a firm's production function shifts to a new, dominant position (i.e., more output can be produced with given inputs, and/or a given output can be produced with less input). To some extent, technological progress can be viewed as a return on investment in research.[60] However, this return is highly uncertain: there may be little or no correlation between a firm's expenditures on research and the actual progress it achieves. Chance discoveries and/or a policy of copying competitors' products may lead to substantial technological progress, even if a firm spends nothing at all on research.

Since the returns from research are so uncertain, and since the decision to invest in research is complex, economic theory provides little assistance in predicting future progress. The extent of past progress is essentially an empirical issue, and only a naive investigator would unquestioningly predict that the future will simply mirror the past (e.g., by extending a "trend" line). The prediction of future progress requires technological sophistication, some "inside" information about the research currently in progress, and a large amount of courage.

In regard to technological progress in the computer industry, two facts are undisputed: (1) improvements have been major and frequent, and (2) greater progress has been achieved in processor and memory technology than in input/output technology. Figure 9-7 shows Armer's estimates of past costs and those that will prevail in the future if the

[60] Note, however, that if research is considered an input in the production function, the very concept of technological progress is in jeopardy.

Cost/Effectiveness

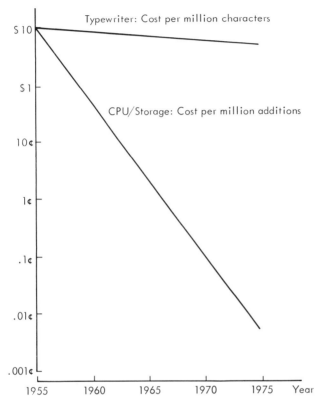

FIGURE 9-7. Estimated trends in cost/effectiveness. Source: Paul Armer, "Computer Aspects of Technological Change, Automation and Economic Progress," A Report Prepared for the National Commission on Technology, Automation and Economic Progress, Sept. 1965, p. 6.

rate of change remains constant. Note that the vertical axis is logarithmic; thus the linear curves reflect a constant annual rate of change. The steeper curve shows approximately an order-of-magnitude improvement (decrease) in the cost of computation every four years equivalent to an annual improvement in effectiveness per dollar of 80% ($1.8^4 \approx 10$). This is intended to refer only to the capability of the central processor plus an associated memory unit, and the rapid improvement is due primarily to changes in the electronic state of the art. The flatter curve shows the (relatively minor) improvement in the costs

TABLE 9-10. Estimates of Improvement in Performance per Dollar *

	Improvement in Performance per Dollar		
Area of Progress	1950–1965	Approximate Average Past Rate per 5-Year Period	1965–1970 (predicted)
Internal high-speed memory	1000–2000	12	20
Logic circuits	100–200	5	10
Magnetic tapes (but in slow stop-start use)	50–100	4	10
Mass storage	50	7	10
Printers (mechanical and nonmechanical)	5–10	2	3 (higher for nonmechanical)
Punched-card machines	5–10	2	?
Programming (coding)	Perhaps 4	1½	?
Input, where character recognition is usable	100	5	2 in large systems; less when extended to smaller systems

* Source: J. Presper Eckert, "The Status of Computer Components and Technology," *DPMA Proceedings,* 1965, p. 37.

of typewriters (intended to represent input/output devices). As Armer points out, "[The typewriter] is not necessarily typical, but will, I believe, become one of the most commonly used I/O devices of the future. . . . Magnetic tape . . . would have shown much greater . . . decreases in cost." [61]

A set of estimates made by Eckert in 1965 is shown in Table 9–10. Again the discrepancy between the rates of progress in electronic and in mechanical technology is clear. The figures are roughly consistent with Armer's (e.g., an order-of-magnitude improvement in logic circuits predicted over the five-year period 1965–1970).

Virtually everyone writing on the subject appears to agree that sub-

[61] Paul Armer, "Computer Aspects of Technological Change, Automation and Economic Progress," a report prepared for the National Commission on Technology, Automation, and Economic Progress, September, 1965, p. 5.

stantial reductions in the cost of basic processing are possible. Sisson's predictions are typical:

In the next five to ten years . . . arithmetic and logical processing components will be developed which can be produced at significantly lower cost than present units. A basic gating unit which cost several dollars in 1955 and is now 50 cents or so will go to 3 to 5 cents. This 10-fold decrease will result from the use of integrated circuitry.[62]

Integrated circuit technology, however, will provide some interesting economic problems for the computer architect. Because of the large volumes in which each component of a current standard microcircuit is produced, marginal production cost is typically only slightly below average cost.[63] Moreover, the start-up costs required to produce a new circuit are relatively small. This is not expected to be the case for integrated arrays. It has been asserted that the cost of processing an individual wafer through the diffusion process will not vary a great deal as a function of what is on it;[64] if so, there will be substantial incentives to include many circuits on each wafer, thus greatly lowering the cost per circuit. However, the start-up cost for a new wafer design may be major. Therefore, in order to obtain major economies from integrated arrays, a relatively few standardized designs may be produced in great numbers. Computer architects and circuit manufacturers will have to consider a great many complicated tradeoffs before a preferred set of circuit and computer designs can be established. In any event, significant changes in the logical design of computer systems are likely to result from such major changes in the underlying economics of circuit production.

Several empirical studies of cost/effectiveness over time have been made. Three will be discussed here. Knight's important work, as mentioned previously, is described in the next section.

1. Gruenberger[65] examined the ratio of his measure of computer effectiveness (E^G, described in Section B-2) to monthly rental cost for a number of systems. Figure 9-8 shows the results for seventeen

[62] Roger L. Sisson, "Planning for Computer Hardware Innovations," *Data Processing Digest*, January, 1967, p. 5.
[63] Robert N. Noyce, "A Look at Future Costs of Large Integrated Arrays," *Proceedings, Fall Joint Computer Conference*, 1966, pp. 111–114.
[64] *Ibid.*
[65] Gruenberger, *op. cit.*

"small" computers; the horizontal axis indicates the date of introduction. The general trend, fitted "free-hand" by Gruenberger, shows an improvement of three orders of magnitude in a decade at a constant annual rate of approximately 100% (note that the vertical axis is logarithmic). A comparable analysis for "large" machines revealed an improvement of only two orders of magnitude in a decade (equivalent to an annual improvement of about 60%). Unfortunately Gruenberger did not show the results of this latter analysis; presumably the trend-line, although flatter, lay above (perhaps well above) that shown in Fig. 9–8. In any event, Gruenberger argued that, given the continuation of such trends, the curves must come closer together each year.

Gruenberger's results imply that economies of scale in computing, if present, are decreasing over time. However, as shown in Section E, Knight's study, based on a much larger data base and the use of more sophisticated techniques of analysis, suggests that, if anything, economies of scale have increased over time.

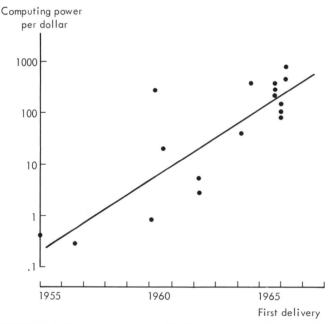

FIGURE 9–8. Ratio of computer effectiveness to monthly rental for 17 small computers. Source: Fred Gruenberger, "Are Small, Free-Standing Computers Here to Stay?" *Datamation*, April 1966, pp. 67–68.

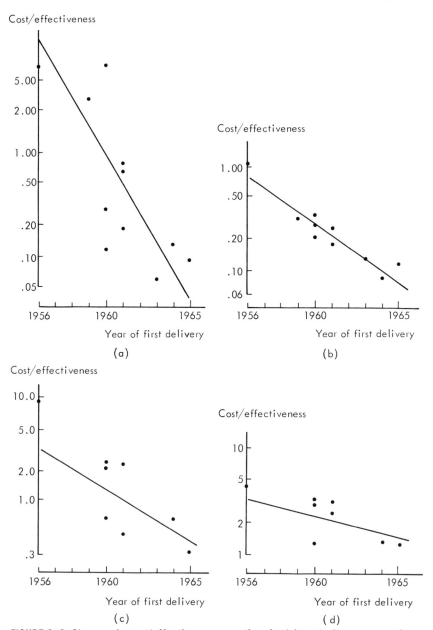

FIGURE 9-9. Changes in cost/effectiveness over time for (a) central processors plus memory, (b) magnetic tape drives, (c) card readers, and (d) line printers. Source: Table 9-11.

2. Schneidewind estimated changes in cost/effectiveness over time for four major components — (a) central processors plus memory, (b) magnetic tape drives, (c) card readers, and (d) line printers — using the measures of effectiveness described in Section B-2 and monthly rental costs. The data, shown in Table 9-11, are plotted in Figs. 9-9a through 9d. Each of the trend lines assumes that cost/effectiveness has fallen by the same percentage every year. The general form is

$$\ln \frac{C}{E} = a + bT$$

or, equivalently

$$\frac{C}{E} = A(B^T)$$

where $A = e^a$, $B = e^b$, and T = first delivery date, measured in terms of the number of years since 1956.

TABLE 9-11. Cost/Effectiveness, Twelve Computer Systems *

Computer System	First Delivery	Cost/Effectiveness †			
		CPU/ Memory	Tape Drives	Card Readers	Line Printers
IBM 650	12/54	152.4	138.4	2.75	2.67
IBM 705II	12/56	7.08	118.4	9.60	4.50
IBM 705III	6/59	3.50	34.4	...	...
IBM 7070	6/60	0.283	34.8	2.36	3.53
IBM 1401	9/60	7.70	28.8	0.69	1.29
Hon. 800	12/60	0.117	21.8	2.19	3.33
IBM 7080	9/61	0.838	26.6	2.36	3.53
IBM 7074	12/61	0.189	...	...	...
Hon. 400	12/61	0.683	18.8	0.50	2.60
Hon. 1800	9/63	0.0617	13.5	...	...
Hon. 200	1/64	0.137	9.04	0.70	1.41
IBM 360/30	9/65	0.0936	12.4	0.32	1.43

* Source: Norman F. Schneidewind, "Analytic Model for the Design and Selection of Electronic Digital Computing Systems," doctoral dissertation, University of Southern California, January, 1966, pp. 204, 205.
† Measures of cost/effectiveness:
CPU/memory: monthly rental dollars per 1000 storage cycles per second per 1000 characters of storage.
Tape drives: monthly rental dollars per 1000 characters per second tape transfer rate.
Card readers: monthly rental dollars per card per minute.
Line printers: monthly rental dollars per line per minute.

TABLE 9–12. Trend Lines *

	Equation	
Device	Form 1: $C/E = A(B^T)$	Form 2: $\ln(C/E) = a + bT$
CPU/memory	$C/E = 14(0.52^T)$	$\ln(C/E) = 2.64 - 0.65T$
Tape drives	$C/E = 0.83(0.76^T)$	$\ln(C/E) = -0.19 - 0.27T$
Card readers	$C/E = 3.4(0.80^T)$	$\ln(C/E) = 1.22 - 0.22T$
Line printers	$C/E = 3.4(0.92^T)$	$\ln(C/E) = 1.22 - 0.08T$

* Source: Norman F. Schneidewind, "Analytic Model for the Design and Selection of Electronic Digital Computing Systems," doctoral dissertation, University of Southern California, January, 1966, pp. 206–209.

The particular equations obtained by Schneidewind (presumably with linear regression) are shown in Table 9–12. The implied rates of change may be expressed in either of two ways. Coefficient B in form 1 shows the ratio of cost/effectiveness at any point of time to that for one time period (here, year) earlier; [66] coefficient b in form 2 ($= \ln B$) indicates the continuous rate of change.[67] According to these results, the cost/effectiveness of a central processor first delivered in year $T + 1$ would be only 52% as great as that of one first delivered in year T (i.e., the annual reduction would equal 48%). On the other hand, the formula indicates a continuous rate of decrease equivalent to 65% per year. Obviously either measure may be calculated from the other; the choice between them is of little importance, as long as the one selected is properly identified.

3. A more extensive analysis of this type was performed by Skattum.[68] Five types of devices were considered—the four covered by Schneidewind plus card punches. The same measures of effectiveness were utilized (those indicated in Section B–2), and cost was again

[66] Since

$$\frac{(C/E)_{T+1}}{(C/E)_T} = \frac{A(B^{T+1})}{A(B^T)} = B$$

[67]

$$\frac{dy/y}{dT} = \ln B = b \quad \text{(where } y = C/E)$$

[68] Skattum, *op. cit.*

measured by monthly rental. But Skattum obtained much larger samples, ranging from 42 to 117 observations. The only other major difference concerns the selected figure of merit: Skattum's results are stated in terms of effectiveness per dollar of cost (i.e., E/C) instead of cost/effectiveness (C/E).

Figures 9–10a through 10e show Skattum's results. The trend lines, determined by least squares regression, reflect a constant percentage increase in effectiveness per dollar over time (again, the vertical axes are logarithmic). The underlying equations are of the form

$$\frac{E}{C} = A(B^T)$$

or, equivalently,

$$\ln \frac{E}{C} = a + bT$$

where $A = e^a$, $B = e^b$, and $T =$ the first delivery date, measured in terms of the number of months since December, 1950.

Table 9–13 shows the equations of the five lines in the latter form, along with sample sizes, percentage of variation explained, and the

TABLE 9–13. Regression Results *

Device †	Number in Sample	Percentages of Variation in ln (E/C) Explained	t Value of Slope Coeff. (b)	Equation: ln $(E/C) = a + bT$
CPU/memory	117	63.1%	14.01	ln $(E/C) = -0.918 + 0.0573T$
Card readers	44	49.9	6.47	ln $(E/C) = -2.064 + 0.0155T$
Tape drives	54	61.4	9.10	ln $(E/C) = -4.389 + 0.0128T$
Line printers	46	37.5	5.13	ln $(E/C) = -2.160 + 0.0105T$
Card punches	42	41.5	5.32	ln $(E/C) = -2.567 + 0.0103T$

* Source: Stein Skattum, "Changes in Performance of Components for Computer Systems" (unpublished).
† Measures of effectiveness/cost:
CPU/memory: storage cycles per second times storage size (in thousands of characters)/ monthly rental (in dollars).
Card readers: cards per minute per dollar monthly rental.
Tape drives: thousand characters per second per dollar monthly rental.
Line printers: lines per minute per dollar monthly rental.
Card punches: cards per minute per dollar monthly rental.

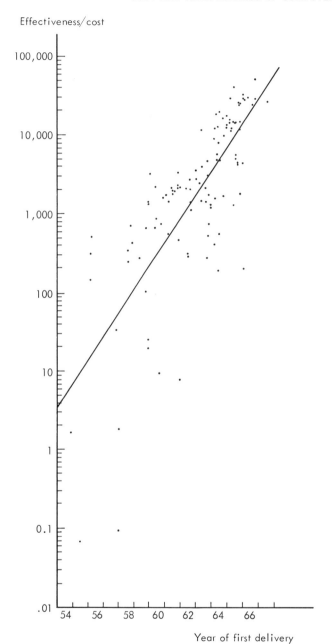

Effectiveness/cost

Year of first delivery

FIGURE 9–10a. Changes in effectiveness per dollar of cost over time for central processors plus memory. Source: Table 9–11.

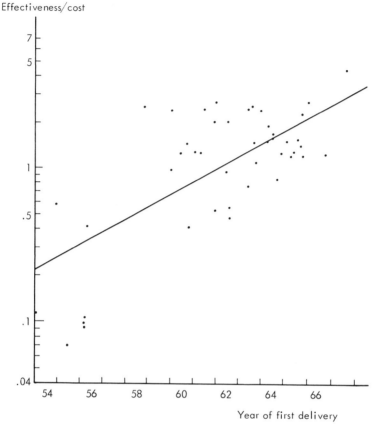

Effectiveness/cost

Year of first delivery

FIGURE 9–10b. Changes in effectiveness per dollar of cost over time for card readers. Source: Table 9–11.

t values of the slope coefficients. Each slope coefficient (b) can be interpreted as a continuous rate of change; for example, the rate for CPU/memory devices was equivalent to 5.73% per month. Table 9–14 gives the implied annual percentage improvement for four of the devices [69] and compares Skattum's results with those obtained by Schneidewind; as shown, the two are very similar.

These results appear to leave little doubt about the past history of the industry. The improvement in processor and memory effectiveness per dollar has been steady and substantial, perhaps as much as 100%

---

[69] Equals 100 ($e^{12b} - 1$).

per year. Compared to this almost fantastic rate, a mere 10–20% annual improvement (the apparent rate of change in effectiveness per dollar of input/output devices) seems insignificant. It is important to remember, however, that in more mature industries an annual improvement of as little as 5% is often considered an impressive achievement.

E. KNIGHT'S STUDY

One of the tasks associated with the analysis of computer cost/effectiveness is the separation of the effects of technological progress from

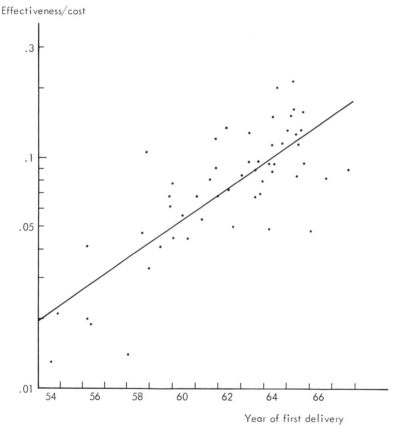

FIGURE 9-10c. Changes in effectiveness per dollar of cost over time for tape drives. Source: Table 9-11.

those associated with economies of scale. Solomon was able to study economies of scale by investigating only a few systems designed at roughly the same time. Gruenberger attempted to avoid capturing some of the possible effects of economies of scale by examining technological progress for small and large machines separately. But such techniques are not wholly satisfactory. If possible, one would prefer to employ data on many systems, differing in both size and date of introduction, and from such data infer the extent of the economies of scale available at various points of time as well as the overall rate of technological progress over time.

Knight attempted to accomplish this purpose in two separate but re-

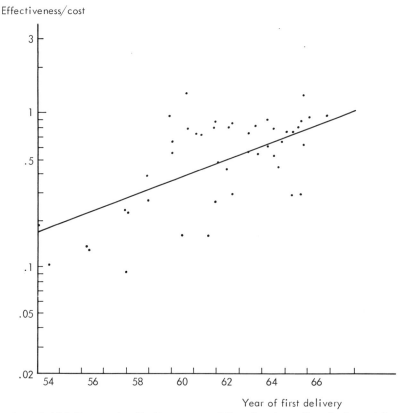

FIGURE 9-10d. Changes in effectiveness per dollar of cost over time for line printers. Source: Table 9-11.

Effectiveness/cost

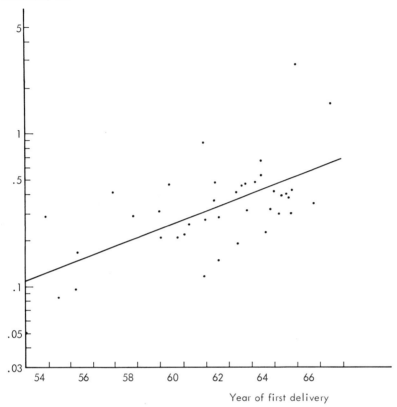

Year of first delivery

FIGURE 9-10e. Changes in effectiveness per dollar of cost over time for card punches. Source: Table 9-11.

lated studies. The first [70] covered 225 computers introduced from 1944 through early 1963; the second,[71] 111 computers introduced between 1962 and 1966 (27 of which were included in the first study).

The performance of each system was measured by using the formula described in Section B-6:

Computing power = memory factor × operations per second

[70] Knight dissertation, *op. cit.*, and "Changes in Computer Performance," *Datamation*, September, 1966, pp. 40–54.
[71] Knight, "Evolving Computer Performance, 1962–1967," *op. cit.*

TABLE 9-14. Annual Changes in Cost Relative to Effectiveness

Device	Annual Improvement in E/C (Skattum)	$\dfrac{(C/E)_{T+1}}{(C/E)_T}$ (Skattum) *	$\dfrac{(C/E)_{T+1}}{(C/E)_T}$ (Schneidewind)
CPU/memory	100%	0.50	0.52
Card readers	20	.83	.80
Tape drives	16	.86	.76
Line printers	13	.89	.92

* Let P be the annual percentage improvement in E/C. Then

$$\frac{(C/E)_{T+1}}{(C/E)_T} = \frac{1}{1 + (P/100)}$$

Since the memory factor is a pure number, computing power (P) is expressed in terms of operations per second. Two values were analyzed, one for commercial data processing (P_c), the other for scientific computation (P_s). Cost (C) is expressed in terms of dollars (rental) per second.[72]

The year in which the first operating version of each system was delivered to a customer was also determined. Thus the following values were obtained for each system:

P_s = scientific power (in operations per second),
P_c = commercial power (in operations per second),
C = cost (in dollars per second), and
Y = year introduced.

[72] Knight chose to measure cost by the reciprocal of this value (i.e., seconds per dollar). Letting C_k be Knight's measure, and using C as above, we have $C = 1/C_k$; thus

$$\ln C = - \ln C_k$$

Knight used ($\ln C_k$) as the dependent variable in each regression analysis; the resultant equations differ from those that would have been obtained if ($\ln C$) had been used only with respect to the signs of the coefficients. Thus Knight's result,

$$\ln C_k = 8.9704 - 0.51934(\ln P_s)$$

is equivalent to

$$\ln C = -8.9704 + 0.51934(\ln P_s)$$

The difference between Knight's measure of cost and that used here (its reciprocal) also accounts for the discrepancies between the diagrams that follow and those provided by Knight.

In general, a "typical" early configuration was selected for each system; no attempt was made to utilize configurations with particularly desirable values of P_s and/or P_c relative to C.

Knight hypothesized that, at any point of time, cost would be related to performance (scientific or commercial) as follows:

$$\ln C = a + b(\ln P) + b^*(\ln P)^2$$

This is equivalent to

$$C = e^a P^{b + b^* (\ln P)}$$

and

$$\frac{C}{P} = e^a P^{b + b^* (\ln P) - 1}$$

Note that $(\ln P)$ is an increasing function of P; if $b^* > 0$, the exponent $b + b^*(\ln P) - 1$ will also increase as P becomes larger. For $b + b^*(\ln P) - 1 < 0$, average cost (C/P) decreases as P rises. For $b + b^*(\ln P) - 1 > 0$, average cost increases as P rises. With $b < 1$ and $b^* > 0$, this function represents a traditional U-shaped average cost curve. On the other hand, with $b < 1$ and $b^* = 0$, the average cost curve is monotonic downward. If many larger-than-optimal machines have been produced, the inclusion of b^* should add significantly to the explanatory power of the equation. But if most systems actually offered for sale lie on the downward-sloping portion of the average cost curve, little will be lost by forcing $b^* = 0$ [i.e., omitting $(\ln P)^2$ from the set of independent variables].

Whatever the relationship between C and P at any given point of time, it presumably shifts over time. Knight hypothesized that any shift reduces the cost of each level of performance by some specified proportion. Thus for year i the equation is

$$\ln C = a_i + b(\ln P) + b^*(\ln P)^2$$

or

$$C = e^{a_i} P^{b + b^* (\ln P)}$$

For year j, it is

$$\ln C = a_j + b(\ln P) + b^*(\ln P)^2$$

or

$$C = e^{a_j} P^{b+b*\,(\ln P)}$$

For any given level of performance, the ratio of cost in year $i + 1$ to that in year i is thus

$$\frac{C_{i+1}}{C_i} = \frac{e^{a_{i+1}} P^{b+b*\,(\ln P)}}{e^{a_i} P^{b+b*\,(\ln P)}} = \frac{e^{a_{i+1}}}{e^{a_i}} = e^{a_{i+1}-a_i}$$

where $e^{a_{i+1}-a_i} < 1$ (presumably).

Shift variables must be used to obtain estimates of a family of equations of this type. For example, assume that a set of computer systems introduced between 1962 and 1966 (inclusive) is to be analyzed. Introduce four shift variables, defined as follows:

$$S_{63} = \begin{cases} 1 \text{ if the system was introduced in 1963,} \\ 0 \text{ otherwise;} \end{cases}$$

$$S_{64} = \begin{cases} 1 \text{ if the system was introduced in 1964,} \\ 0 \text{ otherwise;} \end{cases}$$

$$S_{65} = \begin{cases} 1 \text{ if the system was introduced in 1965,} \\ 0 \text{ otherwise;} \end{cases}$$

$$S_{66} = \begin{cases} 1 \text{ if the system was introduced in 1966,} \\ 0 \text{ otherwise.} \end{cases}$$

Let the regression equation be

$$\ln C = a* + b(\ln P) + b*(\ln P)^2 + \beta_{63}S_{63} + \beta_{64}S_{64} + \beta_{65}S_{65} + \beta_{66}S_{66}$$

In terms of our former notation:

$$\begin{aligned} \text{for 1962:} \quad & a_{62} = a*, \\ \text{for 1963:} \quad & a_{63} = a* + \beta_{63}, \\ \text{for 1964:} \quad & a_{64} = a* + \beta_{64}, \\ \text{for 1965:} \quad & a_{65} = a* + \beta_{65}, \\ \text{for 1966:} \quad & a_{66} = a* + \beta_{66}. \end{aligned}$$

Each value of β will presumably be negative, and larger in the absolute sense than the one preceding it. If systems introduced in any given year cost significantly less than those introduced in the base year (in this example, 1962), the t value of the relevant β coefficient should be large. In Knight's first study, the t values associated with the β coefficients were all larger (in absolute value) than 2. Similar results were apparently obtained in the second study.

As indicated previously, Knight's initial analysis was based on 225 systems introduced before mid-1963. Eight time periods were used to assure sufficient observations in each period, and regression analysis was performed for each of the following equations:

(1) $\ln C = a^* + b(\ln P_s) + b^*(\ln P_s)^2 + \beta_1 S_1 + \beta_2 S_2$

$$+ \beta_3 S_3 + \beta_4 S_4 + \beta_5 S_5 + \beta_6 S_6 + \beta_7 S_7$$

(2) $\ln C = a^* + b(\ln P_s) + \beta_1 S_1 + \beta_2 S_2 + \beta_3 S_3 + \beta_4 S_4$

$$+ \beta_5 S_5 + \beta_6 S_6 + \beta_7 S_7$$

where $S_1, \ldots, S_7$ are shift variables for periods other than the base period.

Equation 1 gave a correlation coefficient of .9596; equation 2, a value of .9569. In other words, very little additional explanatory power was gained by allowing for a U-shaped average cost curve (i.e., using equation 1); the simpler equation, which is consistent with a monotonic average cost curve, represented the data virtually as well. Similar results were obtained for commercial data processing (i.e., using P_c instead of P_s). Knight attributes these results to the reluctance of firms in the industry to build a computer exceeding the size that gives the lowest cost/performance ratio at the time. However, he notes some exceptions: "The AN/FSQ 7 and 8 (the Sage computers), the UNIVAC Lark and the IBM Stretch . . . each obtained a new high evaluation for absolute computing power, but at a considerably [poorer cost/performance ratio]." [73] He also suggests that the optimal (i.e., lowest-cost/performance) size (P) has increased over time.

Since the simpler relationship between cost and performance appeared to fit the data virtually as well as did the more complex equation, Knight used equation 2 for all subsequent analyses. For any year i:

$$\ln C = a_i + b(\ln P)$$

Equivalently,

(a) $C = e^{a_i} P^b$

(b) $P = e^{-a_i/b} C^{-1/b}$

[73] Knight dissertation, op. cit., pp. VI–20, VI–21.

or

(c) $C/P = e^{a_i}P^{b-1}$

The coefficient b provides a direct measure of economies of scale:

$b > 1$: diseconomies of scale (i.e., C/P increases with P),
$b = 1$: constant returns to scale (i.e., C/P unaffected by P),
$b < 1$: economies of scale (i.e., C/P decreases with P).

Note that the method assumes that economies of scale, measured by the value of b, were the same in every period covered in a particular study—no means is provided to determine whether or not this was actually the case.

Four estimates of b were obtained by Knight: [74]

Period	Scientific Computation	Commercial Data Processing
1950–1962	0.519	0.459
1962–1966	.322	.404

The results suggest substantial economies of scale. During the earlier period, Grosch's law ($b = 0.5$) appeared to hold rather well for both scientific and commercial computation. But during the later period even greater economies of scale appear to have been available; for example, the results suggest that cost was proportional to the *cube* root of scientific power. The evidence concerning scientific versus commercial computation is mixed: only for the later period are the results consistent with those described earlier (i.e., greater economies of scale for scientific computing than for commercial data processing).

Knight suggests that relatively little attention be paid to the dif-

[74] Knight actually performed each analysis twice. The first analysis utilized all the data. The cost of each computer system was then compared with the value predicted by the equation obtained from the analysis. If the actual cost exceeded that predicted by more than one-half the standard deviation (error) of predicted cost, the computer system was removed from the sample. The second analysis used only the remaining systems. All the results reported by Knight are based on the second analysis for each of the four cases. This relatively arbitrary procedure was utilized because variation from the hypothesized relationship was presumed to be due to the existence of truly inefficient (i.e., overpriced) systems and to the presence of errors in the estimates of P, C, and the date of introduction. Hopefully the method removed from the sample most of the overpriced systems and few of the others.

ferences among these four values, $b = 0.5$ (Grosch's law) being acceptable as an adequate general approximation. In view of the nature of the data, this is undoubtedly a sensible approach. Although particular numeric values may be disputed, Knight's results lend strong support to the hypothesis that substantial economies of scale exist over most of the range of equipment introduced for sale in any given year.

The extent of technological progress from period to period may be estimated directly from the coefficients obtained for the shift variables. Such progress can be measured in many ways. Two of the more useful are:

(1) the percentage improvement in performance for given cost, and
(2) the percentage reduction in cost for given performance.

The relationship between the two measures is not intuitively obvious. Consider the ratio of the cost in year i to that in year $i + 1$ for given performance:

$$\frac{C_i}{C_{i+1}} = \frac{e^{a_i}P^b}{e^{a_{i+1}}P^b} = e^{a_i - a_{i+1}}$$

Contrast this with the ratio of performance in year $i + 1$ to that in year i for given cost:

$$\frac{P_{i+1}}{P_i} = \frac{e^{-a_{i+1}/b}C^{-1/b}}{e^{-a_i/b}C^{-1/b}} = (e^{a_i - a_{i+1}})^{1/b}$$

Knight found that the average annual improvement in performance for given cost during the period before 1963 was approximately 80% for scientific computation. Since Grosch's law also held approximately,

$$\frac{P_{i+1}}{P_i} = 1.80 = (e^{a_i - a_{i+1}})^{1/0.5}$$

therefore

$$e^{a_i - a_{i+1}} \approx 1.34$$

Thus, for given performance, the cost in the previous year was, on the average, 34% greater than that in any specified year. In other terms, the average annual decrease in cost for given performance was only 25%, that is, $100[1 - (1/1.34)]$.

An interesting, though somewhat academic, question concerns the proper definition of technological progress. The reduction in cost for given performance is based solely on the underlying shift in the curve (i.e., $e^{a_i - a_{i+1}}$), whereas the improvement in performance for given cost depends on both the shift and the extent to which there are economies or diseconomies of scale [i.e., $(e^{a_i - a_{i+1}})^{1/b}$]. Only in the case of constant returns to scale ($b = 1$) are the measures comparable. In view of the nature of the function used by Knight, the reduction in cost for given

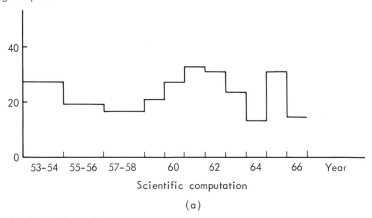

(a)

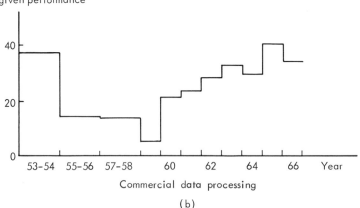

(b)

FIGURE 9-11. Annual percentage reduction in cost for given performance, 1953 through 1966.

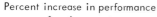

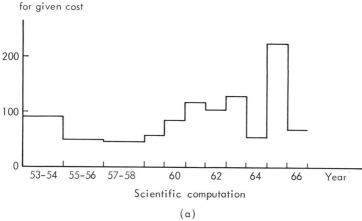

Scientific computation

(a)

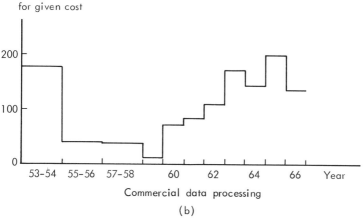

Commercial data processing

(b)

FIGURE 9–12. Annual percentage increase in performance for given cost, 1953 through 1966.

performance appears to be the better measure of technological progress per se, but the choice should, in the final analysis, depend on the question being asked.

Figure 9–11a shows the annual percentage reduction in cost for given performance for scientific computation from 1953 through 1966; Fig. 9–11b shows the results for commercial data processing. Figures 9–12a and b indicate the percentage increases in performance for given cost for the two tasks.[75] Over the period as a whole, the performance obtainable for given cost approximately doubled[76] every year, while the cost of given performance fell about 25%.[77]

As Figs. 9–11 and 9–12 show, the percentage improvement varied considerably from year to year. Relatively little importance should be accorded this variation. Knight found that only two of the annual changes before 1963 differed significantly[78] from the average for the period. Any apparent trend is thus undoubtedly spurious. The overall record, however, strongly supports two hypotheses: (1) that progress has been substantial, and (2) that it has been relatively continuous. The second statement is the more controversial, since it conflicts with the widely held opinion that equates progress with the introduction of a new "generation" of computers. To be sure, there are some peaks in the curves, such as the one for scientific computation in 1965, the year that some third-generation machines were delivered. But significant progress appears to have taken place in every year. From a cost/effectiveness standpoint, the rate of improvement has been remarkably constant over time.

F. THE NATURE OF TECHNOLOGICAL PROGRESS

A number of questions concerning the nature of technological progress in the computer industry have not, thus far, been answered. For example, how rapidly have innovations been dispersed throughout the

---

[75] Each value is stated as an annual change. For example, the ratio of performance in the period 1953–1954 to that in the previous period for given cost was approximately $(1.90)^2$, equivalent to an annual improvement of 90%.

Percentage increases in performance for given cost were taken directly from Knight. The decreases in cost for given performance were calculated as follows: Let

I_p = percentage increase in P, given C (from Knight), and
D_c = percentage decrease in C, given P,

then

$$D_c = 100 \left[1 - \left(1 + \frac{I_p}{100} \right)^{-b} \right]$$

using the value of b appropriate for the period and type of computation.
[76] The average annual increase in P, given C, was 92.5% for scientific computation, and 106.2% for commercial data processing.
[77] The average annual decrease in C, given P, was 23.6% for scientific computation, and 24.7% for commercial data processing.
[78] In the sense of statistical significance.

industry? And to what extent has a firm's ability to manufacture computers been a function of the number of different models designed and built in the past?

Knight's initial studies did not attempt to answer such questions: neither a pattern of technological progress nor a set of causes was assumed. By employing shift variables representing different dates of introduction, Knight simply estimated the actual changes from period to period. And, as shown in Figs. 9–11 and 9–12, such changes followed no simple pattern.

In a subsequent study [79] Knight and James L. Barr considered the phenomenon of technological progress in more detail. The study was limited to equipment introduced before mid-1963,[80] with performance measured solely in terms of scientific computation (i.e., by P_s). The analysis was designed primarily to test the consistency of the data with alternative simple models of technological progress. Among the hypotheses considered were these:

1. Technological progress is a function of calendar time; specifically, cost/effectiveness improves by a constant percentage every time period.
2. Technological progress is a function of the number of different models previously designed (and built) by the firm in question; specifically, cost/effectiveness improves by a constant percentage every time that a new model is introduced by the firm.
3. Technological progress is a function of the number of different models previously designed (and built) by all firms in the industry. In particular, cost/effectiveness improves by a constant percentage every time that a new model is introduced by any firm.
4. Technological progress occurs when specific innovations are incorporated into computer designs. Any major innovation increases the cost/effectiveness of all systems in which it is incorporated by the same percentage.[81]

---

[79] Kenneth Knight and James L. Barr, "Micro-measurement of Technological Change in the Computer Industry," 1967 (unpublished).
[80] Only 223 systems were included (contrasted with the 225 of the earlier study). However, the results are not likely to be affected significantly by this minor difference.
[81] These descriptions refer to percentage increases in "cost/effectiveness"; as shown in the formulas that follow, the precise assumption is that performance will increase by some percentage for given cost.

The equations estimated were of the form

$$\ln P_s = a + b(\ln C) + [\quad]$$

where P_s = scientific performance (in operations per second), a and b are constants, C = cost (in dollars per second),[82] and [   ] represents one or more of the following technological progress functions:

$$(1)\ dT \qquad (3)\ fN_I$$
$$(2)\ eN_f \qquad (4)\ \sum_{i=1}^{6} g_i I_i$$

where d, e, f, g_i = constants,

T = the time of first delivery of a system,

N_f = the number of different models previously produced by the system's manufacturer,

N_I = the number of different models previously produced by all firms in the industry, and

$$I_i = \begin{cases} 1 \text{ if the system incorporates innovation } i, \\ 0 \text{ otherwise.} \end{cases}$$

i	Innovation
1	Magnetic tape
2	Transistorization
3	Index registers
4	Magnetic core
5	Buffering
6	Magnetic drums

The poorest results were obtained by using the simple hypothesis that progress occurs at a constant (percentage) rate over time. With hypothesis 1, only 56.1% of the variation was explained. Moreover, the technological progress function per se (dT) accounted for little of the explanatory power—almost all was attributable to the cost variable.[83]

Good results were obtained when technological progress was hypothesized to be an industry-wide learning phenomenon: 77.2% of

[82] Based on monthly rental adjusted by the U.S. Census of Manufacturers' wholesale price index for electrical machinery.
[83] The t value for coefficient d was only 0.417.

the variation in P_s was explained by using hypothesis 3. Similar success was obtained when progress was assumed to be related solely to the introduction of major innovations (hypothesis 4).[84]

To assess the true importance of the alternative hypotheses, a regression analysis including all of them but hypothesis 1 was performed, using the equation

$$\ln P_s = a + b(\ln C) + eN_f + fN_l + \sum_{i=1}^{6} g_i I_i$$

Approximately 81% of the variation in ($\ln P_s$) was explained, with three of the independent variables accounting for virtually all the explanatory power (i.e., with significant coefficients): cost (C), the total number produced (N_l), and the presence or absence of index registers (I_3).

One of the problems typical of a study of this type involves colinearity among the independent variables. Obviously N_f, N_l, and T were correlated to some extent. But many less obvious correlations were also present. In such situations, whenever a truly important variable is omitted from the analysis, one or more unimportant variables may act as surrogate for it. This makes it extremely difficult to assess the true importance of any variable, let alone the numeric value representing its true impact on the dependent variable. Thus one might be reluctant to conclude, for example, that transistorization was not an unusually important innovation in the computer industry. On the other hand, it appears reasonable to assume that technological progress has been dispersed relatively quickly throughout the industry, with only minor residual benefits accruing to innovative firms.[85]

One interesting sidelight of this study deserves mention. Knight and Barr attempted to determine whether IBM computers differed from those of other manufacturers by performing the analysis again with a shift variable added (equal to 1 if the system was manufactured by IBM, and 0 otherwise). No significant increase in explanatory power was observed. The cost/effectiveness of IBM equipment appears to

[84] Although 79.5% of the variation in P_s was explained by using both hypothesis 1 and hypothesis 4, coefficient d was not significant.
[85] This assumes a reasonable correspondence between cost to the user (rental price) and cost of production. It is possible that some innovative firms have reaped considerable rewards over time through lower costs.

have been neither greater nor smaller on the average than that of other manufacturers—a result consistent with an economist's expectations concerning market prices (used to measure cost in the study), assuming that total effectiveness (i.e., desirability) has been measured correctly.

G. PRICE AND COST

All the studies reported in this chapter use the price or rental charge set by a manufacturer as a measure of cost. Obviously this figure represents cost to the user, but it is not necessarily the cost of production. If all systems were sold in a perfectly competitive market, price would equal both marginal and average cost of production; but the market for computers, although competitive, hardly corresponds to the model of perfect competition. As shown earlier, if the demand curve for a product is downward-sloping, a profit-maximizing seller will plan on a price-quantity combination for which price exceeds marginal cost, the extent of the disparity depending on the difference between marginal and average revenue (i.e., on the elasticity of demand).

Given a price-quantity combination for system i,[86] we have

$$\frac{MR_i}{P_i} = 1 + \frac{1}{e_i}$$

where MR_i = the marginal revenue for system i at P_i, Q_i,

P_i = the price of system i, and

e_i = the price elasticity at P_i, Q_i.

But since the manufacturer will select a price-quantity combination for which marginal cost equals marginal revenue,

$$\frac{MC_i}{P_i} = 1 + \frac{1}{e_i}$$

If the elasticity of demand at current prices were the same for all systems (i.e., $e_1 = e_2 = \cdots$), every price would be a constant multiple of

---

[86] This relationship follows directly from the definitions of MR and e:

$$MR_i \equiv \frac{d(P_i Q_i)}{dQ_i} = P_i + \frac{dP_i}{dQ_i}(Q_i)$$

$$e_i \equiv \frac{dQ_i/Q_i}{dP_i/P_i} = \frac{dQ_i}{dP_i} \cdot \frac{P_i}{Q_i}$$

marginal cost, and relationships concerning marginal costs could be determined by examining prices. But there is no reason to assume that elasticities are, in fact, the same. Thus prices will be imperfect surrogates for underlying costs. This holds, a fortiori, for the prices of individual components, for which cross elasticities of demand are also likely to be relevant (i.e., the price of one component will influence the quantity of another demanded).

What, then, does the price of a system or component represent? It may be regarded as an imperfect measure of cost of production, subject to an expectation of considerable error. On the other hand, it may be considered a measure of value to the user. As shown earlier, if quantity is continuously variable, and price per unit is unaffected by quantity purchased, each purchaser will select a quantity for which marginal value equals price. For those choosing not to purchase, of course, marginal value will be below price. In the case in which integral units must be used (1) for purchasers, the incremental value of one unit less will exceed price; and (2) for both purchasers and nonpurchasers, the incremental value of an additional unit will be less than price.

We conclude that price measures value relatively well and cost of manufacture rather poorly. More properly, price results from the interaction of (1) producers' technological possibilities, input costs, etc., and (2) buyers' values; in other words, it reflects both supply and demand conditions.

This discussion raises some questions concerning the proper economic interpretation of studies such as those confirming Grosch's law. Assume that price is, in fact, proportional to the square root of computing power. Does this relationship reflect economies of scale in manufacturing, or merely suggest that double the computing power is not considered worth twice as much by buyers? It has been suggested that Grosch's law holds only because manufacturers use it to set prices. Others have implied that it is a direct result of the method used to measure power. An obvious case of the latter type would arise if processor power were expressed as the product of memory size and operations performed per second. Assume that one system has memory M_1 and can perform N_1 operations per second, giving a power of P_1 $(= M_1 N_1)$ at a cost of C_1. Now put two such systems in a box and call the result a new computer. Obviously it will cost twice as much $(2C_1)$ and have four times the power $[P_2 = (2M_1)(2N_1) = 4P_1]$. Neither Solomon's nor Knight's approach would yield such results directly; even if one or both did, the conclusion might be correct (in our example, actual power might be quadrupled if both memory modules and both processing units were interconnected).

H. COST-ESTIMATING EQUATIONS

Studies such as those of Knight and Solomon should be viewed primarily as attempts to derive empirical relationships between price and one or more other factors. When price is viewed as cost to the user, the results are cost-estimating equations, reflecting past relationships that have resulted from the complex interplay of demand and supply conditions. Needless to say, their relevance for the future depends on the likelihood of stability in the underlying forces (or, in some cases, on constant rates of change).

Since cost-estimating equations of this type are, at base, empirical in nature (rather than direct tests of simple hypotheses of economic theory), it is not unreasonable to take an even more pragmatic approach than did Knight, Solomon, and others. The general strategy adopted in their studies was to define a relationship between computing power and the basic characteristics of a system (cycle time, add time, etc.):

$$P \equiv f(c_1, c_2, \ldots, c_n)$$

where P = computing power, and c_i = the value of characteristic i. For a given specific definition of P, a cross section of systems was analyzed to determine empirically a relationship between cost and computing power:

$$C = g(P)$$

After completing the analysis, of course, cost could be related to the basic characteristics:

$$C = g[f(c_1, c_2, \ldots, c_n)]$$

or

$$C = h(c_1, c_2, \ldots, c_n)$$

An alternative approach is to remain agnostic about the relationship between basic characteristics and power (i.e., the desirability of each characteristic), estimating directly an equation of the form

$$C = h(c_1, c_2, \ldots, c_n)$$

This approach should result in a better "fit" since it involves fewer constraints;[87] however, the economic meaning of the resulting coefficients may be unclear. Another problem concerns colinearity—systems strong in one characteristic are likely to be strong in some related area, making it difficult to assess the relative importance of each separately. Although this may not affect the value of the equation for estimating cost, it may make the coefficients essentially meaningless as indicators of the relative costs of individual characteristics.

Despite these drawbacks, cost-estimating equations have considerable appeal and can prove valuable if obtained and used wisely. Many such relationships have been derived for computer equipment. We will briefly describe three sets of results.

A preliminary study of this type was performed at the RAND Corporation in 1963.[88] Forty-six different configurations of 19 computers were considered, each comprising a set of modules capable of performing basic computation, storage, and control functions, but not input-output. Approximately 83% of the variance in rental was explained with an equation of the form

$$R = 370 + 0.033N_c + 0.015M_b$$

where $R =$ the monthly rental (in dollars) of the equipment group composed of the central processor, memory, and associated control modules,

$N_c =$ the number of memory cycles per second, and

$M_b =$ the memory core capacity (in bits).

Other forms using the same variables gave somewhat poorer results (for example, only 79% of the variance was explained by using a log-linear version). Including more variables added little to predictive power—in no case was the explained variation increased by more than 1%. Among the variables considered were the number of additions per second, the memory size in words, and the number of bits per word. Their rejection means not that they are unimportant (or free), but simply that they add little to predictive power, given the typical mix of characteristics for computers such as those included in the study.

As indicated in Chapter 6, two of the most widely used summaries

[87] For example, if $P \equiv c_1 + 2c_2$, no simple form of $C = g(P)$ can reflect a relationship in which c_1 and c_2 contribute equally to cost.

[88] Early, Barro, and Margolis, RM–3072–PR (May, 1963), pp. 20–31.

of computer system costs and capabilities are published by Adams [89] and *Computers and Automation*.[90] Since both sources deal with "typical" configurations rather than specific complements of equipment, many items are expressed as ranges and/or "typical" values. Two studies have been made to investigate the usefulness of such data for obtaining cost-estimating equations. The first, by Patrick, covered 53 second-generation systems;[91] the second, by Jacob, 50 third-generation systems.[92]

The reliability of the data given by Adams and *Computers and Automation* is difficult to ascertain. However, in the areas in which the two sources overlap, they at least appear to be reasonably consistent. In particular, the "typical" rental figures are almost perfectly correlated.[93] Thus selection of one source instead of the other should matter relatively little.[94]

Patrick was able to explain 89% of the variation in (ln rent) for second-generation systems by using the following equation:[95]

ln (rent in dollars per month)
= 3.699

$+ 0.253$ ln (space occupied in square feet) $t = 6.675$

$+ 0.017$ (number of months since first installation) $= 5.972$

$+ 0.648 \begin{cases} 1 \text{ if IBM} \\ 0 \text{ otherwise} \end{cases}$ $= 4.196$

$+ 0.168$ ln (thousands of fixed-point additions per second) $= 2.990$

$+ 0.181$ ln (minimum storage capacity in bits) $= 2.354$

$+ 0.154$ ln (maximum storage capacity in bits) $= 2.070$

$- 0.104$ ln (number of similar systems installed to date) $= 1.853$

---

[89] *Computer Characteristics Quarterly.*

[90] *Computers and Automation,* monthly census and annual directory.

[91] James M. Patrick, "Computer Cost/Effectiveness," December 1966 (unpublished). This paper was written as a term project for a seminar given by the author at the University of Washington.

[92] This research was performed by Nancy Jacob of the University of California, Irvine. Errors of interpretation are, of course, the present author's responsibility.

[93] For a sample of 25 systems the correlation coefficient was .992, using data from late 1966. On the average the figures in *Computers and Automation* were 9% higher than those given by Adams.

[94] Except that, as of this writing, Adams no longer gives a single "typical" rental figure (only a range), while *Computers and Automation* continues to give a point-estimate.

[95] Space occupied and number of installations were based on data in *Computers and Automation,* June, 1966; all other figures were based on data in *Computer Characteristics Quarterly,* April, 1966.

These results should be viewed with considerable skepticism because of the small number of observations (53) relative to the number of variables (8) and the known colinearity among the independent variables. Nonetheless it is instructive to see whether the coefficients at least display some expected properties.

Perhaps the most surprising result is the explanatory power provided by the space occupied by a system. A larger computer should not be considered more valuable than a smaller one, *ceteris paribus;* but, given equally space-saving designs, a larger system may be expected to have greater capability than a smaller one (in other words, other things will not be equal). No better example could be obtained to illustrate the fact that correlation need not imply cause and effect.

The second most significant variable in the equation is the number of months since the first installation of the system. This should not be interpreted as a reflection of technological progress per se, since all rental values are supposed to prevail at the same time. The equation suggests that, at any particular time, people will be willing to pay more for older systems than for newer ones with equivalent hardware characteristics. Age is apparently acting as a surrogate for some valuable characteristics not included explicitly in the data—most probably, software support and the reliability of both software and hardware. Interestingly, the numeric value is almost the same as that obtained by Knight using rental charges measured at the date of introduction.[96] The similarity may be attributable to the extremely gross measure used for rental charge. It is notable, however, that the results are consistent with our earlier observation that decreases in rental charges for old systems have been infrequent.

The size and apparent significance of the third variable accord with the expectations of at least some observers. The results suggest that second-generation IBM systems cost approximately 90% more, on the average, than non-IBM systems with comparable hardware characteristics.[97] Many explanations are possible. IBM systems may have had better software, maintenance support, etc.; if so, this coefficient may

---

[96] Knight's results suggest an annual decrease in cost of 20–25% for given performance. Patrick's equation indicates a 1.7% decrease each month—equivalent to about 23% per year:

$$e^{12(0.017)} \approx 1.23$$

[97] $e^{0.648} \approx 1.90$.

provide a measure of the value of such superiority. Another possibility is that typical IBM systems were generally more "complete" (i.e., had more tape drives and other features) and thus more expensive than those of other manufacturers. Finally, the cynic might argue that users were willing to pay significantly more for IBM systems because they did not wish to be nonconformists, or because they had been deluded by IBM's unequaled sales force. The data are essentially neutral on the issue.

The results in regard to the remaining variables conform relatively well to expectations. The number of additions per second appears to represent processing power satisfactorily: the coefficient is positive and significant ($t > 2$). Since Adams did not indicate the memory capacity of a "typical" system, Patrick used the minimum and the maximum values. Both were significant ($t > 2$), with reasonably similar coefficients of the expected type (i.e., suggesting that the larger the memory, the more valuable is the system). The last relationship may be interpreted as a cause (cost per unit falls with the number installed) or as an effect (the lower the rental charge, the more systems are installed). However, the coefficient is neither particularly large nor particularly significant ($t < 2$).

Finally, it is interesting to note that Patrick's equation is consistent with moderate economies of scale. Rewriting the relationship with only the hardware characteristics stated explicitly, we have

$$\text{Rent} = K(\text{space})^{0.253} \, (\text{additions/second})^{0.168}$$

$$(\text{minimum storage})^{0.181} \, (\text{maximum storage})^{0.154}$$

Now, consider two systems, the second having double the hardware capabilities of the first (i.e., $\text{space}_2 = 2 \, \text{space}_1$, etc.). Obviously,

$$\text{Rent}_2 = \text{Rent}_1(2^{0.253+0.168+0.181+0.154})$$

$$= \text{Rent}_1(2^{0.756})$$

Thus doubling the hardware capability (performance) would increase cost (rental) by less than 70% ($2^{0.756} \approx 1.69$).

The results obtained in Jacob's subsequent study of 50 third-generation systems [98] provide some interesting contrasts. Slightly over 85%

---

[98] Defined as those first delivered after December, 1964.

of the variation in (ln rent) was explained with the following equation: [99]

ln (rent in dollars per month)
= 0.481

+0.693 ln (minimum storage capacity in thousands of
 bits) $t = 5.364$

+0.447 ln (memory cycle rate in thousands of bits per
 second) $= 4.219$

−0.447 ln (thousands of additions per second) $= 4.126$

+0.395 ln (number of operation codes) $= 2.349$

+0.017 (number of months since first installation) $= 1.371$

+0.110 ln (maximum storage capacity in thousands of
 bits) $= 0.751$

$+0.098 \begin{cases} 1 \text{ if IBM} \\ 0 \text{ otherwise} \end{cases}$ $= 0.300$

+0.00002 (number of similar systems installed to date) $= 0.087$

Surprisingly, the coefficient indicating the effect of the number of months since first delivery equals that obtained by Patrick (to three places); note, however, that it does not appear to be highly significant ($t = 1.371$). The number of systems installed is clearly insignificant, perhaps because of the relatively short period of time covered. Interestingly, the apparent difference between IBM systems and all others found in Patrick's study is not at all evident — the coefficient for the shift variable is small and insignificant ($t = 0.300$). Second-generation IBM systems may have been more expensive than others, but apparently third-generation systems were not.

As in Patrick's study, rental is clearly related to memory size, but the minimum capacity appears to be far more relevant than the maximum capacity in this case, perhaps because the available ranges have become so great that the typical system's storage is considerably closer to the minimum than to the maximum figure. The inclusion of the size of the instruction repertoire appears to add to predictive power — the t value is 2.349, and the coefficient has the expected sign.

Perhaps the most curious aspect of this study concerns the coeffi-

[99] Rent based on data given in *Computer Characteristics Quarterly,* October, 1966; number of systems installed based on data from *Computers and Automation,* May, 1967; all other data from *Computer Characteristics Quarterly,* Spring, 1967.

cients for computation power and memory cycle rate. Both are significant ($t = 4.126$ and 4.219, respectively), and the two are equal in absolute value (to three significant digits). But they differ in sign. As expected, the equation suggests that rent will increase with the memory cycle rate. It also suggests, however, that rent will decrease with the number of additions performed per second. The implication seems to be that the ability to add rapidly is an undesirable attribute — hardly an expected result.

It might be best to argue that this simply illustrates the danger of too few degrees of freedom, too much colinearity, and the violation of several implicit assumptions of regression analysis. However, at least one rationalization deserves mention. Let R_c be the cycle rate and R_a the addition rate; then the equation may be written as

$$\ln (\text{rent}) = k + 0.447(\ln R_c) - 0.447(\ln R_a)$$

$$= k + 0.447(\ln R_c - \ln R_a)$$

or

$$\text{Rent} = K \left(\frac{R_c}{R_a}\right)^{0.447}$$

As this form indicates, neither the cycle rate nor the addition rate alone may provide much explanatory power, but the ratio may be more helpful. The larger the rate at which information can be transferred into and out of core memory relative to the rate at which addition can be performed, the more valuable the system, *ceteris paribus*. This result may be attributable solely to certain peculiarities of the data, but it is at least a more satisfying interpretation.

The modest economies of scale implied by Patrick's equation do not appear here. The sum of the coefficients for hardware characteristics actually exceeds 1.

None of the results described in this section should be considered definitive. However, these three studies illustrate the approach taken in many empirical attempts to obtain cost-estimating equations. It is, of course, comforting when results consistent with prior expectations are obtained. But the final test of any such equation is its ability to estimate cost more accurately than some meaningful alternative procedure. Given the rapid technological progress in the computer industry, it is not surprising that predictions based on past relationships have rarely proved satisfactory.

I. THE DEMAND FOR COMPUTATION

An interesting attempt to measure the demand for computation was made by Chow, using data covering the period 1954–1965.[100] For each year, two indices were calculated: one representing the price per unit of computing power, the other the total amount of computing power installed.[101] Needless to say, the data indicated that price has decreased over time whereas quantity has increased.

An economist might use price-quantity pairs of this type to estimate a demand curve by means of traditional regression techniques. A likely candidate would be the form exhibiting a constant elasticity:

$$\ln Q = a + b \ln P$$

or

---

[100] Gregory C. Chow, "Technological Change and the Demand for Computers," *American Economic Review*, December, 1967, pp. 1117–1130.

[101] Chow hypothesized that in any given year the price of a system would be related to the values of three basic attributes as follows:

$$\ln P^* = a - b_1 \ln t_m + b_2 \ln M - b_3 \ln t_a$$

or

$$P^* = A \left(\frac{M^{b_2}}{t_m^{b_1} t_a^{b_3}} \right)$$

where P^* = predicted monthly rental,
t_m = multiplication time (in microseconds),
M = memory size (in thousands of bits),
t_a = access time (in microseconds), and
$A = e^a$.

Chow assumed that price could be used as an adequate surrogate for computing power ("effectiveness"). As shown earlier, there appear to be substantial economies of scale in computation; Chow's assumption could thus lead to serious error if the overall mix of systems (in terms of effectiveness) changes radically over time. Barring such a change, the assumption should prove acceptable for the purposes of the study. In any event, the "quantity" of computing power of each system was measured by the rental it would have commanded in 1960. More specifically,

$$\ln Q = -0.1045 - 0.0654 \ln t_m + 0.5793 \ln M - 0.1406 \ln t_a$$

The total quantity of computing power installed was estimated, using IBM data, census figures from *Computers and Automation*, and extrapolation where necessary. An "absolute" price index for each year was calculated by taking a simple average of the price per unit of computing power for each of the models installed, with the actual rental charge of a system divided by its "quantity" of computing power to obtain the relevant measure of price per unit of computing power. Finally, a "relative" price index was obtained by deflating the "absolute" values to reflect changes in the general level of prices. The latter series is meant when the term *price* appears in our discussion of the study.

$$Q = AP^b$$

where $A = e^a$ and b = price elasticity of demand (<0).

A noneconomist might view the computer industry as a "growth" industry, attributing the increase in quantity installed simply to the passage of time. Such an interpretation usually holds that quantity will follow some known curve over time; the problem is simply to select the appropriate form and to estimate the relevant characteristics. One of the more popular forms is the logistic or S-shaped curve.[102] Another is the Gompertz curve, expressed as a differential equation of the form

$$\frac{dQ}{dt} = \alpha Q(\ln Q^* - \ln Q)$$

where Q^* is the equilibrium value of Q, which the actual value (Q) approaches asymptotically.

Using discrete time periods, we can restate the Gompertz relationship as

$$\ln Q_t - \ln Q_{t-1} = \alpha(\ln Q^* - \ln Q_{t-1})$$

Simple regression techniques can obviously be used to estimate the values of α and Q^*, given a series of quantity values ($Q_1, \ldots, Q_n$).

Neither of these simple approaches is likely to prove satisfactory for predicting the growth in computing power. Price has fallen dramatically, a fact that should be taken into account. But the technology has also changed rapidly, and it is difficult for users to comprehend. Moreover, its effective use may require major adjustments; thus it seems unlikely that new equilibrium situations will be reached almost instantly.

The point has been made before, but it is worth emphasizing again. Consider Fig. 9–13; let price-quantity combination P_1, Q_1 represent a

---

[102] Expressed by the differential equation

$$\frac{dQ}{dt} = \alpha Q(Q^* - Q)$$

where Q^* is the equilibrium value of Q, which the actual value approaches asymptotically.

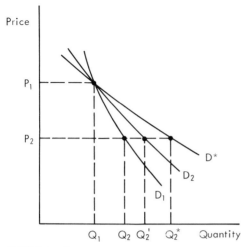

FIGURE 9–13. A long-run and two short-run demand curves.

long-run equilibrium situation. Now assume that price falls to P_2. At the end of 1 year, quantity will have increased to Q_2. If we are interested in response over this period, curve D_1 through these two points should be used as the (1-year response) demand curve. But note that, if price remains at P_2, quantity demanded may very likely increase, say to Q_2'. If we are interested in the situation 2 years after a price change, the relevant demand curve is D_2. If price remains at P_2 forever, and no underlying factors change, quantity will eventually reach some long-run equilibrium value Q_2*. The curve through such points $(D*)$ is often considered *the* demand curve. Clearly, it should not be estimated by simply fitting a curve directly to a series of points (e.g., P_1, Q_1 and P_2, Q_2) that do not represent long-run equilibrium positions.

Figure 9–14 shows an even more complex situation. The actual quantity demanded in period 1 (Q_1) is less than the appropriate long-run equilibrium amount (Q_1*). The increase from Q_1 to Q_2 in period 2 thus represents both a movement toward equilibrium and a response to a decrease in price. In other words, quantity increases from Q_1 to Q_2 in an attempt to approach the now larger equilibrium amount Q_2*.

Chow suggests that both the dynamic adjustment process and the existence of a downward-sloping long-run equilibrium demand curve

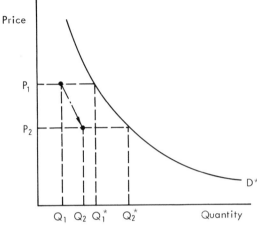

FIGURE 9-14. Movement towards equilibrium.

be recognized explicitly. Following common practice, let the equation of the long-run demand curve be

$$\ln Q_t^* = a + b \ln P_t$$

Now let the adjustment process be represented by the Gompertz curve:

$$\ln Q_t - \ln Q_{t-1} = \alpha \ln Q^* + \alpha \ln Q_{t-1}$$

Combining the two relations, we have

$$\ln Q_t - \ln Q_{t-1} = \alpha(a + b \ln P_t) + \alpha \ln Q_{t-1}$$
$$= \alpha a + \alpha b \ln P_t + \alpha \ln Q_{t-1}$$
$$= c_1 + c_2 \ln P_t + c_3 \ln Q_{t-1}$$

Standard regression methods may be used to estimate the coefficients c_1, c_2, and c_3. From them, the values of α, a, and b may be imputed.[103]

Figure 9-15 shows Chow's results. The long-run demand curve D^* has an elasticity (constant, by assumption) of 1.44. However, as the points representing the actual price-quantity pairs indicate, the adjustment process was relatively slow. The coefficient of the Gompertz

---

[103] $\alpha = c_3$, $b = c_2/c_3$, and $a = c_1/c_3$.

equation was 0.2526 – closer to 0 (representing no adjustment) than to 1 (representing full adjustment in one time period).

Figure 9–16 shows the ratio of the actual quantity installed to the corresponding equilibrium quantity for each year from 1954 through 1965. The dashed curve indicates the future pattern if price is unchanged; it is simply the Gompertz curve for $\alpha = 0.2526$. Needless to say, there is no reason to believe that price will not change; hence actual results are not likely to follow this pattern. If Chow's coeffi-

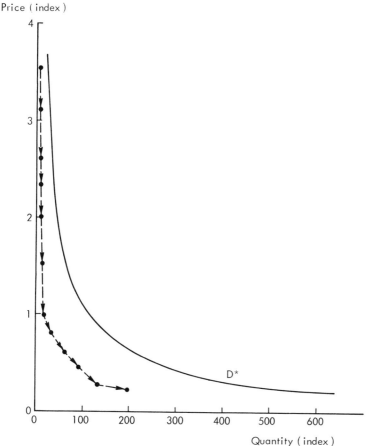

FIGURE 9-15. Relationship between price and quantity, showing actual values over time and an implied demand curve.

Q_t/Q_t^*

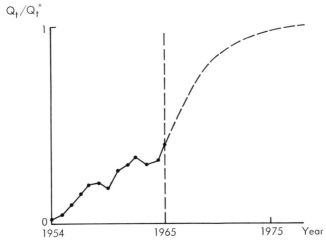

FIGURE 9-16. Ratio of actual quantity of computer power installed to corresponding equilibrium quantity during 1954–1965.

cients are approximately correct, the amount of computer power installed can be expected to triple eventually if its price remains constant. In the more likely event that price continues to fall, quantity can be expected to increase even more.

CHAPTER 10

THE COST AND EFFECTIVENESS OF MEMORY

A. INTRODUCTION

For some purposes it is useful to view a computer as a memory system connected to a series of processors. Input/output processors (e.g., selectors and multiplexors) bring information to the memory system from devices such as card readers, consoles, and metering instruments and/or deliver information to other devices such as line printers and cathode-ray tubes. Arithmetic processors manipulate information in memory, while logic units use such information to control the behavior of the system. The channels over which information can be transferred between memory and various processors differ in both speed and the ability to operate concurrently. One processor may require the use of another—for example, the central processor may be needed briefly to assist an input/output processor. Generally only one processor can be connected to a particular section of memory at a given time; the use of one channel may or may not preclude the use of another, and the use of one processor may or may not preclude the use of another.

The actual composition of a memory system is typically extremely complex. There may be hundreds of components—for example, magnetic tapes, disk units, drums, registers, read-only storage, and each of a potentially large number of logically separate blocks of core memory. Some processors may be able to communicate with only certain devices, requiring other processors to transfer information from component to component within the overall memory system.

The classical distinction between memory and input/output devices is often made on arbitrary grounds, further compounding the problem. Is a tape drive an input/output device? Or does the entire tape library constitute part of the system's memory? If the answer to the latter question is affirmative, in what category should punched-card files be placed?

The exact classification of each memory device is not particularly important. But its intelligent use most certainly is. The key problems associated with the design of both hardware and software are often those of memory management (broadly construed). Such problems are beyond the scope of this discussion; it suffices to say here that the relevant dollar value of any given configuration is that obtainable if it is used efficiently.

Obviously the selection of a preferred set of memory devices requires estimates of value predicated on efficient management. Some estimates of the relative costs of alternative devices, however, will also be needed. This chapter investigates methods for obtaining rough approximations of such costs. The general approach is similar to that used earlier for complete systems. Cost is taken to mean cost to the user – either rental charge or purchase price. It is used as the dependent variable in each regression equation.

Factors relating to cost of production as well as those concerned with value may be expected to influence cost to the user. Thus we consider as independent variables (1) various measures of effectiveness, (2) size (storage capacity), to determine the extent of any economies of scale, and (3) the number of months since first delivery, as a surrogate for reliability, software support, etc.

The empirical studies described in the subsequent sections consider only magnetic devices capable of both storing and retrieving information. Moreover, since most of the data were obtained during 1966 and 1967, only relatively traditional devices were examined.

A number of problems arise in connection with studies of this type. Perhaps most important, the overall value of a memory system is not likely to be related in any simple way to the characteristics of its individual components. It would be surprising to find, for example, that the appropriate measures of effectiveness have the property that the effectiveness of a system is simply the sum of the relevant values for its component devices. Recognition of this problem makes it difficult to establish useful boundaries when categorizing "devices." For example, should a controller be included as part of a "disk drive"? What if the controller can handle several devices concurrently? Worse yet, what if it can handle disk drives and drum units concurrently? In order to obtain empirical results, these questions must be answered, but the choices are usually made on pragmatic (if not arbitrary) grounds.

Similar problems arise with removable media. For example, the device "one tape drive with one tape mounted" has relatively small

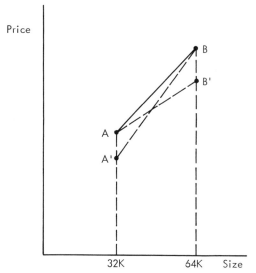

FIGURE 10-1. Possible relationships between computer size and price.

capacity, a relatively high cost per unit of information, and moderate access time. The device "one tape drive with 500 tapes plus an operator to mount whichever one is required" has substantial capacity, a much lower cost per unit stored, and very poor access times under many conditions. In theory both alternatives (and hundreds more) should be considered. In practice this is rarely done.

Another problem concerns the identification of the true cost of additional capacity. Consider two models of a computer system, one with 32K bits of core memory, and the other with 64K bits. Actual prices, shown by points A and B in Fig. 10-1, imply the incremental cost per bit shown by the slope of line AB. But what if one of the two models had been designed simply as a variation of the other? For example, if the original design had been optimized for 64K, the cost of a machine designed explicitly for 32K might be that shown by point A'. The actual prices thus would understate the "true" incremental cost of memory. The opposite situation would apply if the larger machine had been designed by modifying the smaller; then the "true" incremental cost of memory might be that indicated by the slope of the line AB'. This is not simply idle speculation—compatible families of equipment with wide ranges of possible configurations provide great advantages, but they also have drawbacks: for any given task, a member of such a family may be more costly than a machine designed specifically for the job in question. As always in empirical investigations, the law of large numbers may be invoked in this connection: hopefully cases in which incremental cost is understated will be approximately offset by others in which it is overstated.

B. MEASURES OF EFFECTIVENESS

The relative importance of various characteristics of a memory device depends greatly on the details of its intended use. A universally applicable measure of effectiveness cannot possibly be specified. Instead, we will consider two radically different uses of memory and obtain two measures of effectiveness for each.

Consider a memory device capable of storing N bits of information. Let $t_{i,j}$ represent the minimum time between the access of bit i and the access of bit j (for purposes of this discussion we do not differentiate between a reading operation and a writing operation; the term *access* will be used to signify either one). Note that, in general, $t_{i,j}$ need not equal $t_{j,i}$: for example, if bit j follows bit i on a track of a rotating device, $t_{i,j}$ will be very short whereas $t_{j,i}$ will be only slightly less than the time required to complete a revolution.

Now let the bits be numbered from 1 to N in such a manner that the following sum is minimized:

$$T_T = \sum_{i=1}^{N-1} t_{i,i+1}$$

Here T_T is the time required to access all N bits in order; we simply require a numbering system that minimizes this time. Many alternatives may be available (e.g., the choice is completely arbitrary for certain core memory units); or there may be only one such scheme, perhaps for a magnetic tape that can only be accessed while moving forward. In any event, we assume henceforth that the numbering scheme gives the minimum possible value of T_T.

1. Random Access

At a high level of abstraction we may describe the use of a memory device as simply a sequence of accesses. Such a sequence may have a simple pattern or be essentially random. One extreme is represented by a completely sequential pattern:

$$1, 2, 3, \ldots, N$$

The next element in this pattern is completely predictable if the present element is known. The other end of the spectrum is represented by a so-called *random walk*. In such a sequence, knowledge of the previous elements is of no value in predicting the next element. A special case arises when each bit has an equal chance of being accessed:

$$\mathrm{Pr}\ (i = k) = \frac{1}{N} \quad \text{for each } k = 1 \text{ to } N$$

$$\mathrm{Pr}\ (j = k) = \frac{1}{N} \quad \text{for each } k = 1 \text{ to } N$$

We will use the term *random access* to refer to such a case. It is clearly the most demanding in terms of the design (and use) of a memory device. Also, since this case lies at one end of the full spectrum of possible uses, it seems reasonable to attempt to represent the effectiveness of a memory device under such conditions.

In general the object of interest is the interaccess time $(t_{i,j})$. Under the conditions of random access, what will be the probability distribution of $t_{i,j}$ for a given device? Once the distribution is known, it may be summarized in many ways. Following convention, we use two measures:

$E(t_{i,j})$ = the expected value of interaccess time under conditions of random access, and

$\sigma(t_{i,j})$ = the standard deviation of interaccess time under conditions of random access.

As shown below, distributions with radically different shapes may be obtained for different types of devices. Comparisons based solely on these two measures may thus prove unsatisfactory if a choice among very different devices is to be made. However, such measures should suffice for our purpose: to obtain general relationships for broad classes of devices.

Figure 10–2 shows the distribution of $t_{i,j}$ for a core storage unit.

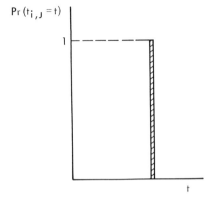

FIGURE 10-2. Distribution of interaccess time for a core storage unit.

This is one of the few types of truly random-access storage devices: $t_{i,j}$ is the same for all values of i and j,[1] hence $\sigma(t_{i,j}) = 0$.

Figure 10-3 shows the distribution for a rotating device with one read/write head per track (assuming instantaneous selection of the proper track).[2] For such a device the distribution of $t_{i,j}$ is the same, regardless of the value of i.[3] Thus Fig. 10-3 could represent the conditional distribution of $t_{i,j}$ for any given i or the unconditional distribution of $t_{i,j}$. The same statement can, of course, be made concerning Fig. 10-2.

For some devices the distribution of interaccess times may be quite complex. Consider a disk or drum unit with fewer read/write heads than tracks; both rotational delay and arm movement must be taken into account. Figure 10-3 indicates the distribution of time required once the appropriate track is selected, but what are the characteristics of the arm-movement time distribution?

Let there be N positions, with a constant rate of arm movement between positions. Let i and j represent numbered arm positions;

[1] This is not precisely true for some systems. For example, the access time for some elements of memory on the IBM 360/67 is 6% greater than that for other elements because of differences in distance from the central processor. We ignore such complications here.
[2] Needless to say, Fig. 10-3 is an approximation; in fact, only certain values of t are possible, but it is convenient to represent t as a continuous variable.
[3] Note that this statement does not imply that the value of $t_{i,j}$ for any given j is unaffected by the choice of i.

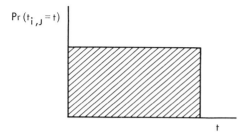

FIGURE 10–3. Distribution of interaccess time for a head-per-track rotating device.

and, for convenience, assume that time is measured so that

$$t_{i,i+1} = t_{i+1,i} = 1$$

As before, we assume completely random accesses.[4]

Figure 10–4 shows the conditional probability distribution of $t_{i,j}$ for $i = i'$. Table 10–1 provides a numeric example for a device with seven positions numbered 0 through 6. Each row in the table corresponds to a conditional probability distribution of the type illus-

[4] That is,

$$Pr\ (i = k) = \frac{1}{N} \quad \text{for each } k = 1 \text{ to } N$$

and

$$Pr\ (j = k) = \frac{1}{N} \quad \text{for each } k = 1 \text{ to } N$$

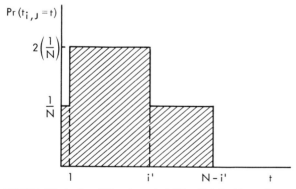

FIGURE 10–4. Conditional probability distribution of arm movement time for a rotating device.

TABLE 10-1. Pr $(t_{i',j} = t)$

				t			
i'	0	1	2	3	4	5	6
0	1/7	1/7	1/7	1/7	1/7	1/7	1/7
1	1/7	2/7	1/7	1/7	1/7	1/7	0
2	1/7	2/7	2/7	1/7	1/7	0	0
3	1/7	2/7	2/7	2/7	0	0	0
4	1/7	2/7	2/7	1/7	1/7	0	0
5	1/7	2/7	1/7	1/7	1/7	1/7	0
6	1/7	1/7	1/7	1/7	1/7	1/7	1/7
Pr $(t_{i,j} = t)$:	7/49	12/49	10/49	8/49	6/49	4/49	2/49

trated in Fig. 10-4 (note the symmetry—row $N - i'$ is the same as row i'). The unconditional probability distribution is shown in the bottom row of the table: it is simply the weighted average of the other rows, with each one weighted by the probability of its occurrence (equal to $1/N$ in each case).

The results can be generalized:

$$\text{Pr}\ (t_{i,j} = 0) = \frac{1}{N}$$

$$\text{Pr}\ (t_{i,j} = t) = \frac{2(N - t)}{N^2}\quad \text{for } 1 \leqq t \leqq N - 1$$

Figures 10-5a and b show the distributions for $N = 7$ and 20. For large values of N a sufficiently close approximation is provided by the following continuous distribution:

$$\text{Pr}\ (t_{i,j} = t) = \frac{2(N - t)}{N^2}\quad \text{for } 0 \leqq t \leqq N$$

The graph of such a distribution is a triangle with altitude $2/N$ and base N. It thus has the required property that the sum of the probabilities equals 1.[5] It is a simple matter to compute the mean and standard deviation of $t_{i,j}$ for such a distribution. The mean is

$$^5 \int_{t=0}^{N} [\text{Pr}\ (t_{i,j} = t)\ dt] = \text{area of triangle} = \frac{1}{2} \left(\frac{2}{N} \cdot N \right) = 1$$

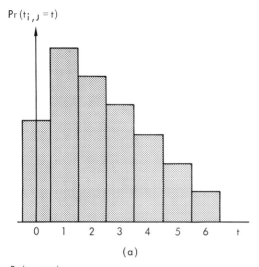

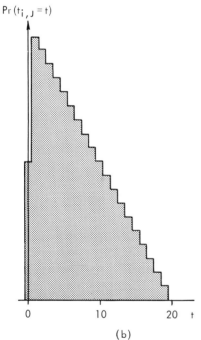

FIGURE 10-5. Probability distribution of arm movement time for a rotating device having (a) 6 and (b) 20 positions.

$$E(t_{i,j}) = \int_{t=0}^{N} \Pr\,(t_{i,j} = t)t \; dt$$

$$= \int_{t=0}^{N} \left[\frac{2(N-t)}{N^2} \right] t \; dt$$

$$= \frac{N}{3}$$

And the variance is

$$\sigma^2(t_{i,j}) = \int_{t=0}^{N} \Pr\,(t_{i,j} = t)[t - E(t_{i,j})]^2 \; dt$$

$$= \int_{t=0}^{N} \left[\frac{2(N-t)}{N^2} \right] [t^2 - 2E(t_{i,j})t + E(t_{i,j})^2] \; dt$$

$$= \frac{N^2}{18}$$

The standard deviation is, of course, the square root of the variance:

$$\sigma(t_{i,j}) = \frac{N}{3\sqrt{2}} = \frac{E(t_{i,j})}{\sqrt{2}}$$

These results apply only to the arm-movement time, but it is a simple matter to compute the expected value and standard deviation for total interaccess time. Since selection of a track and selection of a position on that track are, by assumption, independent events, both the means and the variances are additive:

E(total time) $= E$(arm-movement time) $+ E$(rotational time)

σ^2(total time) $= \sigma^2$(arm-movement time) $+ \sigma^2$(rotational time)

We have discussed only a few of the many possible distributions of interaccess time under conditions of completely random access. In many cases analytic techniques may prove impractical, requiring the use of simulation methods or empirical tests involving the device itself. In any event, the behavior of a system under these stringent conditions is sufficiently important to warrant careful consideration.

2. Sequential Access

Completely random accesses provide the most difficult conditions under which a memory device can operate; to complement the measures of effectiveness based on such conditions we need to consider less demanding tasks. Recall that the bits in each device are assumed to be numbered so as to minimize the time required to access all N bits in order. Clearly no other sequence of N accesses could require less time. We refer to such a situation as the *sequential-access* case.

To formalize, we are concerned here with the distribution of inter-access times when the $(i + 1)$st bit is always accessed after bit i. We denote such a time by $t_{i,i+1}$ and assume that each of the $N - 1$ possible values is equiprobable.

The expected value of $t_{i,i+1}$ is obviously

$$E(t_{i,i+1}) = \sum_{i=1}^{N-1} \left(\frac{1}{N-1}\right) t_{i,i+1}$$

$$= \frac{1}{N-1} \sum_{i=1}^{N-1} (t_{i,i+1})$$

$$= \frac{1}{N-1} (T_T)$$

The final form indicates that the numbering scheme serves to minimize $E(t_{i,i+1})$ as well as T_T.[6]

The standard deviation can be determined from the definition:

$$\sigma^2(t_{i,i+1}) = \sum_{i=1}^{N-1} \left(\frac{1}{N-1}\right) [t_{i,i+1} - E(t_{i,i+1})]^2$$

$$= \frac{1}{N-1} \sum_{i=1}^{N-1} \left(t_{i,i+1} - \frac{T_T}{N-1}\right)^2$$

3. Other Measures

We have suggested four primary measures of storage effectiveness. Two correspond roughly to commonly used definitions:

$$E(t_{i,j}) \approx \text{``average access time''}$$

$$\frac{1}{E(t_{i,i+1})} \approx \text{``average transfer rate''}$$

---

[6] Note that neither $E(t_{i,j})$ nor $\sigma(t_{i,j})$ is affected by the choice of a numbering scheme.

Our other two measures do not appear to have direct counterparts in common use; dispersion is either ignored or stated in terms of maximum and/or minimum values.

Under standard assumptions of risk aversion, all four measures represent undesirable properties: the smaller the average time between accesses the better, and the smaller the dispersion around the average the better.

The problems associated with the use of these measures to compare devices should not be underestimated. As an example, for tape drives should estimates of $t_{i,i+1}$ be based on the assumption that the tape is already in motion? And should $t_{N,1}$, the rewind time, be included in the analysis; if so, how?

For certain classes of devices, one or more of the measures may prove redundant. For most core memories

$$E(t_{i,j}) = E(t_{i,i+1})$$

and

$$\sigma(t_{i,j}) = \sigma(t_{i,i+1}) = 0$$

while for most tape drives

$$E(t_{i,j}) > E(t_{i,i+1})$$

$$\sigma(t_{i,j}) > 0 \quad \text{and} \quad \sigma(t_{i,i+1}) = 0$$

On the other hand, for most moving-arm rotating devices, all four measures are relevant, since

$$E(t_{i,j}) > E(t_{i,i+1})$$

$$\sigma(t_{i,j}) > 0 \quad \text{and} \quad \sigma(t_{i,i+1}) > 0$$

Differences of this type do not indicate that our measures are inappropriate. On the contrary, they suggest useful categories into which devices may be classified.

The four measures of effectiveness described here are not intended to be exhaustive; others will be considered where relevant. However, further generalization would prove of little value. We turn thus to a consideration of each of the major types of magnetic storage in common use.

C. CORE STORAGE

1. Production Costs
The traditional form of high-speed central storage is a stack of ferrite cores. Each core acts as a binary switch, storing either "one" or "zero," depending on the way in which it is magnetized. Generally, each reference to memory involves two steps. In the first, all cores of interest are made to assume a value of zero; all changes are sensed and stored in the relevant position of a register, effectively clearing the selected portion of memory and transferring its contents to the register. The second phase provides for resetting desired cores to the "one" position, based on the contents of a register, effectively transferring its contents to the selected portion of memory. The time to complete both phases is called the memory *cycle time*. Write operations require the full cycle—the first phase clears the selected location, and then the desired information (having been placed in the register) is transferred to memory. Read operations also require both phases if the contents of memory are not to be destroyed: the second phase simply resets memory to its initial value, using the contents of the register set during the first phase. Note, however, that the information is available for use at the end of the first phase. The time required simply to obtain information is typically called the memory *access time*.

A great deal of attention has been given to core memory design. For any given set of requirements, many technologically feasible designs are usually available. For example, mechanical components can often be substituted for electronic elements (or vice versa). Traditional designs include one sense wire and one inhibit wire threaded through each core. But sensing is required only in phase 1, while inhibition is needed only in phase 2. It is thus possible to use one wire for both functions, at the expense of more complicated circuitry. Such a scheme may prove desirable—in one instance a second wire was found to add 0.5 cent per core to costs, whereas the extra circuitry required to share one wire added only 0.2 cent per core.[7]

[7] Dana W. Moore, "Cost Performance Analysis of Core Memories," *Proceedings, Fall Joint Computer Conference*, 1966, p. 271.

The two major phases (interrogation and resetting) must be preceded by the selection of the desired cores in memory. If the number of bits to be read or written (the *bandwidth* or *word size*) is 2^m and the memory unit contains 2^n bits, some means for selecting one from among the $2^w = 2^{n-m}$ words must be found. Here, too, there are complicated trade-offs. The simplest method (*linear selection*) uses a separate wire for each of the 2^w positions, allowing low wiring costs but requiring relatively expensive circuitry for any given speed. The traditional method (*coincident current*) requires more wires to be threaded through each core but economizes on circuit costs.

During the selection operation the *m*-bit address desired must be decoded and an electronic switch set to connect the appropriate *m* cores to the desired registers. In a linear-select system, a 2^w-position electronic switch is required. A coincident-current stack is typically made up of *m* planes, each containing 2^w cores organized in a square array. Any given core in an array is accessed by selecting one of the $2^{w/2}$ wires threaded in one direction plus one of the $2^{w/2}$ wires threaded in the other direction. A small current is sent along each of the two wires; only when the two coincide (at the desired core) is there sufficient current to cause the desired action.

A coincident-current memory requires two $2^{w/2}$-position switches; a linear-select memory, one 2^w-position switch. If the cost of such circuitry is roughly a linear function of the number of positions (as often assumed), this cost will be proportional to the number of words of memory for a linear-select system. But for the more common coincident-current system, cost will be proportional to the square root of the number of words:

$$C_c = 2k \cdot 2^{w/2} = K \sqrt{N_W}$$

where k, K are constants, $N_W = 2^w =$ the number of words in memory, and $C_c =$ the cost of switching circuits.

This formula suggests that considerable economies of scale may be available for coincident-current memories. However, such economies are limited. As array size increases, wire lengths must also, imposing some diseconomies (slower speed and/or higher circuit costs). Most arrays are limited to 4096 cores (64×64). Beyond this point, increases

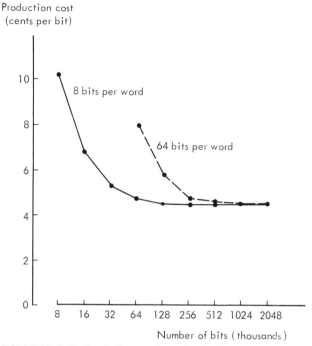

FIGURE 10-6. Estimated cost of production for core units versus number of bits.

in capacity are accommodated by adding new sets of arrays, and marginal cost becomes roughly constant.

Figure 10-6 shows one set of estimated (optimal) costs of production for several alternative core units with roughly 1-microsecond cycle time per word (note that the horizontal axis is logarithmic). As expected, cost per bit declines at a decreasing rate, approaching an asymptote as size increases. The figure also indicates that, for a given capacity in bits, cost per bit increases with word length (at least for small memory sizes), since the number of words will be inversely related to word size. As Fig. 10-7 shows, for equal capacity in words, a system based on a long word may actually cost less per bit than one based on a shorter word.

Figures 10-6 and 10-7 show estimates of minimal costs of production, assuming full use of integrated circuitry. Needless to say, the prices charged by manufacturers for units produced by means of earlier technology are considerably higher. However, economies of scale are

Production cost
(cents per bit)

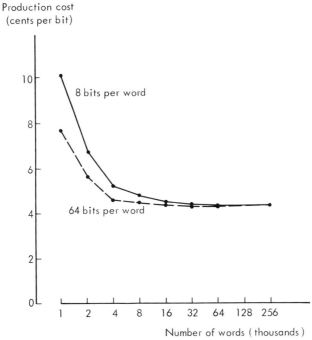

Number of words (thousands)

FIGURE 10-7. Estimated cost of production for core units versus number of words.

still evident, as indicated in Fig. 10-8, taken from a manufacturer's brochure suggesting typical prices for one type of memory unit.[8]

The speed at which a memory operates also has a significant effect on cost. More and better circuitry is usually required to make a given memory faster. Moreover, it is often necessary to use smaller cores: the smaller the core, the faster is the switching time (for given power), and the more compact the array (reducing wire length and hence the time required for a current to travel the length of the wire). But smaller cores are more expensive to manufacture and assemble, because of the need for greater precision.

Other tradeoffs must also be considered. Very fast core memories may require linear selection instead of the cheaper coincident-current organization. And if relatively slow speeds (e.g., 8 microseconds) are

[8] Ferroxcube catalogue M-661 (not dated); the curve indicates the price of memory plus delay-line timing, address storage, drive and logic power supplies, and memory exercisor for 8-μsec, 16-bit systems.

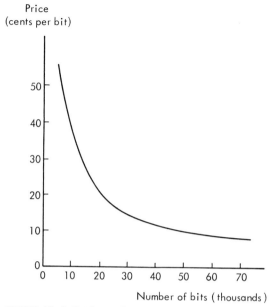

Price
(cents per bit)

Number of bits (thousands)

FIGURE 10–8. Typical prices for second-generation memory units.

acceptable, and the desired amount of memory is large, substantial savings may be achieved by using a system requiring only two wires to be threaded through each core.[9] The relationship between speed and cost for conventional memories of similar size produced by one manufacturer [10] is shown in Fig. 10–9.

To summarize, production cost per bit appears to be inversely related to both memory size (number of bits) and cycle time. Moreover, for small units, cost per bit appears to vary directly with word length. If the cost of electronic circuitry relative to that of mechanical components continues to fall, as expected, the cost of conventionally organized systems will decrease; but the minimal attainable cost will decrease even more rapidly as relatively cheaper electronic circuits are substituted for more expensive elements.

Thus far nothing has been said about rod, plated-wire, and thin-film memories: devices that are equivalent to core memory units in logical

[9] This is the so-called $2\frac{1}{2}$-D, 2-wire system used in most "mass memory" units (Moore, *op. cit.,* p. 273).
[10] Ferroxcube catalogue M-661, *op. cit.*

Relative cost
per bit

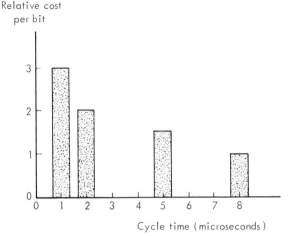

Cycle time (microseconds)

FIGURE 10-9. Relationship between speed and cost for conventional memories of similar size. Source: Ferroxcube M-661, *op. cit.*

operation but can be produced with more automatic assembly methods. All are currently sold commercially. They appear to be more economical (and in many cases the only feasible choice) when high speed is desired. But in the range of speeds for which both types of memory are feasible, core units continue to be the dominant form in use. If noncore devices in this range of speeds are cheaper to produce, the fact was not evident to the customer in 1967: the prices charged for the two most widely used systems (NCR's 315 rod memory and UNIVAC's plated-wire memory) did not differ significantly from those for comparable core units.[11]

2. Prices and Rental Charges

It is important to understand the basic technology of core memory production in order to take into account possible tradeoffs among cost, speed, size, and other variables. But the typical user is not directly concerned with the cost of production; he cares primarily about prices

[11] More correctly, the price per bit of each device was not significantly smaller than the value predicted by the regression equations developed in the study described in Section C-2. Although these devices were included in the study, the regression equations would not have been affected to any major extent had they been omitted. NCR's century series "short-rod" memory, introduced in 1968, appears to be the first exception to the statement in the text. Its price is significantly below that of core units of comparable speed and capacity.

and rental charges. To investigate user costs, empirical analyses were performed by means of standard regression methods.[12] All data were obtained in 1966; thus the results reflect the situation prevailing at that time. This section briefly describes the study.

An obvious problem connected with such an analysis concerns the measurement of cost per bit. Computer manufacturers do not sell memory units by the bit; only substantial increments may be obtained, and often the size of the increment increases with total memory size. The IBM 360/40 provides a typical example. In 1966, users could obtain a central processor with 16K, 32K, 64K, 128K or 256K bytes of memory [13] for the purchase prices shown in Fig. 10–10a. Each pair of adjacent points has been connected with a straight line, the slope of which we define as the marginal cost per bit for the increment. This yields a step function for the marginal cost per bit, for example, that shown in Fig. 10–10b. For the regression analysis, each step is described by its midpoint. Thus the 360/40 provides the four pairs of cost per bit and size shown by points 1–4 in Fig. 10–10b.

In this instance the marginal cost per bit is different for each increment, but this is by no means always the case. We thus define an increment as a range of memory sizes over which the marginal cost per bit is constant.[14] In terms of Fig. 10–10a, an increment begins either at the left-most point or at a point at which there is a "kink" and ends either at the right-most point or at a kink. Using this definition, 222 distinct increments (observations) were obtained for a set of 78 different computer systems. Virtually all general-purpose digital computers manufactured in the United States during 1966 were included, except those for which alternative amounts of core memory were not offered. Only central memory devices were considered; thus high-speed registers and "mass memory" devices such as IBM's large-capacity store were excluded. Although NCR's 315 rod memory and

---

[12] The study was performed by the author in early 1967. However, it benefited considerably from a preliminary study undertaken during the summer of 1966 by the author and Emanuel Sharon under the sponsorship of the Center for Research in Management Science of the University of California (Berkeley). A similar study was performed by John Tennant at the University of Washington at about the same time.

[13] Some manufacturers use K to denote 1000; others, to denote 1024. In the case of the IBM 360 series, the latter meaning applies—thus a 256K system has 262,144 bytes of memory.

[14] Since both purchase price and rental charge are of interest, both price per bit and rent per bit must be constant for a range of sizes to be considered a single increment.

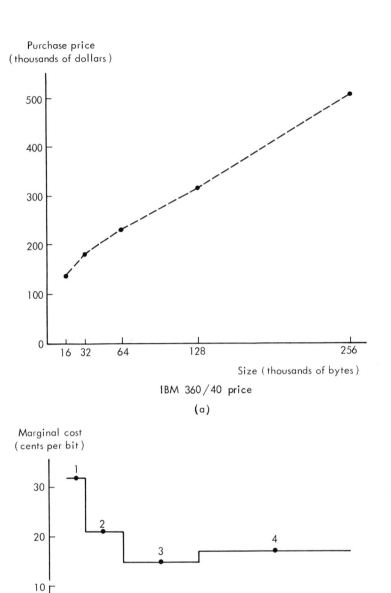

Purchase price
(thousands of dollars)

IBM 360/40 price

(a)

Marginal cost
(cents per bit)

IBM 360/40, price per bit

(b)

FIGURE 10–10. Relationship between size and (a) purchase price and (b) marginal cost per bit, IBM 360/40 core memories.

UNIVAC's plated-wire units were included, as indicated earlier, they did not differ significantly in cost from core units with similar characteristics.

Both rental charges and purchase prices were obtained from GSA price lists.[15] Rental charges include maintenance, but maintenance costs are relatively small for core memory units. For some equipment (e.g., the 360/40), it is impossible to obtain a precise measure of average cost per bit, since memory units and processors are not priced separately. Of course an approximation may be found in such cases by extrapolation (e.g., in Fig. 10–10a the vertical intercept can be estimated). However, we take the more direct approach, relating marginal cost per bit to key attributes of core memory.

To measure effectiveness it would be desirable to use all four measures described earlier. However, a number of problems arise. If the unit of information is taken to be the word (more properly, the "bandwidth"), both measures of dispersion — $\sigma(t_{i,j})$ and $\sigma(t_{i,i+1})$ — will be zero. This need not be the case if the bit is taken as the basic unit, since the time required will typically depend on whether or not the next bit desired is part of the same word as the last one. In true random-access memories, $E(t_{i,j})$ will equal $E(t_{i,i+1})$ when the unit of information is defined as the word; but this need not hold if the unit is defined as the bit.

Independent banks of core memory add further complications; such systems are not truly random access, even when the word is considered the unit of information. In yet other cases, the distribution of $t_{i,j}$ and/or $t_{i,i+1}$ will depend on whether accesses are assumed to be for reading or writing information.

Because of all these problems, and in order to minimize colinearity among the independent variables, only two alternative measures of effectiveness are included explicitly in the regression analyses:

t_c = the cycle time, that is, the time required to select, interrogate, and restore the basic unit of information (2^w bits) for the device, expressed in microseconds; and

$t_{c/b}$ = the cycle time per bit (= $t_c/2^w$), expressed in microseconds per bit.

[15] For Burroughs, IBM, NCR, RCA, SDS, and UNIVAC equipment, the GSA schedules for the period July 1, 1966, through June 30, 1967, were used; for CDC, GE, and Honeywell equipment, the schedules for the period July 1, 1965, through June 30, 1966, were used.

Since a core memory device is typically specific to a single computer system, its value (and hence price) should depend to some extent on the reliability and software support for the overall system. We rely on the time since first delivery to act as a surrogate for such attributes: A = age, expressed as the number of months since first delivery.

To measure economies of scale, size must be included as an independent variable; it is also needed to calculate cost per bit.[16] Hence a decision is required concerning the treatment of parity bits, which are used in almost all core memories to reduce the probability of an undetected error. From the user's viewpoint, they do not store information; but they do increase the reliability of the information stored in the other ("memory") bits. Many users are, in fact, completely unaware of the existence, let alone the number, of parity bits.

The ratio of parity to memory bits differs significantly from system to system. Several machines use 1 parity bit per 8-bit byte; others, 1 parity bit per 36-bit word. A high ratio of parity to memory bits may augur greater effective reliability for the memory unit as a whole. On the other hand, it may indicate that the low reliability of cheap electronic circuits and/or memory elements is being offset to establish adequate overall reliability. Ideally, separate measures of the amount of information stored and the reliability of the storage should be obtained. However, since accurate measures of reliability are not available, such a solution is not practical. Instead, we can only investigate each of the two obvious alternatives:

S_M = average size of the increment (in thousands of memory bits), and

S_T = average size of the increment (in thousands of total, i.e., memory and parity, bits).

Another problem concerns the appropriate measure of cost to the user. Purchase prices are highly correlated with rental charges, but the correlation is far from perfect. Figure 10–11 shows the distribution of purchase/rent ratios of increments of core memory for the 78 computers studied.[17] Since the variation is substantial, it seems wise to

[16] Raising some difficult statistical problems when the latter is used as the dependent variable. We ignore such problems here at some peril.
[17] Basic monthly rental (i.e., the charge for one-shift utilization) was used to measure rent throughout. The purchase/rent ratio for each system was obtained by considering the largest possible increment (i.e., from the minimum to the maximum memory). The distribution has a median of 45, a mean of 44.83, and a standard deviation of 7.52.

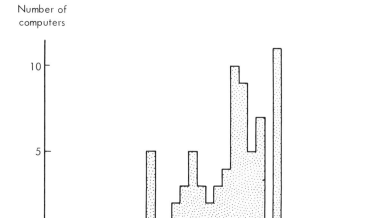

FIGURE 10-11. Distribution of purchase/rent ratios of increments of core memory for 78 computers.

examine both purchase price and rental charge. This decision results in four dependent variables of interest:

P/T = purchase cost per total bit (in cents per bit),

P/M = purchase cost per memory bit (in cents per bit),

R/T = monthly rental charge per total bit (in cents per month per bit), and

R/M = monthly rental charge per memory bit (in cents per month per memory bit).

In each case the corresponding measure of size is selected as one of the independent variables (i.e., S_T for P/T and R/T, S_M for P/M and R/M).

The characteristics of the distributions of the four measures are given in Table 10-2. The distribution of purchase price per memory bit is shown in detail in Fig. 10-12.

The relationships to be investigated can be selected on the basis of hypotheses about the cost of production and/or value of various devices. The discussion of production cost suggests that cost per bit should decrease with size, approaching some lower asymptote, and also with cycle time, again approaching an asymptote. This suggests functions that are linear in the logarithms. In accordance with common

Number of systems

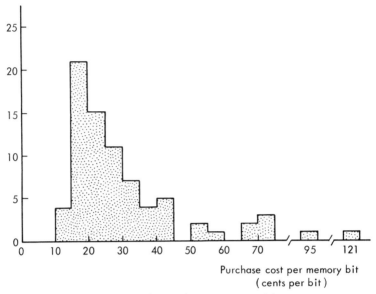

FIGURE 10-12. Distribution of purchase price per memory bit.

practice, the number of months since first delivery ("age") can be used as a surrogate for reliability, software support, etc. Finally, we would expect cost per bit to be greater the longer the word used.

Simple regression analyses give results generally consistent with these hypotheses. Cost per bit is inversely related to size, with the correlation between the logarithms of the two variables considerably greater than that between the variables themselves. Cost per bit is also directly related to age, but no obviously superior form is apparent.[18] There is little correlation between cost per bit and either cycle time or cycle time per bit. However, this is undoubtedly due to the substantial correlation among the independent variables. For example, older systems tend to have longer cycle times,[19] making multiple regression analysis imperative if the effects of these two characteristics are to be properly identified.

---

[18] The correlation coefficients in each case were roughly similar. For convenience, we thus relate the logarithm of cost per bit to age.

[19] The simple correlation coefficient between age and the logarithm of cycle time is .70.

TABLE 10-2. Characteristics of Distributions of Cost per Bit

Attribute	Ratio			
	P/M	P/T	R/M	R/T
Median	24.5	21.7	0.572	0.516
Average	30.95	27.38	.687	.612
Standard deviation	19.36	15.41	.399	.322
Coefficient of variation (standard deviation/ average)	0.628	0.564	.580	.527

The general form of the relationship to be tested is as follows:

$$\ln \begin{Bmatrix} P/T \\ R/T \\ P/M \\ R/M \end{Bmatrix} = a + b_1 \ln \begin{Bmatrix} S_T \\ S_M \end{Bmatrix} + b_2 \ln \begin{Bmatrix} t_c \\ t_{c/b} \end{Bmatrix} + b_3 A + b_4 \begin{Bmatrix} \text{word size} \\ \ln(\text{word size}) \end{Bmatrix}$$

Since the appropriate measure of size depends on the dependent variable selected, only two choices remain: whether to use t_c or $t_{c/b}$ for speed and how to represent word size, if at all.

Table 10-3 shows the percentage of total variation in the dependent variable, explained in each of the four cases by using the alternative measures of speed along with age and the logarithm of size.[20] Cycle time appears to be slightly preferable to cycle time per bit; since the former is also commonly used, we adopt it for the subsequent analyses.

To test the effect of including word size among the independent variables, some analyses using R/M as the dependent variable were performed. The results suggest that word size[21] is a better measure for this purpose than its logarithm. The coefficient (b_4) was positive, as expected, with a value of $+0.00284$. This indicates, for example, that a 64-bit word system would cost about 17% more than a comparable

---

[20] Word size was not included among the independent variables.
[21] Expressed as the number of memory bits per word.

TABLE 10-3. Percentage of Variance in Cost per Bit Explained by Using the Multiple Regression Equation

Dependent Variable	With Cycle Time (t_c)	With Cycle Time per bit $(t_{c/b})$
P/M	42.1%	36.7%
P/T	38.9	36.3
R/M	49.1	46.1
R/T	45.0	45.1

system based on an 8-bit word.[22] However, little importance should be attached to this result, since the coefficient was not very significant—its t value was only 1.38. For this reason it seems best to omit word size from the set of independent variables.

Four equations remain to be estimated, each of the form

$$\ln \begin{Bmatrix} P/T \\ R/T \\ P/M \\ R/M \end{Bmatrix} = a + b_1 \ln \begin{Bmatrix} S_T \\ S_M \end{Bmatrix} + b_2 \ln t_c + b_3 A$$

Table 10-4 shows the resulting equations and the usual statistical measures. Note that all the coefficients are significant (i.e., have large t values) and have the expected signs. Moreover, there is relatively little variation from equation to equation. Rounding each coefficient to two significant digits, we obtain

Variable	Range of Coefficients	Percentage Change in Cost per Bit if Variable Is Doubled [23]
Size	−0.14 to −0.18	−9.3 to −11.7
Cycle time	−0.23 to −0.26	−14.7 to −16.5
Age	+0.015	+1.5

[22]
$$\ln (C_{64}/C_8) = \ln C_{64} - \ln C_8 = 0.00284(64 - 8)$$
Therefore
$$\ln (C_{64}/C_8) = 0.15904 \quad \text{and} \quad C_{64}/C_8 = e^{0.15904} \approx 1.17$$
[23] Let b be a coefficient in an equation of the form
$$\ln y = k + b \ln x$$
and let
$$\ln y' = k + b \ln x'$$
if $x' = 2x$, $y'/y = 2^b$.

TABLE 10-4. Regression Equations

$\ln (P/M) = 4.02168 \quad - \quad 0.15783 \ln S_M \quad - \quad 0.25952 \ln t_c \quad + \quad 0.01551A$
$\qquad\qquad\qquad\qquad\qquad\quad (t = 7.66) \qquad\qquad (t = 5.74) \qquad\qquad (t = 9.12)$
$\sigma_e = 0.39901$
Variation explained $= 42.1\%$

$\ln (P/T) = 3.84691 \quad - \quad 0.14194 \ln S_T \quad - \quad 0.25280 \ln t_c \quad + \quad 0.01494A$
$\qquad\qquad\qquad\qquad\qquad\quad (t = 6.86) \qquad\qquad (t = 5.66) \qquad\qquad (t = 8.91)$
$\sigma_e = 0.39372$
Variation explained $= 38.9\%$

$\ln (R/M) = 0.33732 \quad - \quad 0.17540 \ln S_M \quad - \quad 0.23860 \ln t_c \quad + \quad 0.01522A$
$\qquad\qquad\qquad\qquad\qquad\quad (t = 9.30) \qquad\qquad (t = 5.76) \qquad\qquad (t = 9.78)$
$\sigma_e = 0.36518$
Variation explained $= 49.1\%$

$\ln (R/T) = 0.18201 \quad - \quad 0.16225 \ln S_T \quad - \quad 0.23325 \ln t_c \quad + \quad 0.01466A$
$\qquad\qquad\qquad\qquad\qquad\quad (t = 8.38) \qquad\qquad (t = 5.57) \qquad\qquad (t = 9.33)$
$\sigma_e = 0.36886$
Variation explained $= 45.0\%$

The results suggest that cost (price, rental) per bit will decrease by roughly 10% if memory size is doubled. This relationship is illustrated in Fig. 10-13, which shows the price per memory bit for various sizes, assuming a cycle time of 1 microsecond and 1966 technology (i.e., $A = 0$). Somewhat greater economies of scale appear to be available with respect to speed: doubling cycle time decreases cost per bit by roughly 15%, as illustrated in Fig. 10-14 for 128K units of 1966 design. Finally, every month of age appears to add 1.5% to value (price or rental charge), a result similar to that found earlier for complete computer systems. This suggests that age clearly acts as a surrogate for some desirable feature or features.

Needless to say, none of these equations fits the data perfectly: in each case one-half the original variation in cost per bit remains unexplained. The standard error, which measures the standard deviation of the observations from the values predicted by the equation, provides a measure of this dispersion. On the assumption that errors in predicting the dependent variable will be normally distributed, two out of three actual values will lie within one standard error of the prediction.[24]

[24] Even under the assumed conditions, this is strictly true only in the region of the mean value, as indicated in the Appendix.

P/M (cents per bit)

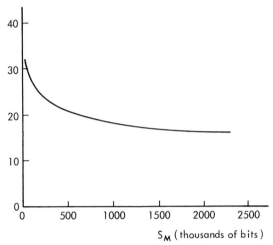

S_M (thousands of bits)

FIGURE 10–13. Relationship between cost per bit and size for 1-microsecond memories of 1966 design.

The standard errors of the four equations range from 0.365 to 0.400; taking the latter value,

$$\ln\left(\frac{C}{b}\right)_e - 0.400 \leq \ln\left(\frac{C}{b}\right)_a \leq \ln\left(\frac{C}{b}\right)_e + 0.400$$

where $(C/b)_a$ = actual cost per bit, and $(C/b)_e$ = cost per bit estimated by using the regression equation. This implies:

$$\frac{(C/b)_e}{e^{0.400}} \leq \left(\frac{C}{b}\right)_a \leq \left(\frac{C}{b}\right)_e \cdot e^{0.400}$$

or

$$0.67\left(\frac{C}{b}\right)_e \leq \left(\frac{C}{b}\right)_a \leq 1.49\left(\frac{C}{b}\right)_e \quad \text{(with probability} \approx .67\text{)}$$

Thus far little has been said about so-called *bulk cores* — devices with relatively large capacities and long cycle times, costing relatively little per bit. Since the technology used for bulk cores is quite different from that employed for central memories, no devices of this type were included in the sample used to derive the regression equations. One rule of thumb holds that bulk core costs about one-tenth as much per bit as does central core. This is approximately correct if "central core" is taken to mean recently designed 1-microsecond storage of moderate size. Perhaps more interesting is the contrast between the actual cost of bulk core and that predicted by the regression equations based on central-core costs and capabilities. For IBM's large-capacity-store (LCS) unit, the actual cost ranges from 30% to 40% of the value estimated in this manner, as shown in Table 10–5. In 1966, core devices in this price range were available only as auxiliary storage, for use with central memory units costing typically ten times as much per bit.

All the calculations in this section have dealt with marginal cost per bit, for the reasons indicated earlier. But it is a relatively simple matter to obtain a rough estimate of the average cost per bit, using the resulting equations. Let C represent the total cost of a memory system and S its total size (in bits). The dependent variable used in the analysis was cost per bit for an increment of memory: $\Delta C/\Delta S$. The measure of size was the midpoint for the increment in question. A reasonable assumption would hold that the derivative of cost with respect to size at that point equals the value obtained for the increment as a whole.

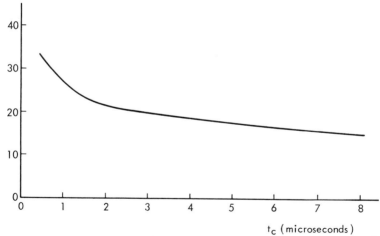

FIGURE 10–14. Relationship between speed and cost per bit for 128K memories of 1966 design. P/M versus t_c for memories with $S_M = 128$ and $A = 0$.

TABLE 10-5. IBM Large-Capacity Store *

Measure	First Million Bytes	Second Million Bytes †
P/M, actual	3.755 cents/bit	2.503 cents/bit
P/M, estimated	8.719	7.331
Actual/estimated	0.43	0.34
P/T, actual	3.338 cents/bit	2.225 cents/bit
P/T, estimated	8.335	7.132
Actual/estimated	0.40	0.31
R/M, actual	0.0775 cent/mo/bit	0.0536 cent/mo/bit
R/M, estimated	0.1975	0.1629
Actual/estimated	0.39	0.33
R/T, actual	0.0689 cent/mo/bit	0.0477 cent/mo/bit
R/T, estimated	0.1872	0.1566
Actual/estimated	0.37	0.30

* Full cycle time = 8 μsec; 1 parity bit per 8-bit byte.
† Based on the differences in costs and capacities of the two models (2361–1 and 2361–2).

Thus, for given values of t_c and A, each equation may be assumed to be of the form

$$\ln\left(\frac{dC}{dS}\right) = a + b \ln S$$

where a and b are constants. This is equivalent to

$$\frac{dC}{dS} = e^a S^b$$

Thus [25]

$$C = \int e^a S^b \, dS = \frac{e^a S^{b+1}}{b+1}$$

which implies

$$\frac{C}{S} = \frac{e^a S^b}{b+1} = \frac{1}{b+1}\left(\frac{dC}{dS}\right)$$

[25] The constant of integration is assumed to be zero since $C = 0$ when $S = 0$.

Since $b \approx -0.16$ in each of the four regression equations, average cost should be approximately 20% greater than marginal cost:

$$\frac{1}{1 - 0.16} \approx 1.19$$

This concludes the analysis of core memory costs and capabilities. Purchase prices for increments to memory range from 2.5 cents per bit (for bulk core) to more than $1.00 per bit, averaging about 30 cents. In general, the results are consistent with prior expectations: the faster, smaller, and older (in design) a unit, the more expensive it will be.

D. ROTATING DEVICES [26]

1. Fixed-Head Units

Rotating disks and drums provide permanent storage at considerably lower cost than core memory units of comparable capacity, although with random-access times that are typically orders of magnitude longer. Frequently disk and drum devices are analyzed separately, but from a cost/effectiveness viewpoint the distinction is not particularly useful. We adopt the more important distinction between (1) units with fixed read/write heads and (2) those with at least some movable heads. This section deals with the first type; movable-head units are considered in Section D-2.

Figure 10–15 illustrates the characteristics of a simple fixed-head drum. Most fixed-head devices can be considered logically equivalent to a unit of this type. We describe such a device in terms of

$t_r =$ the time (in microseconds) required for a complete revolution,
$N_b =$ the number of bands,
$B_b =$ the number of bits stored per band, and
$K = N_b B_b =$ the total capacity (in bits).

The drum is assumed to be rotating continuously at a constant speed

[26] This section incorporates material developed by Robert H. Robinson for a paper submitted for the degree of Master of Business Administration at the University of Washington in 1967: "A Study of Characteristics and Measures of Effectiveness for Electromechanical Random-Access Mass Storage Devices." Although the results reported here are based on different analyses, many of the basic data were obtained by Robinson.

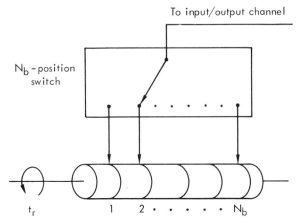

FIGURE 10-15. Characteristics of a simple fixed-head drum.

(typical values for t_r range from 17,000 to 50,000 microseconds). The time required to switch to any desired band is assumed to be zero, since electronic switching can usually be completed before the drum can rotate to a new position.[27]

Figure 10-16 provides more detail. A *band* is composed of T_b separate *tracks*, each with a read/write head. Selection of a band thus involves the connection of a T_b-position channel to the T_b read/write heads of the band in question, as shown in the figure.[28] Obviously

$$B_t = \text{the number of bits per track } (= B_b/T_b),$$
$$N_t = \text{the number of tracks } (= N_bT_b), \text{ and}$$
$$K = N_bB_b = N_tB_t.$$

The simplest possible device uses 1 track at a time (i.e., $T_b = 1$); others use several (values of 2, 3, 4, 6, and 12 have been employed). However, T_b may also be less than 1. If the computer is unable to de-

---

[27] Typical electronic switching times range from 20 to 40 μsec. One device (the Honeywell 270 drum) uses a relay for selection of a group of four bands and an electronic switch for the selection of the appropriate band within the group. The relay switching time is 5000 μsec; the electronic switching time, 40 μsec.

[28] Such a scheme is often described by saying that the device transmits T_b bits in parallel. This will, of course, be true if all T_b bits are written (and thus later read) concurrently. But bits received serially may be written by distributing the first bit to the first track, the next to the second, etc. If this is done, reading will produce serial output. T_b is sometimes called the bandwidth; we avoid this term as well, however, since it seems inappropriate when T_b is less than 1.

liver and receive information as rapidly as the device can provide it, *interlacing* may be used. For example, an interlacing factor of 2 means that positions 1, 3, 5, 7, . . . , etc., on a given track are treated as one band and positions 2, 4, 6, 8, . . . , etc., as another. In the terms used here, such an approach is equivalent to $T_b = \frac{1}{2}$. Values of $\frac{1}{2}$, $\frac{1}{4}$, $\frac{1}{8}$, and $\frac{1}{16}$ have been employed, with alternative values available in some instances for a given device.

The traditional fixed-head device is the drum, but fixed-head rotating disks are becoming increasingly popular. Such devices have one obvious drawback: tracks will differ in length (circumference). One approach ignores this fact, allocating to each track the number of bits that can be stored on the innermost track, as shown in Fig. 10–17a. Such a device is logically equivalent to a drum. Although wasteful of potential storage space, this method is often used to avoid complexity.

Figure 10–17b illustrates an alternative (compromise) solution. The disk is divided into two or more zones; within a zone the number of bits per track is constant, but the number is larger for tracks in outer zones than for those in inner zones. Clearly, each zone can be considered logically equivalent to a drum. For purposes of analysis, it is thus both convenient and simple to describe almost any fixed-head device in terms of one or more logically equivalent drums categorized by the values of four basic parameters: t_r, N_b, B_b, and T_b.

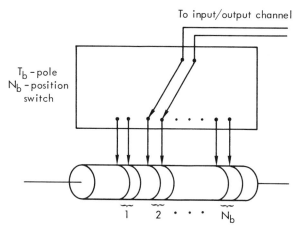

FIGURE 10–16. A fixed-head drum with two tracks per band.

(a)   (b)

FIGURE 10–17. Disks with (a) the same number of bits on every track and (b) more bits on tracks in an outer zone than on tracks in an inner zone.

Most devices require a rather substantial set of electronics to perform functions such as parity checking and code conversion. Moreover, buffers are often needed to match the input/output channel to the device employed. For example, an input/output channel that transfers nine bits at a time (i.e., in parallel), with the ninth bit used for parity, might have to be connected to a drum unit that transfers information serially, with parity bits employed only at the end of a record. Obviously a nine-bit buffer and some rather complicated circuits would be required to match the two devices.

The set of electronics needed to perform common functions is usually packaged separately, along with a switching circuit that allows it to be connected with any one of several devices, as shown in Fig. 10–18. Such *controllers* are generally quite costly, leading to considerable economies of scale in storage of this type. From a cost/effectiveness viewpoint, a controller with two drums, each with N_b bands, is equivalent to a self-contained drum with $2N_b$ bands; the fact that a band is selected by switching first to the appropriate drum and then to a band is of little practical importance.

It is a relatively simple matter to estimate the four basic measures of effectiveness for a device of the type under consideration. The speed at which information can be accessed sequentially depends on both the rotational speed and the number of bits per band:

$$E(t_{i,i+1}) = \frac{t_r}{B_b}$$

Because of the rapid electronic switching from band to band it can be assumed that

$$\sigma(t_{i,i+1}) = 0$$

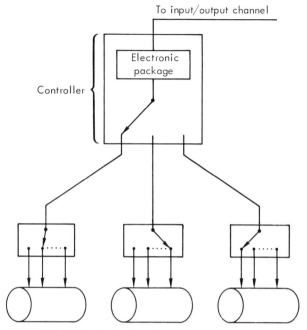

FIGURE 10–18. Controller functions.

Under conditions of completely random access interaccess times will be uniformly distributed between zero and t_r. Thus both the mean and the standard deviation depend solely on rotational speed: [29]

$$E(t_{i,j}) = \frac{t_r}{2}$$

$$\sigma(t_{i,j}) = \frac{t_r}{\sqrt{12}} = \frac{E(t_{i,j})}{\sqrt{3}}$$

[29] The value of $E(t_{i,j})$ is obviously $t_r/2$, and $\sigma(t_{i,j})$ can be obtained directly from the definition of variance. Let x be a value of $t_{i,j}$; then

$$\sigma^2 = \int_{x=0}^{t_r} \frac{1}{t_r}(x - \bar{x})^2 \, dx$$

But

$$\bar{x} = \frac{t_r}{2}$$

It thus follows directly that

$$\sigma^2 = \frac{t_r^2}{12} \quad \text{and} \quad \sigma = \frac{t_r}{\sqrt{12}}$$

As these formulas show, improvements in random-access capability can be obtained only by increasing rotational speed.[30] But sequential-access capability can be improved either by increasing speed or by increasing the number of bits per band. More precise recording techniques (e.g., improved recording surfaces or read/write heads that fly closer to the surface or operate with a smaller magnetic cone) allow more bits to be packed on a given physical track, and significant improvements in the cost/effectiveness of rotating devices have resulted from advances of this type. However, an alternative is available: the number of tracks per band can be increased.

The IBM 2301 and 2303 drums provide good examples of the latter approach. The 2303 has 800 tracks, each storing approximately 41,000 bits; rotational time is 17,200 microseconds. One read/write head may be selected at a time (i.e., $T_b = 1$); thus $E(t_{i,i+1}) \approx 0.420$ microsecond. The 2301 is essentially the same device, but with the 800 tracks grouped into 200 bands of 4 tracks each, reducing $E(t_{i,i+1})$ to approximately 0.105 microsecond. Of course both total capacity and $E(t_{i,j})$ are the same for the two devices.[31]

Figures 10–19a and b show the total cost and cost per bit for 1, 2, 3, and 4 devices of each type, including essential controller costs.[32] Clearly it does not cost four times as much to obtain a device with four times the effectiveness for sequential accesses—i.e., $0.25E(t_{i,i+1})$. Equally clearly, relative costs depend on total capacity. Finally, each device provides considerable economies of scale because of the relatively large controller costs.

[30] There is one apparent exception. Consider a device with M read/write heads per track, spaced evenly around the drum. Assume that at every point of time the location of the drum is known, so that the preferred head on any given track can be selected. If the device has N_t tracks, each with B_t bits, and a rotational time of t_r, it is logically equivalent to a system with

$$t_r' = \frac{t_r}{M}, \quad N_t' = N_t M, \quad B_t' = \frac{B_t}{M}$$

and, of course

$$E'(t_{i,j}) = \frac{E(t_{i,j})}{M}$$

[31] The manufacturer's quoted capacities differ slightly, since they do not include space required for record keys, track identification, etc., which are not precisely the same on the two devices.

[32] The figures for the 2301 include the cost of one 2820 controller; those for the 2303, the cost of one 2841 controller with a 2303 attachment. All are expressed in terms of purchase price.

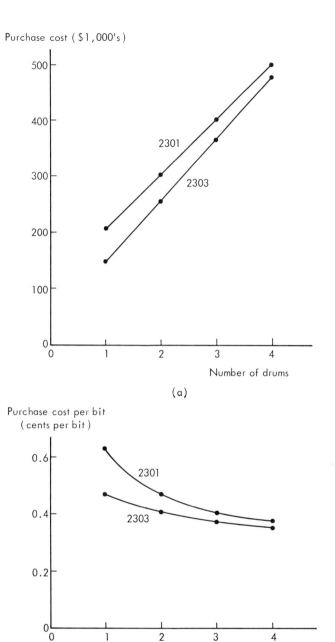

Purchase cost ($1,000's)

2301

2303

Number of drums

(a)

Purchase cost per bit
(cents per bit)

2301

2303

Number of drums

(b)

FIGURE 10–19. Total cost and cost per bit for 1–4 drums.

Number of devices

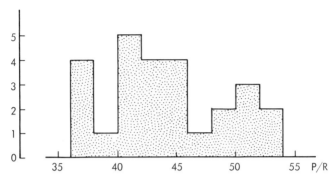

FIGURE 10-20. Distribution of purchase/rent ratios for 26 fixed-head units.

This comparison hardly provides a general relationship between cost and effectiveness for fixed-head units. To find one and to assess the manner in which it has changed over time, a sample of 26 different devices (21 drums and 5 disks) was analyzed. Almost all fixed-head devices delivered by computer manufacturers before 1968 were included. Only two measures of effectiveness, $E(t_{i,j})$ and $E(t_{i,i+1})$, were used for the analysis, since $\sigma(t_{i,j})$ would be perfectly correlated with $E(t_{i,j})$ and $\sigma(t_{i,i+1})$ would equal zero in every case.[33] As usual, an estimate of the year in which the first system was delivered was employed.[34]

For convenience, purchase price was used as the dependent variable throughout. However, an examination of the data suggests that the results would not have differed significantly had rental charges been used instead. Figure 10–20 shows the distribution of purchase/rent ratios for the 26 devices.[35]

Not surprisingly, a number of approaches have been taken by manufacturers, to assure data reliability. Some devices append a parity bit to every basic group of bits (e.g., 6, 8, or 12). Others use check bits at the

---

[33] This is not strictly true for disks with more than one zone. In the single case of this kind, each track was simply assumed to have the same (average) number of bits.
[34] In many cases, for lack of a better estimate the figure was based on the first GSA Price List in which the device was included. For example, a unit first listed in the July 1, 1965, through June 30, 1966, schedule was assumed to have first been delivered in 1966.
[35] Based on gross monthly rental (i.e., including basic maintenance) for one-shift operation and on purchase price for storage devices only (i.e., not including controllers). The median value is 43.5.

end of every record, the ratio of parity to memory bits depending thus partly on data format. As with core memory, a high ratio of parity to memory bits may indicate high overall reliability. On the other hand, it may signal a need for compensation, leading to equal overall reliability. Since insufficient evidence exists to reject either approach, an essentially arbitrary selection is required. We choose to exclude bits (and, in some cases, entire tracks and even surfaces) reserved exclusively for parity, format control, timing, etc. Our measure of capacity thus refers to capacity for storing the user's data; figures showing cost per bit should be interpreted similarly.

As indicated earlier, many devices require a separate controller that can often be switched to any one of several units. Each configuration up to the maximum number of devices per controller may thus be considered a separate device. By including all such combinations,[36] the sample was enlarged to 111 devices.[37]

Historically there has been little change in random-access capability $-E(t_{i,j})-$ over time, although sequential-access capability $-E(t_{i,i+1})-$ has improved.[38] Cost per bit has declined significantly.[39]

Multiple regression analysis provides at least some indication of the impact of each of the factors affecting cost per bit. A priori considerations and the results obtained by using alternative forms suggest an equation expressing the logarithm of cost per bit as a linear function of the years since first delivery and of the logarithms of $E(t_{i,j})$, $E(t_{i,i+1})$, and capacity. Approximately 79% of the variation in the logarithm of cost per bit was explained by the following equation:

[36] Configurations including more than one controller were not included, since they provide potentially greater capability. For example, if four drums are attached to one controller, only one band on one drum may be used at any given time. But if two drums are attached to one controller and two more to another, it is at least possible for two bands to be used concurrently. This matter is considered in greater detail in section E.
[37] Needless to say, for some purposes the degrees of freedom should be based on a sample of 26 rather than one of 111 observations, since the latter are hardly independent random draws. Since we refrain here from speaking of significance except in the vaguest sense, this problem does not arise explicitly.
[38] Less than 1% of the variation in either $E(t_{i,j})$ or ln $E(t_{i,j})$ was explained when the year of first delivery was used as the independent variable; 31% of the variation in $E(t_{i,i+1})$ was explained by an equation in which this is a decreasing function of the year of first delivery.
[39] Approximately 31% per year, in spite of the concurrent decrease in $E(t_{i,i+1})$. As the subsequent multiple regression results show, part of this decline is attributable to secular increases in total capacity.

ln (cost/bit)

$$= 7.052 + 0.169A - 0.655 \ln E(t_{i,j}) - 0.089 \ln E(t_{i,i+1}) - 0.500 \ln (\text{cap.})$$
$$(t = 5.83) \qquad (t = 5.67) \qquad (t = 1.71) \qquad (t = 10.20)$$

where cost/bit = purchase cost (in cents per bit),

A = years since first delivery (1967 = 0),

$E(t_{i,j})$ = expected value of $t_{i,j}$ (in microseconds),

$E(t_{i,i+1})$ = expected value of $t_{i,i+1}$ (in microseconds), and

cap. = capacity (in millions of bits).

The following data indicate the range of values for devices first delivered in 1966 or 1967:

Parameter	Low Value	Median Value	High Value
Cost/bit	0.06 cent/bit [40]	0.42 cent/bit [41]	1.60 cents/bit
$E(t_{i,j})$	4250 μsec	17,000 μsec	20,000 μsec
$E(t_{i,i+1})$	0.08 μsec	0.43 μsec	1.52 μsec
Cap.	6 million bits	50 million bits [41]	600 million bits [42]

The coefficients accord reasonably well with prior expectations. Cost per bit has been decreasing significantly over time at a rate of approximately 15% per year.[43] Increasing random-access capability adds more to cost than increasing sequential-access capability: halving $E(t_{i,j})$ raises cost per bit by more than 50%,[44] whereas halving $E(t_{i,i+1})$ adds less than 10%.[45] Finally, there are significant economies of scale—cost per bit falls by approximately 30% when capacity is doubled.[46]

As these results indicate, the costs of fixed-head storage devices vary considerably. An order-of-magnitude difference in cost per bit between two devices is not impossible, even if they are of roughly the same vintage. This precludes the use of any simple rule of thumb for the cost of such storage. However, much of the variation can be ex-

---

[40] One controller plus five disk units.
[41] Figures indicate median values based on all configurations considered.
[42] One controller plus eight drums.
[43] Since $e^{-0.169} \approx 0.845$.
[44] Since $2^{0.655} \approx 1.57$.
[45] Since $2^{0.089} \approx 1.06$. Note, however, that the relatively low t value for this coefficient raises doubts concerning the significance of the result.
[46] Since $2^{-0.5} \approx 0.707$.

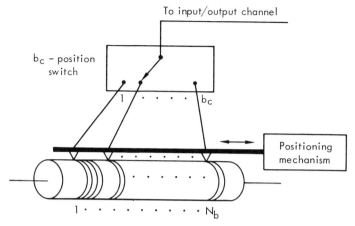

FIGURE 10–21. A rotating device with movable heads.

plained by differences in size, effectiveness, and/or age: the regression results provide at least a rough indication of the impact of each of these factors on the overall cost of devices of this type.

2. Movable-Head Units

In order to consider movable-head units we must extend the specifications for rotating devices. It is convenient to continue to cast the description in terms of drum devices, although most movable-head units utilize disks. The logical equivalence of the two can be readily shown.

As before, the device has N_b bands, each storing B_b bits on T_b tracks; total capacity is thus $K = N_b B_b$. Now, however, we consider the read/write heads to be mounted on a comb, such as that shown in Fig. 10–21. The number of bands that can be accessed without comb movement is b_c; any such group is called a *cylinder*. The comb can be moved mechanically to any of N_p positions (cylinders); clearly, if $N_p = 1$, we have as a special case a standard fixed-head unit.

The time required to switch electronically to the desired band on a given cylinder is assumed to be zero. But the time required to mechanically position the comb over the desired cylinder will in general be substantial (100,000 microseconds is not uncommon). For analytic convenience we assume that

$$\text{if } N_m = 0, \quad t_m = 0$$

$$\text{if } N_m > 0, \quad t_m = a + \frac{N_m}{N_p} \quad (b)$$

where N_m = number of positions moved,

t_m = time required to complete the movement,

N_p = maximum number of positions that the comb can move, and

a,b are parameters.[47]

A number of mechanisms have been adopted for comb movement. In most devices the relationship between t_m and N_m is not strictly linear.[48] The assumption should thus be viewed as a simple, though probably acceptable, approximation. Further simplification would, however, be unwise; for example, t_m is seldom proportional to N_m (i.e., $a = 0$), since most devices require a significant fixed time to allow for head settling, etc.

[47] Let

t_{min} = the minimum comb-movement time (i.e., the time required to move to an adjacent cylinder), and

t_{max} = the maximum comb-movement time (i.e., the time required to move in the worst — max t_m — case).

Estimates of t_{min} and t_{max} are usually provided by manufacturers; the value of N_p is, of course, readily obtained. Given these values, good estimates of a and b are

$$b = \frac{(t_{max} - t_{min})N_p}{N_p - 1}$$

$$a = t_{min} - \frac{b}{N_p}$$

However, since N_p is typically large, we utilize the simpler estimates

$$b = t_{max} - t_{min}$$

$$a = t_{min}$$

[48] That is, for $N_p \geqq 1$. Some devices employ several mechanisms, one for each level of movement; the larger the distance moved, the more likely is the need to employ additional mechanisms. The relationship between t_m and N_m for such devices will therefore contain significant steps. In other devices the comb must return to a "home" position before moving to a new one. For such units, t_m depends on the locations of the initial and the terminal position, not just on the number of positions between them. Both these approaches appear to have poor survival properties: recently introduced devices employ neither type of mechanism.

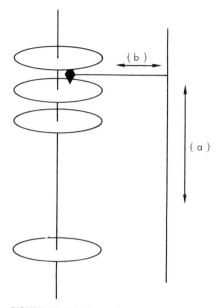

FIGURE 10-22. An early movable-head unit.

Most (but not all) movable-head devices utilize one or more disks. Figure 10-22 illustrates the strategy employed in one of the earliest devices. The comb carried only two read/write heads ($b_c = 2$); two positioning mechanisms were employed, one (a) to move the arm to the appropriate space between disks and another (b) to position the read/write heads over the desired bands on the disks selected. The number of disks was large (50), so that comb-movement time was likely to be substantial.

To reduce access times, two or three independent mechanisms, each of the type shown in Fig. 10-22, were incorporated in later systems. Careful utilization of such a device could, in theory, provide substantial improvement in performance. However, the merits of allowing more than one comb to access a given location appear to be more than offset by the difficulties involved in avoiding conflicts: virtually no device currently being manufactured includes such a feature. It is possible, thus, to consider a single comb and the cylinders that it can access as a device for the purposes of analysis; units with more than one

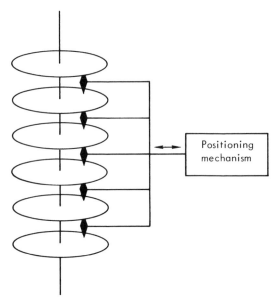

FIGURE 10-23. Typical movable-head unit in current production.

comb are best treated as combinations of (logically) separate devices.[49]

Figure 10–23 illustrates a typical configuration for units currently being produced. To reduce access time, the number of bands per cylinder is increased (here to ten) and only one positioning mechanism employed.

Early devices utilized relatively large disks (e.g., 30 inches in diameter); thus considerable storage space was wasted when the same number of bits was stored on each track. In several units tracks were grouped into two or more zones, with more bits stored per track in outer zones. In some systems the computer and/or an input-output channel was required to accommodate the variation in transfer rate among zones. In others some method was employed to avoid this problem. One device stored twice as many bits per track in the outer zone but employed an interlacing factor of 2 when such a track was utilized (i.e., $T_b = 1$ for bands in the inner zone, $T_b = \frac{1}{2}$ for bands in the outer

---

[49] Only one unit included in the analysis described below provided for the access of a given location by alternative combs—the IBM 7300 (–1 and –2). For consistency, this unit was treated as three devices, assuming that each of the access mechanisms was restricted to one-third of the total storage area.

zone). Another system coupled an inner-zone track with an outer-zone track when forming a band, allowing a constant transfer rate, regardless of the band selected.

There appears to be a trend toward smaller disks (e.g., 14 inches in diameter), reducing the disparity between the storage capacities of inner and outer tracks. Since the effort required to accommodate tracks with different numbers of bits is no longer as worthwhile, the use of zones appears to be dying out.[50] Thus our simple model serves to describe most devices currently being produced.[51]

Perhaps the most important single trend in movable-head devices is the increasing use of removable media. The first device of this type, the IBM 1311 drive, was initially delivered during 1963. The basic storage medium is a "disk pack" of six disks. Since neither the top nor the bottom surface is used for storage, each cylinder includes ten bands ($T_b = 1$, $b_c = 10$). Figure 10–23 illustrates the basic mechanism employed.

Until late 1967, only IBM manufactured disk packs; now, however, they are produced by a number of firms. New packs have traditionally sold for $490 and rented for $15 per month.[52] During 1967 an unanticipated increase in demand forced equilibrium prices up, with brokers handling rentals at $1 per day, even though IBM (the only manufacturer at the time) continued to rent packs at $15 per month to those fortunate enough to have placed orders sufficiently far in advance. Needless to say, this demand created substantial incentives for new firms to enter the market and for IBM to increase its production.

Since there is no reason to expect the long-run cost of production to increase significantly with industry output, and since there appear to be no effective barriers to entry, one would expect rental rates to be established at or below $15 per month (and price at or below $490) in the long run. The rapid response of suppliers in 1968 suggests that long-run equilibrium can be reached rather rapidly. If future increases in de-

[50] A notable exception is the UNIVAC Unidisk. Eighty-character records are stored on the inner tracks, and 120-character records on the outer; a buffer is employed to accommodate the variation. The device also incorporates a track with a fixed head ("fastband"); some of UNIVAC's movable-head drums use a similar strategy.
[51] Six of the 38 devices included in the sample for the analysis described below used zones in the traditional manner (i.e., B_b was not the same for all bands). For purposes of the analysis, each band was assumed to store the average number of bits for all bands.
[52] However, some manufacturers offer packs only for sale.

Estimated value of shipments
(millions of dollars)

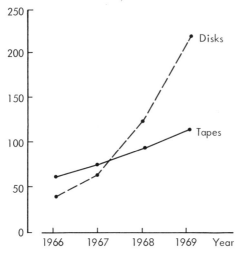

FIGURE 10-24. Estimates of the dollar values of disk pack and magnetic tape shipments during 1966–1969. Source: *EDP Industry and Market Report,* Nov. 10, 1967, p. 1.

mand are predicted properly, price should remain unchanged or decrease because of technological advances.[53]

Figure 10–24 shows one set of estimates of the dollar value (purchase price) of disk pack shipments for the period 1966–1969, along with comparable estimates for the value of magnetic tape shipments. Many observers share the view reflected in the figure: the value of disk pack shipments will rapidly surpass that of magnetic tapes.

Both IBM and Control Data Corporation manufacture drives for standard disk packs. Both sell their equipment to other manufacturers, sometimes with modifications. Early drives, such as the IBM 1311 and CDC 852, stored less than 20 million bits on a pack. With improved reading techniques, newer drives (e.g., the IBM 2311, CDC 854, and variants thereof) store from 50 to 60 million data bits on a single pack. In 1968 several other firms began to manufacture disk drives of this type.

A drive employing removable disks is presumably both more

[53] In the latter part of 1968 one manufacturer (Athana) announced a price of $300 per pack. The long-run viability of this policy is subject to some question in the industry.

valuable and more expensive than one with permanently installed disks. However, the evidence seems to indicate that with current technology the increase in value typically exceeds that in cost. Perhaps the best indication is the decision by IBM in 1967 to employ removable media for all movable-head devices intended for use with its third-generation systems.[54] As we will show later in this section, there is also some evidence that devices with removable media do not cost significantly more than others. Of course relative reliability is of interest; as usual, little evidence is available.[55] Removable devices require more complicated mechanisms, but they allow simple replacement of defective disks. No a priori argument can thus be advanced concerning the comparative reliability of the two approaches.

The standard disk pack is the most popular removable unit, but others are also in use. Several single-disk units are available, and IBM offers an 11-disk unit (the 2316) for use with the 2314 drive system. The 2314 includes 9 separate drive mechanisms; 1 is assigned as a spare, leaving 8 available for use. Each 2316 cartridge can store over 200 million data bits, giving the 2314 a total capacity of over 1.6 billion accessible bits. Viewed strictly as a disk drive (i.e., not taking into account the fact that the cartridges are removable), the 2314 provides a lower cost per bit (approximately 0.015 cent) than any other movable-head device introduced before 1968.

Table 10–6 provides data for several removable disk units produced in 1967 and 1968.

In the rest of this section, all drive mechanisms will be treated alike, whether or not they employ removable disk units. The ability to rapidly replace a disk (or set of disks) will be considered simply an additional feature.

The effectiveness of movable-head devices may be stated in terms of the basic measures described earlier. The distribution of sequential-access times is relatively simple to categorize. If bits i and $i + 1$ are stored on the same cylinder,[56]

---

[54] The 2310, 2311, and 2314 drives were retained; the 2302 was dropped.
[55] The majority of such evidence is anecdotal; for example, some assert that IBM's 2314 unit is subject to errors caused by dust particles if opened too frequently.
[56] For devices with more than one track per band the formula given may hold precisely or only on the average, depending on the manner in which data are organized on the tracks.

TABLE 10–6. Removable Media: Cost and Capacity, 1968

Unit	Number of Disks	Capacity (millions of data bits)	Purchase Price (dollars)	Rental Charge * (dollars/month)	Purchase Cost per Million Bits (dollars)
IBM 2315	1	8.2	90	N/A	10.98
GE DCT 100	1	9.4 †	260	N/A	27.66
UNIVAC Unidisk	1	12.0 †	300	N/A	25.00
GE DCT 150	1	47.2	400	N/A	8.47
IBM 1316	6	58.0	490	15	8.45
IBM 2316	11	207.0	650	20	3.14

　* N/A indicates that the device is not available for rental from the manufacturer.
　† Figures given represent total capacity. Only one side of the disk can be accessed without removing it and turning it over.

$$t_{i,i+1} = \frac{t_r}{B_b}$$

If they are stored on adjacent cylinders:

$$t_{i,i+1} = t_{min}$$

where t_{min} = the time required to move the comb to an adjacent cylinder. These values typically differ significantly: a ratio of 30,000 to 1 is not uncommon.

To assess the probabilities associated with the two alternatives, only one cylinder need be considered, since each cylinder is the same, and the use of each is equiprobable. A single cylinder stores $B_b b_c$ bits, all but one followed (in sequence) by a bit on the same cylinder. Thus

$$\Pr\left(t_{i,i+1} = \frac{t_r}{B_b}\right) = \frac{B_b b_c - 1}{B_b b_c}$$

$$\Pr\left(t_{i,i+1} = t_{min}\right) = \frac{1}{B_b b_c}$$

These probabilities also differ significantly: $B_b b_c$ may be well over 1 million.

The distribution of $t_{i,i+1}$ is thus binary, with a large probability of a small value and a small probability of a large value. The mean and standard deviation are not particularly well suited to summarize such a distribution, but we use them for consistency. The values can be computed directly from the definitions:

$$E(t_{i,i+1}) = \left(\frac{B_b b_c - 1}{B_b b_c}\right)\left(\frac{t_r}{B_b}\right) + \frac{1}{B_b b_c}(t_{min})$$

$$\sigma(t_{i,i+1}) = \sqrt{\sigma^2(t_{i,i+1})}$$

where

$$\sigma^2(t_{i,i+1}) = \left(\frac{B_b b_c - 1}{B_b b_c}\right)\left[\frac{t_r}{B_b} - E(t_{i,i+1})\right]^2 + \frac{1}{B_b b_c}[t_{min} - E(t_{i,i+1})]^2$$

The distribution of random-access times is somewhat more complex. Two independent operations must be considered: (1) positioning the comb over the appropriate cylinder, and (2) waiting for the desired position to come under a read/write head. The time for the second operation was considered earlier, in the analysis of fixed-head devices. Letting t_{rot} stand for the required rotation time,[57] we have

$$E(t_{rot}) = \frac{t_r}{2} \quad \text{and} \quad \sigma(t_{rot}) = \frac{t_r}{\sqrt{12}}$$

Comb-movement time (t_m) is, by assumption, a linear function of N_m, the number of positions moved:

$$t_m = a + \frac{N_m}{N_p} \quad (b) \quad \text{if } N_m > 0$$

$$= 0 \qquad\qquad \text{if } N_m = 0$$

If accesses are completely random, N_m will be triangularly distributed, as shown in Section B–1. Adapting the formulas derived there, we obtain

$$E(t_m) = a + \frac{b}{3} \quad \text{and} \quad \sigma(t_m) = \frac{b}{3\sqrt{2}}$$

Note, however, that there is a probability of $1/N_p$ that no comb movement will be required. When this is taken into account, the overall expected value for comb-movement time (t_{cm}) becomes

$$E(t_{cm}) = \frac{1}{N_p}(0) + \frac{N_p - 1}{N_p}\left(a + \frac{b}{3}\right)$$

---

[57] Proofs are given in Section D–1.

As shown in the footnote,[58] the standard deviation will be:

$$\sigma(t_{cm}) = \sqrt{\sigma^2(t_{cm})}$$

where

$$\sigma^2(t_{cm}) = \frac{1}{N_p}[0 - E(t_{cm})]^2 + \frac{N_p - 1}{N_p}\left[a + \frac{b}{3} - E(t_{cm})\right]^2$$

$$+ \frac{1}{N_p}(0) + \frac{N_p - 1}{N_p}\left(\frac{b^2}{18}\right)$$

Combining and simplifying, we have

[58] The general case is as follows. Consider the following probabilistic process:

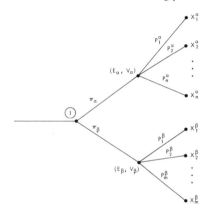

A decision is made at point 1 to take either path α or path β with probabilities π_α and π_β, respectively ($\pi_\alpha + \pi_\beta = 1$). If path α is taken, the outcome will be X_i^α with probability $p_i^\alpha \left(\sum_{i=1}^{n} p_i^\alpha = 1\right)$. If path β is taken, the outcome will be X_j^β with probability $p_j^\beta \left(\sum_{j=1}^{m} p_j^\beta = 1\right)$. The expected value and the variance of the outcome at point α are E_α and V_α, respectively. The values at point β are E_β and V_β, respectively. What are the mean and the variance of the overall outcome?

The problem is best considered as a required selection of path and its associated expected value, followed by the selection of the deviation from this expected value. For the former selection,

$$\text{Exp}_1 = \pi_\alpha E_\alpha + \pi_\beta E_\beta$$

$$\text{Var}_1 = \pi_\alpha(E_\alpha - \text{Exp}_1)^2 + \pi_\beta(E_\beta - \text{Exp}_1)^2$$

There is probability π_α that an additional variance of V_α will be encountered, and probability π_β that V_β will be encountered. Total variance is thus

$$\text{Var} = \text{Var}_1 + \pi_\alpha V_\alpha + \pi_\beta V_\beta$$

This is the basis for the formula given in the text.

$$E(t_{i,j}) = \frac{t_r}{2} + E(t_{cm})$$

$$\sigma(t_{i,j}) = \sqrt{\sigma^2(t_{i,j})}$$

where

$$E(t_{cm}) = \frac{N_p - 1}{N_p}\left(a + \frac{b}{3}\right)$$

$$\sigma^2(t_{i,j}) = \frac{t_r^2}{12} + \frac{1}{N_p}[E(t_{cm})]^2 + \frac{N_p - 1}{N_p}\left[a + \frac{b}{3} - E(t_{cm})\right]^2 + \frac{N_p - 1}{N_p}\left(\frac{b^2}{18}\right)$$

To relate cost to these and other measures, a sample of 38 movable-head devices (34 disks and 4 drum systems) was analyzed.[59] Sixteen of the units utilized removable media; in such cases the cost of the basic number of disks was included as part of the overall system cost. The sample was expanded to 186 observations by considering all possible configurations utilizing a single controller for reasons similar to those given for the comparable treatment of the sample of fixed-head devices. The following variables were considered to be at least potential factors influencing cost:

A = years since first delivery (1967 = 0),

$E(t_{i,j})$ = expected value of $t_{i,j}$ (in microseconds),

$\sigma(t_{i,j})$ = standard deviation of $t_{i,j}$ (in microseconds),

$E(t_{i,i+1})$ = expected value of $t_{i,i+1}$ (in microseconds),

$\sigma(t_{i,i+1})$ = standard deviation of $t_{i,i+1}$ (in microseconds),

$R = \begin{cases} 1 \text{ if removable disks utilized,} \\ 0 \text{ if not,} \end{cases}$

combs = number of independent combs included in the configuration, and

cap. = capacity (in millions of bits).

For simplicity, purchase price was used to measure cost. Figure 10–25 shows the distribution of the purchase/rent ratios for the 38 devices.[60]

Many regression analyses were performed; the results were gen-

---

[59] Only units offered by the major computer manufacturers were considered. The sample included the majority of such devices introduced between 1960 and 1968.

[60] Based on gross monthly rental (i.e., including basic maintenance) for one-shift operation and on purchase price for storage devices only (i.e., not including controllers). The median value is 45.0.

Number of devices

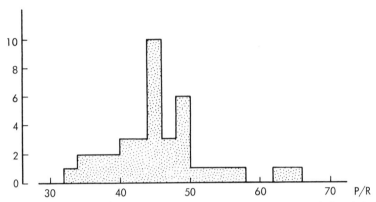

FIGURE 10-25. Distribution of purchase/rent ratios for 38 movable-head devices.

erally disappointing. The four measures of effectiveness were highly intercorrelated, leading to spurious and/or insignificant coefficients in multiple regressions. The simple correlation coefficients for the logarithms of the measures were as follows:

	$\ln \sigma(t_{i,j})$	$\ln E(t_{i,i+1})$	$\ln \sigma(t_{i,i+1})$
$\ln E(t_{i,j})$	.96	.75	.85
$\ln \sigma(t_{i,j})$		.74	.84
$\ln E(t_{i,i+1})$			.74

The simple correlation coefficient between cost per bit and the shift variable R was positive, suggesting that devices with removable disks are more expensive than others. But this result may simply reflect the fact that such systems are typically relatively small and hence not subject to economies of scale. Multiple regression analysis suggests quite the opposite relationship. In one instance the equation indicated that the ability to replace disks would lower cost by 16%.[61] This

---

[61] The equation was of the form:

$$\ln (\text{cost/bit}) = K - 0.169R$$

where K represents all other terms. The t value for the coefficient for R was 2.15; an increase in R from 0 to 1 would lower cost/bit by roughly 16%, since

$$e^{-0.169} \approx 0.84$$

value clearly cannot be correct. It does suggest, however, that the true cost, though not negative, may be quite small.

Because of the extensive colinearity among independent variables it proved essential to consider very simple multiple regression equations. Only technological progress and economies of scale proved to be sufficiently important (and independent) to be easily identified by means of regression techniques.[62] Approximately 81% of the variation in ln (cost/bit) was explained with the following equation:

$$\ln (\text{cost/bit}) = -0.847 + 0.132A - 0.375 \ln (\text{cap.})$$
$$(t = 11.23) \qquad (t = 25.49)$$

where cost/bit = purchase cost (in cents per bit),
A = years since first delivery (1967 = 0), and
cap. = capacity (in millions of bits).

The following data indicate the range of values for devices first delivered in 1966 or 1967:

Parameter	Low Value	Median Value	High Value
Cost/bit	0.015 cent/bit	0.073 cent/bit [63]	0.483 cent/bit
$E(t_{i,j})$	73,800 μsec	83,500 μsec	339,200 μsec
$\sigma(t_{i,j})$	23,900 μsec	29,500 μsec	153,400 μsec
$E(t_{i,i+1})$	0.13 μsec	1.04 μsec	4.34 μsec
$\sigma(t_{i,i+1})$	5.7 μsec	49.9 μsec	572.9 μsec
Cap.	6 million bits	230 million bits [63]	9660 million bits [64]

The coefficients obtained for the regression equation are slightly smaller than the corresponding values for fixed-head devices. Cost per bit decreases significantly over time at a rate of approximately 12% per year.[65] Economies of scale appear to be significant, though moderate: cost per bit falls by approximately 23% when capacity is doubled.[66]

It is unfortunate that the data do not allow some assessment of the

---

[62] None of the four measures of effectiveness gave significant results with expected characteristics.
[63] Figures indicate median values based on all configurations considered.
[64] One controller plus eight disk units.
[65] Since $e^{-0.132} \approx 0.88$.
[66] Since $2^{-0.375} \approx 0.77$.

relative cost of alternative levels of effectiveness as represented by our four measures. Regression analysis requires a sample with adequate (uncorrelated) variation in the independent variables; apparently manufacturers assumed that it would be unprofitable (or perhaps even impossible) to produce devices with a wide range of such capabilities. If this continues to be the case, the simple formula derived here may prove reasonably adequate for predicting the cost per bit of movable-head devices. Otherwise the formula may, of course, be seriously inadequate.

3. Magnetic Strip Units [67]

Movable-head disks provide moderate access times at relatively low cost. Removable disk units allow the storage of large amounts of information off-line, but the data can be accessed only after the unit is mounted on a drive, a procedure requiring 1–2 minutes. Magnetic strip devices provide a compromise. The recording medium is a flexible magnetic strip 2–4 inches wide and 7–16 inches long. The strips are mounted in cartridges which may be stored off-line. One or more cartridges are mounted on a drive mechanism; upon command any desired strip may be selected and wrapped around a drum, forming the recording surface for a rotating drum similar in many respects to those described in the previous sections. When the strip is no longer required, it is released from the drum and returned to the appropriate cartridge.

The time required to select a strip and then position it on the drum, ready for reading and/or writing data, ranges from 100 to 540 milliseconds, depending on the device. Drum rotation speeds are similar to those of conventional devices; recently introduced units employ a movable comb of read/write heads, instead of the fixed heads used on early devices. In no case does the strip completely cover the drum. Depending on the device, from 15% to 40% of the drum rotation time may be "wasted" while the gap between the trailing edge and the leading edge of the strip passes under the read/write heads.

Only four computer manufacturers have produced devices of this type, and one (Honeywell) terminated production in 1968. Since a great deal of high-speed mechanical action is employed, poor reliability

---

[67] This section incorporates material developed by Gordon Parkhill and Stein Skattum for a seminar given by the author at the University of Washington in 1966.

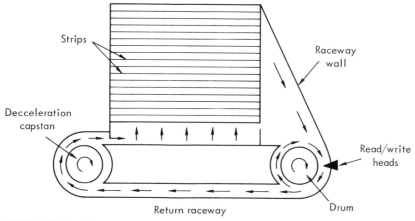

FIGURE 10-26a. Honeywell mass memory file, top view.

and extensive maintenance requirements have been experienced by some users. All devices provide for automatic recording of the utilization of each strip; one manufacturer (RCA) explicitly recommends replacement of a strip after 30,000 selections or 100,000 revolutions (whichever comes first).

Figures 10-26a through 10-26d show the basic mechanisms used in the four systems. Strips are loaded in cartridges, one or more of which can be placed in a drive unit. Each strip within a cartridge is uniquely identified by a series of notches and/or tabs. A strip is selected by specifying the cartridge (if two or more are mounted) and the strip number. Gating rods, pusher rods, and/or gripping arms then extract the desired strip and start it toward the drum. After one or more revolutions the strip is returned to the appropriate cartridge.

In NCR's CRAM units, the time required to select a strip varies relatively little with the location of the strip. In both the RCA and Honeywell units the time depends primarily on the distance between the drum and the cartridge in which the strip is located. In the IBM system the time depends on the relative locations of the present strip and the last one used—the tub-like mechanism can be rotated (in either direction) to any of 200 positions; in each position, ten strips are accessible by the selection mechanism.

The devices differ considerably with respect to allowable concurrent action. In an NCR unit three strips may be active at once—one falling toward the drum, one on the drum, and one being returned to the cartridge. Two strips may be active concurrently in the RCA and Honeywell devices. No concurrent action is possible in IBM's data cell—the selection mechanism may not be repositioned until the currently active strip is returned to the appropriate position in its cartridge.

During the six-year period following the delivery of the first magnetic strip device, recording densities have increased considerably, alleviating the need to use bands made up of several tracks in order to achieve high performance for sequential accesses. Recently introduced devices use one track per band, storing from 1 to 3 million bits on each strip.

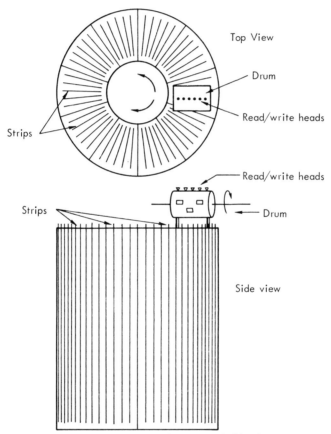

FIGURE 10-26b. IBM data cell drive, top and side views.

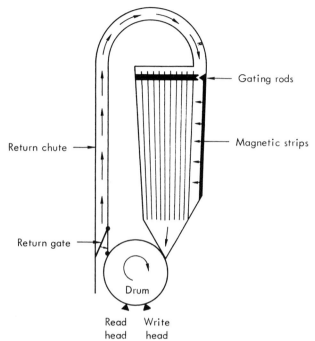

FIGURE 10-26c. NCR CRAM (card random access memory), side view.

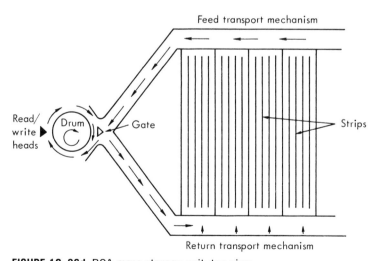

FIGURE 10-26d. RCA mass storage unit, top view.

TABLE 10-7. Magnetic Strip Devices: Basic Characteristics

Device	Hon. 251	Hon. 252	Hon. 253	IBM 2321
First delivery (year)	1966	1966	1967	1966
Strip width (in.)	3.25	3.25	3.25	2.25
Strip length (in.)	7.38	7.38	7.38	13
Data tracks/band	1	1	1	1
Bands/strip	32	128	128	100
Thousands of data bits/strip	186	743	743	1600
Strips/cartridge	512	512	512	200 †
Cartridges/device	1	1	5	10 †
Number of comb positions	2	8	8	5
Drum rotation time (msec)	16.7	16.7	16.7	50
Head positioning time (msec)				
Minimum	25	25	25	95
Maximum				
Time to select and mount				
strip (msec)				
Minimum				175
Maximum	95	150	225	400
Peak transfer rate ‖	100KC	100KC	100KC	54.7KB

Table 10–7 indicates the basic characteristics of twelve major units produced between 1962 and 1968.[68] Table 10–8 shows the capacity, purchase cost, and cost per bit for alternative configurations. The purchase cost includes the prices of the drive unit(s), the required controller (if any), and the number of cartridges and strips that can be mounted at one time. For devices requiring a controller, both a minimum configuration (a controller plus one device) and a maximum configuration (a controller plus the maximum number of devices that can be attached) are included. Capacity is measured by the maximum number of data bits that can be stored on-line.

Casual inspection of Table 10–8 suggests that economies of scale are present in magnetic strip storage and that costs have fallen over time. It is, of course, impossible to assess adequately the impact of any specific variable on cost per bit since the sample is so small and the variables are so interrelated (for example, average card selection time and capacity are positively correlated). However, there is no doubt

[68] Every attempt was made to obtain accurate data for Table 10–7; however, it was necessary to rely on secondary sources to some extent so that there may be errors.

NCR 353-1	NCR 353-2	NCR 353-3	NCR 353-5	NCR 653-101	RCA 3488-1	RCA 3488-2	RCA 70/568-11
1962	1964	1964	1967	1968	1964	1964	1967
3.5	3.5	3.5	3.65		4.5	4.5	4.5
14	14	14	14		16	16	16
6*	1	1	1	1	2	2	1
7	56	56	144	144	64	64	128
130	376	376	1296	2600	998	998	2097
256	128	256	384	384	256 ‡	256 ‡	256 ‡
1	1	1	1	1	8 ‡	16 ‡	8 ‡
1	1	1	4	4	16	16	16
48.4	48.4	48.4	48.4		60	60	60
N/A §	N/A §	N/A §			20	20	20
							35
235	235	235	125	90	290	290	439
				125	360	465	538
100KC	38KC	38KC	50KC	72KB	80KC	80KC	70KB

* Plus one parity track and one clocking track per band.

† 200 strips per data cell, 10 cells per drive. Addressing is by subcell; thus a subcell of 10 strips constitutes a logical cartridge.

‡ 256 strips per magazine, 8 or 16 magazines per unit. Addressing is by half-magazine; thus a group of 128 strips constitutes a logical cartridge.

§ N/A indicates that head-positioning time is not applicable for fixed-head units.

‖ KC: thousands of 6-bit characters per second; KB: thousands of 8-bit bytes per second.

about the relative expense of this type of rotating storage. Each manufacturer offers a device providing on-line storage for considerably less than 0.01 cent per bit; for example, the costs for the IBM 2321, the Honeywell 253, the NCR 653-101, and the RCA 70/568-11 range from 0.0034 to 0.0074 cent per bit. Magnetic strip storage typically costs an order of magnitude less than storage using movable-head disk units of comparable capacity and age.

Table 10-9 shows the cost and storage capacity of several cartridges. The final column indicates the cost per million bits of off-line storage, assuming that all strips are stored mounted in a cartridge. For most recently introduced systems the values are between $1 and $2 per million bits. The cost advantage of magnetic strips over removable disk units, though present, is less pronounced in this regard: as shown earlier, the IBM 2316 disk pack can be used to store information for $3.14 per million bits.

TABLE 10-8. Magnetic Strip Devices: Cost and Capacity, 1968

Device	First Delivered (year)	Num- ber of Drives	Capacity (millions of data bits)	Purchase * Cost (dollars)	Cost per Bit (cents/bit)
Hon. 251	1966	1	95.16	44,500	0.0468
Hon. 251	1966	8	761.28	252,925	.0332
Hon. 252	1966	1	380.64	65,875	.0173
Hon. 252	1966	8	3,045.12	423,925	.0139
Hon. 253	1967	1	1,903.14	117,000	.0061
Hon. 253	1967	8	15,225.12	832,925	.0055
IBM 2321	1966	1	3,200	175,900	.0055
IBM 2321	1966	8	25,600	1,167,450	.0046
NCR 353-1	1962	1	33	38,150	.1156
NCR 353-2	1964	1	48	30,695	.0639
NCR 353-3	1964	1	96.6	35,675	.0369
NCR 353-5	1967	1	372	63,350	.0170
NCR 653-101	1968	1	1,000	74,450	.0074
NCR 653-101	1968	8	8,000	497,600	.0062
RCA 3488-1	1964	1	2,040	170,300	.0083
RCA 3488-1	1964	4	8,160	583,700	.0072
RCA 3488-2	1964	1	4,080	238,100	.0058
RCA 3488-2	1964	4	16,320	854,900	.0052
RCA 70/568-11	1967	1	4,488	182,900	.0041
RCA 70/568-11	1967	8	35,904	1,217,500	.0034

* Includes drive, controller (if required), and the number of cartridges and strips that can be mounted in the unit(s). Figures for RCA devices are based on an assumed cost of $350 per magazine.

Table 10-10 indicates the minimum time between access of bits in sequence. The actual time will, of course, be much larger if the next bit to be accessed is located (1) at the beginning of another track on the same cylinder, (2) on another cylinder, or (3) on another strip. In case 1, $t_{i,i+1}$ will range from 8000 to 20,000 microseconds, depending on the device; in case 2, it may be as large as 95,000 microseconds; in case 3, several hundred thousand microseconds may be required. Clearly, average values of $t_{i,i+1}$ will be considerably greater than the values shown in Table 10-10.

The complexity of magnetic strip devices makes it difficult to compute accurate values for our four measures of effectiveness. In general, $E(t_{i,i+1})$ and $\sigma(t_{i,i+1})$ will be larger than the values obtained for comparable movable-head disk units. However, the more important

TABLE 10–9. Magnetic Strip Cartridges: Cost and Capacity, 1968

Device on Which Cartridge Is Used	Cartridge Capacity (millions of data bits)	Purchase Price per Cartridge (dollars)	Purchase Cost per Million Bits (dollars)
Hon. 251	95.16	375	3.94
Hon. 252, 253	380.64	375	0.98
IBM 2321	320	515	1.61
NCR 353–1	33	150	4.55
NCR 353–2	48	95	1.98
NCR 353–3	96.6	175	1.81
NCR 353–5	372	350	0.94
NCR 653–101	1000	450	0.45

differences concern the other two measures. Both $E(t_{i,j})$ and $\sigma(t_{i,j})$ are likely to be much larger for a magnetic strip device than for a comparable disk unit. This difference and a possible lack of reliability are the major penalties that must be incurred to obtain the substantial reduction in cost offered by such systems.

E. MAGNETIC TAPE DRIVES

Magnetic tape is the major medium for storing data in machine-readable form. Punched cards and punched tape require considerable space, are subject to physical damage, cannot be easily altered, and cannot be read rapidly. Magnetic ink characters are best suited for common information on preprinted forms. Printed or typewritten records are not used widely for this purpose at present, although improvements in the price and/or performance of optical character rec-

TABLE 10–10. Sequential-Access Times: Magnetic Strip Devices

Device	Minimum Value of $t_{i,i+1}$* (microseconds)	Device	Minimum Value of $t_{i,i+1}$* (microseconds)
Hon. 251, 252, 253	1.67	NCR 353–5	3.33
IBM 2321	2.29	NCR 653–101	1.74
NCR 353–1	1.67	RCA 3488–1, –2	2.08
NCR 353–2, –3	4.39	RCA 70/568–11	1.79

* Time between bits which equals (peak transfer rate in bits/microsecond)$^{-1}$.

ognition devices may make such a strategy more attractive. As indicated earlier, removable disk units are being used increasingly for storing data that are not inherently sequential. Unless relative costs change dramatically, however, magnetic tape will remain the most popular medium for storing data that are sequential or are used relatively seldom. Punched cards and paper tape will be employed for small amounts of information and, to some extent, as temporary forms of storage. However, the use of punched cards as a transitional medium between keyboard entry and magnetic storage appears to be declining.

Magnetic tape is commonly utilized for the interchange of programs and data. This provides strong incentives for standardization. It is thus not surprising that many tape drives accommodate alternative modes of operation, the desired mode being selected by setting a switch. In view of IBM's market position, it is also not surprising that other manufacturers tend to adopt the characteristics of this company's tape systems as *de facto* standards.

Figure 10-27 summarizes the characteristics of a typical tape drive. Logically, the entire tape constitutes a single band of (usually) 7 or 9 tracks. All read/write heads are fixed in place; [69] only the tape moves. Data are recorded in blocks of varying lengths separated by gaps in which no data are recorded. After a block of data is written on the tape, the required gap is created automatically. When a "read" instruction is received, the drive is started and data are transferred until the next gap is encountered. Most devices have the capability to read the tape while it is moving in either direction, but can write data only when the tape is moving forward. Rewind speed is typically two to three times as great as the speed at which the tape moves while reading or writing data.

Recording density is generally stated in terms of the number of bits per inch (bpi) on a given track. However, other measures may be used. Early drives employed 7 tracks—6 for data and 1 for parity bits; thus the number of bits per inch per track equaled the number of (6-bit) characters per inch. Current drives typically use 9 tracks—8 for data and 1 for parity bits, with the number of bits per inch per track equal to

[69] The typical drive has a separate set of heads for each operation. When moving forward, the tape comes under the writing heads first. This allows an automatic check of data written on the tape; any errors are detected immediately, and the data are automatically rewritten.

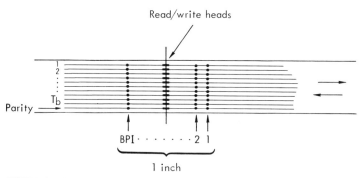

FIGURE 10-27. Magnetic tape storage.

the number of (8-bit) bytes per inch. The first drives used a recording density of 200 bpi. Densities of 556 and 800 bpi were the most popular for second-generation equipment. Many drives used with currently produced machines allow recording at a density of 1600 bpi.[70] A device intended to record at over 3000 bits per inch (the IBM 7340 "hypertape" drive) was withdrawn in 1968 after mixed results. To achieve compatibility, most drives include provisions for reading or writing data at different densities.

The rate at which data may be transferred depends on both the recording density and the speed of tape movement past the read/write heads. Values range from slightly more than 18 inches to 200 inches per second. Since data written at one speed may be read at another,[71] there is no need to accommodate alternate speeds on a given drive. Most manufacturers provide drives of various speeds; the user selects the one appropriate for his overall system.

The product of recording density and tape speed — the maximum attainable transfer rate — is usually stated in terms of thousands of bytes per second (for 9-track systems) or thousands of characters per second

[70] The method of recording is usually different. Phase encoding, used for recording at 1600 bpi, requires tape of better quality than the non-return-to-zero (NRZ) method used for lower densities. See Clarence B. Germain, *Programming the IBM 360*, Prentice-Hall, Englewood Cliffs, N.J., 1967, p. 70. Some difficulties have apparently been encountered with the higher recording density: "Of no small obstacle to higher packing densities is the difficulty the computer industry is having in developing read-write heads to handle efficiently the available 1600 bit densities" (G.A. Jaggers, quoted in "Magnetic Tape: a Message about the Medium," by Jan Snyders, *Business Automation*, February, 1968, pp. 36, 37).

[71] Assuming, of course, that both drives can accommodate the same recording density.

(for 7-track systems). As mentioned in the footnote to Table 10–7, common abbreviations are KB for the former and KC for the latter, although practice is far from consistent.

Both the time required to actually transfer a large amount of information and the amount that can be stored on a single tape depend critically on the manner in which the data are organized into blocks. Each interblock gap requires considerable space, usually $^6/_{10}$ inch.[72]

The effect of block size on the capacity of a tape is easily shown. Let N_{bb} be the number of bytes per block and bpi the number of bytes per inch of tape (equal, for 9-track tapes, to the number of bits per inch per track). If an interblock gap requires G inches, the amount of tape required for N_{bb} bytes will be

$$\frac{N_{bb}}{\text{bpi}} + G$$

and the portion used for storage will be

$$P_u = \frac{N_{bb}/\text{bpi}}{(N_{bb}/\text{bpi}) + G} = \frac{N_{bb}}{N_{bb} + G(\text{bpi})}$$

Figure 10–28a shows the relationship between the proportion utilized and the number of bytes per block for the two most popular recording densities (bpi = 800 and 1600), assuming $G = 0.6$. Note that doubling the recording density requires twice as many bytes per block to obtain a given utilization (P_u).

A standard reel contains 2400 feet of $^1/_2$-inch-wide tape. If 2300 feet is usable, with 9-track recording such a reel could store 22 million bytes at a density of 800 bpi or 44 million bytes at a density of 1600 bpi if all data were stored in a single block. In practice the amount actually stored is usually much smaller, depending primarily on the average block length.[73] Figure 10–28b relates the number of bytes actually stored on a standard reel of tape to the number of bytes per block for densities of 800 and 1600 bpi.

Interblock gaps not only reduce the storage capacity of a reel of

[72] This is the standard gap for 9-track, $^1/_2$-in. tapes. The earlier 7-track, $^1/_2$-in. tapes generally used a gap of $^3/_4$ in.

[73] It will also depend on the amount of "bad" tape. Areas in which recording cannot be accomplished without error are skipped over automatically, leaving gaps much longer than 0.6 in. We assume here that such areas total 100 ft.

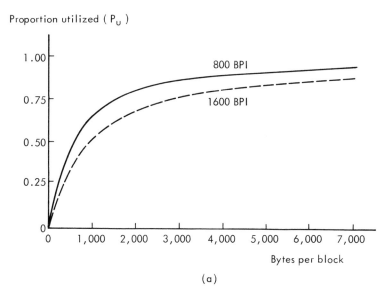

(a)

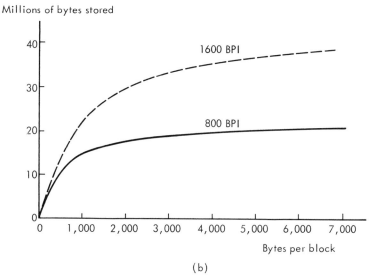

(b)

FIGURE 10–28. The number of bytes per block versus (a) proportion utilized and (b) number of bytes actually stored for densities of 800 and 1600 BPI.

tape but also make the average transfer rate lower than the "nominal" or "peak" rate obtained by multiplying recording density by read/write speed. If the tape is kept in motion while passing over gaps, the ratio of average to maximum transfer rate will equal P_u. If it is stopped between blocks, additional time will be required (typically from 2 to 5 milliseconds), reducing the average rate even more. Of course the overall effect on transfer rate will depend heavily on the nature of the application.

Since the capacity of a reel of tape depends so strongly on the organization of the data stored,[74] simple estimates of cost per bit are difficult to specify. However, some ranges can be given. A tape drive with required controller equipment typically costs between $10,000 and $60,000. In practice, from 5 to 40 million bytes will be stored on a standard reel. Considering a drive plus one reel of tape as a device for on-line storage, cost will fall between 0.003 and 0.150 cent per bit.

The market for magnetic tape appears to be highly competitive. In 1968 there were 13 manufacturers in the United States.[75] At the time it was reported that

One user estimates that the price of tape is down 20 percent from a year ago, and a tape supplier notes that two years ago he was selling tape for about $40 a reel; now the price is $20 to $25 a reel. Increasing competition is the major factor. Most industry sources trace this to the move by IBM into tape manufacturing which, in turn, caused 3M Co.—formerly IBM's supplier—to increase marketing activities directed at the consumer.[76]

In 1968 the General Services Administration awarded contracts for as much as 1 million reels of tape for federal government agencies. Prices ranged from $12.25 to $15.10 per reel.[77]

Depending on block size and reel price, the cost of off-line storage on magnetic tape will range from 5 to 50 cents per million bits.[78] This is significantly smaller than the cost of storage on magnetic strips

[74] Tape is by no means unique in this regard. The figures shown in Section D assume that data are organized to maximize the amount stored. This typically requires one record (block) per band. But a band on a rotating or magnetic strip device holds far less than an entire reel of tape (which constitutes the sole band on a tape drive).

[75] Jan Snyders, "Magnetic Tape: a Message about the Medium," *Business Automation,* February, 1968, p. 39.

[76] *Ibid.*   [77] *Datamation,* February, 1968, p. 97.

[78] For example, 5 million bytes stored on a reel costing $20 gives a cost of 50 cents/million bits; 40 million bytes stored on a reel costing $16 gives a cost of 5 cents/million bits.

TABLE 10–11. Cost and Effectiveness: IBM Tape Drives

	A. Purchase Prices		B. Relative Cost Effectiveness		
	Maximum Recording Density		Speed (inches/ second)	Maximum Recording Density	
Device *	800 bpi	1600 bpi		800 bpi	1600 bpi
Tape drive, 37.5 ips	$16,100	$18,500	37.5	1.000	0.583
Tape drive, 75 ips	23,400	25,800	75	0.681	.382
Tape drive, 112.5 ips	37,900	40,300	112.5	0.694	.374
Tape drive, 200 ips	N/A †	54,600	200	N/A †	.260
Controller	32,600	40,100			

* The 200-ips drive is the IBM 2420-7; all others are models of the 2401 series. Controllers are model 2403 (1 × 8).

† N/A indicates that a drive with a speed of 200 ips and maximum density of 800 bpi was not available.

(from $1 to $2 per million bits) or removable disk units (from $3 to $25 per million bits). Given the disparity in costs, there is no reason to expect that the total amount of data stored on removable disks will exceed that stored on magnetic tape in the near future, even if the value of disk shipments exceeds that of tape shipments by a considerable margin.

Tape drives vary with respect to both speed and recording density. If peak transfer rate (speed times maximum density) is taken as a measure of effectiveness, clear economies of scale are evident, especially those resulting from increases in recording density. Section A of Table 10–11 shows the 1968 purchase prices of seven IBM tape drives differing primarily in speed and density. The final entry gives the cost of a controller capable of handling eight drives; as indicated, the cost depends on the recording density to be used. Section B of the table shows the cost/effectiveness of each unit relative to that of the drive with the lowest speed and density.[79]

Several manufacturers offer stations housing two or more tape drives; this allows some sharing of common functions, such as power supplies. The reduction in cost is suggested by Table 10–12. Section A

[79] Peak transfer rate was used as the measure of effectiveness. The cost of each drive included that of one drive and one-eighth the cost of the appropriate controller.

TABLE 10–12. Relative Costs: * Multidrive Stations

A. IBM 2401 and 2402 Systems

Speed (inches/ second)	Density (bits/inch)	Cost of Two Separate Drives (model 2401) (dollars)	Cost of One Station with Two Drives (model 2402) (dollars)	Difference in Cost (dollars)	Ratio of Costs
37.5	800	32,200	29,800	2400	0.925
75	800	46,800	44,200	2600	.944
112.5	800	75,800	73,300	2500	.967
37.5	1600	37,000	34,600	2400	.935
75	1600	51,600	49,000	2600	.950
112.5	1600	80,600	78,100	2500	.969

B. Burroughs 9380 Systems †

Speed (inches/second)	Density (bits/inch)	Number of Drives per Unit	Cost (dollars)	Relative Cost per Drive
45	800	2	43,200	1.000
45	800	3	52,800	0.815
45	800	4	62,400	0.722
45	1600	2	52,800	1.000
45	1600	3	67,200	0.848
45	1600	4	81,600	0.773

* Costs do not include separate controller prices.
† The 800-bpi Burroughs units are models 9381; the others, models 9382.

contrasts the cost of two separate tape drives with that of one unit housing two drives. Section B shows the relative costs of units housing two, three, and four drives. IBM equipment is used for the former comparison; Burroughs equipment, for the latter. All costs are based on 1968 prices.

Many controllers are sold as separate units, but limited economies can sometimes be obtained by combining a controller and one or more drives in the same unit. Table 10–13 suggests the possible magnitude of such savings on the basis of the 1968 prices of IBM equipment.

As these comparisons indicate, the cost of a controller is not insignificant—the cheapest typically costs as much as one tape drive or

TABLE 10-13. Relative Costs: Controller/Drive Units

Speed (inches/ second)	Density (bits/inch)	Cost of One Tape Drive (model 2401) plus One Controller (model 2803) (dollars)	Cost of One 2403 Unit (includes one tape drive plus one controller) (dollars)	Difference in Cost (dollars)	Ratio of Costs
37.5	800	48,700	43,400	5300	0.891
75	800	56,000	50,900	5100	.909
112.5	800	70,500	65,700	4800	.932
37.5	1600	58,600	53,300	5300	.910
75	1600	65,900	60,800	5100	.923
112.5	1600	80,400	75,600	4800	.940

even more. In addition to the requisite electronics, a controller includes a switching mechanism for connecting any of several drives to an input/output channel. Possible combinations are usually indicated with the standard notation for switches. Thus a 1 × 8 (1 by 8) controller can connect one input/output channel to any one of eight drives; a 2 × 8 can connect either of two channels to any of eight drives, with the connected drives operating concurrently if desired. Multichannel controllers may or may not include sufficient circuitry to allow concurrent operations of the same type (e.g., reading two tapes at once). IBM equipment provides a good example of the relative costs, as shown in Table 10-14. In general, concurrent operations of any type require additional cost; for example, a 2 × 16 controller will cost more than two 1 × 8 units.[80]

Significant controller costs lead to substantial economies of scale. An indication of the potential magnitude is provided by the results of an analysis of 93 different tape drives produced during 1968.[81] For each unit, two configurations were considered: (1) the one giving the minimum overall cost per drive—typically 8, 10, or 16 units plus a controller, and (2) the one giving the maximum overall cost per drive—the

---

[80] No comparable 2 × 16 controller was manufactured by IBM in 1968; however, the costs of such controllers produced by other manufacturers follow the expected pattern.
[81] Virtually all drives sold by major computer manufacturers at the time were included.

TABLE 10-14. IBM Controller Costs: * Concurrent Operations

Capability	Maximum Recording Density	
	800 bpi	1600 bpi
1 × 8 (one 2803 controller)	$32,600	$40,100
2 × 8 Concurrent read and write (one 2804 controller)	46,700	54,200
2 × 8 Concurrent read and write Concurrent read and read Concurrent write and write (two 2803 controllers plus one 2816 switching unit)	91,700	106,700

* All costs based on 1968 prices.

smallest number of drives obtainable plus any required controller. Figure 10–29 shows the distribution of the ratio of the two costs; the median value, 0.65, provides a measure of the potential economies.

Regression analysis is of limited value for assessing the impact of several tape drive characteristics on cost. For example, most nine-track systems, but few seven-track systems, have the capability to read tape moving in the reverse direction. Moreover, early systems used a variety of tape sizes (½-inch, ¾-inch, and 1-inch were all employed); later systems generally use ½-inch tape. Clearly it would be difficult to separate the effects of technological progress from cost differences due to differences in capabilities. No more accurate estimate of technological progress is likely to be obtained than that found by using the simple regression analysis described in Chapter 9. As shown there, the annual improvement in the cost/effectiveness of tape drives (calculated in this manner) has been approximately 16%.

An extensive regression analysis of magnetic tape drive cost and effectiveness was performed by Takaki in 1967.[82] A great many combinations of drives and controllers were evaluated on the basis of four

[82] Steven T. Takaki, "Cost versus Effectiveness of Digital Magnetic Tape Devices," June, 1967, research report submitted to the Graduate School of Business, University of Washington, in partial fulfillment of the requirements for the degree of Master of Business Administration.

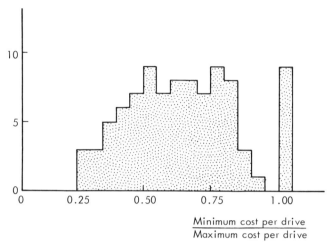

FIGURE 10-29. Distribution of the ratio of minimum to maximum cost per drive for 93 tape units.

measures. Dominated configurations were excluded, one configuration being considered to be dominated by another if the latter was better with respect to at least one of the four measures and no worse with respect to any other. The four measures employed were as follows:

cost = for each configuration, the purchase price of all drives plus any required controllers,

capacity = the maximum number of characters or bytes that could be stored if each tape drive contained one single block of data,

TR = the peak-load transfer rate for the configuration, measured in thousands of characters or bytes per second, and

AR = accessibility ratio, the proportion of potential concurrent operations actually possible.

The accessibility ratio provides a means for differentiating between, for example, a configuration with 8 drives and two 1×4 controllers and one with 8 drives and one 2×8 controller. In the latter case any of the 28 different pairs [83] of drives can be used concurrently. In the

[83] Given N drives, the number of different pairs is

$$\frac{N^2 - N}{2}$$

former case only 16 different pairs can be used concurrently.[84] The values of AR are thus $28/28 = 1$ and $16/28 = 0.57$, respectively.

No more than 38% of the variation in the logarithm of cost could be explained in Takaki's analysis, even when shift variables were used to allow a different intercept for each manufacturer's equipment.[85] The best equation was of the form

$$\ln (\text{cost}) = a_i + b_1 \ln (\text{capacity}) + b_2 \ln TR + b_3(AR)$$

where a_i = the intercept for the ith manufacturer. The three slope coefficients were significant and had the expected signs:

Coefficient	Value	t Value
b_1	0.658	15.96
b_2	0.689	14.68
b_3	1.496	11.00

The results suggest clear economies of scale: doubling total capacity increases cost less than 60%;[86] doubling the peak transfer rate increases it slightly more than 60%.[87] The coefficient for the accessibility ratio appears to be excessively large, however: according to these results, a system with all potential combinations accessible $(AR = 1)$ costs 45% more than one in which 75% are accessible [88] – the average figure for the sample as a whole. Presumably AR acted as a surrogate for one or more excluded factors.

Whatever the true values of the coefficients relating cost to effectiveness, it seems likely that the qualitative results are correct. As we have found repeatedly when examining computer equipment, systems that

[84] If N_1 drives can be connected to channel 1 and N_2 drives to channel 2, and no single drive can be connected to more than one channel, the number of possible pairs is $N_1 N_2$. To maximize this value, drives should be distributed equally (or as equally as possible) among controllers. For example, given N drives,

$$N_1 + N_2 = N$$

Hence to maximize $N_1 N_2$ requires $N_1 = N_2 = N/2$.
[85] The results showed only insignificant differences among manufacturers with two exceptions – Burroughs and UNIVAC equipment appeared to be more expensive than that of other manufacturers. The results may have been spurious. However, both firms subsequently introduced new drives and controllers.
[86] $2^{0.658} \approx 1.58$.
[87] $2^{0.689} \approx 1.61$.
[88] $e^{1.496(1.00-0.75)} \approx 1.45$.

TABLE 10-15. Random-Access Times: Tape Drives

Tape Length (feet)	Read/Write Speed (inches/ second)	$E(t_{i,j})$ (seconds)	$\sigma(t_{i,j})$ (seconds)
2400	18.75	512	362
2400	37.5	256	181.02
2400	75	128	90.51
2400	112.5	85.3	60.34
2400	150	64	45.25
2400	200	48	33.94
1200	18.75	256	181.02
1200	37.5	128	90.51
1200	75	64	45.25
1200	112.5	42.67	30.17
1200	150	43	22.63
1200	200	24	16.97

are twice as large or twice as effective in some respect cost less than twice as much as others. Magnetic tape is apparently no exception.

Given the dependence of the effectiveness of tape drives on the organization of the data stored and the manner in which the data are used, it is preferable to conduct analyses in terms of basic capabilities, as we have done thus far. For purposes of comparison with other devices, however, some indication of effectiveness in terms of our standard measures is desirable.

Since data must be read and written in blocks, and since tape-movement time is not simply a function of the distance to be moved (start/ stop time may be required, some movement may be accomplished at rewind speed, etc.), no simple model will yield the exact distribution of interaccess times under conditions of completely random selection. For purposes of analysis, however, it may suffice to assume that data are uniformly distributed on the tape and that tape is moved between any two locations at read/write speed. Under these conditions the previous results apply:

$$E(t_{i,j}) = \frac{t_{\max}}{3} \quad \text{and} \quad \sigma(t_{i,j}) = \frac{E(t_{i,j})}{\sqrt{2}}$$

where

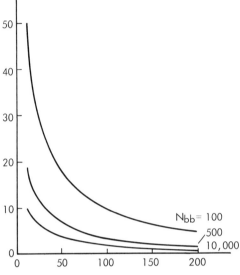

$E(t_{i,\,i+1})$
(microseconds)

Nbb= 100
500
10,000

Read/write speed (inches/sec)

FIGURE 10–30a. Relationship between expected value of sequential access time and read/write speed.

$$t_{max} = \frac{\text{length of tape}}{\text{read/write speed}}$$

Table 10–15 provides values for several cases.

The distribution of sequential-access times for tape storage is affected by data organization as well as by density and read/write speed. If bits i and $i + 1$ are in the same block of data, the peak transfer rate may be assumed to be [89]

$$t_{i,i+1}^{min} = \frac{1}{\text{bpi} \cdot T_B \cdot \text{ips}}$$

where bpi = bits per inch per track,

T_B = data tracks (thus bpi $\cdot$ T_B = data bits per inch of tape), and
ips = read/write speed (in inches per second).

[89] The formula given here indicates the average time; $t_{i,i+1} = 0$ if bits i and $i + 1$ lie beside one another on different tracks.

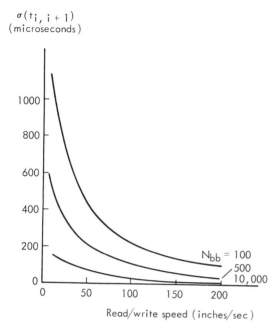

$\sigma(t_i, i+1)$
(microseconds)

Read/write speed (inches/sec)

FIGURE 10–30b. Relationship between standard deviation of sequential access time and speed, for 800-BPI units with a 0.6-inch gap.

If bit $i+1$ is at the beginning of the next block of data, the time required may be assumed to be [90]

$$t_{i,i+1}^{\max} = \frac{G}{\text{ips}}$$

where G = interblock gap length in inches.

Letting N_{bb} be the number of bytes per block (as before), we have

$$t_{i,i+1} = \begin{cases} t_{i,i+1}^{\max} & \text{with probability } 1/8N_{bb} \\ t_{i,i+1}^{\min} & \text{with probability } (8N_{bb} - 1)/8N_{bb} \end{cases}$$

Figure 10–30a shows the relationship between $E(t_{i,i+1})$ and read/write speed for 800-bpi units with a 0.6-inch gap; Fig. 10–30b indicates the relationship between $\sigma(t_{i,i+1})$ and speed.

---

[90] If the drive must stop and then restart between blocks, a different time may be required.

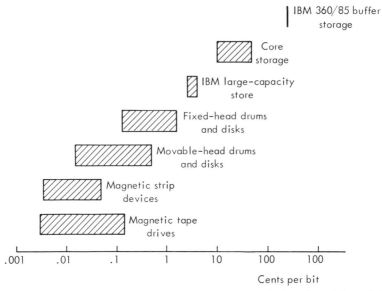

FIGURE 10-31a. Ranges of cost for magnetic storage devices first delivered during 1966-1968. Cost of on-line storage.

F. COST AND EFFECTIVENESS OF MAGNETIC STORAGE, 1966-1968

Figures 10-31a through 10-31c indicate the ranges of cost and effectiveness for magnetic storage devices first delivered from 1966 through 1968. The IBM 360/85 buffer storage was included to represent the cost and effectiveness of very high-speed (80-nanosecond cycle time) circuitry. The other data were derived from the results of

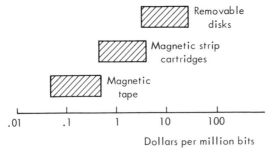

FIGURE 10-31b. Ranges of cost for magnetic storage devices first delivered during 1966-1968. Cost of off-line storage.

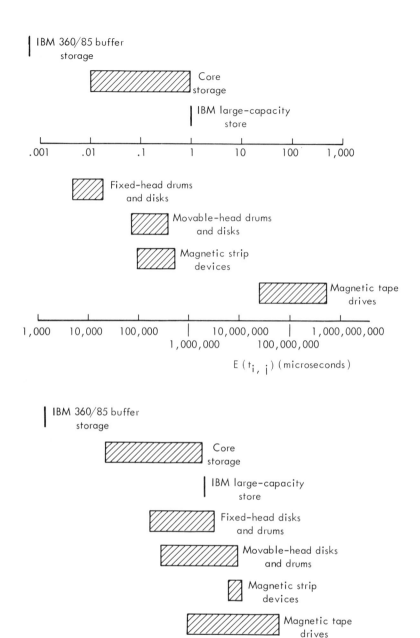

FIGURE 10–31c. Ranges of effectiveness for magnetic storage devices first delivered during 1966–1968.

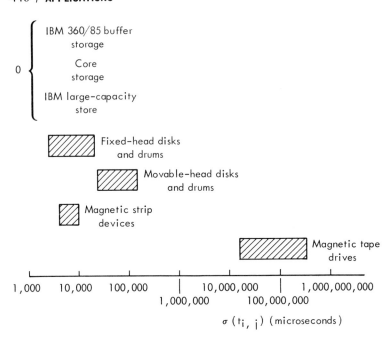

$\sigma\,(t_{i,\,j})\ (\text{microseconds})$

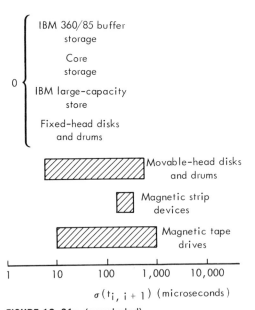

$\sigma\,(t_{i,\,i+1})\ (\text{microseconds})$

FIGURE 10–31c. (concluded)

the studies described in previous sections. Each figure is plotted to a logarithmic scale.

The results conform to prior expectations. By and large the less expensive a device, the poorer is its performance in all respects, that is, the larger the values of $E(t_{i,j})$, $\sigma(t_{i,j})$, $E(t_{i,i+1})$, and $\sigma(t_{i,i+1})$. It is noteworthy, however, that the most dramatic differences in effectiveness concern $E(t_{i,j})$. This relationship is, of course, well known: high-cost storage is most likely to prove desirable under conditions of random access.

Figures 10–31a through 10–31c provide only rough estimates of the measures for devices introduced in 1966, 1967, and 1968. Those introduced in later years will undoubtedly have values lying outside some or all of the indicated ranges. But the relative magnitudes may change less dramatically than the absolute values. In any event, there will always be choices to make, and they will rarely be simple. Devices will vary in effectiveness and in cost, with better ones more expensive than their poorer counterparts. Hence the selection of an optimal mix of devices will remain one of the most important and difficult problems facing the system designer.

A. INTERNAL AND EXTERNAL PRICING

Managers of most computer installations should consider carefully both *external* pricing for services provided to those outside the firm or agency of which the installation is a part and *internal* pricing for services provided to other members of the firm or agency. External prices bring money into the organization and thus serve both an income and an allocation function; internal prices simply allocate computer use, since only transfer payments are involved. Nonetheless the similarities are greater than the differences.

The key to the use of internal pricing is the concept of the "profit center." A firm is divided into a number of reasonably autonomous divisions, with each allowed to "sell" or "buy" goods and services from other divisions at appropriate transfer prices. Accounts are kept for each division, and its profit or loss is calculated accordingly. Since every manager is assumed to have considerable discretion over his division, its profit or loss can be used to assess his performance.

In practice the profit center concept is difficult to implement. Although boundaries must be drawn so that each division is small enough to be meaningfully managed, a proliferation of divisions with its attendant increase in bookkeeping must be avoided. Also, the manager of each' division must have real discretion over its operation if he is to be held responsible for its performance, but the firm may thereby be vulnerable to a catastrophic error on the part of one of the division managers. Finally, there is the matter of the transfer prices themselves — how should they be set? And should a division be allowed to buy or sell outside the firm if it prefers, rather than dealing with another division?

Figures 11–1a and b illustrate a typical problem connected with internal pricing. Assume that programming is produced by one division and purchased by another. The total cost (TC) and marginal cost (MC) to the selling division, and hence to the firm as a whole, are as shown. The total value (TV) and marginal value (MV) to the buying division,

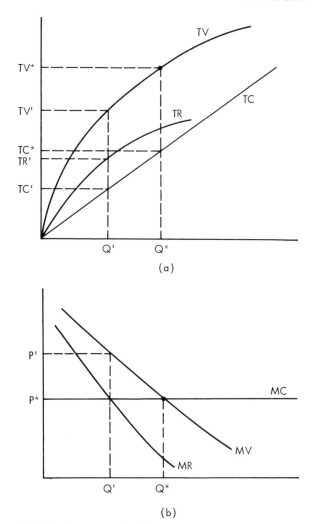

FIGURE 11-1. Internal pricing.

and hence to the firm as a whole, are also as shown. Clearly, from the standpoint of the firm, the quantity bought and sold should be Q^* and the transfer price should be P^*, equal to the marginal cost. Then the selling division would break even, and the buying division would be credited with "profit" equal to $TV^* - TC^*$. Unfortunately, this will probably not be the outcome. Usually the selling division will set the

price, and since its manager is encouraged to maximize his "profit"—
total revenue (TR) less total cost (TC)—he will attempt to do so. The
price that will accomplish this goal is P', which will lead the buying
division to purchase Q' units; the total "profit" to the firm as a whole,
equal to $TV' - TC'$, will be split between the divisions, with $TV' - TR'$
going to the buying division and $TR' - TC'$ to the selling division. But
the total amount will be smaller than the maximum possible $(TV^* -
TC^*)$.

The problem is the seller's monopoly over the buying division. The
profit center concept in this case encourages exploitation of one division by another, to the detriment of the firm's overall profits. The
magnitude of the problem may be reduced by allowing the buying division to deal with outside suppliers if it wishes, thus reducing the selling
division's monopoly power. But the full solution usually requires that
one of the two divisions behave in a "statesmanlike" manner.[1] In this
instance the selling division could simply set its price equal to the
(constant) marginal cost, agreeing to provide any amount of service at
that price. Note, however, that the opposite procedure would not work.
The buying division could present its entire marginal value schedule
to the selling division; but the latter would still elect P' and Q', as we
have argued. In the more common case in which the marginal cost
curve is not flat, a presentation of the cost curve to the buying division,
with the latter selecting the transfer price, could have similar (undesirable) effects.[2]

It may be unwise, therefore, to provide incentives for a division
selling its product to other divisions to "make a profit." A better approach may be to instruct its manager to set prices to maximize the
value of the firm as a whole (or, for a government agency, to minimize
the overall cost of providing a required level of service). This can be
accomplished in a relatively straightforward manner if the demand
(marginal value) curve of each buying division can be assumed to indicate the value to the firm as a whole. Needless to say a number of con-

[1] Or else discriminate perfectly against the other, an interesting but relatively impractical
objective.
[2] From the standpoint of the buying division, the relevant cost is the product of transfer
price times quantity; this need not equal total cost to the firm. Thus the optimal solution
from the viewpoint of the buying division may not be the best solution for the firm as a
whole.

ditions must be met for this identity of interests to hold. Throughout this chapter we will assume that it does, stating only that in practice the assumption is sometimes violated to such an extent that questions concerning internal pricing lose much, if not all, of their relevance.

If the demand curves of internal buyers reflect marginal value, the relationship between external and internal prices can easily be determined. Assume that there are N_i internal buyers and N_e external buyers. The object is to maximize net value, which is equal to (1) the total value obtained by internal users plus (2) the total revenue obtained from external users less (3) total cost:

$$\text{Maximize:} \quad \sum_{i=1}^{N_i} TV_i + \sum_{j=1}^{N_e} TR_j - TC$$

subject to

$$TV_i = f_i(Q_i) \quad \text{for each internal user } i$$
$$TR_j = f_j(Q_j) \quad \text{for each external user } j$$
$$TC = f(Q_T)$$
$$Q_T = \sum_{i=1}^{N_i} Q_i + \sum_{j=1}^{N_e} Q_j$$

The optimum will be reached when output is divided so that the following conditions hold:

$$\frac{dTV_i}{dQ_i} = \frac{dTC}{dQ_T} \quad \text{for each } i = 1 \text{ to } N_i$$

$$\frac{dTR_j}{dQ_j} = \frac{dTC}{dQ_T} \quad \text{for each } j = 1 \text{ to } N_e$$

Obviously the appropriate internal price will equal the marginal cost (dTC/dQ_T), and it should be applied uniformly for all internal users. However, the appropriate price for an external user is the one that leads him to purchase the quantity at which marginal revenue equals marginal cost. Thus each external user should be charged a price greater than marginal cost (and hence greater than the internal price), and it is possible that each external user should be charged a different price. In general, the less elastic an external user's demand curve, the greater should be the discrepancy between external and internal price.

Some of the theoretical aspects of internal pricing will be discussed more fully in later sections. First, however, it will be useful to describe a particularly important debate concerning the pricing policies of university computer centers.

B. UNIVERSITY COMPUTER CENTER PRICES

A substantial portion of the costs of university computer centers has been financed by the federal government. The estimated breakdown for 1966 was as follows [3]

Source	Percentage of Total Cost
Federal government	57%
Universities	29
Computer manufacturers (educational discounts)	14

Part of the federal contribution (19% of the total) was made in the form of direct facility grants; however, the larger portion was paid indirectly, through purchases of computer time by holders of government research grants and contracts. Naturally the price at which such time is purchased is of interest to both the university and the government, and there is ample room for a conflict of interest between the parties. It is thus not surprising that the subject has received continuing attention, although the government's policy toward universities in this regard is merely a special case of its general policy toward cost-reimbursement-type contractors.

The basic policy in cases involving cost-reimbursement contracts and shared facilities relies on an "equitable" sharing of costs. In particular, the government expects to pay no more than its proportional share of costs, where this proportion is based on some acceptable measure of utilization. For computers, time has been the traditional measure. Let H_g be the hours during a month devoted to government use, and H_n the hours devoted to nongovernment use $- H_g + H_n = H_T$ (total hours used). Then, if the total cost of running the computer for

[3] "Digital Computer Needs in Universities and Colleges," NAS-NRC *Publication* 1233.

the month is $TC[=f(H_T)]$, the government will pay

$$TP_g = TC\left(\frac{H_g}{H_T}\right)$$
$$= H_g\left(\frac{TC}{H_T}\right)$$
$$= H_g(AC)$$

where AC = average hourly cost (= TC/H_T). The price to government users is thus required to equal average cost; no explicit restrictions are placed on the price (or prices) charged to other users in the simple case in which the product (e.g., "computer hours") is considered homogeneous.

One of the earliest controversies concerning this policy involved the appropriate measure of total cost. In 1956 the Carnegie Institute of Technology leased a model 650 computer from IBM; the company granted a 60% discount, termed an "educational contribution." Carnegie used the total commercial base rental as its monthly cost when calculating an hourly charge for government users, arguing that the IBM contribution was intended to pay for student use. In 1957 the Navy Department, sponsor of some of the research performed with the equipment, disallowed the practice. Carnegie appealed and lost its case (in 1964). The Armed Services Board of Contract Appeals held that the educational "contribution" was simply a trade discount; thus only the university's actual costs could be included when calculating the relevant average cost. The Carnegie decision was the first of a series of setbacks for universities attempting to fund computer centers almost entirely from federal sources, thus providing "free" computation for students and nonsponsored faculty research.

A second issue in the Carnegie case concerned off-peak prices. The university argued that its equipment had been rented for use during the prime shift (in fact, operators were not employed at other times — students and faculty using the machine off-shift ran it themselves); thus all rental costs should have been allocated to the prime-shift users. The Board upheld this assertion:

While it is recognized that value and pricing are not identical with costing, the principle that the products or services which generate the cost should bear the cost is not violated when a larger share of the cost is assigned to the more valuable services which are the principal justification for the incurrence of the cost.

The Board did, however, acknowledge its inability to provide a general rule for ". . . the much more difficult problem of how to prorate the costs so that each class of service will bear its proper share of costs."

The Carnegie decision settled some of the outstanding issues, but a great many were left unresolved. In an attempt to clear the air, the National Association of College and University Business Officers met with representatives of the Bureau of the Budget; the result was BOB *Circular* A–21, which specified in paragraph J–37 that

The costs of [facilities such as electronic computers] . . . normally will be charged directly to applicable research agreements based on actual usage or occupancy of the facilities at rates that (1) are designed to recover only actual costs of providing such services, and (2) are applied on a nondiscriminatory basis as between organized research and other work of the institution. . . .

The requirement that rates recover only actual costs dictated an overall policy of average costing; although off-peak rates were allowed, they generally had to be based on cost differentials. The Defense Department's instructions [4] for implementing the new policy were representative of the requirements imposed by most federal auditors:

General operating costs of those facilities . . . should generally be charged to users by means of actual or predetermined billing or costing rates covering a period not normally in excess of twelve months (not necessarily a calendar or fiscal year), as provided below:

a. Where only one rate for the facility is to be applied, it should consist of the actual or estimated applicable costs divided by the actual or estimated number of hours or other units composing the basis.

b. Where real cost differentials (such as certain services furnished during prime shifts only or by different facilities) exist and can be readily demonstrated, separate rates for such cost differentials may be used. In the case of educational institutions, moreover, where rental or lease costs are based upon prime-shift usage, second- and third-shift usage may, with appropriate approval, be charged at reduced rates.

c. Under certain situations, furthermore, reasonably estimated differential

---

[4] Defense Contract Audit Agency Regulation 7640.9, reported in Herschel Kanter, Arnold Moore, and Neil Singer, "The Allocation of Computer Time by University Computer Centers," *The Journal of Business,* July, 1968, pp. 383–384.

costs may be used where cost differentials logically exist but cannot be determined precisely by the contractor. For example, as regards a computer facility, such differentials would permit priority or interrupt or short turn-around time runs at premium rates and/or non-priority or non-prime-time or large-volume runs at reduced rates.

d. Whether a single rate or several rates are used, the rates should be so designed as to recover or closely approximate total recovery of costs from all uses of the facility. Where differing rates are used, they should be applied to all users on a non-discriminatory basis. The costing of accommodations sales at reduced rates is not considered appropriate.

e. Any underabsorption or overabsorption of costs resulting from application of predetermined rates may be charged or credited to an appropriate category of indirect expense.

f. Where the manufacturer leases or sells the equipment below commercial prices to an educational institution as an allowance to education, the application of this allowance should be treated as a reduction of the cost of leasing or purchasing.

g. Where the contractor (normally a university) has received a grant from the Government to be used in connection with a particular facility, the application of the funds provided should be made in accordance with the terms of the grant.

Whatever the merits of this set of policies, implementation has been far from simple. One problem concerns the calculation of monthly costs when some or all of the equipment is owned—what depreciation formula is applicable? In more than one instance the price charged for a machine already heavily utilized had to be greatly lowered to reflect the "decrease" in costs that took place after the depreciation period had ended. Another problem arises in connection with multipro-grammed, multiprocessor, and multiuser machines—what measures of use are relevant, and how can costs be allocated "logically" among them? These and other questions have been resolved primarily on an ad hoc basis, as might be expected, since the "correct" answers are, by and large, inconsistent with the basic philosophy behind federal policy.

C. THE "STANFORD CRISIS"

One of the more dramatic instances of the perverse effects of average-cost pricing occurred in the spring of 1966. Stanford University's computers were heavily utilized by holders of government grants and contracts (approximately 70% at the time). Total costs for the fiscal year were virtually unaffected by utilization. Since federal policy required that research users be charged at a rate determined by dividing total cost by the total hours utilized, the larger the utilization by students, the lower was the income per hour from federally sponsored users. The Stanford administration had budgeted a fixed dollar amount toward defraying some of the costs of the computer center in order to provide computation for students and unsupported faculty research, an amount based on the assumption that federal grants and contracts would provide roughly the same proportion of total costs as they had in the previous year. However, student and nonsponsored faculty use proved to be greater than anticipated; and it appeared that, unless this type of computation was drastically curtailed, federal use would fall below the anticipated percentage of total use, requiring a larger proportion of the expense to be paid by the university. Although the equipment was literally idle much of the time, with a true marginal cost of zero, Stanford chose to deny students further computation, arguing that the situation was indeed a crisis, one directly attributable to the unwise federal policy of average-cost pricing.

One element rarely considered explicitly in this type of situation concerns the demand for computation by federally sponsored users. Some implicitly assume that this demand is perfectly inelastic, that is, the user will not alter his purchases of computation if the price is changed. This is seldom strictly true; whatever inelasticity there is may result from another peculiarity of federal policy. Computer centers can set price exactly equal to average cost only after the fact, since total utilization cannot be predicted perfectly. If a price is to be set in advance, it can be at best an estimate of average cost. Once the accounting period (usually a year or less) has come to an end, federal auditors may require a university to refund the difference if the amount charged proves to be greater than the average cost. But errors in the other direction rarely result in additional income for the computer center, since the holders of grants and contracts have usually exhausted their budgets by the time the average cost has been determined. The effective charge is thus the smaller of (1) the price announced in advance and (2) the average cost, computed at the end of the accounting period.

The impact of federal policy with a totally inelastic demand by sponsored users can readily be found. Assume that total use (H_T) is less than the capacity of the system. For convenience, assume moreover that the actual charge is always equal to average cost (AC) and that total cost for the period (TC) is fixed. The income received from government-sponsored users will be

$$TP_g = H_g(AC) = \frac{H_g(TC)}{H_g + H_n}$$

and the marginal cost of a non-government-sponsored job in terms of foregone income will be

$$MC_n = \left| \frac{dTP_g}{dH_n} \right| = \frac{H_g(TC)}{(H_g + H_n)^2}$$

$$= \frac{H_g}{H_T}(AC)$$

This illustrates in a somewhat different manner the inefficiency resulting from the overall policy — although the true (social) marginal cost of a non-government-sponsored job is zero, the actual cost to the university is not. Figure 11–2a shows the marginal cost of such a job as a proportion of average cost for alternative values of H_g/H_T (the proportion of total hours of government-sponsored use). Given this situation, the university administration might charge nongovernment users this marginal cost instead of denying them access entirely. The income from such users would then be

$$TP_n = (MC_n)H_n = \frac{H_g H_n}{H_T}(AC) = \frac{H_g H_n(TC)}{H_T^2}$$

and

$$\frac{TP_n}{TC} = \frac{H_g}{H_T} - \left(\frac{H_g}{H_T} \right)^2$$

Letting TP_T be total income ($= TP_g + TP_n$), we have

$$\frac{TP_T}{TC} = 2 \left(\frac{H_g}{H_T} \right) - \left(\frac{H_g}{H_T} \right)^2$$

This relationship is shown in Fig. 11–2b. Note that total cost will be recovered only if government-sponsored researchers are the sole users of the equipment; in general the university would have to make up the difference (e.g., in Fig. 11–2b, D' for H_g'/H_T).

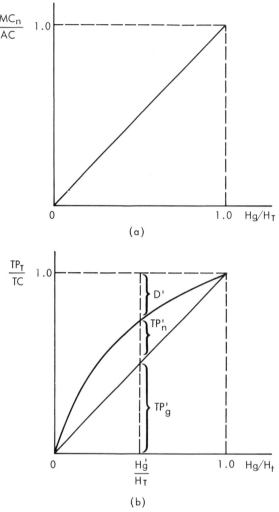

(a)

(b)

FIGURE 11-2. Effects of average-cost pricing for government use with marginal-cost pricing for nongovernment use.

This example indicates the complexity of the problem faced by a government contractor attempting to allocate equipment efficiently by means of this type of federal policy. The solution clearly lies in a revision of the policy, but the best form for such a revision is not entirely obvious. Optimal allocation dictates that prices be divorced from costs, both for the short and the long run. But equity (in the opinion of many) dictates that charges to users be somehow related to costs. Moreover, there is an ever-present danger that some university will take advantage of a relatively captive (federal) customer if mechanical rules for costing are dispensed with entirely. In this type of situation there is no obvious best solution, and we will not attempt to suggest one here.

D. INTERNAL PRICING: FIXED CAPACITY

We return now to the more abstract discussion of pricing, concentrating for the rest of the chapter on problems connected with internal pricing.

The simplest case involves a given computer system with use measured simply in clock time (hours). In almost every instance of this type the total cost over some period (e.g., a year) increases less than proportionately (if at all) with utilization. Thus average cost is always greater than marginal cost.

As indicated in Chapter 2, the appropriate internal price in such a situation is marginal cost if and only if an equilibrium point can be found at a utilization for which marginal cost is defined. Marginal cost is not defined at points at which the total cost curve exhibits a kink (e.g., 176 hours per month for rented IBM equipment), and it is clearly not defined when utilization reaches capacity.

Figures 11-3a and b illustrate these relationships. Three possible total and marginal value curves are shown. In each case total value exceeds total cost over some range of utilization (and, a fortiori, at the optimal utilization). In the case shown by curves TV_1 and MV_1, the optimal utilization (U^*) is less than capacity (C), and the price (P_1) should equal marginal cost. But in the other two cases the system should be used to capacity, and the appropriate price is the one that rations this capacity. In one case it falls below average cost ($P_2 < AC$); in the other it exceeds the average ($P_3 > AC$).

The situation shown in Figs. 11-3a and b is typical of cases involving economies of scale:[5] average cost decreases with utilization. But

---

[5] Note, however, that both rate and volume vary along the horizontal axis. This differs from the situation in which volume is varied and rate held fixed; we have previously used the term *economies of scale* to refer only to the latter case. The term is used here in a manner more consistent with its common meaning.

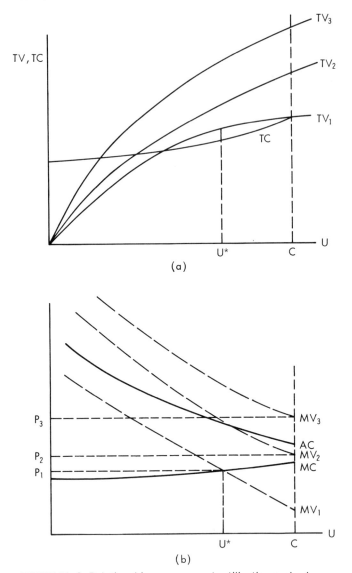

FIGURE 11-3. Relationships among cost, utilization and price.

it immediately follows that marginal cost must lie below average cost at every point; if marginal cost constitutes the appropriate internal price, the computer center should in such cases incur a deficit. This, briefly, is the argument presented by a number of observers. Proposals for "making up" the deficit vary (although the consensus seems to hold that the federal government should provide direct grants to university computer centers to cover at least a portion of their deficits). In any event, most agree that a center should be allowed to sell time at less (often far less) than average cost.

As we have indicated, this argument does not hold when marginal-cost pricing results in demand in excess of capacity (in which case the appropriate price may be more or less than average cost). It thus follows that, in any situation in which the argument does hold, the computer is not (and should not be) used to capacity. This raises a second question: why was such a large system obtained in the first place? Several reasons may be invoked. To understand them we must consider the longer-run problem of selecting optimal capacity.

E. INTERNAL PRICING: VARIABLE CAPACITY

To say that capacity is variable means, in this case, that computers of different size and capability are available and/or that more than one of a given type may be obtained. For convenience assume that possible uses are known and stable over time; in other words, the total value and marginal value curves are given. To begin, assume that only one

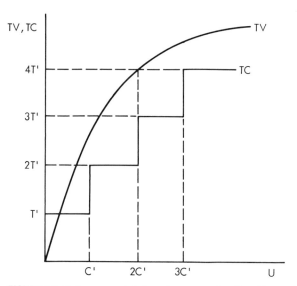

FIGURE 11–4. Long-run total cost curve, reflecting the options of using more than one computer.

type of computer is available, with capacity C', and that T'—its total cost (e.g., monthly rental)—is unaffected by utilization. The long-run total cost curve, reflecting the options of using more than one computer, will be that shown in Fig. 11–4. In the situation illustrated, net value $(TV - TC)$ is maximized if two computers are obtained and used to capacity $(U = 2C')$. The appropriate rationing price equals marginal value (i.e., the slope of the total value curve); in this case it is greater than marginal cost (which equals zero) but somewhat less than average cost, although with a different total value curve it might exceed average cost.

Figure 11–5 shows a situation in which additional utilization of a given computer increases total costs. In this case it would pay to have idle capacity if three or more systems were obtained (i.e., $U > 2C'$). But the optimal capacity is $2C'$; two systems should be obtained and used to capacity. Here the appropriate price is approximately equal to marginal cost and less than average cost, but this is due solely to the nature of the particular total value curve. The other relationship is much more common, however: unless the cost of using capacity rela-

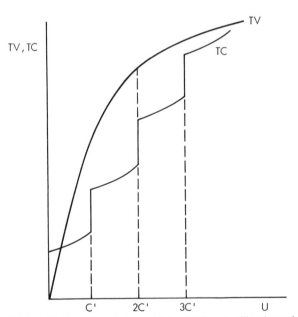

FIGURE 11–5. A situation in which additional utilization raises total costs.

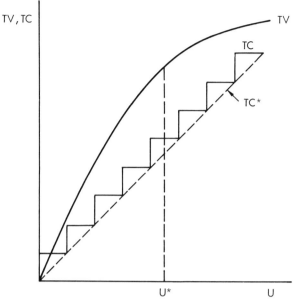

FIGURE 11-6. A situation in which demand is large relative to the capacity of a single machine.

tive to that of obtaining it is very large, it will be unwise to constrain utilization so much that idle capacity is created.

It is interesting to note the effect of a demand that is large relative to the capacity of a single machine. Figure 11-6 shows such a situation (for simplicity total cost is assumed to be unaffected by utilization[6]). Actual total cost is shown by the step function TC. The straight line TC^* is an optimistic approximation of total cost; it is correct only when all systems are utilized to capacity. Note, however, that, if TC^* is assumed to represent the total cost curve, it is a simple matter to find the optimal utilization (here, U^*). Moreover, there will be relatively little difference between this and the truly optimal utilization. Finally, the slope of the total value curve (the marginal value) at this point equals that of TC^*, which is an (optimistic) approximation of the average cost. Thus the appropriate internal price will be equal to or slightly below average cost.

The situation shown in Fig. 11-6 obviously applies if a single user

---

[6] This assumption is not required, however, for the argument that follows.

has a great many valuable computational jobs. It also holds, however, if curve *TV* represents the jobs of many users. And in a world in which there are economies of scale in computation substantial incentives exist for users to share equipment. The average cost of an underutilized system exceeds that of a fully utilized system, and eventually the user will probably have to bear this higher cost. Two users, each with a half-utilized system, have good reasons to consider consolidating their computation. Service bureaus, computer utilities, computer time exchanges, etc., all exist to facilitate such sharing. Of course problems of allocation, communication, and transportation tend to reduce the advantages to be gained. But in large metropolitan areas in which many users are in close proximity it may make little sense for an organization to operate equipment at a substantially higher cost per unit of computation than that obtainable by operating the most efficient system available at its effective capacity.

This conclusion holds even in the more realistic case in which there are computers of alternative designs, with those of larger capacity offering lower costs per unit of capacity. A case involving five designs is shown in Fig. 11–7 (again for convenience we assume that total cost is unaffected by utilization).[7] The step function is, of course, the true total cost curve; however, for some purposes one of the two (optimistic) approximating functions shown may be used. The solid curve connects the points representing capacity use of multiples of all machines installed; the dotted line connects only the points representing capacity use of multiples of the most efficient (largest-capacity) machines available. Clearly the larger the total value curve relative to the total cost function, the greater is the relevance of the approximating functions. If a user (or group of users) has jobs with relatively small total value, the step function should be utilized, and the appropriate internal charge may be less than, equal to, or greater than the average cost. If the available jobs have a somewhat greater total value, the

---

[7] The computers are assumed to have the following capacities and costs:

Capacity	Total Cost
1	10
2	18
3	24
4	28
5	30

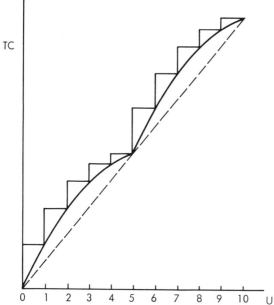

FIGURE 11-7. A situation involving five computers having different capacities and costs.

appropriate capacity may be found approximately by using the smooth curve; again, the associated internal price may be less than, equal to, or greater than average cost. Finally, if total value is large, the dotted line may be adequate for selecting the approximate capacity, and the appropriate internal price will be equal to or slightly less than average cost.

The conclusion to be drawn is essentially negative: economies of scale, in the use of given equipment and/or in the selection of equipment, do not necessarily imply that the appropriate internal price will be substantially below average cost.

F. TURNAROUND TIME

Throughout the discussion of internal pricing we have spoken of the "capacity" of a system and assumed that little or no additional cost was incurred if the system was used to full capacity. Unfortunately this is rarely the case; typically the average turnaround time increases as the load on a computer approaches capacity. Although this is not an explicit cost, it is clearly an economic cost and one that should be carefully considered.

If jobs were submitted at the most desirable intervals during the day (week, month, year), turnaround time would equal run time for all jobs. In particular, assume that job $j + 1$ is submitted t_{j+1} minutes after job j and that job j requires T_j minutes of computer time. A necessary and sufficient condition for all jobs to receive immediate service is

$$t_{j+1} \geqq T_j \quad \text{for all } j$$

Obviously this will rarely hold. And the greater the load (i.e., the smaller the average value of t_j and/or the greater the average value of T_j), the greater is the likelihood that some jobs will have to wait for access to the computer. Turnaround time is defined as the sum of (1) the time that the job is running on a machine and (2) the time that it must wait for service. The former is determined by the characteristics of the job itself, but the latter is related to the other jobs to be run, since an additional job may impose external diseconomies on other jobs by increasing their waiting times.

The situation can be illustrated with the simplest possible case of queueing. Assume that jobs are processed on a first-come, first-served basis (i.e., there is only one queue), and that each job is run to completion (e.g., there are no priority interrupts) on a single processor. Assume further that there are no predictable peak-load periods and that variations in arrivals and run times are predictable only in a probabilistic sense. Let λ equal the average number of jobs submitted per unit time (e.g., per day) and μ the average number of jobs that can be run per unit time (e.g., per day). Then the proportion of the time that the processor is utilized will be

$$p = \frac{\lambda}{\mu}$$

Under commonly assumed conditions [8] it can be shown that the average time a job must wait for service will be

---

[8] That is, that both arrivals and services are distributed according to a Poisson distribution or, equivalently, that the time between arrivals (and services) is distributed exponentially.

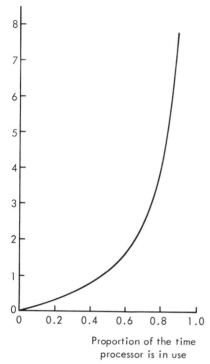

Average waiting time
expressed as a multiple of
average job computer time

Proportion of the time
processor is in use

FIGURE 11-8. Relationship between average waiting time and proportion of the time processor is utilized.

$$\bar{W} = \left(\frac{p}{1-p}\right)\frac{1}{\mu}$$

or

$$\bar{W} = \left(\frac{p}{1-p}\right)\bar{T}$$

where $\bar{T} = 1/\mu =$ the average computer time per job.

This relationship, shown in Fig. 11-8, will hold if a single-queue, first-come, first-served discipline is to be followed. The computer center must select the preferred utilization of the system on the basis of the relative desirability of (1) running many jobs versus (2) providing fast

Cost per minute of execution
expressed as a multiple of cost per
minute at full capacity = c/k

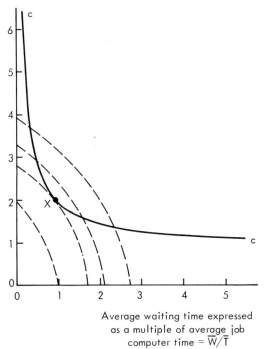

Average waiting time expressed
as a multiple of average job
computer time = $\overline{W}/\overline{T}$

FIGURE 11-9. Relationship between average waiting time and relative cost of use.

turnaround. Once the preferred utilization has been determined, of course, it may be obtained by setting the internal price at a level that elicits the desired number of jobs.[9]

Figure 11-9 provides a somewhat different view of the situation. Assume that total cost is unaffected by utilization; then cost per minute of computer time (c) will be inversely proportional to utilization:

$$c = \frac{k}{p}$$

where k is a constant. Using the relationship between average waiting time ($\overline{W}$) and p, we obtain

---

[9] The problem is complicated, however, by the fact that the quantity demanded will typically depend on both the price and the average turnaround time.

$$\frac{c}{k} = \frac{1 + (\bar{W}/\bar{T})}{\bar{W}/\bar{T}}$$

shown by curve cc in Fig. 11–9.

One organization's preferences might be those shown by the indifference curves in Fig. 11–9, with curves lying to the left and below representing preferred combinations (lower costs per minute and/or shorter waiting times). The optimum lies at the point of tangency (point X in Fig. 11–9). The marginal cost (and value) of waiting time may be represented by the slopes of the two curves at point X, which show the reduction (increase) in cost per minute of computer time associated with an increase (decrease) in waiting time.

Note that in this situation the *average* waiting time equals the *expected* waiting time for each user, since jobs are run strictly on a first-come, first-served basis. The computer center manager has the option of incurring a higher or lower cost per minute of computer time and thereby obtaining a lower or higher average turnaround time, but once the decision is made the user has no such option.

Alternative schemes can preserve some options for the user. One possibility would involve a number of similar computers, each with a different charge per minute of machine time. After some period of time an equilibrium would be reached—lower-priced machines having heavier utilization and thus longer expected turnaround times. The user could then choose the preferred one among the available combinations of price and turnaround time for each job that he wished to run.

Similar schemes can be implemented on a single computer. Several queues can be maintained, each associated with a specified price per minute of computer time—the higher the price, the higher the queue's priority. The discipline might be to service a queue only when all higher-priority queues were empty and, within a queue, to service jobs on a first-come, first-served basis. Such a scheme would offer users the option of paying a higher (lower) price to obtain a smaller (larger) expected turnaround time.

The number of possible queue disciplines is, of course, virtually infinite; the final choice should depend on many factors, including, for example, users' preferences concerning uncertainty in regard to turnaround time and/or price, and simple schemes versus complicated ones. We will describe some of the systems that have been implemented or proposed in later sections; first, however, we reconsider the question of peak-load pricing.

G. PEAK-LOAD PRICING AND TURNAROUND TIME

In most situations it is misleading to consider computer time as a homogeneous commodity; time during the day is usually preferred by the majority of users to time at night. Given equal prices, users will submit more jobs per hour during more attractive periods (e.g., daytime) than during less attractive periods, such as nighttime and weekends, giving rise to the classic peak-load problem discussed in Chapter 5. One solution to this problem is to adjust prices so that computer time is cheaper during (ordinarily) off-peak hours. However, even if no adjustment in price is made, other forces will bring about an equilibrium of sorts.

Assume that the price charged for computer use is the same at all times. Initially more jobs will be submitted during some periods than during others. But this will lead to average turnaround times that are larger during peak than during off-peak hours. As the disparity grows, some users will switch from peak to off-peak hours, so that eventually an equilibrium will be reached. The result may be viewed in either of two ways. If "price" is taken to mean only the charge, the services may be considered equally desirable overall (at the margin) — one involving a long turnaround time expected during a desirable period, the other a short turnaround time expected during an undesirable period. On the other hand, if "price" is taken to mean both the charge and the expected turnaround time, one alternative involves a high price for computation during a desirable period whereas the other involves a low price for computation during an unattractive period. In any event, no matter how charges are set (equal or not) by the computer center, loads will adjust appropriately. Hence the optimal pricing policy is not at all obvious, and the presence of disparities in utilization among periods is not necessarily a sign of inefficiency.

An interesting variation of this type of self-equilibrating system occurs with some commercial time-sharing systems. For example, in 1967 General Electric charged users of the 265 system $10 per hour of terminal connection time plus 4 cents per second of central processor time. With such a system, as the number of users increases, so, of course, does turnaround time, making the service not only less desirable but also more costly (since more terminal connection time is required to complete a given job).[10] Thus, although GE's prices were the same at all times, the user's cost per unit of service varied considerably, reaching high levels at (otherwise) attractive times and low levels at (otherwise) unattractive times.

H. PRICING SCHEMES

One of the simplest multiple-price schemes uses the time of day or the day of the week as a surrogate for the load that would be encountered in the absence of differential pricing. For example, in 1966 ITT Data Services' basic rates for IBM 7094 time were $650 per hour during the "prime shift" (8:30 A.M. to 5:00 P.M.) and $550 per hour "off-shift" (all other times). The Service Bureau Corporation's IBM 7094 rates at the time were the same, with one exception—weekend use was provided at an even lower basic rate ($505 per hour).[11]

Control Data Corporation's Palo Alto Data Center followed a different policy. Price was based, not on the time that the job was run, but on the category of service requested; the categories were, in turn, defined in terms of turnaround time exclusive of computer time actually used. Charges for the CDC 3800 were as follows:

Category	Turnaround Time Requested (excluding computer time) hours	Charge (dollars/hour)
A	≦24	580
B	≦ 6	715
C	≦ 2	820

Presumably the actual charge was the minimum of (1) the charge for the requested turnaround time and (2) the charge for the actual turnaround time.

A scheme similar to CDC's was used during 1964 by Electricité

---

[10] The system used time slicing, in which each job being executed receives a quantum of time and then is suspended until all other jobs in execution have been provided with some service.

[11] Both companies also provided substantial quantity discounts.

de France (EDF) for the internal allocation of time on an IBM 7094 among departments. Four priority classes were used, each based on total delivery time: [12]

Priority Class	Maximum Turnaround Time (hours)
1	$2 + 4T$
2	$3 + 6T$
3	$8 + 16T$
4	$16 + 32T$

where T = actual run time for the job in hours. Initially prices were set as follows:

$$P_1 = 3P_4, \quad P_2 = 2.33P_4, \quad \text{and} \quad P_3 = 1.66P_4$$

However, relative prices were revised at the end of every month. The revision procedure took account of the previous month's experience, summarized in a table of values indicating the extent to which priority requests were met, that is, the entry in row i, column j, indicated the total hours of computer time requested for priority class i but delivered within the range relevant for class j. An ideal system would yield zeros everywhere except along the diagonal; the greater the values in other cells, the greater would be the desirable revision in relative prices. Rather complex procedures were used for the calculations; the basic philosophy was, however, relatively simple — the percentage revision in each price was a function of the percentage discrepancy between users' requests and actual performance.

The EDF scheme included a rather complex method for selecting jobs to be run. For example, a priority 2 job that had waited almost 3 hours might be run before a priority 1 job that had just arrived. The problem was complicated by the need to prepare fairly large batches of jobs on magnetic tape on another machine. It was also complicated by a common source of uncertainty — the actual computer time required by any given job is rarely known precisely before it is run.

Almost all installations require that jobs be submitted with "es-

[12] Vivian Saminaden, "Operating Techniques and Experience of the Electricité de France Computation Center," presented to the SHARE Installation Management Division, Operations Management Project.

timates" of time required, lines printed, memory used, etc. In many cases these figures are used by the operating system or the operators as maximum limits: the job is terminated if one or more is exceeded. Such a policy gives the user an incentive to provide estimates considerably greater than expected values. Some installations use such estimates in according priorities, however—the lower the estimate(s), the higher the priority—a policy that obviously provides a counteracting incentive.

Experience at EDF indicated that users' estimates averaged about twice actual requirements; similar results have been obtained elsewhere. Although this type of relationship may be used for planning, the method is relatively crude. Assume, for example, that a user's prediction of time required is characterized by a (subjective) probability distribution. Given the usual incentives, he may wish to submit an estimate K standard deviations above the mean of the distribution in order to keep the probability of premature termination below a given level and still obtain reasonable turnaround time. The ratio of estimated time to expected time will thus be

$$R = \frac{E + K\sigma}{E} = 1 + K\left(\frac{\sigma}{E}\right)$$

where E = expected time, and σ = standard deviation. Obviously the greater the relative uncertainty (measured by σ/E), the larger will be this ratio. For planning purposes it would be useful to have a relatively unbiased estimate of E. Some installations have attempted to obtain such a value by requiring users to provide both estimated and maximum figures. A variation of the method would penalize the user for errors by charging an amount related to the absolute value of the discrepancy between actual and estimated values, thus providing a greater incentive for careful estimation (however, no such scheme appears to have been actually implemented).

Another pricing scheme involves the use of numerous queues, each with an associated price. Jobs are serviced on a first-come, first-served basis within each queue, no queue being serviced unless all higher-priority (i.e., higher-priced) queues are empty. The user is able to observe the current state of the system before selecting a queue and is allowed to move his job from one queue to another at any time before execution. Such a scheme provides the user with a

Price per minute
of computer time

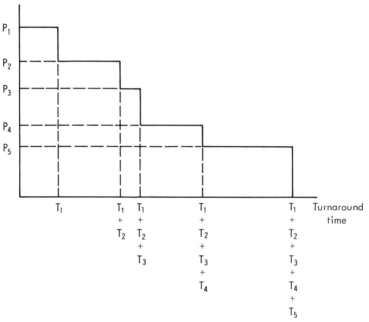

FIGURE 11-10. Pricing scheme involving five queues.

picture similar to that shown in Fig. 11-10. In this example there are five queues; P_i is the price for jobs in queue i, and T_i is the total *estimated* time required to run all jobs *currently* in queue i. If all estimates were correct, and if no further jobs were submitted, the function shown in Fig. 11-10 would represent precisely the relationship between price and turnaround time available to a user. However, neither assumption is likely to hold in practice. Errors in estimated running times lead to uncertainty regarding the turnaround time associated with every queue. Also, the likelihood that additional jobs will be submitted suggests that the actual turnaround time associated with every queue but the first (highest-priority) may exceed the time shown, perhaps by a considerable margin. The user is thus left with substantial uncertainty.

Stanford University proposed a multiple-queue system of this type in 1967.[13] A variation, suggested by Seymour Smidt,[14] would allow the user to specify either the maximum price (as in the example above) or the maximum turnaround time. In the first case price would be known and turnaround time uncertain; in the second, maximum turnaround time would be known but price would be uncertain.

To a considerable extent the selection of a pricing scheme rests on the type of uncertainty to be borne by the user, as these examples demonstrate. However, it is possible for users to be allowed to ensure against certain types of uncertainty. As an example, the Stanford flexible pricing proposal included a file storage charge expressed in cents per disk track per day; the charge would be adjusted monthly, on the basis of anticipated demand and capacity. Users planning to institute major file-based systems would thus be faced with uncertainty regarding the total cost. However, the proposal included a provision for long-term contracts: the user could purchase file storage capacity for a one-year period at a firm price, subject to the provision that he pay for the storage whether it was used or not.

It is interesting to note in passing that a computer center need not necessarily offer options of this sort. For example, an enterprising student might well offer similar long-term contracts, acting as a broker of file storage space. If sufficient competition existed, the resulting charges would presumably equal the expected sum of the monthly costs plus a premium for the risk involved.

I. VALUE-BASED ALLOCATION

Most pricing schemes present the user with one or more prices and actual or estimated turnaround times; he is then expected to choose among them. Presumably the chosen combination will be the one for which the difference between value (to him) and cost (price) is the greatest. An alternative approach would have users indicate the *values* of alternative types of service, with the computer facilities allocated so as to maximize overall value to the organization. Although such an approach may in some situations prove impractical, its characteristics

---

[13] Stanford University Computation Center, "A Flexible Pricing Proposal."
[14] Seymour Smidt, "A Flexible Price System for Computer," (unpublished), May, 1967.

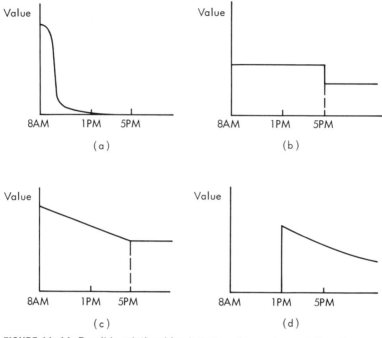

FIGURE 11-11. Possible relationships betwen value and completion time.

are of considerable interest; moreover, it can be shown to be closely related to some more traditional schemes.

To begin, assume that each user is willing to describe the value (to him) associated with the completion of a job at various times of the day, and that such values are expressed in dollar units. Assume moreover that all the conditions for a satisfactory profit center operation are met, so that the value to a user is equal to the value to the overall organization. Figures 11–11a through 11–11d illustrate some possible relationships. Figure 11–11a is typical of so-called "real-time" applications, in which results not obtained within a short period of time are of little value. Figure 11–11b illustrates a case in which the user would like to see the results before he goes home but will not have time to look at them earlier in the day; moreover, he does not plan to come back before the next morning, even if the results become available during the evening. Figure 11–11c represents another situation in which the user refuses to return during the evening but would like to see the results as soon as possible during the day. Note that in all cases of this sort, value is monotonic downward with completion time (e.g., if a user says completion at 10 A.M. is better than completion at 9 A.M., the center can hold the results for an hour if need be; thus the higher value for 10 A.M. completion can be considered relevant for 9 A.M. completion as well). Figure 11–11d represents a job that will not become available until 1 P.M. Here the horizontal axis must be interpreted as representing the time at which computation facilities are allocated to the job.[15]

Relationships such as those shown in Figs. 11–11 allow a complete specification of the "priority" or "importance" of a job. Attempts to classify jobs as "real-time," "batch," "low-priority," etc., represent at best crude approximations. Conceptually, jobs can best be scheduled if the value of each one is given as a function of the time at which it is completed.

For purposes of analysis it is convenient to assume that each "job" requires the entire computer facility for one unit of time. Under these conditions the value curves can be described by a set of values of the form

$V_{ij} \equiv$ the value of running job i during time period j.

Assume that the number of jobs equals the number of time periods ($= N$). Then the optimum allocation of jobs to time periods is a standard assignment problem, a straightforward exercise in linear programming. Let

$$X_{ij} = \begin{cases} 1 \text{ if job } i \text{ is run during time period } j, \\ 0 \text{ if job } i \text{ is not run during time period } j, \text{ and} \end{cases}$$

$V^T \equiv$ total value.

Then

$$V^T = \sum_{i=1}^{N} \sum_{j=1}^{N} X_{ij} V_{ij}$$

Since a job should be run only once (i.e., during only one time period), we require

$$\sum_{j=1}^{N} X_{ij} \leq 1 \quad \text{for each job } i$$

---

[15] The curve is, of course, monotonic downward only after 1 P.M.

And since only one job can be run during a given time period, we require

$$\sum_{i=1}^{N} X_{ij} \leq 1 \quad \text{for each time period } j$$

The problem is simply to select a set of values X_{ij} that gives the maximum value (V^T) subject to the constraints above. This is clearly a linear programming problem, although a large one (N^2 decision variables and $2N$ constraints). A number of special-purpose algorithms exist, however, for efficiently solving problems of this type.[16]

As described in Part I, most linear programming codes provide as output a series of shadow prices, one associated with each of the constraints. Each shadow price indicates the change in the optimum level of the objective function per unit change in the constant (right-hand side) of the constraint. A basic theorem of linear programming holds that, if the constant of each constraint is multiplied by its shadow price and all such products are summed, the result will equal the optimal value of the objective function. Moreover, if use of a unit of a constraint is "charged" for according to its shadow price, decision variables in the solution will just break even (i.e., total "costs" will equal value), whereas others will exhibit losses (i.e., total "costs" will exceed value).[17] The shadow prices can thus be used to rediscover the preferred decision variables.

These relationships are of more than academic interest in connection with the allocation problem. There will be $2N$ shadow prices, one for each constraint:

P_i = the price of job i ($i = 1$ to N), and
P_j^t = the price of time j ($j = 1$ to N).

A number of these prices (those associated with nonbinding constraints) will be zero. Since the right-hand side of each constraint equals 1, it follows that

---

[16] In particular, the out-of-kilter (OKA) network algorithm described in L. R. Ford, Jr., and D. R. Fulkerson, *Flows in Networks*, Princeton University Press, Princeton, N.J., 1962.

[17] There will sometimes be variables out of the solution that could be exchanged for one or more variables in the solution without altering the value of the objective function. The total "costs" for such variables will equal value.

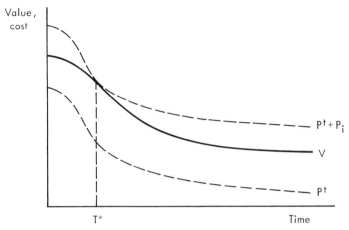

FIGURE 11-12. Relationships among value, cost, and time.

$$\sum_{i=1}^{N} P_i + \sum_{j=1}^{N} P_j^t = V^{T*}$$

where V^{T*} = the optimal (maximum) total value.

Now assume that each job is required to pay two costs (either or both of which may be zero)—one regardless of the time at which it is run, the other related to this time. In particular, if job i is run during time period j, let the cost be

$$C_{ij} = P_i + P_j^t$$

Given the structure of the problem and the characteristics of linear programming problems, it follows that

if $X_{ij} = 1$ in the solution, then $C_{ij} = V_{ij}$, and
if $X_{ij} = 0$ in the solution, then $C_{ij} \geq V_{ij}$.

Now consider a particular job, such as the one illustrated in Fig. 11-12. Curve V represents the value of the job as a function of the time at which it is run ($V_{ij}, j = 1$ to N). Curve P^t represents the price of running the job at various times (i.e., $P_j^t, j = 1$ to N). The upper curve ($P^t + P_i$) represents the total cost, including the charge levied on the job itself (P_i). Presented with *either* of the two cost curves, the user would choose to run his job at time T^*, since the difference between value and cost would then be maximized. If the relevant curve is

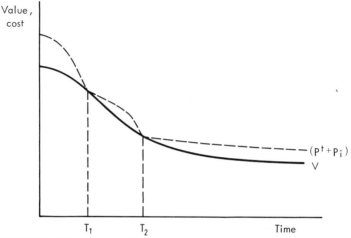

FIGURE 11-13. A relationship among value, cost, and time with alternative optimal solutions.

$(P^t + P_i)$, the optimal difference is zero (indeed, P_i will be such that this will be exactly the case). But a cost function obtained by adding any constant to the set of prices for computer time will lead each user to select the same preferred time or times (there can be ties, such as T_1 and T_2 in Fig. 11–13). In any event, if each user is presented with the set of shadow prices for times and asked to select one or more "best" times, all requests can be met, that is, each job can be run during one of the times selected by the user, although finding a feasible allocation that accomplishes this goal may not be a trivial problem. If each job is required to pay the full shadow price (P_i) as well, total income to the computer center will equal total value; if the total cost of providing the service is greater than this, the system should be discontinued. If, on the other hand, total cost is less than total value, the computer center may wish to be fair to its users, adjusting prices so as to lower costs to them. No obvious criterion for "fairness" is available; however, certain types of adjustments will not alter the allocation process and thus are to be preferred, *ceteris paribus*, to alternatives that will. Examples of the preferred type are (1) changes in the charges levied on jobs per se, including the dropping of all such charges, and (2) lowering or raising all time charges by a *constant* amount (equal percentage changes are very likely to alter the allocation and hence reduce the total value of the operation).

Comparable statements can be made concerning the effects of altering the values attributed to the jobs (i.e., the V_{ij}'s). Most important, if all the values associated with running a given job at various times are increased or decreased by a constant (not percentage) amount, there will be no change in the overall allocation. This is obvious once it is noted that the total value of a job is completely unimportant as long as each job is to be run sometime: the relevant figures concern the loss in value if a job is run later rather than sooner.

A simple example may help to illustrate these relationships. Section A of Table 11-1 indicates the value associated with running each of six jobs at each of six times. An optimal solution is shown in Section B; it uses the time in the most valuable way, giving a total value of 51. Note, however, that there are other allocations giving equal value

TABLE 11-1. An Example of Value-Based Allocation.

	A. Values							B. Solution		
	Time Run								Run at	
Job	1	2	3	4	5	6		Job	Time	Value
1	5	5	5	5	5	5		1	4	5
2	9	8	7	7	7	7		2	6	7
3	12	10	6	2	1	0		3	2	10
4	13	0	0	0	0	0		4	1	13
5	13	11	9	9	9	4		5	5	9
6	7	7	7	5	1	1		6	3	7
										51

	C. Shadow Prices				D. Breakeven Times	
Job	Price (P_i)	Time	Price (P_j')		Job	Times
1	0	1	13		1	4, 5, 6
2	2	2	10		2	4, 5, 6
3	0	3	7		3	2
4	0	4	5		4	1
5	4	5	5		5	4, 5
6	0	6	5		6	3, 4

(e.g., job 1 could be run during period 6 and job 2 during period 4 with no change in overall value); but no other allocation can give a greater value. The shadow prices are shown in Section C. Note that only jobs 2 and 5 must make a payment in addition to that required for the time period used. Section D shows the time or times at which each job can "break even" given the prices in Section C – at all other times the total cost (shadow price) of running the job exceeds the value. Any feasible selection from among this set (i.e., one job per time period) will give the maximum total value; the solution shown in Section B is one such set.

In this example, the required information (V_{ij}'s) concerning each job is available before the first time period, so that a truly optimal allocation can be found. Even if some of the other simplifying assumptions are relaxed, this may still be the case. A job not yet ready to be run (e.g., the one shown in Fig. 11–11d) can be accommodated if the relevant information about it is known. Jobs requiring more than one time period, situations in which there are more or fewer jobs than time periods, etc., can also be handled.[18] But the common case in which there is uncertainty regarding the characteristics of jobs yet to be received poses considerably greater problems.

Consider the following situation. Two jobs, a and b, are available at the beginning of time period 1. A third, c, will become available at the beginning of time period 2. Nothing is now known about job c. Should a or b be run during time period 1? Assume that the relevant values are as follows:

	Time Period	
Job	1	2
a	5	3
b	7	6

Considering only these two jobs, the obvious solution is to run job a first and b second, giving a total value of 11 instead of 10. This may in fact turn out to have been the correct policy, as in the following case:

---

[18] Although perhaps at the expense of requiring an integer linear programming code for the solution.

	Time Period		
Job	1	2	3
a	5	3	2
b	7	6	1
c	0	10	10

Here the appropriate sequence is (a, b, c), giving a total value of 21. But consider this possibility:

	Time Period		
Job	1	2	3
a	5	3	2
b	7	6	1
c	0	10	1

The optimal sequence here is (b, c, a), giving a total value of 19. If job a had already been run during time period 1, a total value of only 16 could be obtained, via sequence (a, c, b). Obviously allocation schemes should attempt to anticipate the characteristics of jobs to be submitted at later periods. Equally obviously, no simple technique can be expected to perform this function perfectly.

One relatively simple method for allocating computer resources is a variation of the so-called Dutch auction, in which the auctioneer calls off ever-lower prices until the first (and winning) bid is received. Assume that each of the six users in the example of Table 11–1 has before him a price meter. At the beginning of each time period it goes to infinity and then begins to drop; the first user to press his "bid" button is given the time period.

How will the users bid? One possibility is that each will bid the value of the time period for his job, that is, V_{ij}, except that once a job is run it will be removed from the bidding. This will typically not result in the optimal use of the system. In our example such behavior would yield a total value of only 38 instead of the maximum possible value of 51.[19]

---

[19] Assuming that, in each case of a tie, the lower-numbered bidder won. The resulting sequence is (4, 5, 2, 1, 3, 6).

In all likelihood bidders will not behave in this way. At the very least each will try to bid slightly above the next highest bid instead of the most that he is willing to pay.[20] Moreover, this type of behavior assumes implicitly that, if a bid is lost, the job will not be run at all. This is rarely the case; the more likely alternative is that the job will be run later. The user will typically have some expectations about the prices in later time periods. Therefore, the greatest net value to be obtained if job i is not run in period 1 will be

$$V_n{}^* = \underset{j=2 \text{ to } N}{\text{Max.}} \{V_{ij} - P_{ij}^t\}$$

where P_{ij}^t represents user i's expectation concerning the price charged for time period j.

The user concerned only with expected values will be unwilling to bid an amount for time period 1 that will result in a smaller net gain than $V_n{}^*$; the most likely bid will give just this gain, letting B_{i1} represent user i's bid for time period 1:

$$B_{i1} = V_{i1} - \underset{j=2 \text{ to } N}{\text{Max.}} \{V_{ij} - P_{ij}^t\}$$

This merely illustrates in a formal manner the complexity of any bidding and/or pricing scheme used to sequentially ration items (time periods) that are to some extent substitutes for one another. Users' reactions may depend heavily on their expectations regarding future prices, turnaround times, etc. If, over time, they find that experience is inconsistent with their previous expectations, they will revise their expectations and, correspondingly, their actions. Hopefully the process will eventually converge to a stable pattern, although no theorem of economics can guarantee such a happy solution. Of course, if users share common expectations about future prices, and if these expectations are in fact correct, the Dutch auction system will lead to the optimal allocation of computer time.

The possibility of complex bidding strategies is also present when users are asked to submit specifications concerning value as a function of completion time. If no charges are to be levied, the user is given an incentive to vastly overstate the relative value of early com-

[20] Of course no bidder is likely to know the amount that every other bidder is willing to pay, hence the statement in the text (that he will *try* to enter such a bid).

pletion (e.g., $V_{i1} = 1000$, $V_{i2} = 1$) in order to "outbid" other jobs for the initial time periods. On the other hand, if the user is to be charged his stated value for the time period during which the job is run, he has some incentive to understate all values. Fortunately this may not lead to improper allocation. Although the user may wish to understate all values, he may not want to indicate that the value of running sooner rather than later is either greater or less than it really is. Thus user i may submit bids V_{ij}^b related to actual values V_{ij} as follows:

$$V_{ij}^b = V_{ij} - k_i$$

where k_i is a constant. In general, the user can be expected to select the largest positive value of k_i possible, subject to the constraint that he retain some reasonable likelihood that the job will be run at some time. If the computer center will guarantee that all jobs will be run, the user will probably select the value of k_i that makes one or more V_{ij}^b's zero. As indicated earlier, this type of behavior will not lead to an undesirable allocation of the computer facility. But it will lead to an understatement of the total value of the facility, since the latter will be based on V_{ij}^b values instead of the true V_{ij} figures.

It is important that practical issues not be lost in the somewhat rarefied atmosphere of this discussion. Whether time is divided into two periods (e.g., "on-shift" and "off-shift") or thousands (e.g., one per minute or one per second),[21] as long as decisions must be made about the order in which jobs will be run, the problem will remain. If users are to submit some type of information about values, an algorithm designed to somehow anticipate future submissions must be designed; and the possibility that users will employ bidding strategies to subvert the system to their advantage must be considered. On the other hand, if prices are to be set by the computer organization, some method must be devised for eventually finding the "right" set of prices; the

---

[21] The formulation given earlier is easily generalized to accommodate such an arrangement. The constraint for each time period becomes

$$X_{ij} \leq K_j \quad \text{for each time period } j$$

where K_j is the maximum number of jobs that can be run during time period j. The larger K_j, the fewer are the time periods and hence the prices. On the other hand, the longer each time period, the blunter will be the formulation, since V_{ij} must refer to the value of completing job i at *any* time during period j. An important but difficult question concerns the appropriate length (number) of such time periods.

shadow prices associated with the overall allocation problem are, in an important sense, one of the possible sets of "right" prices. No matter how the problem is approached, it is clearly both difficult and worthy of considerable attention.

J. THE SHORT-JOB-FIRST RULE

The discussion of the preceding section allows us to deal summarily with one of the more popular methods for allocating computer time. Many installations grant top priority to "short" jobs. One or both of the following reasons for this policy is usually given: (1) value is assumed to increase less than proportionately with job length, so that short jobs are "worth" more per unit of computer time, and (2) this scheme provides a lower average turnaround time.[22] The first argument is not particularly relevant if all jobs are to be run sometime — the differential value of short versus long turnaround time is the relevant variable, not the total value. The second argument may or may not hold; for example, if the loss from delayed receipt of a long job greatly exceeds that associated with short jobs, a larger average turnaround time may be preferred. Like all simple allocation schemes, the short-job-first rule may lead to quite undesirable results.

K. PRICING MULTIPROGRAMMED, MULTIPROCESSOR, AND TIME-SHARED SYSTEMS

We have assumed throughout most of the discussion in this chapter that a computer system can be regarded as an entity, with "computer time" used as a measure of service and thus of value. Such a simplification becomes less and less tenable with every advance in computer technology. The typical system is now a complex of separate devices capable of being used concurrently and/or sequentially for one or more jobs.

Consider, for example, the relationship among processing, input,

---

[22] Assume a mix of six 5-minute jobs and one 30-minute job. If the former are run first, average turnaround time will be slightly less than 24 minutes; if they are run last, it will be 45 minutes. If jobs are selected randomly to be run, the expected average turnaround time will be slightly more than 34 minutes.

and output: most jobs are structured in such a way that at one or more points processing must be stopped until further input is received (in some cases this must, in turn, come after output—for example, when a user sitting at a console wishes to see results before specifying the next input). The time required to obtain input may be short (e.g., if it is available in high-speed memory), moderately long (e.g., if it is to be obtained from magnetic tape or a card reader), or very long (e.g., if it must be typed by a user sitting at a console). If the delay is substantial, the processor can usefully be employed on one or more additional jobs in the interim. It is even possible that during the calendar time required to complete one job another can also be finished. Even if this is not the case, the time required to run two jobs together will often be considerably less than the sum of the times required to complete each separately.

The last example illustrates *multiprogramming,* in which a single processor serves two or more jobs by switching to a new one when the processing of the first must be temporarily suspended because of some delay. A variation of the scheme, termed *time sharing* or, more properly, *time slicing,* forces such a switch after a predetermined amount ("quantum") of time if no other type of delay arises. Finally, more than one processor may be available for concurrent operation; this type of arrangement is termed *multiprocessing.*

How should a system with some or all of these features be priced? As indicated earlier, this type of question cannot be answered without posing another: how should such a system be used? The answer is obvious—the components should be allocated among jobs so as to maximize total value, where the value of each job is related to the time of its completion. Any real problem is, of course, very complex, primarily because complementarities must be taken into account in detail, that is, it will be possible to run more than one job in time period j, but only if the right kinds of jobs are selected. In any event, there is some best allocation, and some set of prices that will lead to the appropriate use of the system.

An extreme view would regard each component and time period separately. For example, during any single microsecond only one job can occupy the card reader, only one can use the adding circuitry, and only one can use cell 593 in core memory. Each component might be allocated to the job for which it is most valuable (i.e., the highest bidder) in each time period.[23] Of course all the problems that may arise when such a scheme is used for a simple (homogeneous) computer system are likely to occur in this case as well.

It is instructive to consider a simple example of this type of problem more formally. Assume that there are four jobs, each requiring one time period if run alone. Two jobs, 1 and 2, use the central processor almost exclusively and are said to be processor-bound. The other two, 3 and 4, use the input and output facilities almost exclusively and are said to be input/output-bound. If either job 1 or 2 is run with either job 3 or 4, both can be completed within one time period. Obviously the jobs should be paired, and the best pairing will be that giving the greatest total value. As before, the decision can be formulated as a linear programming problem:

$$\text{Maximize:} \quad V^T = \sum_{i=1}^{4} \sum_{j=1}^{2} X_{ij} V_{ij}$$

subject to constraints that each job should be run just once:

$$\sum_{j=1}^{2} X_{ij} \leq 1 \quad \text{for each job } i = 1 \text{ to } 4$$

and that only one processor-bound job and one input/output-bound job be run in each time period:

$X_{11} + X_{21} \leq 1$ (only one processor-bound job in time period 1)

$X_{31} + X_{41} \leq 1$ (only one input/output-bound job in time period 1)

$X_{12} + X_{22} \leq 1$ (only one processor-bound job in time period 2)

$X_{32} + X_{42} \leq 1$ (only one input/output-bound job in time period 2)

Shadow prices associated with the first four constraints may be used as charges levied against the jobs, regardless of the time at which each is run, as in the earlier example. But note that now two shadow prices will be associated with each time period: one for processor-bound jobs, the other for input/output-bound jobs.

It is not essential that the computer center manager attempt to ration

[23] If the time periods are sufficiently short, such a scheme may give very poor results, since it does not take into account the time required to reallocate a component from one task to another.

his facilities at such a detailed level (either directly on the basis of value or by means of a complex pricing scheme) if others are willing to perform the function. For example, assume that the computer center simply rents the entire facility at a given charge per time period and that each of the four jobs comes from a different user. If the rental is sufficiently high, it is possible that no single job will be worth running. But whether this is the case or not, there will be incentives for someone to pair a processor-bound job with an input/output-bound job. One or more of the users may attempt to find a complementary job, arranging some mutually agreeable sharing of costs. Or an intermediary (perhaps an enterprising student) may act as a broker. As in many other situations, decision-making may be decentralized, with different organizations and/or individuals performing specialized tasks and bearing different types and/or degrees of risk.

An interesting issue connected with pricing complex facilities arises with certain time-shared systems which a number of people concurrently utilize from remote consoles. Many feel that the charge for running a given job should be predictable, simply computed, and unaffected by the other activities of the system at the time that the job is run. These goals clearly conflict with efficient allocation of the computer facilities. For example, remote terminals should be charged for tying up communication channels, but only if a charge is required to ration the available channels; and if a charge is required, it should be based on the strength of the demand at the time. From the standpoint of efficient allocation of communication channels, this charge should be allowed to vary frequently as demand changes. But this may lead to very unpredictable costs. Users may well prefer a less efficient but more predictable scheme (e.g., with prices revised only every hour, every 12 hours, or perhaps never).

A similar situation concerns processor time. For efficient allocation, users should be charged for processor time (in addition to communication channel time) whenever a charge is needed to adequately ration the use of the processor. This gives rise to added uncertainty, however, since the cost per second of processor time will not be completely predictable. Even if this charge were never changed, there would still be some uncertainty, since the user can rarely predict precisely the time required for his problem, and in some systems the processor time required for one job depends on the overall mix of jobs being serviced at the time.

The argument could be extended, but the basic issue involved is clear. Efficient allocation calls for a number of prices—one for each of many components—each allowed to change frequently over time. But predictability and simplicity are also virtues; hence the best strategy, all things considered, will depend to a major extent on the cost of implementing a complex system and users' attitudes toward such a system.

It is far too early to tell just where the appropriate balance lies (moreover, the optimum will probably differ among various groups of users). Some commercial time-sharing firms, such as Tymshare, charge primarily for terminal connection time. Others (e.g., Keydata) go even further, charging on the basis of lines printed, file queries, etc., so that cost is almost completely predictable. General Electric charges for terminal connection time, processor time, and disk storage used for semipermanent files. Users of Allen-Babcock Computing, Inc., do not pay for terminal connection time per se; charges are based only on processing time and the amount of high-speed (temporary) storage used.[24] Experimentation and competition may lead to somewhat greater uniformity in this area over time; but as long as users differ in the strength of their distaste for uncertainty, there will be ample room for systems with different pricing structures.

L. EXPANSION AND PRICING

We conclude this chapter with a discussion of another real problem that has been ignored here thus far. Demand has been assumed to be stable over time and known with certainty; in most practical situations, however, it is neither certain nor stable. Here we deal with only one of these aspects: the problem of accommodating expected increases in demand over time.

Consider first a seemingly simple situation. Assume that only one type of disk storage device is available for an installation's computer system, and that each such device has a rather large capacity. Assume,

---

[24] This policy and all the others described in this paragraph were in effect in 1968. Present pricing methods may, of course, differ.

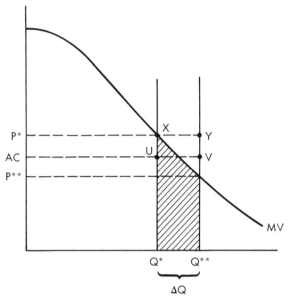

FIGURE 11-14. The effect of an expansion of capacity.

however, that the manager can rent as many or as few of these storage devices each year as he wishes, that the demand (marginal value) at any point of time can be predicted with certainty, and that it is expected to rise over time (i.e., the curve will shift to the right and upward). Finally, assume that the manager always selects the internal price per unit of storage that just rations current capacity. When will it be worthwhile to increase capacity, and how will the rationing price behave over time?

Figure 11-14 illustrates the situation faced by the manager at any given time. Assume that current capacity is Q^*; given the current demand (marginal value) curve, the appropriate price (marginal value) is P^* per unit of storage (we assume that the marginal cost of *using* capacity is well below the price required to just fully utilize capacity). Should another storage device be added, increasing capacity by ΔQ units (from Q^* to Q^{**})? Only if its value will exceed (or equal) its cost. The value associated with adding ΔQ units is shown by the shaded area in Fig. 11-14. Note that it will be less than the area of rectangle Q^*XYQ^{**}—and the steeper the demand (marginal value) curve, the greater will be the disparity. The area of this rectangle is equal to the product of (1) the current price per unit of storage (P^*), and (2) the number of units of storage per device (ΔQ). It follows that an additional device should not be purchased if the current rationing price just equals the incremental cost per unit of storage. In this case incremental cost will equal average cost; thus additional storage should be obtained only if the price required to ration current storage exceeds its average cost. Unfortunately the magnitude of the required excess depends on the shape of the demand curve to the right of the point representing current capacity; in other words, it depends on the value associated with storing information not currently being stored. And this value is not easily discovered.

Whenever it does become worthwhile to increase capacity, price will of course have to be lowered, and the new price will be below incremental (and in this case, average) cost. Assume that the shaded area under curve MV in Fig. 11–14 just equals the cost of adding one device of capacity ΔQ. Prior to the time shown, such an addition would not have been desirable, since the marginal value curve lay below curve MV. Before adding the capacity, price would be P^*, afterwards P^{**}. But average cost in this case equals incremental cost, which is simply the cost of a device divided by its capacity. If AC is average cost, the cost of a device will equal $AC \cdot \Delta Q$, shown by the area of rectangle Q^*UVQ^{**}. Since this area equals that of the shaded area (incremental value), $P^* > AC > P^{**}$.

Figures 11–15a, b, and c provide an illustration of an expansion of this type over time. Figure 11–15a shows marginal value curves for five time periods ($t = 1, 5, 10, 15,$ and 20), stated in terms of the ratio of price to average cost. The assumed relationship is

$$\frac{P}{AC} = \frac{4+t}{10\sqrt{Q}}$$

where Q is capacity in number of devices. Figure 11–15b shows how the optimal capacity (Q) changes over time. The price required to ration the optimal capacity at each point of time is shown in Fig. 11–15c. In this case, at least, the fluctuations in price diminish in amplitude over time.

Note that in Fig. 11–15c price is below average cost much of the time. This is not due to increases in capacity justified only on the basis of predicted expansion of demand; the capacity at each point of time

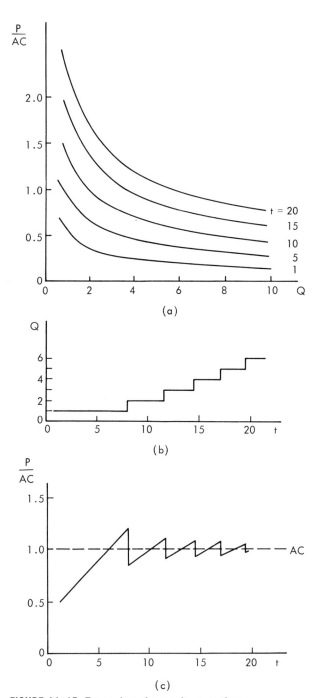

FIGURE 11-15. Expansion of capacity over time.

is optimal for the current demand. If the expansion of demand ceased at any time, the capacity and price shown in Figs. 11–15b and c would remain optimal. This is consistent with the earlier analysis of cases of stable demand, in which we argued that the optimal price may be (and remain) below, above, or equal to average cost.

Although this analysis has been cast in terms of components such as storage units, much of the approach can be applied to the overall problem of selecting and pricing an entire computer system. For example, assume that systems are available with capacities $Q = 1, 2, 3, \ldots$ and that the rental cost of each is proportional to its capacity. Finally, assume that the installed system may be replaced at any time with a larger system at no cost other than the increased rental charge. Then both the analysis and the results of the preceding discussion apply directly.

Over at least some range of capacities, of course, cost does not rise proportionately with capacity. Thus the incremental cost of raising capacity from $Q = 2$ to $Q = 3$ may exceed that of a further increase from $Q = 3$ to $Q = 4$. It is entirely possible that capacity should be enlarged even if the added value of the smallest increase possible is less than its cost. Let ΔV_{ij} be the increase in total value if capacity is raised from $Q = i$ to $Q = j$, and ΔC_{ij} be the corresponding increase in cost. The nature of the marginal value curve ensures that

$$\Delta V_{23} > \Delta V_{34}$$

Now, if

$$\Delta V_{23} < \Delta C_{23}$$

it follows that

$$\Delta V_{34} < \Delta C_{23}$$

but since there are economies of scale,

$$\Delta C_{23} > \Delta C_{34}$$

Thus it is possible that

$$\Delta V_{34} > \Delta C_{34}$$

and even that

$$V_{24} = \Delta V_{23} + \Delta V_{34} > \Delta C_{23} + \Delta C_{34} = \Delta C_{24}$$

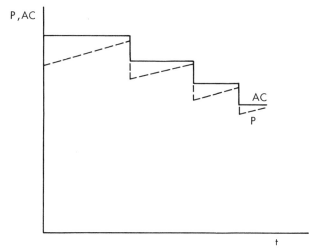

FIGURE 11-16. Possible pattern of price and average cost over time with economies of scale.

In simple terms, in the presence of economies of scale it is dangerous to consider merely the smallest possible increase in capacity, since only a larger increase may prove worthwhile.

To what extent are the conclusions reached under the previous assumptions valid in the presence of economies of scale? Recall the argument concerning price and average cost before and after an expansion in capacity. Expansion (of whatever magnitude) will be worthwhile as soon as the incremental value equals incremental cost. As shown earlier, this implies that, before the expansion, price must exceed incremental cost per unit (i.e., the cost of adding capacity divided by the increase in capacity) and that, after the expansion, price must fall below it. If there are neither economies nor diseconomies of scale, incremental cost will equal average cost and average cost will be unaffected by capacity. But if there are economies of scale, average cost will decrease when capacity is increased, and will exceed incremental cost. Thus it may pay to expand capacity before price exceeds (or even equals) average cost, although (as before) price will be below average cost immediately after each expansion. Figure 11-16 illustrates a possible pattern of price and average cost over time under these circumstances.

An additional complication arises when a fixed cost is associated with the transition from one system (capacity) to another. Such costs are likely to be considerable: they include not only shipment and installation charges, but also – and more important – the costs, monetary and other, associated with conversion. The latter may be very large indeed if the new system is not highly compatible with the old one. Although computer manufacturers have devoted a great deal of attention to the minimization of such costs by designing "compatible," "modular," and "expandable" sets of equipment, the problem is still significant.

An example will illustrate how difficult it is to determine the appropriate method of expansion if there are major transition costs. Consider a situation involving three computers of capacities Q_1, Q_2, and Q_3. At present computer 1 is installed; eventually computer 3 must be installed. The prime question concerns the interim period – should computer 2 be used or not?

Each of the alternatives must be analyzed to determine the best timing. Let policy A be the use of all three systems, and policy B the use of only the smallest and the largest. Obviously the optimal timing of changes for either policy is independent of the transition costs;[25] this part of the analysis is thus essentially the same as that used in the earlier examples. Two times must be determined for policy A: t_{12}, the optimal time to switch from computer 1 to computer 2; and t_{23}, the optimal time to switch from computer 2 to computer 3. Only one time need be found for policy B: t_{13}, the optimal time to switch from computer 1 to computer 3.

Figure 11–17 shows the marginal value curves associated with each of these times. Area Q_1abQ_2 equals the added (rental) cost per time period of the additional capacity obtained by replacing computer 1 with computer 2. Area Q_2cdQ_3 equals the added cost per time period of the additional capacity obtained by replacing computer 2 with computer 3. As shown in Fig. 11–17, t_{13} will be less than (that is, earlier than) t_{23}. The added cost per time period resulting from the replacement of computer 1 with computer 3 (in this case, via computer 2) equals the sum of the two shaded areas. But the added value of such a replacement at time t_{23} is considerably larger (area Q_1ycdQ_3). Thus

[25] With one minor qualification: see footnote 26.

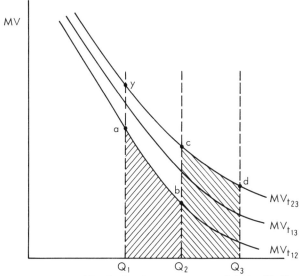

FIGURE 11-17. Marginal value curves associated with three alternative times of switching to gain additional capacity.

the replacement should be made at some time before t_{23}. The conclusion is hardly surprising: the largest computer should be installed sooner if an interim system is not utilized.

The two plans can now be compared directly. In summary, they involve the following:

		Computer Installed	
From	To	Plan A	Plan B
0	t_{12}	1	1
t_{12}	t_{13}	2	1
t_{13}	t_{23}	2	3
t_{23}	...	3	3

The alternatives differ only from t_{12} through t_{23}: from t_{12} through t_{13} policy A yields higher costs and greater values than policy B; from t_{13} through t_{23} the situation is reversed. The transition costs must also be considered: policy A requires such expenditures at t_{12} and t_{23}; policy B requires only one, at t_{13}. If the time span involved is relatively short, all these costs and values may be simply summed algebraically and the results compared directly. If not, the present values should be used instead.[26]

Even more complex (and realistic) cases could be covered, but we choose instead to conclude both this section and the chapter with two brief points — one concerning profit-maximizing behavior, the other federal policy regarding cost recovery.

Most of the discussion has been concerned with problems of internal pricing, in which the total value of the installation was of prime interest. Relatively little has been said about external pricing, for which total revenue is more relevant. The changes required to cover the latter situation are not major, however. For purposes of determining optimal capacity, the marginal value curve is simply replaced by the marginal revenue curve. The appropriate price will be the one that rations the optimal capacity, unless marginal revenue at that point is less than the marginal cost of using capacity; in the latter event, the appropriate price is that associated with the quantity for which marginal revenue equals this marginal cost.

The final point concerns federal policy regarding pricing by cost-reimbursement contractors. Whatever the relationship between optimal price and average cost, whenever demand increases during a period of fixed capacity, price should be allowed to rise. And at the time capacity is increased, price should be lowered. Unfortunately federal policy in the past has made it difficult to vary price. In general, average price over a year has had to equal average costs. Such a policy is likely to lead to underutilized capacity in the early years of a system's life when demand is small and price should be below average cost. In later years it may lead to the use of additional methods for rationing time if the appropriate price is greater than average cost; and these rationing methods are likely to be less efficient than price, leading to an allocation of the capacity among users that is less than optimal. In both situations the total value obtained from the system will be lower than it can (and should) be.

One partial remedy for this problem is to allow price variation subject only to a requirement that average price equal average cost over

---

[26] Strictly speaking, if expenditure timing is to be taken into account, the problem cannot be dichotomized, since the time at which each transition is made will affect the present value of the transition cost. However, this is clearly a second-order effect.

a relatively long period, such as five years. This type of a policy has been endorsed by a number of federal agencies and managers of university computer centers. Note, however, that although such a change may reduce inefficiency, it is not likely to eliminate the problem entirely. As we have shown in a number of contexts, the appropriate internal price need not equal average cost, even if the average is taken over a very long period.

CHAPTER **12** **THE COMPUTER INDUSTRY**

□ □ SERVICES, MARKETS, AND COSTS

□

□
□ **A. LEASING COMPANIES**

One of the first contracts for the lease of a computer from a "third party" (i.e., neither the manufacturer nor the user) was drawn in 1961.[1] By the end of 1968, according to one estimate,[2] equipment with a purchase cost of almost $1 billion was leased in this manner.

One of the most common arrangements is the sale/lease-back transaction. The using firm purchases its previously rented equipment from the manufacturer and then sells it to a third firm, which in turn leases it to the user. This is not the only arrangement currently in practice. Several leasing firms maintain an inventory of equipment (some of it returned by previous customers), delivering new or used systems to customers on demand. The user of the equipment is termed the *lessee;* the leasing firm is the *lessor.*

According to one source, leasing companies hold title to about 5% of all computers in use.[3] Most lessors prefer to contract for widely used systems, in order to minimize the difficulty associated with finding another lessee (or a purchaser) if the equipment is returned. One estimate[4] indicates that IBM 360 series computers accounted for 75–85% of the total value of leased systems in 1968.

Few computer-leasing companies base their charges on equipment utilization. The Levin-Townsend Computer Corporation is a major exception: "Leases generally provide for a minimum rental plus additional use charges for usage in excess of 176 hours a month."[5]

Traditionally, leasing companies provide capital, leaving main-

NOTE: This chapter covers several topics that could not be made to fit naturally into previous chapters.

[1] Angeline Pantages, "An Introduction to Leasing," *Datamation,* August, 1968, p. 30.
[2] *Ibid.,* p. 26.
[3] *Business Week,* June 1, 1968, p. 100.
[4] Pantages, *op. cit.,* p. 26.
[5] *Prospectus, Levin-Townsend Computer Corporation Common Stock,* April 7, 1966, p. 8.

tenance, software support, etc., to the manufacturer. The lessee is expected (and usually required) to sign a maintenance contract with the equipment manufacturer. There are exceptions, however. In 1968, Management Assistance, Inc., not only leased but also maintained peripheral devices (tape drives purchased from Potter Instruments and disk drives purchased from Memorex) although the company did not lease computers per se.[6]

The attitude of IBM toward leasing companies appears to change periodically, perhaps because of changes in the likelihood of antitrust action. In January, 1968, IBM salesmen were apparently told to consider third-party lessors as competitors.[7] Three months later the company established a Leasing Company Relations Department "to insure an effective relationship between IBM and purchasers of its equipment."[8] Then in May, 1968, IBM agreed that henceforth the second user of a purchased system would receive free training and programming support.[9] This latter change removed one of the few remaining disadvantages of leasing equipment previously returned to a lessor. It is reported to have been agreed upon only after an antitrust suit on the matter had been prepared.[10]

Almost any kind of lease contract can be written, and many different types have been employed. They differ primarily in the manner in which risk is borne by the two parties. There are two major categories:

1. The full-payout lease, in which the lessee contracts to make payments with a present value at least equal to the current value of the equipment.
2. The nonpayout lease, in which the lessee contracts to make payments with a present value smaller than the current value of the equipment.

Full-payout leases are like secured loans. The lessee usually insures the equipment, pays personal property taxes on it, and arranges for maintenance. A full-payout lease is usually termed a *net lease* if the lessor retains ownership of the equipment at the end of the lease period; it is usually called a *financial lease* if ownership is vested in the lessee at the end of the period. Net leases are apparently more popular than

[6] Pantages, *op. cit.*, p. 29.
[7] *Ibid.*, p. 27.   [8] *Ibid.*   [9] *Ibid.*   [10] *Ibid.*

financial leases for computer equipment.[11] Although a full-payout lease is virtually equivalent to the purchase of equipment and the creation of a new debt, the lessee's financial statements need not show either component. Some accountants contend that such transactions should be shown explicitly to avoid giving an overoptimistic indication of the firm's credit position.

Nonpayout leases require the lessor to bear some of the risk associated with the future value of specific equipment; the general credit of the lessee is somewhat less important. The term *nonpayout lease* is sometimes restricted to describe contracts in which the lessee agrees to pay most, but not all, of the equipment cost; others are called *short-term contracts*.[12] A lessor who depends on income from the sale or release of equipment will generally take on many of the functions of ownership. Issuers of nonpayout leases often pay personal property taxes, take out insurance, and contract with the manufacturer for required maintenance.[13]

Figure 12–1 suggests the relationship between cost and the length of the lessee's commitment. The vertical axis indicates the ratio of (1) the required monthly payment throughout the contractual period to (2) the current monthly rental charged by the manufacturer. The horizontal axis indicates the length of the commitment. The relationship is based on leases for IBM equipment in late 1967. The variation in ratios for a given commitment can be explained in part by the presence or absence of other conditions in the lease contract.

Most discussions of third-party leases deal rather extensively with tax considerations. Payments made to a lessor may be deducted by the lessee as an expense, thereby reducing taxes. But the assumed depreciation on owned equipment is also deductible, as is interest paid on any loan used to obtain the funds for purchasing the equipment. It is important to remember that lessors also pay taxes. A procedure that saves taxes for the lessee may very well increase the lessor's taxes. Third-party leasing does not automatically provide a tax advantage (although it may in specific instances).

From time to time, Congress has authorized tax credits to stimulate investment. In 1967, the credit for new computers ranged from 2⅓%

[11] George H. Heilborn, "The Art of Leasing Computers," *Computers and Automation,* January, 1967, p. 42.
[12] *Ibid.,* p. 44.   [13] *Ibid.,* p. 45.

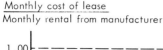

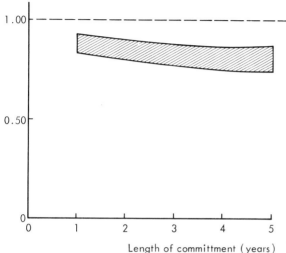

FIGURE 12-1. Relationship between cost and length of lease for IBM equipment, late 1967. Source: *Automatic Data Processing Newsletter,* Management Science Publishing, Inc., Vol. XII, Number 7 (Dec. 4, 1967).

of purchase price (for new equipment with a life of 4 years) to 7% (for equipment with a life of 8 years).[14] Such credit can be used to reduce tax payments by an equal amount. It may be taken by the manufacturer, the user, or a third-party lessor, or it may be divided among them.

Leasing companies obtain capital from a variety of sources. Bank credit has been used rather heavily, as has equity capital. Many companies finance their purchases of equipment directly from the manufacturer. In 1967, IBM apparently would finance up to $7.5 million dollars' worth of equipment for any single customer. The terms were 25% down and payment over 4 years or less, with interest on the balance at a rate 1½% above that of the "prime" rate charged by New York City banks at the time of the purchase.[15]

What accounts for the popularity of third-party leases? One answer is that they provide credit that need not be shown explicitly on the

[14] *Ibid.,* p. 44.
[15] *Wall Street Journal,* Feb. 20, 1967, p. 24.

lessee's financial statement. Also, they may offer tax advantages. But more fundamental causes are undoubtedly more important.

People differ in their aversion to risk. Third-party leases allow those with relatively little risk aversion to take on some or all of the risk associated with the future value of computer equipment.

But people also differ in their assessment of risk. Those with a relatively optimistic view of the future value of current computer equipment will consider it desirable to lease such equipment to others with a less optimistic view. If third-party lessors are more optimistic than equipment manufacturers, users will be able to obtain better terms by dealing with them rather than with the manufacturers.

The following statements from a prospectus issued by the Levin-Townsend Computer Corporation are typical of the attitudes and policies of many computer-leasing companies:

> The Company's business premise is that the revenue producing life of its computers will be long enough to permit the Company to recover the cost of such computers together with an appropriate return on its investment. The Company may incur substantial loss if computers it leases as principal are returned by present lessees and the Company is unable to place the computers with new lessees or dispose of them at satisfactory prices.
>
> The Company expects that the average revenue producing life of computers leased through its efforts will be in excess of ten years after acquisition.
>
> To recover the acquisition cost of newly acquired computers and the carrying cost of its investment, the Company estimates that, at present rent schedules, these computers must be continuously on lease to others for six to seven years.[16]

It is extremely difficult to predict the eventual profitability of such companies. The earnings reported in the first few years of operation may be deceptively large, if revenues reflect the rental value of new equipment while costs include only 10% of the cost of acquisition. Some feel that the glamor associated with the securities of computer leasing companies from 1966 through 1968 reflected an overly optimistic assessment of reported earnings. Needless to say, only in time will it be possible to tell whether the optimism was, in fact, justified.

---

[16] *Prospectus, Levin-Townsend Computer Corporation Common Stock,* Apr. 7, 1966, pp. 3, 8.

B. THE USED-COMPUTER MARKET

Before 1960, few computer systems were produced in large numbers. Moreover, vacuum-tube equipment required more maintenance as it aged. There was little reason, therefore, to develop a market for used computers. In the early 1960's, however, a great many systems were installed. From 8000 to 12,000 IBM 1401's are reported to have been produced.[17] Smaller, but significant, quantities of UNIVAC 1004's, Honeywell 200 series, and others were installed. And all these systems were transistorized. By the latter part of 1967, IBM 360 series systems were being installed at a rate in excess of 1200 per month [18] (many replacing IBM 1401 systems). The conditions for a viable market in used computers were finally present.

No adequate measure of the extent of this market is available. Estimates for 1967 sales of used computers ranged from a low of $10 million to a high of $75 million.[19]

Some of the earliest computers eventually sold for 1 or 2% of their original list price; IBM 650 and 700 series machines (all of which used vacuum tubes) often sold for less than 10% of original price.[20] The value of solid-state equipment appears to decline somewhat less rapidly. Advertisements listed during 1967 and 1968 provided the following evidence:

System	Age (years)	Asking Price as a Percentage of Original List Price
UNIVAC 1004	4	45
IBM 1410	4	25
IBM 1401 (several systems)	6–7	20–30
IBM 1620	7	23
CDC 1604 plus⎱ CDC 160A ⎰	8	16

[17] Arlene Hershman, "Boom in Used Computers?" *Dun's Review*, December, 1967, p. 63.
[18] Michel Feuche, "Second-Generation Computers Live Again—in the Resale Market," *Computers and Automation*, September, 1967, p. 24.
[19] *Ibid.*
[20] Nicholas H. Dosker, Jr., "The Used Computer Market: How IBM Shapes It," *Computers and Automation*, July, 1964, p. 26.

A firm that no longer wants to use an installed computer has several options. If the system is rented from the manufacturer, it may be returned or purchased (often at a substantial discount) and then sold to another user. If the system is owned, it may be used as a trade-in on new equipment, sold directly to another user, or sold to a used-computer dealer. The most common practice, however, is for the user to obtain the services of a broker to help locate a buyer.

In 1968 there were approximately twenty used-computer brokers.[21] They offer services similar to those provided by real estate brokers. The seller lists his equipment for some period of time, promising to pay the broker a percentage (usually 10%) of the final sales price.[22] The broker advertises the equipment, establishes contact with prospective buyers (and checks their credit), and then attempts to bring buyer and seller together on mutually acceptable terms.

Relatively few brokers maintain large inventories of used-computer systems. However, some do maintain stocks of components, primarily peripheral equipment. (In 1968, the IBM 1402 card reader/punch, the IBM 1403 line printer, and IBM 729 tape drives were particularly popular.)

The eventual position of leasing companies in the market for used computers is difficult to predict. To quote one authority:

The leasing firms have not been too active in the resale field, largely because the market was too thin and leasing was a much more attractive proposition. As the market grows it will be easier for them to use their sizable resources to purchase used equipment on a risk basis for later resale. In this way, they will gradually establish a trading market in which a dependable supply will be promptly available to meet normal demand. They may thus also emerge as the major factors in the resale "industry."[23]

Some computer manufacturers sell returned systems—in 1967 Sperry Rand (UNIVAC) had "an aggressive program for outright sales of both new and used equipment."[24] On the other hand, IBM refrained from selling used systems to new customers. Dealers were given an opportunity to buy returned equipment, but apparently the terms were not too attractive.[25] Users renting equipment were al-

[21] Hershman, *op. cit.*, p. 63.   [24] Hershman, *op. cit.*, p. 63.
[22] Feuche, *op. cit.*, p. 25.   [25] Feuche, *op. cit.*, p. 25.
[23] *Ibid.*

lowed to exercise their purchase options—often at rather attractive prices.[26] But through 1968, most of the used second-generation systems returned to IBM were either rerented, scrapped, or used for parts.

Systems produced in large quantities with relatively standard configurations can be marketed most efficiently. In 1968 the most popular used computers were the IBM 1400 series, the UNIVAC 1004, and the Honeywell 200 series systems. Although IBM 7000 series computers were also traded, smaller numbers were involved. By the latter part of 1968, transactions in used IBM 360 series computers (primarily models 20 and 30) had begun.

In 1967, one company was reported to be preparing "a price list for major data processing equipment models and options similar to the used car and office machine 'blue books.' "[27]

The market for used computers should continue to grow. As it does, the cost of arranging a transaction should decrease, perhaps substantially. All brokers disseminate information; some also hold inventories of goods of uncertain value. Both activities may be subject to economies of scale. It is thus possible that a relatively few firms will capture the majority of the market as it matures.

C. THE MARKET FOR COMPUTER SERVICES

Economies of scale appear to be significant for computing in general. They may also be substantial for applications of a particular kind. Users thus have an incentive to share equipment. This may be accomplished through cooperative operation and use, with joint responsibility for the installation and joint risk-bearing. A more common arrangement relies on a single agent (user, entrepreneur) to assume both the responsibility and the risk. Other users are expected to purchase services, hopefully on terms that will adequately compensate the owner (renter) of the equipment.

Entrepreneurs of this type may be divided into two groups for purposes of analysis: (1) those who buy equipment primarily for their own use, selling "excess" capacity, and (2) those who buy equipment pri-

---

[26] In 1968, IBM offered federal agencies purchase options on all 1401 central processors produced before Jan. 1, 1964 for approximately 25% of the original list prices (source: IBM Federal Supply Schedule Price List, 1968–1969).

[27] Feuche, *op. cit.*, p. 26.

marily as a commercial venture, hoping to sell most of its capacity. Often the distinction is difficult to make: anyone who purchases equipment with more capacity than he needs, intending to sell some of the excess, has chosen to act as an entrepreneur. Marketing policy provides the best basis for classification. If sales are of primary importance, the firm will usually rely for publicity on its own sales organization; otherwise it will depend on word of mouth, relatively inexpensive advertisements, or brokers.

Firms that do not rely significantly on their own sales forces may be termed *excess-capacity sellers*. Others are *service bureaus, time-sharing vendors,* or possibly both. Service bureaus rely on physical movement (e.g., via a delivery service) of data between the location of the user and that of the computer equipment. Time-sharing vendors provide for at least some electronic movement of data. Input may be via teletypewriter, card reader, paper tape reader, or some other device located at a remote site. Output may be returned on a teletypewriter, card punch, paper tape punch, line printer, graphical display, or some other device at the remote site. Depending on the speed of response, such a service may be termed *true time-sharing, remote-job-entry,* or *remote-batch processing.*

A single firm may act as a service bureau and also furnish time-shared services (perhaps several varieties). Both types of service may even be provided on the same computer.

1. Computer Time Brokers
Some excess-capacity sellers locate potential buyers without the services of a broker. Weekly and monthly periodicals include special sections for advertising computer time for sale. Users' organizations provide a means for identifying those owning similar equipment who may want to either buy or sell time, depending on the (perhaps temporary) relationship between their current capacity and demand. Many buyers and sellers, however, prefer to utilize the services of a computer time broker.

The first such brokerage firm was formed in 1964.[28] By 1968 this firm's quarterly listing of available systems was distributed to over

---

[28] William P. Hegan, "Buying . . . and Selling . . . Computer Time," *Computers and Automation,* September, 1968, p. 33.

TABLE 12-1. Computer Time Report Listings, Fall, 1968 *

Computer Type	Number of Listings	Computer Type	Number of Listings
IBM 360/30	82	IBM 1460	2
IBM 360/40	37	Burroughs 5500	2
IBM 360/50	16	UNIVAC 1108	2
IBM 360/20	14	Honeywell 120	2
IBM 1401	11	IBM 7010	1
IBM 1130	8	IBM 7070	1
Honeywell 200	8	IBM 7074	1
IBM 360/65	5	IBM 7090	1
IBM 1440	5	IBM 7094	1
RCA Spectra 70/45	4	DEC PDP-9	1
Honeywell 1200	4	GE 635	1
RCA Spectra 70/35	3	CDC 3300	1
IBM 360/44	2	Honeywell 125	1
IBM 360/75	2	Honeywell 2200	1
		Total	219

Location	Number of Listings
New York	81
Boston	40
Los Angeles	33
Washington, D.C.	26
New Jersey	16
Philadelphia	13
Chicago	10
	219

* Source: Time Brokers, Inc., *Computer Time Report,* Fall, 1968.

12,500 potential buyers.[29] Table 12-1 provides some information on the computers listed in the fall of 1968.

The excess-capacity seller must usually pay a fee of 10% to the broker and agree never to charge less to an outside user than to one of the broker's customers.[30] In 1968, most sales were apparently based on "wall-clock time"—the buyer was expected to reserve a system for

[29] Time Brokers, Inc., *Computer Time Report,* Fall, 1968, p. 23.
[30] Hegan, *op. cit.,* p. 33.

TABLE 12-2. Data on Transactions Made by One Computer Time Broker, 1968 *

Shift	Period	Price as a Percentage of Prime-Shift Price	Approximate Percentage of Time Sold
Prime shift	Working days, 8:00 A.M.–6:00 P.M.	100	42
Second shift	Mon.–Fri., 6:00 P.M.–midnight	85–90	28
Third shift	Any job starting after midnight	60–90	25
Weekend	Saturday and Sunday	Negotiable	5

* Sources: Shift definitions and prices—Time Brokers, Inc., *Uniform Guide for Computer Time Marketing,* 1968, pp. 3, 5.
Percentages of time sold—derived from figures given in Time Brokers, Inc., *Computer Time Report,* Fall, 1968, p. 6.

a given block of time and pay accordingly. A typical agreement required such a buyer to pay for half the block of time in the event of a cancellation with less than an hour's notice.[31] Table 12-2 provides data on the transactions made with the aid of one brokerage firm in 1968.

Competition should provide reasonable uniformity of price for comparable services throughout a city, but it is entirely possible for prices to differ among cities. Table 12-3 shows the intercity variation in 1968 for three popular systems.

The relationship between the price charged for computer time and the cost of the equipment should depend on (perhaps temporary) demand and supply conditions. According to one authority, "a good rule of thumb . . . is five or six dollars per hour for each thousand dollars of monthly rental." [32] At such a price, sales of 200 hours per month would cover the cost of renting equipment. Since other costs must be assumed in running an installation, and since both expense and risk are associated with the sale of computer time, the price quoted should not be considered exhorbitant.

The problems associated with selling (or buying) computer time should not be minimized, as the following statement by a broker indicates:

A pressing problem is the problem of compatibility. It is ironic that when the IBM 360 was first announced, it was hailed as a computer with both up-

[31] *Ibid.,* p. 34.   [32] *Ibid.,* p. 33.

TABLE 12-3. Intercity Variations in Prices for Computer Use, 1968 *

Location	Prime-Shift Price as a Percentage of New York Price		
	360/30, 32K	360/30, 65K	360/40, 131K
New York	100%	100%	100%
Boston	113	103	108
Chicago	105	105	87
Philadelphia	101	105	87
Washington, D.C.	100	84	95
Los Angeles	76	86	74

* Source: Time Brokers, Inc., *Computer Time Report,* Fall, 1968, p. 1.

ward and downward compatibility, yet it comes in so many versions that from the standpoint of time sales, it is harder to match than most other computers. Sometimes it is a question of 1401 compatibility feature, or possibly the tape drives are 7 track, when the buyer requires 9 track format. It may also be that the seller uses the wrong tape density, or lacks any one of the many special features. A similar problem is the non-standard method of assigning addresses in the operating system. . . . Finally, failures may occur because different releases of the operating system are used.[33]

2. Service Bureaus

Service bureaus accounted for estimated revenues of $534 million in 1966, $640 million in 1967, and $765 million in 1968.[34] According to one source, there were over 800 of them as early as 1966.[35] Size varies considerably, however. In 1968, almost half the total revenue went to 13 firms, with another 70% of all firms accounting for less than 15% of the revenue.[36]

In 1968, over 200 companies were represented by ADAPSO, the Association of Data Processing Service Organizations. This association publicizes the activities of its members, lobbies for legislation consistent with their interests, and engages in legal action on their behalf.

By definition, banks are not independent service bureaus. Those

[33] Time Brokers, Inc., *Computer Time Report,* Summer, 1968, p. 4.
[34] Edward J. Menkhaus, "Banks versus Bureaus," *Business Automation,* May, 1968, p. 56.
[35] Manley R. Irwin, "The Computer Utility," *Datamation,* November, 1966, p. 23.
[36] Menkhaus, *op. cit.,* p. 56.

banks offering computer services thus constitute a clear competitive threat to the members of ADAPSO. Not surprisingly, the association has attempted to obtain court rulings and/or legislation to preclude banks from offering computer services. No substantial success in these efforts had been achieved by the end of 1968.

Banks have substantial peak-load problems. Hence they are often willing to sell off-peak computer time at seemingly "cut-rate" prices. Charges may or may not be explicit. In 1968, 6% of the banks in one sample provided data-processing services "free" to account holders with acceptably large balances, while another 37% offered lower charges to holders of large balances.[37]

The most important service bureau is undoubtedly the wholly owned IBM subsidiary, Service Bureau Corporation (SBC). Originally set up under the terms of the 1956 consent decree, SBC is required to purchase equipment from IBM on terms available to other customers, in order to avoid "unfair competition." Moreover, it must keep separate books and set prices and rates based on its full costs.

Opinions about the impact of the last provision differ. Some assert that IBM's service bureau activity had been based on rates established on the basis of the production cost of equipment—a cost possibly far below price. Others argue that such a policy would have been foolish since the relevant cost of retaining a computer for service operations is the foregone revenue. If IBM had been trying to maximize profit, decisions would have been based on foregone revenue, not production cost.

Both arguments may be considered correct, given appropriate interpretations. The relevant value is, of course, foregone revenue—in more formal terms, marginal revenue. But this will be less than price unless the demand for IBM computers is perfectly elastic. The less elastic the demand, the greater is the disparity between marginal revenue and price. Moreover, output should be selected so that marginal cost equals marginal revenue (average cost may be smaller or larger). In sum, an unfettered service organization operated by a manufacturer should assume that it obtains equipment at either marginal cost or marginal revenue (since the two should be equal).

If IBM attempts to maximize profits (a reasonable assumption),

[37] *Ibid.*

what impact did the consent decree have on its service bureau operation? To shed some light on the issue, we consider a highly simplified case.

Assume that marginal cost is unaffected by quantity. Let P_c be the price charged for a computer and Q_c the quantity of computers sold. Let service be measured in computer units, with P_s the price of a computer unit of service and Q_s the number of such units sold. Figure 12–2 shows the maximum-profit solution in the absence of constraints: quantities will be Q_c^* and Q_s^*; prices will be P_c^* and P_s^*. Under such conditions, P_s might be greater than P_c, equal to it, or smaller, depending on the nature of the demand for computers (shown by curve D_c) vis-à-vis that for service (shown by curve D_s).

The intent of the consent decree called for the Service Bureau Corporation to regard P_c as its true marginal cost of equipment. This imposes a constraint on the maximum-profit problem. But IBM's overall objective would presumably be unchanged.

Assume that the constraint is satisfied. Clearly, this will result in a value of P_s greater than that of P_c unless the demand for service is perfectly elastic. The smaller the elasticity of demand for service, the greater will be the disparity between the two prices.

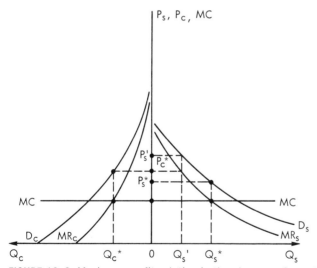

FIGURE 12–2. Maximum-profit solution in the absence of constraints.

Total revenue,
  Total cost

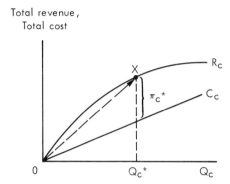

(a)

Total revenue,
  Total cost

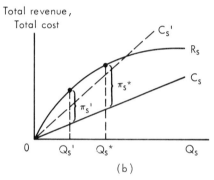

(b)

FIGURE 12–3. The effect of changes in computer price on the profit situation in (a) the market for computers and (b) the market for computer services.

It is difficult to predict the effect on P_c. It might be left unchanged. In Fig. 12–2, such a decision would lead to a reduction in the quantity of service (to Q_s') and an increase in its price (to P_s').

Figures 12–3a and b illustrate the impact of changes in P_c. The two cost curves (C_c and C_s) reflect the assumption of constant marginal cost. The two revenue curves (R_c and R_s) reflect downward-sloping and independent demand curves. In the absence of constraints, the maximum-profit situation involves quantities Q_c^* and Q_s^*, with profit equal to the sum of π_c^* and π_s^*. The slope of ray OX in Fig. 12–3a indicates the price of a computer (P_c). Given that price, the Service Bureau Corporation must act as if its cost curve were C_s' in Fig. 12–3b — a ray with the same slope as OX in Fig. 12–3a. This leads to a quantity of Q_s' and true profits in the service business of π_s'.

Now consider an increase in P_c. This would lead to smaller values of Q_c and π_c. It would also cause Q_s to be reduced below Q_s', and π_s to be reduced below π_s'. Thus an increase in P_c would reduce total profit and would not be desirable.

A decrease in P_c would reduce π_c, but it would increase π_s (above π_s'). Thus it might be desirable.

Needless to say, a complete analysis would have to account for other factors — in particular, the interdependence of the demand for computers and the demand for service. However, the simple case considered here illustrates at least one crucial relationship. The elasticity of demand is of major importance. In the late 1950's, it is possible that IBM enjoyed a rather substantial monopoly position. If so, the consent decree's provisions regarding the company's service bureau business may have had a major impact. But the greater the competition faced by IBM, the smaller will be the importance of these provisions. Their impact may thus be less substantial now.

3. Time-Sharing Vendors

We have defined time sharing to include all systems using remote input/output stations. Typically, more than one such station is connected to a system at one time. The central facility is designed to receive input and/or transmit output at a considerably faster rate than that of any single remote station. In order to keep all stations busy, a round-robin technique is utilized, with the input/output stations given small amounts of service in rotation.

Procedures vary, but many systems can be adequately described with a very simple model. Tasks are divided into priority classes. A resource may service tasks in one or more classes. If a single resource is assigned to more than one class, it accepts tasks in a lower-priority category only if none remains to be serviced in any of the higher-priority classes. Within a class, tasks are serviced in order. Once a resource is assigned to a task, it continues on assignment until either (1) no more can be accomplished (e.g., because another resource is required) or (2) a given amount of time, called a *quantum* or *time slice*, has elapsed.

General Electric was the first company to offer time-shared services extensively on a commercial basis. According to one authority, GE was still the largest supplier of such services in 1968, with IBM rank-

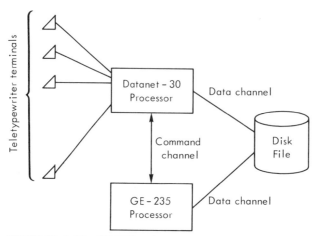

FIGURE 12–4. The GE 265 system.

ing second.[38] But there are many seemingly viable independent companies in the industry.

Initially IBM offered time-sharing services directly, through its Information Marketing Department. However, a number of competitors argued that the company was violating the provision of the 1956 consent decree concerning service bureau activities. In the latter part of 1968, the Information Marketing Department was transferred to the Service Bureau Corporation.

Figure 12–4 shows the major components of the GE 265, the first commercially successful time-shared system. One processor—a Datanet 30—is devoted to input, output, and certain editing tasks. The quantum is small and the speed of the processor large relative to the time needed to perform the required tasks. In essence, tasks in the input/output/editing class can be performed almost as rapidly as the remote teletypewriter stations can function. Other tasks—compiling and executing programs—are treated differently: they are performed by the GE 235 processor. The quantum is relatively large and the speed of the processor small relative to the time needed to perform such tasks.

Some systems use a single processor in much the same manner, with

[38] Alan F. Hammersmith, "Selecting a Vendor of Time-Shared Computer Services," *Computers and Automation,* October, 1968, p. 16.

a high-priority program servicing input and output requirements and a
low-priority program servicing more time-consuming functions. Others use many input/output processors, each servicing a particular set
of terminals. And some systems employ more than one processor to
handle the more time-consuming tasks.

The size of the quantum (time slice) will have a major impact on the
responsiveness of a system. Highly interactive (fast-response) systems devote a small amount of time to each task, allowing rapid response to relatively simple requests. Batch-processing systems can be
viewed as time-shared systems with exceedingly long time slices.

The amount of high-speed storage required for a particular task may
be very large or very small. Most systems impose upper bounds on the
amount of such storage used. If each task requires the entire capacity
of a system's high-speed storage, information must be "swapped"
between high- and low-speed memories whenever a new task is begun.
This "swap time" is lost — no other processing can be performed. The
smaller the time-slice used, the greater is the number of swaps required to complete a given task and the smaller the amount of regular
processing performed during a given period of time. Processor efficiency may often be increased, however, by increasing the amount of
high-speed storage. One task may be swapped out of high-speed memory and another swapped into it while the processor works on a task
in another part of memory.

In general, the designer of a time-shared system must attempt to
find an optimal combination of (1) maximum task size, (2) length of
time slice,[39] (3) amount of high-speed memory, and (4) processor
speed.

Time-sharing systems are sometimes judged on the basis of the
processor time "lost" (for swapping, overhead, etc.). Such an approach is likely to be inadequate. A given processor may be used more
efficiently by adding more high-speed memory and/or by reducing
maximum task size. The relevant measures concern the tasks that
can be performed, the cost of performing them, and the speed with
which they can be completed.

General-purpose time-sharing systems are typically more expensive

[39] In some cases, it may be desirable to use a more complex algorithm, for example,
one that varies the length of time according to the priority of the task, the number of
time slices it has received, etc.

than special-purpose systems. A system using only one language may be designed so the language-processor program is always in high-speed memory, with only information unique to each task moved back and forth between high- and low-speed memories. A system using many languages will require either more high-speed memory (to store all the required language-processor programs) or more movement of information between high- and low-speed memory (since the processor programs may have to be swapped).

For these and other reasons, it is not easy to compare competing services. In 1968 a number of vendors offered time-shared use of the BASIC language. Rates differed considerably. One vendor charged only for terminal connection time. Others charged for both terminal connection time and central-processor time, but relative costs differed. On some systems, top priority was reserved for input, output, and minimal editing tasks, with execution of programs performed in a relatively traditional manner, making on-line diagnosis difficult or time-consuming. On other systems, each statement was completely checked as it was entered; moreover, the user was provided with a number of features to facilitate program debugging. The languages themselves differed. One version allowed only numeric data to be manipulated, whereas another included sophisticated constructs for analyzing strings of characters.

Figure 12–5 shows the total time required to complete a test program using a number of competitive systems; the total cost is also shown. The program performed 100 regression analyses, each using 100 pairs of random numbers; no output was required. A different program would undoubtedly have given different results.

The responsiveness of a time-shared system (and often the cost of completing a given job) is usually highly dependent on the load — more precisely, on the relationship between the task under consideration and all others active at the same time. Unfortunately, the precise impact of one task on another is likely to be difficult to assess after the fact and virtually impossible to predict in advance.

Charges vary considerably. In 1968 Tymshare, Inc., charged $13 per terminal-hour for service on an SDS 940 system. Pillsbury's Call-a-Computer offered service on a GE 265 system in the daytime at rates varying from $6.50 to $9.00 per terminal-hour (depending on

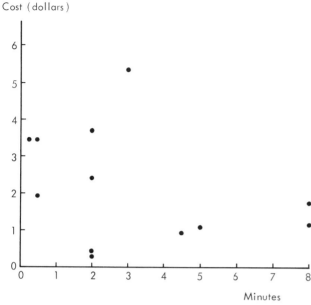

Cost (dollars)

Minutes

FIGURE 12-5. Total time and cost required to complete a test program, using competitive systems.

total monthly utilization) plus 3 cents per second of central-processor (GE 235) time. Night rates were $4.50 per terminal-hour plus 2 cents per second of central-processor time. Educational institutions were offered 24-hour, 7-day-per-week service for $890 per terminal per month.

In 1968 IBM's Call/360:Basic service cost $11.00 per terminal-hour plus $7.00 per minute of central-processor (IBM 360/50) time. General Electric offered service on both the GE 265 and GE 635 systems. Charges were $10.00 per terminal-hour plus 4 (GE 265) or 40 (GE 635) cents per second of central-processor time. Applied Logic offered service on a PDP 10 for $10.00 per terminal-hour plus 1.5 cents per 10,000 machine instructions executed.

Allen-Babcock bases its charges on processor time and core storage used. In 1968, rates for service on an IBM 360/50 varied from $5.50 per minute (using 8K bytes) to $15.50 per minute (using 32K bytes).

Keydata bases its charges on the nature of the task performed. In

1966, rates for typical transactions were as follows: [40]

Basic invoice charge	$0.075 per invoice
Invoice item line charge	0.025 per line
File maintenance	0.025 per entry
File queries	0.015 per inquiry
Off-line report generation	3.00 per 1000 lines

File storage charges also vary. A vendor may provide some "free" storage (often in return for a guaranteed minimum monthly utilization). In general, rates are greater, the smaller the average access time. In 1968 Allen-Babcock charged $4.00 per month to store 100,000 characters on an IBM 2321 data cell and $12.00 per month to store the same amount of data on an IBM 2314 disk. In the same year IBM's Call/360:Basic service charged over $30.00 per month to store 100,000 characters, while Tymshare charged $100.

Some vendors offer quantity and/or educational discounts. The following offer was made to an educational institution for 24-hour dedicated terminals:

Number of Terminals	Average Cost per Terminal per Month
1–8	$2200
9–16	2000
17–24	1800
25–32	1600
33–40	1400

The system to be utilized rented for approximately $30,000 per month and could serve up to 40 users. The vendor was willing to provide the full system for approximately twice its rental cost ($40 \times \$1400 = \$56,000$). This seems reasonable, in view of the costs of operating even a relatively simple computer installation. The higher rates required if the user is unwilling to make a major commitment reflect risk, added marketing costs, and possibly the cost of unused capacity.

Users of time-shared systems behave very differently. Figures 12–6a through 12–6d provide evidence of such differences obtained

[40] D. F. Parkhill, *The Challenge of the Computer Utility*, Addison-Wesley, Reading, Mass., 1966, p. 81.

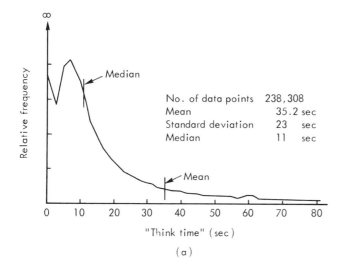

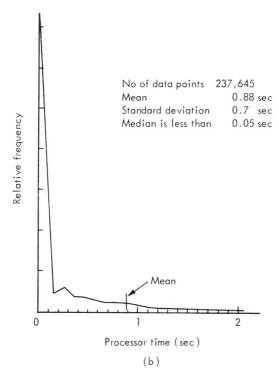

FIGURE 12-6. Characteristics of Project MAC utilization, 1964-1965.

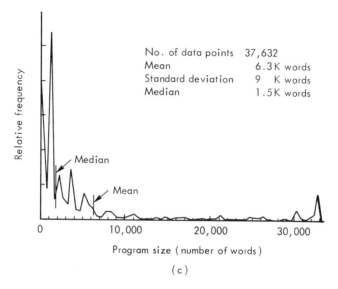

No. of data points   37,632
Mean   6.3K words
Standard deviation   9   K words
Median   1.5K words

Median

Mean

Program size (number of words)

(c)

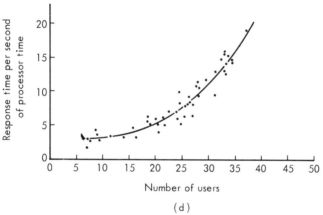

Number of users

(d)

FIGURE 12-6. (concluded)

during 1964 and 1965 on M.I.T.'s Project MAC system.[41] Figure 12-6a shows the distribution of "think time"—roughly, the time a user requires to complete an input after being requested to provide one by the system.[42] Figure 12-6b shows the distribution of processor

[41] Taken from A. L. Scherr, *An Analysis of Time-Shared Computer Systems,* The M.I.T. Press, Cambridge, Mass., 1967.
[42] Approximately 12% of the observations required zero "think time"; they represented automatic responses to computer-initiated instructions.

time required to service an input; Fig. 12–6c, the amount of storage required. The relationship between the number of users and response time is shown in Fig. 12–6d. As expected, response time increases at an increasing rate as the number of users goes up.

Time-shared service clearly costs more than traditional batch processing. To decrease average response (turnaround) time, capacity must be increased relative to utilization. As Fig. 12–6d shows, if a small response time is desired, the cost of a given system must be shared by relatively few users. Moreover, there are additional costs, such as those for communications processors and extra storage.

Clearly, such systems cost more. But are they worth more? The answer depends primarily on the value of fast response. For example, a typical programmer can finish a job sooner by using a time-shared system. Ratios from 3:1 up to 7:1 have been reported for programming time when conventional systems are tested in comparison to time-shared systems.[43] In some cases, rapid response is its own reward—it is worth the extra cost to obtain the desired result sooner. In other situations, rapid response is worthwhile only if it reduces other costs (e.g., programmer's salaries) by at least as much as it adds to computer service costs.

Generalization is impossible. Suffice it to say that systems with a wide range of response times (and costs) are available, and that the number of each type is increasing. Some sophisticated users already purchase service from several vendors, selecting the best one for each task on the basis of both cost and value. In the future this approach is likely to become more widespread.

Figure 12–7 provides estimates [44] of the number of general-purpose time-sharing systems in the United States. The prediction that the number will double every year through 1972 (the vertical scale is logarithmic) seems reasonable enough in the light of past experience.

D. THE MARKET FOR SOFTWARE

Broadly defined, *software* denotes any set of instructions for a computer, whether written using the code of a particular machine or ex-

---

[43] Walter F. Bauer and Richard H. Hill, "Economics of Time-Shared Systems," *Datamation,* November, 1967, p. 49.

[44] Taken from T. James Glauthier, "Computer Time-Sharing: Its Origins and Development," *Computers and Automation,* October, 1967, p. 24.

Number of systems

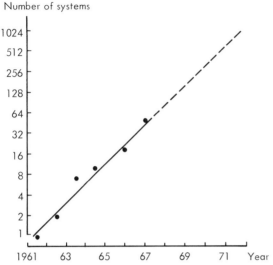

FIGURE 12–7. Estimates of the number of general-purpose time-sharing systems in the United States.

pressed in some higher-level language. Certain types of software may be essential to the very operation of a computer (e.g., an operating system). Other types may be extremely valuable to most, if not all, users (e.g., a FORTRAN or COBOL compiler). Still other types may be valuable to only a few users (e.g., an airline reservation system).

The importance of software cannot be overemphasized. Computer manufacturers spend large sums on it. For example, the president of IBM says, "We are investing nearly as much in System/360 programming as we are in the entire development of System/360 hardware." [45] A representative view from the other side of the market is the following: "For users, software has become the most important factor in system selection." [46] But problems abound: "We have no standard measures of performance, inadequate tools for performance evaluation, and little ability to predict or guarantee performance before or during its development." [47] Moreover,

[45] Mark I. Halpern, "The Future of Software," *Data Processing Digest,* February, 1967, p. 2.
[46] J. D. Tupac, *An Approach to Software Evaluation,* The RAND Corporation, P–3581, April, 1967, p. 2.
[47] Halpern, *op. cit.,* p. 2.

. . . on-time machine delivery is the rule nowadays. Software, on the other hand, is seldom quite on time, and slippages measured in years are not hard to find. . . . Even when a delivery date is apparently met, all that can be said is that a deck or tape has been delivered that does some small fraction of what was promised. . . . No machine manufacturer could hope to lease a machine half as effective as its competitors in price—but even wider anomalies exist in software.[48]

Software is developed by computer manufacturers, computer users, independent software producers, research institutions, and universities, among others.

Traditionally, computer manufacturers have given software to users of their equipment without (further) charge. In 1968 there was only one major exception—Scientific Data Systems required extra payment for a COBOL compiler for the Sigma 7 computer.

Users considering the development of software have generally been concerned more with its value in their own operation than with its possible worth to others. Independent software companies perform much of their work under contract to users and/or manufacturers. Universities and some nonprofit research institutions are often concerned as much with educational as with practical value. A great deal of important software has been developed at such institutions, much of it with federal support; in general it is provided to others at little or no cost.

Some types of software are clearly valuable. Moreover, software development entails considerable cost (although its distribution and reproduction may cost relatively little). The primary conditions for a viable market are thus present. But a market presumes that property rights exist (they are, after all, the real object of exchange). Moreover, the enforcement of such rights must be relatively simple—theft must be both illegal and costly, relative to the value of the good stolen. An important question thus concerns the status of property rights in respect to software.

Once a good has been created, public policy usually favors a maximum of competition. However, the process of creation may be enhanced by the promise of monopoly control over the good, once created. In the case of inventions and artistic endeavors, public policy

[48] Ibid.

usually favors a compromise between competition and monopoly. The major questions concern the degree of monopoly granted and the length of time over which it may be exercised. An "optimal" solution would be difficult enough to determine in any specific case; it would be impossible to determine in general. Public policy on this issue must be viewed as a practical attempt to provide an appropriate balance.

In the United States, an *"invention* which is *novel, useful* and *unobvious"* [49] may be patented; the inventor is then allowed to preclude others from "making, vending or using" [50] the invention for a period of 17 years. The protection is substantial. Lack of knowledge of a patent is no defense against a claim of infringement. Even a completely independent development is of no value.

Patents are awarded only after examination by the U.S. Patent Office to ensure that all requirements have been met. Particularly troublesome is the determination of sufficient novelty. In 1968 the Office issued a patent for a particular sorting technique. This was widely viewed as a major precedent. However, a Patent Office official suggested otherwise: "It may be invalid. We issue invalid patents every day. . . . We'll just have to wait for the court to decide. . . . We have not changed our guidelines and we do not think that a program is patentable." [51] Clearly, software does not fit neatly into the classification "inventions." Until new legislation and/or court rulings clarify the issue, the patentability of software will be open to serious question.

There is, however, another avenue for protection: software may be copyrighted. Copyrights "protect authors from unauthorized *copying* of their *published* writings." [52] The copyright owner has exclusive control for 28 years of the right to reproduce the "form of expression . . . but it is not a violation of copyright to express the same idea in other words." [53] Copyrights may be registered with an administrative agency—the U.S. Copyright Office. In 1964 the Office agreed to

---

[49] Allen W. Puckett, "Protecting Computer Programs," *Datamation,* November, 1967, p. 56.

[50] *Ibid.*

[51] First Assistant Commissioner Edwin L. Reynolds, quoted in *Computerworld,* June 26, 1968, p. 3.

[52] Puckett, *op. cit.,* p. 56.

[53] Robert B. Bigelow, "Legal Aspects of Proprietary Software," *Datamation,* October, 1968, p. 32.

register copyrights on computer programs, on the grounds that in doubtful cases registration was to be preferred.[54] The decision is by no means binding. The issue can be settled only by court rulings and/or new legislation. A copyright revision bill which appeared to include computer programs as copyrightable material was passed by the House of Representatives in 1968 but not voted on in the Senate.[55]

A copyright makes it illegal for someone to copy the published work of another. Independent development, however, is not precluded. The dividing line between copying and independent development is far from clear, and will undoubtedly remain imprecise until a number of cases have been taken to court. The value of copyright protection for software is thus extremely difficult to assess.

A software developer may be able to bring suit against those who obtain his product without authorization, under the statutory provisions pertaining to patents and copyright. Alternatively, he may bring suit against the source of such an unauthorized disclosure. Common law provides for damages whenever a trade secret is divulged without approval. More important yet is the contract authorizing the use of software:

Although a contract between vendor and vendee or licensor and licensee cannot be binding on third parties who gain access to the program through the vendee or licensee and without notice of the contractual agreement, a contract can surely provide for appropriately heavy damages to be obtained from the vendee or licensee in the case of such disclosure. This contractual protection should undoubtedly prove the most useful device in meeting the needs of most companies and computer programmers.[56]

Vendors frequently offer software for lease—in some cases, over an extremely long term (several years) for a single payment. Court rulings may very well lead to the conclusion that such a lessor is better protected against unauthorized disclosure than a developer who sells his software outright.[57]

Obviously the legal situation concerning property rights in software

[54] *Ibid.*, p. 33.   [55] *Ibid.*
[56] Puckett, *op. cit.*, p. 58.
[57] Time-shared services may provide even greater protection. The developer of an application program may choose to sell its *use* via a time-shared system of his own, rather than selling the program itself. If the system is well designed, the developer will know who is using his program and when, and can charge accordingly.

is confused. However, a market has developed, and transactions are being made at significant prices. Some apparently believe that property rights in this area are reasonably secure.

Precise data about transactions are difficult to obtain. According to one source:

> . . . prices range from several hundred dollars to $10,000 and more. Most commercial application packages fall within a range of $2000 to $20,000. For this expenditure, the purchaser should expect to receive a fully operational system, good documentation and a reasonable amount of technical support. . . . For packages in this price range, the purchase price usually represents *one-fifth* to *one-tenth* of the total cost of developing an equivalent package.[58]

As might be expected, there are software *brokers,* who act primarily as go-betweens, and software *dealers,* who carry "inventory" and provide some sort of guarantee that the software will serve its intended function. Some dealers buy software outright from developers; others share the risk via royalty payments. Inexpensive listing services and nonprofit program exchanges also facilitate the joint use of software.

Independent software companies sometimes make their products available generally, for a price. However, the majority of their work is performed under contract. Much of the risk may be borne by the firm: "More and more, the fixed-price contract has come to dominate the software industry."[59]

In 1968 eleven firms, with sales of more than $100 million annually, formed the Association of Independent Software Companies (AISC) to "handle common problems such as competition with 'not-for-profit organizations' and protection for proprietary programs. The firms . . . chose Washington as the natural site for their joint operations because of the need to work with government and other official bodies."[60]

It is generally felt that independent software companies can attract better people than manufacturers or firms that use computers. One reason may be noneconomic: computer people are said to prefer to work for other computer people. Another reason is clearly economic. Small independent companies are able to easily capitalize their suc-

[58] Robert V. Head and Evan F. Linick, "Software Package Acquisition," *Datamation,* October, 1968, p. 24.
[59] Richard H. Hill, "Contracting for Software," *Data Processing Magazine,* March, 1966, p. 28.
[60] *Computerworld,* May 22, 1968, p. 1.

cess. Employees are paid moderate wages and given stock or stock options; payment thus comes partly in the form of capital gains, as the value of a company's stock increases. Income tax legislation favors long-term capital gains — the effective tax rate is at most half that on ordinary income. Venturesome and/or confident software developers are thus likely to be attracted to independent companies.

A recurring theme in trade publications concerns the desirability of separate pricing of software and hardware. Should computer manufacturers — especially IBM — be required to produce software in divisions that keep separate books and are expected to at least break even? If not, should manufacturers be required to make all software equally available to all users, those outside the firm as well as those inside?

Software for certain time-sharing applications (Call/360:Datatext and Call/360:Basic) was originally developed by the Information Marketing Division of IBM. The software was initially classified proprietary — no IBM customer could obtain it. Under considerable pressure from those using IBM equipment to offer competitive services, the company finally agreed to release both systems on an "as is" basis with no program support. However, "an IBM spokesman denied that any part of the company's change in policy had been caused by a consideration of the antitrust situation and said that it had occurred simply because 'we found there was an appreciable interest in the software.' " [61]

As mentioned previously, software development for the IBM/360 series is reported to have cost as much as hardware development. But this hardly implies that total software cost will equal total hardware cost. The production of an additional computer of a given design clearly costs something; the production of an additional copy of a given item of software costs almost nothing. One observer argues that, overall, the cost to IBM of System/360 programming will not exceed 2.5% of revenue.[62] The reason is obvious: the marginal cost of software is nearly zero.

[61] *Computerworld,* Oct. 2, 1967, p. 2. The services were subsequently transferred to the Service Bureau Corporation, which is under no compulsion to make its software available to other IBM customers.

[62] Melvin E. Conway, "On the Economics of the Software Market," *Datamation,* October, 1968, p. 30.

Large fixed costs and low marginal costs often give rise to a natural monopoly. There are substantial economies of scale in the production of any specific item of software. In such a case, considerable advantage may be achieved via discriminatory pricing. Consider Figs. 12–8a and b. In each figure, curve D shows the demand for software and curve MR the marginal revenue if a single price is chosen. In the absence of price discrimination, the quantity sold would be q^*, and total

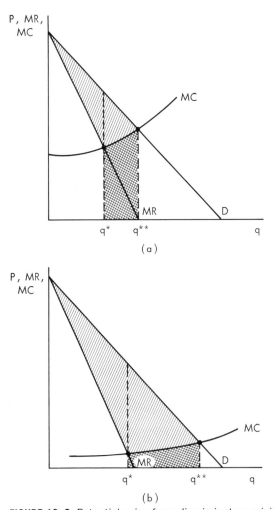

FIGURE 12–8. Potential gains from discriminatory pricing.

revenue would equal the area under the marginal revenue curve up to q^*.

Now consider the impact of a change to a perfectly discriminatory pricing policy. The demand curve becomes the marginal revenue curve. Quantity will be increased, to q^{**}, and total revenue will equal the area under the demand (marginal revenue) curve up to q^{**}. In each diagram, total revenue increases by an amount equal to the total shaded area, total cost increases by an amount equal to the cross-hatched area, and net profit increases by an amount equal to the difference. Clearly, the lower the marginal cost curve, the greater is the potential gain from price discrimination.

Any developer has substantial incentive to price software discriminatorily, charging customers primarily on the basis of value. But how can the value of a specific item to a given customer be determined? One possible surrogate is the cost of the system on which the software is to be used. A FORTRAN compiler may be of some value to an IBM 360/40 user, of more value to a 360/65 user, and of even more value to a 360/85 user. A reasonable working hypothesis would be: the greater the equipment cost (rental charge or purchase price), the more valuable the software.

As a practical approach, a manufacturer might invoke software charges proportional to hardware costs. A less obvious alternative would be to simply raise the cost of the hardware appropriately and "give away" the software. IBM appears to prefer the latter policy, perhaps in order to avoid explicitly discriminatory pricing. Thus far the Justice Department has taken no stand on the legality of IBM's "free" software.

What if free software were outlawed, at least for IBM? To the extent that major economies of scale exist, software production would tend to be concentrated in relatively few firms. To the extent that hardware and software production are complementary, hardware manufacturers would enjoy a competitive advantage over other software firms that develop software only. If discriminatory pricing (explicit or implicit) is precluded, some users will benefit, whereas others will lose; and some types of software may not be produced at all.

Should software be priced separately? Unfortunately (but not surprisingly), economic theory alone cannot provide a direct answer.

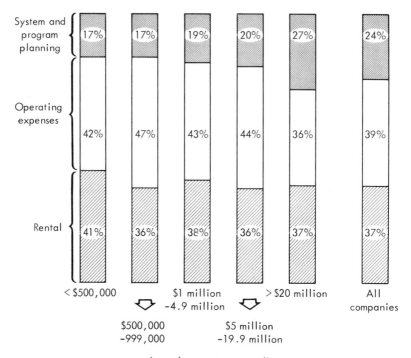

Annual computer expenditures

FIGURE 12-9. Expenditures of 33 firms for computer services in 1966. Source: Taylor and Dean, *op. cit.*

E. PERSONNEL COSTS

Two major inputs are required to provide computer service: equipment and manpower. For development, employees such as programmers and systems analysts are needed; for operation, the services of managers, operators, etc., are essential. In practice the two activities usually coexist. Some sort of computer installation is required to check out development efforts. And almost every installation engages in continuing development as old systems are modified and new ones begun.

Within limits, manpower may be substituted for equipment, and vice versa. The optimal combination will clearly depend on relative costs and on the services which the installation is supposed to provide. There is no uniformly "correct" ratio of hardware costs to total expenditures. Most installations managers devote one-third to one-half their budget to equipment. Figure 12-9 provides some information

TABLE 12-4. Data Processing Personnel Costs *

Classification	Average Annual Salary	Percent- age of Total Personnel	Percentage of Total Personnel Cost
Manager of data processing	$14,400	5.0%	8.5%
Assistant manager of data processing	11,800	2.3	3.1
Manager of systems analysis	12,800	4.1	6.3
Senior systems analyst	9,900	19.9	23.4
Manager of computer programming	11,100	4.5	6.0
Senior computer programmer	8,900	8.5	8.8
Computer programmer	6,900	13.6	11.1
Coder	5,300	14.0	8.9
Supervisor, computer operations	9,100	4.7	5.0
Computer operator	5,800	17.0	13.7
Tab and peripheral equipment supervisor	8,300	3.2	3.1
Tape librarian	5,400	3.2	2.1
		100.0	100.0

* Source: *Data Processing Salary and Compensation Guidebook* (1968), *Computerworld,* Newton, Mass.

about the expenditures of thirty-three firms surveyed in 1966. Overall, from 0.13% to 1.33% of annual revenue was devoted to computer activities.[63] A survey taken in 1967 found that, in a typical installation, salaries for data-processing personnel were approximately equal to the rental value of the equipment.[64]

Table 12-4 presents some data obtained from a "nation-wide census of data processing personnel" conducted during 1967.[65] Three figures are shown for each classification. The first indicates the average annual salary;[66] the second, the percentage of total personnel so classified; and the third, the percentage of total personnel cost spent on those in the classification. Overall, the average salary was approximately $8500 per year.[67]

[63] James W. Taylor and Neal J. Dean, "Managing to Manage the Computer," *Harvard Business Review,* September–October, 1966, p. 101.
[64] *Data Processing Salary and Compensation Guidebook* (1968), *Computerworld,* Newton, Mass., p. 16. On the average, salaries equaled 96% of computer equipment rental value.
[65] *Data Processing Salary and Compensation Guidebook, op. cit.,* p. 12.
[66] Obtained by multiplying the average weekly salary (given in the report) by 52, then rounding to the nearest one hundred dollars.
[67] The figure was obtained by dividing total personnel cost by the total number of persons employed.

TABLE 12-5. Computer Personnel Salaries *

| | Annual Salaries | | |
| | 15th Percentile | Median | 85th Percentile |
Position			
Management positions			
Systems managers			
Installation size:			
Medium	$14,600	$17,000	$20,500
Large	15,900	22,100	26,700
Programming managers			
Installation size:			
Medium	13,900	15,700	17,900
Large	15,100	18,100	21,600
Operations managers			
Installation size:			
Small	8,300	10,200	12,500
Medium	10,100	11,800	14,800
Large	14,200	17,600	21,800
Information systems directors			
Installation size:			
Small	12,600	14,900	17,600
Medium	18,900	23,100	26,600
Large	21,000	30,500	44,000
Nonmanagement positions			
Commercial programmers and programmer/analysts			
Experience:			
6 months–1 year	7,200	8,400	9,300
1–2 years	8,800	9,800	10,700
2–4 years	10,300	12,200	13,200
Over 4 years	10,800	12,900	14,800
Scientific-OR programmers and analysts			
Experience:			
6 months–1 year	9,400	10,600	11,800
1–2 years	10,500	12,100	13,900
2–4 years	12,200	14,600	16,900
Over 4 years	14,300	16,600	20,400
Systems programmers			
Experience:			
1–2 years	10,100	11,400	12,700
2–4 years	12,300	13,800	15,400
Over 4 years	13,400	15,900	18,800
Senior systems analysts and project leaders			
Experience:			
2–4 years	11,900	14,000	15,900
Over 4 years	12,800	15,600	18,300

* Source: *EDP Computer Salary Survey and Opportunities Analysis,* 1968 Edition.

Table 12–5 presents data on salaries earned by those applying for new positions during 1967 with the assistance of a firm specializing in recruiting computer personnel.[68] The figures describe the salaries being earned at the time of application; typical increases obtained when a new job was accepted ranged from 5% to 15%.[69] Management salaries appeared to be related to the size of the installation. The classifications used were:

Size	Monthly Rental Value of Equipment
Small	Up to $15,000 per month
Medium	$15,000–$60,000 per month
Large	Over $60,000 per month

For nonmanagement positions, experience appeared to be more relevant.

Computer people have tended to change positions relatively often. The cost is not trivial. The average relocation expense per person hired in 1966 was estimated by one source to be $2045.[70] The cost of hiring professional computer people is also high; one estimate placed the average (not marginal) cost at $2087 per person employed in 1966.[71]

It is particularly difficult to estimate the cost of programming a given task or set of tasks. Many alternatives are available. Higher-level languages reduce development time but may increase the time required to run the program. Special-purpose languages reduce the time required to produce programs of certain types, but the fixed cost of learning the language may not be worth the reduction in variable cost associated with its use. Ideally, one would like to have quantitative estimates of the impact of such decisions in order to select the best policy in each case. In fact it is difficult to even predict the impact of a given policy.

Figure 12–10 shows the cumulative distribution of man-months per 1000 machine instructions required to prepare and debug a group of programs. Table 12–6 summarizes data concerning 123 programs

[68] *The Source EDP Computer Salary Survey and Opportunities Analysis,* 1968 Edition, Source EDP, New York.
[69] *Ibid.*
[70] *Data Processing Salary and Compensation Guidebook, op. cit.,* p. 6.
[71] *Ibid.*

Percent

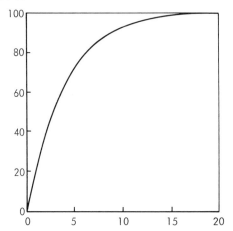

Man-months per 1000 machine instructions

FIGURE 12-10. Cumulative distribution of man-months per 1000 machine instructions required to prepare and debug a group of programs. Source: E. A. Nelson, *Management Handbook for the Estimation of Computer Programming Costs,* System Development Corporation Technical Memorandum TM-3225/000/00 (Oct. 31, 1966), p. 69.

written in machine-oriented languages (MOL's) and 46 programs written in higher-level procedure-oriented languages (POL's). Programs written in higher-level languages required fewer man-months, less computer time for development and debugging and less elapsed time per 1000 machine instructions. However, two cautionary notes are in order. First, the number of machine instructions generated by a translator from a program written in a higher-level language will usually exceed the number written by a programmer working in a machine-oriented language. Estimates for a "mature" translator designed to produce efficient code range from 10 to 15% above the number of instructions produced by a machine-oriented language programmer.[72] The second drawback concerns efficiency: instructions produced by a translator from a program written in a higher-level language may require more time to complete a given task than a comparable set of instructions written in a machine-oriented language.

[72] V. LaBolle, *Development of Equations for Estimating the Costs of Computer Program Production,* System Development Corporation Technical Memorandum TM-2918/000/00 (Apr. 5, 1966), p. 25.

TABLE 12-6. Comparison of Times Required for Programs Written in Machine- and Procedure-Oriented Languages *

Man-months per 1000 machine instructions:

	Maximum	Minimum	Std. Dev.	Median	Mean
123 MOL programs	100	0.14	10.18	4.00	5.89
46 POL programs	9.49	0.07	2.61	1.16	2.13

Computer-hours per 1000 machine instructions:

	Maximum	Minimum	Std. Dev.	Median	Mean
123 MOL programs	294.04	0.05	42.75	15.00	29.52
46 POL programs	52.50	0.30	13.74	2.86	9.76

Elapsed time (months) per 1000 machine instructions:

	Maximum	Minimum	Std. Dev.	Median	Mean
123 MOL programs	40.00	0.06	5.81	1.33	3.55
46 POL programs	18.43	0.06	3.71	0.92	2.30

* Source: E. A. Nelson, *Management Handbook for the Estimation of Computer Programming Costs,* System Development Corporation, Technical Memorandum TM–3225/000/00 (Oct. 31, 1966), p. 67.

In spite of these drawbacks, an increasing proportion of programs appear to be written in higher-level languages. Partly this is due to technological progress: new languages and new translators make this alternative relatively more attractive than formerly. But there is another factor at work. The relative cost of machine time vis-à-vis programmer time has fallen. Not surprisingly, there has been a substitution of the former for the latter. A change from a machine-oriented language to a procedure-oriented language is an obvious case in point.

In an ambitious series of studies, the System Development Corporation attempted to provide estimating equations for the design, coding, and testing of computer programs. Multiple regression analysis was used, with a sample of 169 programs. The selected equations explain 58% of the variance in man-months required, 56% of the variance in computer-hours required, and 60% of the variance in elapsed time.[73]

[73] E. A. Nelson, *Management Handbook for the Estimation of Computer Programming Costs,* System Development Corporation Technical Memorandum TM–3225/000/00 (Oct. 31, 1966), pp. 77–79.

Unfortunately, each equation requires values for a number of variables, some of them rather subjective. For example, to estimate the number of man-months one must provide values for the following:

Lack of knowledge of operational requirements (0, 1, or 2).

Stability of design (0, 1, 2, or 3).

Per cent mathematical instructions.

Per cent information storage and retrieval functions.

Number of subprograms.

Programming language (MOL or POL).

Business program? (yes or no).

Stand-alone program? (yes or no).

First program on computer? (yes or no).

Hardware components to be developed concurrently? (yes or no).

Random-access device used? (yes or no).

Different computers for programming and operation? (yes or no).

Number of man-trips required.

Program data point developed by military organization? (yes or no).

Major programming projects require artistry as well as scientific ability. Uncertainty will probably continue to plague those required to predict the time and cost associated with such undertakings.

F. COMMUNICATIONS COSTS [74]

The subject of communications is becoming increasingly important to computer users. Remote-batch, remote-job-entry, and true time-sharing systems require reliable and accessible communications. The lower their cost, the greater is the use of such systems.

In the United States, a firm offering communications services for sale is generally considered a public utility. Under the Communications Act of 1934, the Federal Communications Commission is empowered to regulate all communications common carriers. State and local agencies exercise additional regulatory authority. Such actions are based on the assumption that communications carriers are natural monopolies, subject to considerable economies of scale, and should thus be regulated.

[74] This section has benefited from a paper written as a term project for a seminar given by the author at the University of Washington: Larry Granston and Robert M. Johnson, "Data Communication Channels, Cost and Service Considerations" (December, 1965).

The major carrier in the United States is the American Telephone and Telegraph Company (AT & T) and its affiliated companies, known collectively as the Bell System. Western Union, dealing primarily in telegraph services, is a distant second. Most remote computer services utilize the facilities of the Bell System in order to obtain the greatest possible coverage.

The information-carrying capacity of a circuit between two points can be measured in bits per second. Some telegraph circuits can transmit only 75 bits per second; others, 150 bits per second. Standard ("voice-grade") telephone circuits can transmit approximately 2000 bits per second. Several voice-grade circuits may be leased as a group; the resulting circuit may be used to transmit correspondingly large amounts of information per unit time.

Voice-grade circuits may be purchased from telephone companies in several different ways. The most familiar is the standard "toll service." One party dials the other. Charges are based on the amount of time that a connection is maintained, the distance between the two locations, and the time when the connection is made. Practice differs from location to location (and telephone company to telephone company), and rates change periodically. Figure 12–11 shows the cost in 1968 of a 3-minute station-to-station call originating from Santa Ana, California.[75] Two curves indicate the approximate relationship between cost and distance for in-state calls. The two classifications are:

Day: Monday through Saturday, 6:00 A.M. to 6:00 P.M.

Night: Every night, 6:00 P.M. to 6:00 A.M.

    All day Sunday.

The other curves indicate the approximate relationship between cost and distance for out-of-state calls. The four classifications are:

Day: Monday through Friday, 7:00 A.M. to 5:00 P.M.

Evening: Monday through Friday, 5:00 P.M. to 7:00 P.M.

Night: Monday through Friday, 7:00 P.M. to midnight.

    All day Saturday.

    All day Sunday.

---

[75] The curves were derived from sample rates given in the Orange County telephone directory (Pacific Telephone) for November, 1968. The curves for in-state rates were fitted free-hand to the sample points. The solid portions of the curves for out-of-state rates fit the data points exactly; the dashed portions are approximations. All rates are for station-to-station calls; tax is not included.

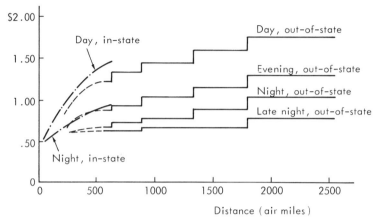

FIGURE 12-11. Relationship between cost and distance for a 3-minute call.

Late Night: most dialed calls, every night, midnight to 7:00 A.M.

Within many metropolitan areas, telephone calls may be made for zero marginal cost—a flat monthly fee entitles the subscriber to unlimited local calls.

Voice-grade circuits may also be leased on a monthly basis. A "private line" between two specific points, available at all times, costs between $1.50 and $3.00 per mile per month. The following estimates may be useful for planning purposes: [76]

Distance (miles)	Cost per Mile per Month (dollars)
0–25	3.00
25–250	2.00
250–500	1.75
Over 500	1.65

Leased circuits may be conditioned to increase their information-transmission capacity. Rates of 2400 bits per second are easily accommodated, and some users have transmitted data at rates as high as 9600 bits per second. [77]

[76] The figures shown are based on data provided the author by an employee of a Bell System telephone company.

[77] Walter E. Simonson, "Data Communications: the Boiling Pot," *Datamation*, April, 1967, p. 25. Much (perhaps all) of the difference may be due to the greater freedom given to private-line users. Before 1968, users of the regular dial-up network were precluded from transmitting data at rates exceeding 2000 bits per second.

The companies of the Bell System offer a special billing arrangement, termed Wide Area Telephone Service (WATS), for use with the dialed network. The customer is provided with an access line to be used only for outgoing calls. He selects one of six *areas*. Area 1 includes nearby out-of-state locations. Area 2 includes additional locations. Each area includes all locations in lower-numbered areas; area 6 includes the entire continental United States except Alaska and the subscriber's home state. In general, ". . . the calling areas are determined by a percentage of the total number of telephones a customer can reach and by geographical boundaries." [78]

Two contractual arrangements are offered. A *full-time* WATS line may be used at any time; the monthly fee depends only on the area (1–6) selected. A *measured-time* WATS line may be used up to 15 hours per month for the basic fee; there is an extra charge for each additional hour.

Figure 12–12 indicates the approximate cost of a WATS line as a function of the hours it is used each month and the area covered.[79] In every case the cheaper service (full-time or measured) is assumed to have been chosen. Generally, the measured-time option is cheaper for utilization below 50 hours per month; the full-time option, for utilization above 65 hours per month. The curves are similar to those relating the monthly cost of rented computer equipment to utilization, before 1965. We have suggested that the latter relationship can be explained partly in terms of discriminatory (value-based) pricing. The argument can be applied in this case as well.

Comparison of the three types of communication service is not a simple matter. Toll service allows calls between virtually any two points, with either party originating the call. Cost depends on distance, length of call, and the time when it is made. More than one call may be made concurrently. Leased lines connect two specific points, either party may originate the call, concurrent calls are precluded, and cost is based solely on distance. Wide Area Telephone Service allows various selections of destination points, but each call must originate at a common point; concurrent calls are precluded. Cost is based on coverage and, with the measured-time option, on utiliza-

---

[78] Edgar C. Gentle, Jr. (Editor), *Data Communications in Business,* The American Telephone and Telegraph Company, New York, p. 134.
[79] The curves shown, based on data provided the author by an employee of a Bell System telephone company, assume that the subscriber is in the Southern California area.

Cost per month (dollars)

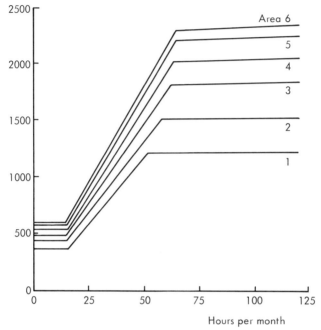

FIGURE 12-12. Relationships between cost and number of hours used per month, for six WATS areas.

tion. No general conclusion about the best choice can be offered. Each case must be considered separately to find the most desirable service (or combination of services).

However obtained, a voice-grade line connecting two points a substantial distance apart is not inexpensive. Moreover, such a line can transmit more information per unit time than many input/output devices can originate or accept. Properly used, a single voice-grade line can accommodate twenty model 33 teletypewriters operating concurrently at full speed.[80] To take advantage of this capability, a communications computer can be employed. Such a device (sometimes called a multiplexor or concentrater) includes a buffer storage and a commutator to service remote terminals in round-robin fashion.

[80] Michael M. Gold and Lee L. Selwyn, "Toward Economical Remote Computer Access," July, 1967, Department of Computer Science, Carnegie Institute of Technology.

Characters are accepted from the terminals and stored in the buffer for later transmission along the line. Characters received from the line are stored in the buffer for later transmission to the appropriate terminal.

The average transmission rate of a terminal is typically far below its maximum capability. Taking advantage of this fact, time-sharing companies have successfully shared a voice-grade line among as many as forty teletypewriter users. The greater the number of users, of course, the larger is the required buffer (or the higher the probability that some information may be lost).

Computer communication equipment capable of handling from 25 to 50 terminals costs from $1000 to $2000 per month. Several time-sharing companies have decided to place their main computers in a central location, using remote communications computers to provide service in major cities. One advantage is redundancy — if a computer requires service, another can perform its work. Perhaps more important, highly valued periods (e.g., 10:00 A.M. to noon, 2:00 P.M. to 5:00 P.M.) in one section of the country may coincide with less highly valued periods in some other area.

Both the telephone network and the present rate structure were designed primarily for voice communications. Neither is particularly suitable for data communications. Until 1968, AT & T insisted that special equipment be leased by users planning to transmit data on the dial-up network. The company claimed the policy was necessary to avoid transmissions that would affect other lines. Some users charged that the company was, in effect, charging more for data transmission than for voice communication by requiring the use of overpriced equipment. The development of devices requiring no physical connection facilitated evasion. And in 1968 the FCC ruled that AT & T could no longer require the use of its own equipment, with the possible exception of relatively inexpensive protection devices.

According to one source, the average local telephone exchange is designed so that 12% of the subscribers can use their telephones at one time; the average holding time (length of a call) is 5 minutes for residences and 3 minutes for businesses.[81] Data transmissions are likely to last longer. The relevant factor for pricing is, of course,

[81] *EDP Analyzer,* October, 1967, p. 8.

use during peak periods. If data communications subscribers are likely to use their lines more during peak hours, they should probably pay relatively more per month than other subscribers. Some telephone companies have begun to explore ways to identify such users and charge them accordingly.

A great deal of attention is being devoted to the impact of data communications. Rates for broadband services with capacities many times that of a voice-grade line are the subject of extended negotiations between AT & T and the Federal Communications Commission. The extent to which the FCC should regulate computer services offered by or in conjunction with communications carriers is another subject of widespread interest.[82] A warning is in order for the impatient. The history of the U.S. communications industry and its regulators suggests that change will come relatively slowly.

G. COMPUTERS ABROAD

We conclude with a few comments about the use and manufacture of computers outside the United States. Not surprisingly, IBM plays a major role internationally. The company has important manufacturing facilities in Britain, France, Germany, and Japan. In 1967, IBM was estimated to have 80% of the market in Germany,[83] 65% in France,[84] 40% in Australia,[85] and somewhat less than 40% in Britain [86] and Japan.[87]

Britain has by far the most important domestic computer-manufacturing industry outside the United States. The major firm, International Computers, Limited (ICL), was formed in 1968 by merging two previously independent companies: International Computers and Tabulators and English Electric Computers. The merger was encouraged by the Ministry of Technology in order to create a large (and hopefully competitive) domestic computer-manufacturing firm. The government contributed $41 million, the majority as a grant toward research and development over a 5-year period; the remainder was

---

[82] A formal inquiry into the matter was initiated by the FCC in 1967.
[83] *Computers and Automation,* March, 1968, p. 33.
[84] *Ibid.*
[85] *Computers and Automation,* February, 1968, p. 37.
[86] *Computers and Automation,* August, 1967, p. 36.
[87] G. B. Levine, "Computers in Japan," *Datamation,* December, 1967, pp. 22–24.

used to purchase 10.5% of the common stock of the new company.[88] Computers made by ICL are widely used in Britain, eastern Europe, and Australia. The company had assets of $240 million in 1968, making it the fourth largest computer manufacturer in the world [after IBM, Sperry Rand (UNIVAC), and Honeywell], according to one source.[89]

The French government also supports a domestic computer industry. The major manufacturer, Compagnie Machines Bull, encountered difficulties in the early 1960's; the government subsequently allowed it to be taken over by General Electric. This left only two French-owned companies of any size — Compagnie Européene d'Automatisme (CAE) and Societé Européene d'Automatisme (SEA). Together, they held 15% of the market in 1966. A crisis of sorts was reached when the U.S. State Department refused to grant export licenses for large scientific computers ordered by the French Atomic Energy Commission. Although the problem was subsequently solved, a viable domestic industry became a major government goal. The result was the "Plan Calcul," whereby CAE and SEA were merged and promised a total of approximately $100 million over a 5-year period. The government plans to invest most of its funds in research and development and to share any profits. A Délegate Génerale, appointed by the government, acts as "computer overlord." [90] Specifications for the first machine produced by the new company were made public in 1968.

The West German government also provides support. Under a 5-year plan covering the period 1967–1971, the government plans to spend $100 million for "research and development in the public sector of the computer industry." [91]

In 1968, the giant Dutch firm, Philips Industries, began deliveries of the first of a major series of computers. According to one source, the company spent about $10 million annually during the period 1965–1968 on its "buildup for the assault" on the computer market.[92]

Only one (Fujitsu) of the several Japanese manufacturers can be considered virtually independent. Hitachi, the leading company,

[88] *Computers and Automation*, May, 1968, p. 39.
[89] *Common Ground* (published by KLM Airlines), June, 1968, p. 1.
[90] "40m for French Computers," *The Economist*, Aug. 13, 1966, p. 659.
[91] "Comment," *Computer Survey*, March/April, 1968, p. 197.
[92] *Common Ground, op. cit.*, p. 3.

relies heavily on RCA designs. Nippon Electric Company uses some Honeywell designs; Toshiba and Mitsubishi have close arrangements with General Electric; and the Oki Electric Company is affiliated with Sperry Rand (UNIVAC).[93] The government has chosen to protect the domestic computer industry: "new foreign investments in computer manufacture in Japan, even as a minority partner in a joint venture, are basically prohibited."[94]

In a world of pacific international relations, government protection and/or support of computer-manufacturing firms would be difficult to justify. The standard arguments of economic theory could easily be invoked against such policies. But the realities of international politics must be acknowledged, as well as the existence of national pride.

[93] Levine, *op. cit.*
[94] *Ibid.*

APPENDIX

REGRESSION ANALYSIS

Much of the empirical analysis described in Part II of this book relies on the technique of regression analysis, a major tool of classical statistics. The method is briefly described here for the reader with little or no background in the area. The discussion is addressed to the pragmatist who wishes to obtain at least a minimal understanding of the results reported in this book. Those interested in the details of statistical inference, hypothesis testing, and more advanced techniques are advised to look elsewhere.[1]

A. CURVE FITTING

Assume that Fig. A–1 represents the cost and throughput (somehow measured) for each of ten computer systems. An analyst might like to argue that cost is some relatively simple function of throughput:

$$C = f(T)$$

Expressing the problem differently, we could say that he wants to "fit" a curve through the points. But what kind of curve? And which one of the family of curves of the "right" kind should be selected?

It is important to recognize that a perfect or nearly perfect fit can always be obtained. If only one Y value is associated with each X value, and there are N points, it is possible to find an $(N-1)$th degree polynomial of the form

$$Y = a_0 + a_1 X + a_2 X^2 + \cdots + a_{N-1} X^{N-1}$$

that passes through each point. If there are multiple Y values for some X value, it is a simple matter to "move" such points slightly to the right or left and then fit an $(N-1)$th-degree polynomial to the resulting

---

[1] For example:
Gerhard Tintner, *Econometrics,* Science Editions, Wiley, New York, 1965.
Sylvain Ehrenfeld and Sebastian B. Littauer, *Introduction to Statistical Method,* McGraw-Hill, New York, 1964.
Edward C. Bryant, *Statistical Analysis,* McGraw-Hill, New York, 1960.

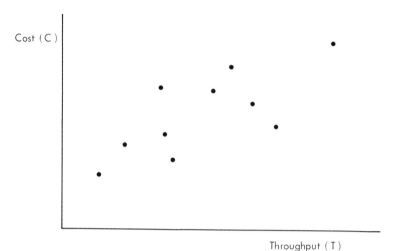

FIGURE A–1. Hypothetical relationship between cost and throughput for ten computer systems.

points; although the curve will not pass through some of the original points, it can be made to come very close to them.

But why fit a curve at all? The usual reason is that available data represent only part of the full set of data of interest. For example, the points in Fig. A–1 show the cost and throughput for ten computers, but the analyst may be interested in the cost and throughput of all computers (including some not even built yet). Alternatively, he may be interested in the cost of a computer with a throughput differing from that of any of the ten machines for which data are available. The object is thus to *infer* something about the relationship that holds for a larger group (often called the *universe* or *population*) from data describing a subset of this group. The subset is typically called the *sample*.

As indicated earlier, the process of making such inferences should begin with one or more hypotheses about the expected relationships, and these should be derived from some sort of theoretical model. For example, cost may be expected to increase with throughput, *ceteris paribus*. If efficient production methods are employed, a machine with smaller throughput and higher cost than an alternative one will not be built. Even if one was built, the seller would presumably have lowered its price below that of a higher-throughput computer in order to sell it. Thus, if "cost" refers to cost to the user (i.e., price charged by the seller), economic theory would imply that cost increases with throughput:

$$C = f(T) \quad \text{and} \quad \frac{dC}{dT} > 0$$

Note that relatively little is implied about the form of this function, except that it is monotonic and upward-sloping. Selecting the appropriate function from among those meeting these criteria is essentially an empirical problem.

If the throughput and cost of the ten systems have been measured precisely, and if no other factors influence cost, the points should fall along an upward-sloping curve, and systems with equal throughput should have identical costs. Even under these stringent conditions the appropriate curve relating cost to effectiveness is not obvious, for many curves (an Nth-degree polynomial, an $(N + 1)$th-degree polynomial, etc.) can be drawn through all the points. However, discussion of such a case is decidedly academic, since measurement is seldom perfect and rarely can all relevant factors be included in the data sample.

Consider the following modification of the problem posed. Assume that throughput (T) refers to the efficiency of a system when it is operating, while reliability (R) measures the expected portion of the time that the system will be operable. Arguments similar to those given earlier lead to the conclusion that economic theory implies:

$$C = f(T, R), \quad \frac{dC}{dT} > 0, \quad \text{and} \quad \frac{dC}{dR} > 0$$

If the sample data include figures on reliability for the ten systems, and if all variables (C, T, and R) have been measured without error, all points should lie on the true surface relating C to T and R. The problem is then to select some surface passing through the ten points in the three-dimensional diagram with C, T, and R on the axes. But data on reliability are often unavailable. In such cases the analyst must resign himself to attempting to indicate the relationship between cost and throughput for a system of "typical" reliability, with the expectation that the relationship will predict too low a cost for a highly reliable system and too high a cost for a system of low reliability.

Moreover, he must assume that, to the extent that the systems in his sample vary in reliability, the variation is reasonably random: if some systems in the sample have less-than-average reliability, others are likely to have greater-than-average reliability; moreover, those with less-than-average reliability are not likely to fall primarily within one range of costs while those with greater-than-average reliability fall primarily in another. More formally:

(A–1a) $\qquad C_i^a = C_i^p + d_i$

(A–1b) $\qquad C_i^p = f(T_i)$

(A–1c) $\qquad \text{Exp}(d_i) = 0$

(A–1d) $\qquad \text{Correlation } (d, T) = 0$

Equation A–1a is a definition of d_i, the difference between the actual (C_i^a) and the predicted (C_i^p) cost of system i. Equation A–1b is the prediction equation; it indicates the relationship between cost and throughput for systems of typical reliability. Equation A–1c states that the expected difference should be zero, while equation A–1d states that there should be no relationship between the cost differences and the throughput values.

In this example differences are assumed to be due to a single unmeasured factor—reliability. But no significant change is required if differences are assumed to be due to several unmeasured influences or to errors in measuring cost. In general, letting X_1 through X_K be measured factors (called *independent variables*) and Y a variable assumed to be influenced by these factors (Y is the *dependent* variable), we have

(A–2a) $\qquad Y_i^a = Y_i^p + d_i$

(A–2b) $\qquad Y_i^p = f(X_{1i}, X_{2i}, \ldots, X_{Ki})$

(A–2c) $\qquad \text{Exp}(d_i) = 0$

(A–2d) $\qquad \text{Correlation } (d, X_j) = 0 \quad \text{for } j = 1 \text{ to } K$

Models of the type indicated in equations A–2a through A–2d include only variables on which data are to be collected, assuming that other influences and errors in measurement may be considered equivalent to a single random variable (d). For some purposes an additional specification concerning d is made: in the entire population (but not necessarily the sample), values of d_i are assumed to follow a normal distribution.[2]

B. SELECTING THE BEST MEMBER OF A FAMILY OF CURVES

Assume for the present that a particular form has somehow been selected for the prediction equation—for example, a linear form:

(A–2b') $$Y_i{}^p = a + b_1 X_1 + b_2 X_2 + \cdots + b_K X_K$$

Which of the alternative members of this general family provides the best fit, that is, what are the best values of the coefficients $a, b_1, \ldots,$ b_K? More to the point, how shall "fit" be measured?

For a number of reasons most analyses utilize the sum of the squared deviations of actual from predicted values of the dependent variable— the smaller this sum, the better is the fit. To some extent the selection of this measure is based on its computational properties. However, a more compelling reason can be given: under certain conditions its adoption can be shown to lead to the selection of an equation with the greatest likelihood of success in prediction. The details of this rationale are beyond the scope of this discussion; we note merely that standard statistical analyses assume that the sum of the squared deviations pro- vides the most appropriate criterion.

The best equation of any given family is assumed to be the one mini- mizing the sum of the squared deviations. The problem for a linear form can be stated as follows.

Select values of $a, b_1, \ldots, b_K$ that

$$\text{Minimize:} \quad \sum_{i=1}^{N} (Y_i{}^a - Y_i{}^p)^2$$

subject to

$$Y_i{}^p = a + b_1 X_{1i} + \cdots + b_K X_{Ki} \quad \text{for each } i \text{ from 1 to } N$$

where $(Y_i{}^a, X_{1i}, \ldots, X_{Ki})$ is the ith one of N observations. Such a prob- lem is not difficult to solve; it requires the solution of $K + 1$ simul-

---

[2] If d represents the net effect of many independent effects, appeal to the central limit theorem may be made to support this assumption.

taneous linear equations in $K + 1$ unknowns. A number of standard computer programs have been written for such analyses.

The process of determining a function of this type is known as *regression analysis* by the method of least squares. If only one independent variable is employed, the technique is *simple* regression; if $K > 1$, the analysis is termed *multiple* regression.

In practice, linear equations are used most frequently; fortunately, a wide variety of relationships can be accommodated by judicious choice of variables. For example, consider a problem involving only one independent variable (X); the data consist of N observations — $Y_i{}^a$, X_i pairs. To fit a quadratic function, merely add a third variable for each observation:

$$V_{1i} = Y_i{}^a, \quad V_{2i} = X_i, \quad \text{and} \quad V_{3i} = X_i{}^2$$

Then regress:

$$V_{1i} = a + bV_{2i} + cV_{3i}$$

The resulting equation is, of course:

$$Y_i{}^a = a + bX_i + cX_i{}^2$$

The following examples suggest other transformations that can be used to fit nonlinear curves by means of linear regression techniques.

	Linear Regression	*Equation*
(A–3a)	$\ln Y = a + b(\ln X)$	$Y = AX^b$, where $A = e^a$
(A–3b)	$\ln Y = a + bX$	$Y = AB^X$, where $A = e^a$ and $B = e^b$
(A–3c)	$Y = a + b(\ln X)$	$e^Y = AX^b$, where $A = e^a$

Form A–3a is particularly useful, since it assumes a constant relationship between percentage changes in X and Y. As shown in Chapter 3, the coefficient b can, in this case, be interpreted directly as the percentage change in the dependent variable (Y) associated with a 1% change in the independent variable (X). Form A–3c is also of interest; in this case the coefficient b indicates the absolute change in the dependent variable associated with a 1% change in the independent variable. These interpretations hold also in cases involving more than one independent variable, for example:

Linear Regression	Equation

$\ln Y = a + b_1(\ln X_i) + b_2(\ln X_2)$ $Y = AX_1^{b_1}X_2^{b_2}$,   where $A = e^a$

Here b_1 = percentage change in Y associated with a 1% change in X_1, *ceteris paribus;*

b_2 = percentage change in Y associated with a 1% change in X_2, *ceteris paribus;* and

$b_1 + b_2$ = percentage change in Y associated with a 1% change in both X_1 and X_2.

One minor qualification concerns the fitting of curves in which the dependent variable has been transformed. For example, to fit the curve $Y = AX^b$ we regress ($\ln Y$) on ($\ln X$). The resulting coefficients give a curve that minimizes the squared deviations of the actual values of ($\ln Y$) from the predicted values. This curve will typically differ slightly from the one that minimizes the squared deviations of Y from the predicted values. However, the difference is usually small and is generally disregarded.

In certain instances linear regression methods may be used to analyze influences expressed only with ordinal measures. For example, the analyst may feel that IBM computers cost more than others of comparable performance. Such a relationship may be accommodated by defining a binary variable:

$$Z_i = \begin{cases} 0 \text{ if computer } i \text{ is not made by IBM, and} \\ 1 \text{ if computer } i \text{ is made by IBM,} \end{cases}$$

and then regressing an equation such as

$$C = a + b_t T + b_z Z$$

This implies that

$$C = \begin{cases} a_1 + b_t T \text{ for IBM computers, and} \\ a + b_t T \text{ for non-IBM computers,} \end{cases}$$

where $a_1 = a + b_z$.

Further examples could be given, but the point has been made — clever use of linear regression methods allows the fitting of relationships of considerable complexity.

C. SELECTING THE TYPE OF CURVE

Even though reasonably simple procedures are available to provide the "best" curve of any given kind, the best type of curve must still be chosen. If the criterion were solely the extent to which the curve fits the sample data, one would merely select one of the functions giving a perfect (or nearly perfect) fit, for example, an $(N - 1)$th-degree polynomial, since the sum of the squared deviations could then be made to be zero. But we are usually interested in the extent to which the selected curve will fit all points in the population, even though only a subset is available for the analysis. Intuitively it would seem that the more complex the curve used, the more likely the curve is to reflect peculiarities of the sample at hand instead of the underlying relationship for the full (unavailable) set of data. *Ceteris paribus*, the simpler the form of the equation, the better it is.

A desirable measure of simplicity in this connection is the number of coefficients in the equation being estimated.[3] A related measure is the difference between the number of observations and this sum:

$$\text{df} = N - n_c$$

where df = degrees of freedom,

N = number of observations, and

n_c = number of coefficients estimated.

Other things being equal (especially the goodness of fit), the greater the degrees of freedom, the more significant is the fit. An extreme case arises when df = 0. We have argued that a perfect or nearly perfect fit can be made to any set of N points (Y_i, X_i) if an $(N - 1)$th-degree polynomial is used. Such a curve would fit very well, but a good fit hardly guarantees that the true relationship for the population as a whole has been discovered. This is immediately apparent: since N coefficients have been estimated (including the intercept), there are *no* degrees of freedom (df = 0).

The concept of degrees of freedom leads directly to the choice of the "best" curve. For a specified type of curve, we select the one minimizing the sum of the squared deviations of actual from predicted

---

[3] Equal, in the case of multiple regression, to the total number of variables (independent plus dependent).

values of the dependent variable. Now we divide this sum by the number of degrees of freedom for the equation; the result is defined as the square of the *standard error of estimate:*

$$(se)^2 \equiv \frac{\displaystyle\sum_{i=1}^{N} (Y_i^a - Y_i^p)^2}{N - n_c}$$

This is the measure used to select the best type of curve: the smaller the standard error, the better is the curve. Its use ensures that among curves with the same number of coefficients the one giving the smallest sum of squared deviations will be selected. Moreover, among curves giving the same sum of squared deviations, the one with the fewest coefficients will be selected. Most important, the measure provides a method for selection among curves differing in both respects. The theoretical basis for its use will only be alluded to here: under certain assumed conditions it represents the best estimate of the standard deviation of points in the entire population around the curve in question.

D. STATISTICAL SIGNIFICANCE

We have suggested that the appropriate curve is the one minimizing the standard error of estimate. But once such a curve is found, one often would like to determine its importance. Two types of questions arise, those having to do with the significance of the entire equation and those dealing with the significance of particular coefficients in the equation. Before addressing these questions, however, we must briefly consider the meaning of *statistical significance.*

Central to the notion is the concept of a *null hypothesis.* For example, we might assert that, if all the points in the population were available, there would be no relationship between cost and throughput. Typically the sample will show some relationship. But even if the null hypothesis were true, there would be some chance that a sample showing at least as great a relationship would be found. For example, there might be 5 chances out of 100; if so, we say that the relationship found in the sample differs from that specified by the null hypothesis at the 5% *level of significance.* A greater difference might be significant at, say, the 1% level. The analyst might (rather arbitrarily) decide to reject a null hypothesis if the sample results differ by at least the amount significant at the 5% level. Or he might insist on a difference large enough to be significant at the 1% level.[4] In general, the assertion that some relationship is *significant* indicates that the sample result differs enough from an assumed value of zero (no relationship) to be significant at some preselected level, usually 5% or 1%.

Measures of significance may seem to have little practical value, for they must be based on characteristics of the entire population, about which little is actually known. To overcome this problem, statisticians sometimes utilize sample results (plus a substantial set of assumptions) to make inferences about the essential features of the population, and hence about the significance of the sample results. Neither the basis for such procedures nor the computations used will be considered here; a discussion of the rationale would be far too lengthy, and the formulas are of more interest to programmers of statistical routines than to users.

E. THE PREDICTIVE ABILITY OF THE REGRESSION EQUATION

If the goal is to predict future values of a dependent variable, given values for the independent variables, the relevant question is simple: how much will the use of the equation improve predictive ability? Such a question presumes an alternative method of prediction; this is typically assumed to be simply a prediction that every value of Y will equal the average value in the sample. The sum of the squared deviations around the mean of Y provides a measure of the errors associated with this predictive method. Hopefully the sum of squared deviations around the fitted curve will be considerably smaller. It is useful to refer to the latter as the sum of squared deviations *unexplained* by the curve. We

---

[4] An important question concerns the alternative: if the null hypothesis is rejected, what hypothesis will be selected? Denote the null hypothesis as H_0 and the alternative as H_1. Let the selected level of significance be α. A desirable statistical test

maximizes the probability of rejecting H_0 (and thus selecting H_1) when H_1 is in fact correct,

subject to the constraint that the probability of rejecting H_0 when it is in fact correct must be less than or equal to α.

A typical null hypothesis asserts that no relationship exists between two variables. A possible alternative is the hypothesis that there is some relationship—positive *or* negative. The usual test of significance is consistent with the choice of such an alternative.

have thus

$$S_T = \sum_{i=1}^{N} (Y_i^a - \bar{Y})^2$$

$$S_U = \sum_{i=1}^{N} (Y_i^a - Y_i^p)^2$$

$$S_E = S_T - S_U$$

where Y_i^a = the actual value of the independent variable for the ith observation,

$\bar{Y}$ = the mean observed value of $Y (= \Sigma Y_i/N)$,

Y_i^p = the value of Y_i predicted by the fitted curve,

S_T = the total sum of squared deviations of Y_i around $\bar{Y}$,

S_U = the sum of squared deviations of Y_i unexplained by the curve, and

S_E = the sum of squared deviations of Y_i explained (implied) by the curve.

Of the total variance, the proportion "explained" by the curve is

$$\frac{S_E}{S_T}$$

This ratio, usually called the *coefficient of determination,* can range from 0 to 1. A value of 0 signifies that the curve does not fit at all; a value of 1 indicates a perfect fit for the sample data.

For some purposes it is convenient to take the squre root of the co-efficient of determination. This measure, the (multiple) correlation coefficient, is typically denoted by R. Hence the coefficient of deter-mination (proportion of variation explained) is often represented as R^2. It is important to note that a high correlation between two variables indicates association but need not imply causality (e.g., X may affect Y, Y may affect X, or both may be affected by a third factor).[5]

[5] Although related mathematically, the coefficient of determination and the correlation coefficient rest on quite different philosophical bases. Regression analysis usually as-sumes that measurement errors are associated with the dependent variable, but that independent variables have been measured precisely. The regression equation is thus arranged to minimize the sum of the squared deviations of actual values of the dependent variable from those predicted by the equation. If an analyst feels that errors of measure-

Clearly the significance of a coefficient of determination will depend on the degrees of freedom. Thus a value close to 1 is not necessarily an indication of substantial predictive ability. The assumptions required to perform a test of significance for the coefficient of determination are sufficiently stringent to seriously limit the utility of the approach for applications of the type discussed in this book. The coefficient of determination should thus be regarded primarily as a measure of the extent to which a regression equation fits the sample data.

A prediction equation attempts to provide the best single estimate (i.e., the expected value) of the dependent variable for given values of the independent variables. Of course, when new data are obtained, actual values are likely to differ from those predicted by the regression equation. But by how much? Recall that the standard error of estimate is an estimate of the standard deviation of such differences. Now assume that these differences are normally distributed in the same manner all along the regression line. Under these conditions we might assert that

$$Y^p - (\text{se}) \leqq Y^a \leqq Y^p + (\text{se}) \quad \text{with probability of 0.68}$$
$$Y^p - 2(\text{se}) \leqq Y^a \leqq Y^p + 2(\text{se}) \quad \text{with probability of 0.95}$$

where Y^a = actual value of Y,

Y^p = predicted value of Y, given specified values of the independent variables and using the regression equation, and

se = standard error of estimate.

Confidence intervals, constructed by using assumptions such as these, are widely employed. However, even more sophisticated methods[6] should be viewed as providing, at best, rough estimates of the likely range of outcomes. We note in passing that regressions per-

---

ment are connected with the values of Y in his sample, but not with the values of X, he should regress Y on X. On the other hand, if he believes that there are measurement errors in X, but not in Y, he should regress X on Y. This will give a different regression equation (unless the values fit the curve perfectly), but the coefficients of determination (and hence the correlation coefficients) will be the same. In cases in which errors occur in the measurement of two variables, standard (simple) regression techniques may be completely inapplicable, but the correlation coefficient can still be used to measure the association of the two variables.

[6] Careful analysts take into account the fact that the slope of the regression line itself is subject to error. When predicting values distant from the mean, the likely error caused by faulty estimation of the regression line should be added to that due to variation of values around the line.

formed by using the logarithm of a variable as the dependent variable lead to confidence intervals stated in terms of the likely percentage deviation of the actual value of the original variable from the value predicted by the equation.

F. THE IMPORTANCE OF INDIVIDUAL VARIABLES

Often one is interested not only in the predictive ability of the regression equation as a whole but also in the "importance" of individual variables.[7] For example, does throughput really influence cost, or is only reliability important? Questions of this type can be formalized. Assume that the true relationship for the population as a whole is

$$C = \alpha + \beta_t T + \beta_r R$$

where $C = $ cost
$\quad T = $ throughput
$\quad R = $ reliability
and α, β_t, β_r are constants.

From the sample at hand we obtain a least-squares equation:

$$C = a + b_t T + b_r R$$

Now assume (as the null hypothesis) that throughput really does not affect cost; this is equivalent to assuming that $\beta_t = 0$. Even if this were the case, it might be possible for a regression analysis performed on a sample to give a (spurious) relationship similar to that actually found. But how probable is such a result? To answer this question, statisticians compute a statistic from the sample data known as the *standard error of the regression coefficient*. For example, a regression equation might be reported as follows:

$$C = 35.6 + 20.2T + 9.3R$$
$$(10.1) \quad (11.9)$$

Each figure in parentheses indicates the standard error of the regression coefficient above it. To estimate the extent to which such a co-

---

[7] Note, however, that, if there is only one independent variable (i.e., simple regression), the two questions are equivalent. Thus the t test described in this section can serve as a test of the significance of the coefficient of determination for simple regression equations. Note also that, for multiple regression equations, if one or more independent variables is significant, the entire equation should also be significant (*a fortiori*).

efficient differs from the value assumed in the null hypothesis, we divide the difference by the associated error to obtain a *t value*. For example, taking as the null hypothesis $\beta_t = 0$, we have

$$t \text{ value} = \frac{20.2 - 0}{10.1} = 2.0$$

The larger the *t* value, the less is the likelihood that the true value of the regression coefficient (e.g., β_t) is really the hypothesized value (in this case, zero). Under certain conditions statements concerning statistical significance can also be made. If the *t* value exceeds 3.0, the coefficient is often significant at the 1% level; if it exceeds 2.0, the coefficient is often significant at the 5% level. The qualifications are included partly to account for the fact that the number of degrees of freedom influences the result. The minimum *t* values significant at the 5% and 1% levels for some alternative degrees of freedom are as follows:

Degrees of Freedom	Minimum Value Significant at the 5% Level	Minimum Value Significant at the 1% Level
10	2.23	3.17
20	2.09	2.84
30	2.04	2.75
∞	1.96	2.58

Needless to say, these assertions rest, as usual, on assumptions, some of which may not apply in any given case.

G. REGRESSION ANALYSIS: ART OR SCIENCE?

A great deal of statistical theory has been developed to cope with problems involving regression analysis. In practical, empirical work, however, the use of this technique remains more of an art than a science. It is often far too easy to find an equation giving a large coefficient of determination. For example, a regression of total cost on some measure of effectiveness is likely to yield a large coefficient, for the assumed alternative is the hypothesis that effectiveness does not influence total cost at all. On the other hand, a regression of average cost on effectiveness may give quite a low coefficient, for the assumed alternative is the much more sensible hypothesis that effectiveness does not influence average cost. Another danger is the attribution of a cause-and-effect relationship to regression results.

In practice, investigations seldom follow the procedures of classical statistics. The investigator is supposed to formulate a detailed hypothesis before examining the data in question. This rarely happens. Usually the data are examined, hypotheses tested, new ones formed and tested, and so on. The final (reported) results typically concern an hypothesis formulated after extensive analyses of the data used to test the validity of the hypothesis.

Another problem can best be described by means of an example. In a study of core memories a regression of cost per bit on cycle time gave a good fit (large R^2) with indications that the regression coefficient was clearly significant (large t value). However, the coefficient was positive, suggesting that slower memories cost more per bit than faster ones. This result was unexpected, to say the least. It arose because slow memories tended to be older memories, and older memories typically had higher costs (per bit) than newer ones. Thus the measure of speed was acting partly as a surrogate for the date of first introduction. The problem was easily solved by including the date of first introduction as an additional independent variable. When this was done, the value of R^2 became even larger, both regression coefficients appeared to be significant, and (happily) they exhibited the expected signs. Having reached such a point, an analyst is likely to assert that he has captured the "true" cause-and-effect relationship. But how does he know that the date of introduction, for example, is not simply acting as a surrogate for something else, which is the real determinant of cost? The answer is that he does not and cannot know. Investigations typically are concluded when results consistent with our expectations are obtained; additional analysis is performed primarily when the initial findings cause discomfort.

Although regression analysis is fraught with hazards, it does provide a convenient method for summarizing data and attempting to focus on key relationships. Its use in empirical work is thus virtually unavoidable. Many of the results in this book are based on regression analysis. In such cases we have generally reported only the equation, the t

values,[8] the coefficient of determination, and the standard error of estimate, for example:

$$Y = 1.76 - \underset{(t=10.1)}{0.20X_1} + \underset{(t=3.2)}{0.16X_2} - \underset{(t=9.6)}{0.01X_3} \begin{cases} R^2 = 0.45 \\ se = 0.37 \end{cases}$$

When describing studies lacking some of this information, we sometimes indicate statistical significance (as reported in the original study). However, such interpretations have been avoided whenever possible; the reader may furnish them if he chooses.

---

[8] Relative to the hypothesis that the variable is insignificant, that is,

$$t \text{ value} = \frac{\text{coefficient} - 0}{\text{standard error of coefficient}}$$

SELECTED RAND BOOKS

Arrow, Kenneth J., and Marvin Hoffenberg. *A Time Series Analysis of Inter-industry Demands*. Amsterdam, Holland, North-Holland Publishing Co., 1959.

Bellman, Richard. *Dynamic Programming*. Princeton, N.J., Princeton University Press, 1957.

Bellman, Richard. *Introduction to Matrix Analysis*. New York, McGraw-Hill Book Co., 1960.

Bellman, Richard. *Adaptive Control Processes: a Guided Tour*. Princeton, N.J., Princeton University Press, 1961.

Bellman, Richard (ed.). *Mathematical Optimization Techniques*. Los Angeles, Calif., University of California Press, 1963.

Bellman, Richard, and Stuart E. Dreyfus. *Applied Dynamic Programming*. Princeton, N.J., Princeton University Press, 1962.

Bellman, Richard, and Robert E. Kalaba. *Quasilinearization and Nonlinear Boundary-Value Problems* (Vol. 3). New York, American Elsevier Publishing Co., 1965.

Bergson, Abram, and Hans Heymann, Jr. *Soviet National Income and Product, 1940–48*. New York, Columbia University Press, 1954.

Dantzig, George B. *Linear Programming and Extensions*. Princeton, N.J., Princeton University Press, 1963.

Dorfman, Robert, Paul A. Samuelson, and Robert M. Solow. *Linear Programming and Economic Analysis*. New York, McGraw-Hill Book Co., 1958.

Dresher, Melvin. *Games of Strategy: Theory and Applications*. Englewood Cliffs, N.J., Prentice-Hall, 1961.

Dreyfus, Stuart. *Dynamic Programming and the Calculus of Variations*. New York, Academic Press, 1965.

Edelen, Dominic G. B. *The Structure of Field Space: an Axiomatic Formulation of Field Physics*. Los Angeles, Calif., University of California Press, 1962.

Ford, L. R., Jr., and D. R. Fulkerson. *Flows in Networks*. Princeton, N.J., Princeton University Press, 1962.

Gale, David. *The Theory of Linear Economic Models*. New York, McGraw-Hill Book Co., 1960.

Galenson, Walter. *Labor Productivity in Soviet and American Industry*. New York, Columbia University Press, 1955.

Gruenberger, Fred, and George Jaffray. *Problems for Computer Solution*. New York, John Wiley & Sons, 1965.

Gruenberger, Fred J., and Daniel D. McCracken. *Introduction to Electronic Computers: Problem Solving with the IBM 1620*. New York, John Wiley & Sons, 1963.

Hastings, Cecil, Jr. *Approximations for Digital Computers*. Princeton, N.J., Princeton University Press, 1955.

Hearle, Edward F. R., and Raymond J. Mason. *A Data Processing System for State and Local Governments*. Englewood Cliffs, N.J., Prentice-Hall, 1963.

Hirshleifer, Jack, James C. DeHaven, and Jerome W. Milliman. *Water Supply: Economics, Technology, and Policy*. Chicago, Ill., The University of Chicago Press, 1960.

Hitch, Charles J., and Roland McKean. *The Economics of Defense in the Nuclear Age*. Cambridge, Mass., Harvard University Press, 1960.

Hoeffding, Oleg. *Soviet National Income and Product in 1928*. New York, Columbia University Press, 1954.

Jorgenson, D. W., J. J. McCall, and R. Radner. *Optimal Replacement Policy*. Amsterdam, Holland, North-Holland Publishing Co., and Chicago, Ill., Rand McNally & Co., 1967.

Kershaw, Joseph A., and Roland N. McKean. *Teacher Shortages and Salary Schedules*. New York, McGraw-Hill Book Co., 1962.

Markowitz, Harry M., Bernard Hausner, and Herbert W. Karr. *SIMSCRIPT: a Simulation Programming Language*. Englewood Cliffs, N.J., Prentice-Hall, 1963.

Marschak, Thomas A., Thomas K. Glennan, Jr., and Robert Summers. *Strategy for R & D*. New York, Springer-Verlag New York, 1967.

Meyer, John R., Martin Wohl, and John F. Kain. *The Urban Transportation Problem*. Cambridge, Mass., Harvard University Press, 1965.

McKean, Roland N. *Efficiency in Government through Systems Analysis: with Emphasis on Water Resource Development*. New York, John Wiley & Sons, 1958.

McKinsey, J. C. C. *Introduction to the Theory of Games*. New York. McGraw-Hill Book Co., 1952.

Newell, Allen (ed.). *Information Processing Language-V Manual*. Englewood Cliffs, N.J., Prentice-Hall, 1961.

Novick, David (ed.). *Program Budgeting: Program Analysis and the Federal Budget*. Cambridge, Mass., Harvard University Press, 1965.

Pincus, John A. *Economic Aid and International Cost Sharing*. Baltimore, Md., The Johns Hopkins Press, 1965.

Quade, E. S. (ed.). *Analysis for Military Decisions*. Chicago, Ill., Rand Mc-
Nally & Co., and Amsterdam, Holland, North-Holland Publishing Co.,
1964.

Quade, E. S., and Wayne I. Boucher (eds.). *Systems Analysis and Policy
Planning: Applications in Defense*. New York, American Elsevier Publishing Co., 1968.

Rush, Myron. *Political Succession in the USSR*. New York, Columbia University Press, 1965.

Williams, J. D. *The Compleat Strategyst: Being a Primer on the Theory of
Games of Strategy*. New York, McGraw-Hill Book Co., 1954.

INDEX OF NAMES

SUBJECT INDEX